PRESSURE COOKER

PRESSURE COOKER

Why Home Cooking Won't Solve Our
Problems and What We Can Do About It

Sarah Bowen

Joslyn Brenton

Sinikka Elliott

OXFORD
UNIVERSITY PRESS

OXFORD
UNIVERSITY PRESS

Oxford University Press is a department of the University of Oxford. It furthers
the University's objective of excellence in research, scholarship, and education
by publishing worldwide. Oxford is a registered trade mark of Oxford University
Press in the UK and certain other countries.

Published in the United States of America by Oxford University Press
198 Madison Avenue, New York, NY 10016, United States of America.

Library of Congress Cataloging-in-Publication Data
Names: Bowen, Sarah, 1978– author. | Brenton, Joslyn, author. | Elliott, Sinikka, author.
Title: Pressure cooker : why home cooking won't solve our problems and what
we can do about it / Sarah Bowen, Joslyn Brenton, and Sinikka Elliott.
Description: New York, NY, United States of America : Oxford University Press, [2019] |
Includes bibliographical references.
Identifiers: LCCN 2018008311 | ISBN 9780190663292 (hard cover) |
ISBN 9780190663322 (epub)
Subjects: LCSH: Grocery shopping—Cross cultural studies. |
Dinners and dining—Cross-cultural studies. | Cooking—Cross-cultural studies. |
Food security—Cross-cultural studies. | Equality—Cross-cultural studies. |
Homemakers—Interviews.
Classification: LCC TX356.B66 2019 | DDC 641.5/4—dc23
LC record available at https://lccn.loc.gov/20180083119780190663292

1 3 5 7 9 8 6 4 2

Printed by Sheridan Books, Inc., United States of America

CONTENTS

ACKNOWLEDGMENTS

Authorship of the book is listed alphabetically as a testament to the process we followed in writing it. None of us took the lead, and the book represents a melding of our voices and expertise into one. In fact, by the end, it was difficult to identify even a single sentence written solely by one of us. We share equal credit, and take equal responsibility, for the book's content.

We hold great admiration for the women and families who contributed to this research by sharing their stories and allowing us to conduct observations with them. We owe them a tremendous debt for giving us such intimate access to their lives. Much of the research for this book was funded by a grant from the US Department of Agriculture for a participatory outreach and research project, Voices into Action. We are grateful to all of the people who have been part of Voices into Action over the span of the project. Annie Hardison-Moody was central to developing the vision for Voices into Action and seeing it through.

The book would not have been possible without the dedication of the graduate students and research staff who recruited participants and conducted interviews and observations over the course of the study: Erinn Brooks, Gloria Cardona, Ashley Coleman, Daniela García-Grandón, Helen Herrera, Cassandra Johnson, Tashara Leak, Lillian MacNell, Blake Martin, Josephine Ngo McKelvy, Mari Kate Mycek, Emilia Cordero Oceguera, Rachel Powell, Kathryn Rosenbaum, Chaniqua Simpson, and Casey Strange. Many other research assistants and staff members helped with data collection, data entry, coding, and other aspects of the research: Alecia Anderson, Janine Baldino, Aysha Bodenhamer, Shaqueeta Brantley, Allyson Corbo, Angel Cruz, Madeleine Eldrige, Kim Eshleman, Lauren Frey, Ariel Fugate, Doretta Gaudreau, Courtney Gold, Scott Grether, Dayne Hamrick, Micaela Hayes, Kellie Leavitt, Patricia Parker, Marissa Sheldon, and Amanda Wyant.

We also thank the large network of community mentors, extension staff, and community partners who contributed to the participatory outreach aspects of Voices into Action: Zandra Alford, Mary Jane Bartlett, Alvin Bean, John Blevins, Dara Bloom, Gina Dean, Frances Harrington, Renée Hein, Demetrius Hunter, Susan Jakes, Lorelei Jones, Kristin Larson, Crystal McIver, Tremika Middleton, John O'Sullivan, Tawanna Petty, Kelley Richardson, Vidya Sanka, Lonnie Sessoms, Debbie Stephenson, and Lisa Valdivia, as well as students in the Food and Society class at North Carolina State University in spring 2012 and spring 2014 and students in the public health program at Campbell University in spring 2014.

Interviews with middle-class mothers were conducted by Joslyn Brenton for her dissertation, which was partially funded by a Doctoral Dissertation Completion grant from the Graduate School at North Carolina State University. The College of Humanities and Social Sciences, the College of Agriculture and Life Sciences, the Department of Sociology and Anthropology, the Sociology Graduate Student Association, and the Department of Agricultural and Human Sciences at North Carolina State University provided crucial administrative support and small grants to fund aspects of this research. North Carolina State University, Ithaca College, and the University of British Columbia provided us with time off from teaching to focus on the book. Our colleagues and friends at North Carolina State University, the University of British Columbia, Ithaca College, and the University of Gothenburg provided encouragement and support as we wrote the book.

Thanks to Arlene Stein and Jodi O'Brien at *Contexts* magazine for their assistance with the article that inspired this book. Matt Shipman wrote a press release about that article, and the attention it received convinced us we needed to write a book. Anne-Marie Slaughter and Liz Mundy at New America invited us to present our initial findings for the book at the 2014 "Homemaker Mystique" event in Washington, DC.

Our editor at Oxford University Press, James Cook, championed the book from the beginning. We are grateful for his stewardship, advice, and willingness to share his own kitchen stories with us. Several reviewers provided constructive feedback along the way that pushed us to reorganize the book and better articulate its focus. We also acknowledge the following friends and colleagues for their insightful conversations about the book, as well as their generosity in reading parts (and in some cases, all) of the manuscript and sharing their feedback: Katherine Cohen-Filipic, Kathryn DeMaster, Sarita Gaytán, Max Garrone, Patrick Grzanka, Eleanor Henderson, Kate Kallal, Emily Mann, Vrushali Patil, Jyoti Puri, Stephen Sweet, and Alicia Swords.

We dedicate the book to all the home cooks whose work is too often invisible and underappreciated, and to our families, who sustained us as we wrote the book. For inspiration, encouragement, and much needed distraction during the book's writing, Sinikka Elliott thanks Patrick, Zak, Jude, Joshua, Aubrey, and Karine. In memory of Victoria, who hated cooking, and Dinah, who loved it. Joslyn Brenton thanks Peter for feeding our family delicious meals and for his support while writing the book, and Quinn and Clara, who cheered her on, and whose dinner table antics have helped her to appreciate the work of feeding young children! She also thanks her parents and sisters for their encouragement. Sarah Bowen is thankful to Mark for being a great partner and for all the late-night conversations about this book, and to Simon and Anna, her favorite dinner companions. She also thanks her dad, grandma, sisters, and the Wirt family for their support. This book is in memory of her mom.

The nine families who are featured in the book leave us inspired and in awe. We thank them and have taken much care to honor them and do their stories justice.

PRESSURE COOKER

1 INTRODUCTION

(BACK) TO THE KITCHEN?

It started with pancakes and eggs when she was five. By the time she was nine, Leanne Armstrong was making fried chicken for her family. At least that's how she tells it, her gold-flecked, green eyes flashing. A hand on her hip, she says, "Girl! I can *cook*."

Leanne's mother walked out on the family when Leanne was young. There were many years when she was absent. As the only daughter, Leanne felt called to replace her in the kitchen. "I had to cook for the whole family," she recalls. It was a big responsibility, one she's proud of handling on her own.

Still resentful about her mom leaving, Leanne nevertheless fondly remembers the slow but steady process of gaining mastery over the kitchen. Under her grandmother's tutelage, she even learned how to make her dad's beloved southern foods. "I can make chitlins, I can make pigs' feet. I'm telling you, I can throw down!" she says, grinning confidently.

Today, Leanne's favorite dishes are the ones that put a smile on her children's faces. "Sometimes I fry chicken wings. That's the boys' favorite, my chicken drumettes! I make roasts. They like hamburgers, or hotdogs and French fries, but that's easy. I mean, I can cook!"

She also likes to experiment with new dishes. "I've made baked potato casserole before. We cut up the potatoes and put it in a casserole dish with all our favorites on it. This past week I made Buffalo wings. I made a nice little taco casserole."

The daughter of a white mother and a black father, Leanne has curly, auburn hair and light brown skin, with a spray of freckles across her cheeks. She often dresses in blue scrubs and white sneakers, the required uniform at the technical college she attends. In the summer of 2013, Leanne was working part-time as a cashier at

McDonald's and taking classes. Her husband, Latrell, was unemployed. Like millions of others, their family was still struggling in the wake of the financial crisis that began in 2007. The largest economic upheaval in the United States since the 1930s, the Great Recession affected all American households, but it hit those on the lowest rungs of the economic ladder the hardest.[1]

Leanne's usually cheery disposition often bends under the weight of her daily struggles. She doesn't like her neighborhood, describing it as dangerous, noisy, and "drug infested." There is never enough money to go around, and Leanne is constantly forced to make hard choices. Buy groceries or pay the collection agency? Get new school clothes for the kids or hire an exterminator to get rid of the cockroaches?

Her marriage is another source of stress. Leanne and Latrell "bump heads," as Leanne puts it, especially when Latrell won't watch the kids or help around the house. There are moments when Leanne wonders if she made a mistake by marrying him.

But when the topic turns to food, Leanne is self-assured. She adores cooking, and the kitchen is one place where she feels a semblance of control in her life.

Like many Americans, Leanne spends a lot of time thinking about and preparing food. She doesn't subscribe to any parenting or cooking magazines, and she doesn't read the "mommy internet,"[2] but she's well aware of the dominant messages about what mothers should be doing in the kitchen. Good moms cook for their children. And not just any food, but food that is appealing, healthy, and made from scratch. Leanne has embraced many of these messages. She apologizes for using canned food, saying she'd prefer fresh or frozen, and dreams of having more money to make creative meals, like baked fish on a cedar plank. Leanne wouldn't call herself a foodie, but if you spend some time talking to her, you just might conclude that she is. Like self-professed foodies, she cares deeply about cooking and eating.[3] But these days, she doesn't have much money to spend on food. When the cupboards run low, as they often do, Leanne skips a meal so the kids and Latrell have enough to eat. There are days when all she has for lunch are two hard-boiled eggs. When her food stamps run out, Leanne calls someone for a ride across town to the food pantry. But help from the pantry comes at a cost. She waits around, her three children by her side, for her number to be called. She never knows what kind of food she will get, which makes it hard to plan meals or work around her family's preferences. Being poor chips away at Leanne's pride.

The kitchen restores her dignity and her confidence. But it doesn't solve her problems. And it creates new dilemmas, like when she can't reliably get the food she needs to make home-cooked meals, the kind of meals that good mothers are supposed to make for their children.

Now, perhaps more than ever, food is a matter of national concern and a political and cultural flashpoint.[4] One out of every eight people in the United States doesn't have enough to eat.[5] Food recalls, conflicting nutritional advice, and unpronounceable ingredients make people anxious about the food they're ingesting.[6] The impacts of large-scale food production also raise alarm bells. Consumers are afraid of pink slime in their hamburger meat,[7] chemicals in their strawberries,[8] and whether their food decisions are contributing to climate change. There is also panic about our growing waistlines. Since the 1980s, rates of obesity have doubled among adults and tripled among children, which many people attribute to the ubiquity of cheap, processed foods and the fast-food restaurants that stretch from coast to coast.[9]

Not everyone agrees about how to reform the food system and restore the nation's health, but one message often rises above the din: We need to get back in the kitchen. From celebrity chefs to home cooks, lots of people seem to have the feeling that our country has lost its way and that returning to the dinner table will get us back to healthy kids and strong families.

It's an alluring message.

Michael Pollan, arguably the most influential foodie in the United States, implores us to slow down and rediscover the joy of cooking and eating together. Cooking is a meaningful act, Pollan says, that can deepen our connection to nature and to ourselves. In his bestselling book *Cooked*—now also a documentary series on Netflix—Pollan takes readers into his own kitchen on a Sunday afternoon, evocatively demonstrating the pleasures cooking can bring.

As his teenage son, Isaac, works on his laptop at the kitchen island, Pollan stirs a *sugo* (the Italian word for "sauce"). They are planning to make fresh pasta later. "Sometimes Isaac wanders over to one pot on the stove with a tasting spoon," Pollan writes. "But mostly we work in parallel, both of us absorbed in our respective tasks, with occasional breaks for conversation." There is something about this kind of slow-paced work that alters the experience of time, he ruminates. "Our hours at the kitchen island have become some of the easiest, sweetest times we've had together."

Pollan's message is inspirational, seeking to convert readers by appealing to the healing power of cooking. Other food reformers aren't so gentle. They accuse people who fail to cook of being selfish, of neglecting their responsibilities as parents or citizens.

For example, farmer-author Joel Salatin points a finger at a general culture of laziness, which he and others believe is responsible for the high rates of obesity and diabetes among American children and adults. Salatin routinely blasts families for failing to capitalize on modern kitchen technology to cook good food at home. "With slow cookers, indoor plumbing, timed-bake [ovens], and refrigerators, today's techno-enabled kitchens allow busy people to cook from scratch and eat with integrity far easier than during Great Grandma's time," he chastises.

"She had to fetch water from the spring, split stove wood, start a fire and churn the butter and she still managed to feed a large family very well. If our generation can't do at least as well with our 40-hour work week and kitchen tech, then we deserve to eat adulterated pseudo food that sends us to an early grave." In a jab aimed directly at parents, Salatin concludes, "I don't know that anyone's children deserve this, however."[10]

Food reformers frame cooking from scratch not as a culinary choice or a hobby, but as an issue of morality.

The crux of the problem, food evangelists say, is the increasing number of people who have turned their backs on cooking. Jamie Oliver, Pollan's charismatic British contemporary, paces the stage, throws his hands in the air, and points dramatically at the audience during his TED Talk, viewed more than eight million times. There is a catastrophe in the United States, he tells them, with three generations of people who were never taught to cook. "We need to "start passing on cooking [skills] again," Oliver exhorts an enraptured audience.[11]

But what does it really take to achieve the foodie ideal of a home-cooked meal?

Home-cooked meals have acquired an almost mythical status. Yet it's worth thinking for a moment about what it takes to put a home-cooked, foodie-worthy meal on the table.

At a minimum, it takes a working stove and enough money to pay the electric bill to run the stove. Poor families like Leanne's are sometimes forced to make difficult choices: pay the electric bill or the rent? Buy groceries or pay a medical bill?

The foodie version of a home-cooked meal also takes the right ingredients. Foodies tell us to cook like our great-grandmothers did, using mostly fresh, unprocessed ingredients.[12] But who were these great-grandmothers? Certainly they weren't the vast numbers of immigrant women living in tenement slums in cities like Chicago and New York at the turn of the twentieth century.

They weren't the African American and white sharecroppers barely eking out a living on land they didn't own. Far too many of our great-grandmothers had diets marked by scarcity and deprivation, not nutritious foods plucked straight from the garden.

Universalized images of Great-Grandmother notwithstanding, the foodie ideal assumes that everyone has access to fresh food. Leanne's neighborhood no longer has a supermarket, although the wealthier neighborhoods a few miles away have plenty. Within walking distance, all Leanne has are a few corner stores. They sell soda and cigarettes and some processed staples, but they have little or no fresh produce. Leanne's not going to grow her own vegetables, because she has no land for a garden.

Leanne shops at the supermarket, because it's cheaper than the corner stores, but she can't go grocery shopping very often. Without a car, it's hard to get there. Sometimes she takes a taxi, but that eats up money she would rather spend on groceries. Leanne's mother, now back in her life, will give her a ride, but that comes with a cost too. She usually expects some money for gas and harangues Leanne for how she raises her children. The bus is an option, but it takes hours, and then she'd have to lug the grocery bags home from the bus stop, several blocks from her house.

Like many poor moms, Leanne shops once a month and, as noted earlier, sometimes goes to a food pantry to supplement whatever remains in her cupboards at the end of the month. She appreciates the help, but she has no control over the type of food she gets at the pantry. They dole out what they've received in donations. Sometimes the food is good, sometimes it's expired or stale, and often it's just not what Leanne would ordinarily choose. Most of it is canned or boxed food. Leanne would prefer fresh, but she also has a hard time storing it, given the cockroaches overrunning her kitchen.

Cooking according to the foodie ideal takes adequate space and functioning kitchen tools. Leanne has an older fridge, and it doesn't hold much. When she does her big monthly shop, she has a hard time wedging everything in. Her tiny crisper drawers don't keep the veggies very crisp or fresh. She has almost no counter space, making food prep challenging, but she manages, sometimes by sitting at the kitchen table to chop vegetables. She feels lucky to have a table; some of her neighbors don't have a dining table or even enough chairs for everyone in the family. But chopping veggies is like sawing logs with the dull knife she uses, the only one they have.

Making a foodie-worthy meal also takes time. Foodies assume that most people have enough time to cook from scratch and that everyone is home in time for dinner. Leanne's work schedule varies from day to day. She often

finds out only a few days in advance when she'll be working, making it difficult to plan ahead. Her classes at the technical college are typically held in the
late afternoon or at night. Often Leanne doesn't get home in time for dinner.
Many Americans share Leanne's predicament.

The foodie ideal is based on the notion that food is, or should be, at the
top of everyone's priority list. Food matters to Leanne. It matters a lot. But so
do other things. While she cooks, she's making lists of what she needs to do
the next day. She's totaling up how she is going to get through the month with
the money she has. Her kids clamor for her attention. One needs a signed per-
mission slip and $15 for his school field trip. Another says she's supposed to
listen to him read and then mark the checklist for his teacher, showing that he
completed the assignment. Her one-year-old wants cuddles.

Finally, foodies often seem to assume that if we just take the time to prepare good food, our families will flock to the table and contentedly eat it.
However, as many weary parents can attest, a lot can go wrong at dinner.
"Though everyone likes to think of the family table as a place of harmony and
solidarity," writes anthropologist Richard Wilk, "it is often the scene for the
exercise of power and authority, a place where conflict prevails."[13] The work of
sociologist Marjorie DeVault reminds us that the dinner table is a place where
parents teach children manners and convey the particular eating habits and
tastes of their social class group.[14]

Kids are often tired and cranky at the end of the day, just when parents
are at their most frazzled. Sitting together for a meal, parents feel frustrated
when kids subvert, and sometimes outright ignore, their efforts to get them
to eat with a fork, use a napkin, talk quietly, and stay in their seat. In the old
days, parents may have used a heavy hand—forcing kids to sit at the table until
all the food was eaten, or even spanking them—to get children to conform.
But modern parenting advice condemns such tactics, urging parents to reason
with their children, give them choices, and explain the consequences of their
behavior.[15] And even when children do stay in their seats and eat with their
silverware, many parents struggle to get them to eat the food they've made.

Even with cooking skills and motivation, a lot of people find that achieving
the foodie ideal of a home-cooked dinner is consummately out of reach. And
yet many Americans feel the pressure to get it right.

For centuries, people have been telling Americans that we need to change
the way we cook: cook more at home, cook more efficiently, cook more fru-
gally, cook more American.[16] These messages are directed mostly to women,
who continue to do the bulk of the work of feeding the family, including

planning, shopping for, and cooking meals.[17] And women take this work seriously. "Failing" at food—whether that means eating too much or not making home-cooked meals—means failing at motherhood.[18] Even when women, like Leanne Armstrong, enjoy cooking, they also internalize the judgments of others who condemn them for not cooking enough, not cooking the right food, or not assembling their families around the dinner table nightly.

Whereas nineteenth-century dietary reformers worried that we'd stopped baking our own bread, today's food evangelists worry that we've stopped cooking altogether. It's true that families eat out more than in the past. And women spend less time cooking than they did a few generations ago. But oversimplified comparisons of today's families with those of previous generations fail to acknowledge the fact that Americans have long depended on the labor of others to get dinner on the table. Poor white women and women of color prepared many people's meals a century ago, just as they do today. The difference is that these women previously worked inside the home, as domestic laborers, rather than in restaurants. At the peak, almost two million domestic workers were employed in American households.[19] Anthropologist Amy Trubek notes that idealized visions of home cooking persistently neglect "the many generations of paid cooks who first worked in homes and then in commercial settings to make these meals possible."[20]

Beyond *whether* we cook, debates about *what* we cook and eat have long simmered in the United States. What people eat and who gets to set the standards reflect larger economic and racial inequalities. The money in our pockets shapes the types of food we buy. On average, rich people in the United States have healthier diets than poor people, and the gap has widened in recent years, as the diets of middle-class and wealthy Americans have improved, but the diets of poor Americans have not. Researchers say this gap is largely due to the high cost of healthy foods.[21] It's more expensive to prepare a dinner with lots of fresh fruits and vegetables and lean proteins like fish or chicken than it is to make some ramen noodles or heat up a jar of pasta sauce and boil some spaghetti. There are other reasons, too. For example, it's more important to avoid wasting food if you don't have a lot of money, so poor people may be less likely to introduce something new to their families, because they might not like it.[22]

Class stereotypes about food also shape our ideas about people's food choices. In experimental studies, people automatically assume that more expensive foods are healthier than less expensive foods (even when the descriptions are identical).[23] Similarly, because people know that fast food is not very healthy, it is stereotyped as being the preferred fare of the poor. But

Americans across the income spectrum have a soft spot for McDonald's and Taco Bell. Still, this comes as a surprise to many. When a study revealed that the middle class eat more fast food than the poor, media headlines conveyed shock. "No, Poor People Don't Eat the Most Fast Food," proclaimed one.[24]

Ideas about food and what people eat are also shaped by legacies of racism. The foods traditionally associated with black culture, for example, are frequently denounced as unhealthy, simple, or backward, rather than as symbols of resilience, creativity, and sustenance. Psyche Williams-Forson, an American Studies scholar, argues that stereotypical black foods like fried chicken and watermelon have also been used to perpetuate racist images of blacks as primitive, predatory, or backward in their thinking.[25] Racist caricatures involving food have a long history[26] and persist today, such as when a white fraternity in New Orleans hosted a Martin Luther King Jr. Day party and served fried chicken, watermelon, and "forties" (40-ounce bottles of beer).[27] Unsurprisingly, given this racist context, many African Americans have a complex relationship with these foods.

Historically, food has carried symbolic weight for the many waves of immigrants who have made their way to the United States. Figuring out what to eat is one of the first challenges new immigrants face, and specific dishes and recipes from a person's country of origin can serve as a tangible source of memory and identity for immigrant communities. These foods have also long been used as symbols of immigrants' success or failure to assimilate. Starting in the late nineteenth century, nutrition reformers mounted campaigns to teach working-class immigrant populations from Eastern Europe and Italy how to "Americanize their diets in an economical fashion."[28] Italian food was described as "garlicky," "overstimulating," and "a real tax on digestion." "Still eating spaghetti, not yet assimilated," wrote one social worker after visiting an Italian household.[29]

Nowadays, dishes once derided as too "exotic" or "foreign" are widely embraced. American's favorite comfort food is pizza, introduced to the United States by Italian immigrants.[30] Mexican restaurants are now the second most common type of restaurant in the United States, edging out both pizzerias and hamburger joints.[31] Food scholars also argue that high-end cuisine is more "omnivorous" than ever before, with Indian, Mexican, and Thai restaurants available not just in New York or San Francisco, but in smaller cities like Raleigh or Des Moines.[32]

But the rising popularity of foods from around the world doesn't reflect a real movement toward equality or a genuine embrace of different cultures.

As food studies scholar Krishnendu Ray argues, there is a "hierarchy of taste" in terms of "ethnic" cuisine; as immigrant groups move up the economic and cultural ladder in the United States, so do the prices consumers are willing to pay for their food, but not before.[33] Immigrants, many undocumented, also disproportionately work in jobs that feed others: as farmworkers, meat processors, or restaurant kitchen staff.[34] These job sectors are among the lowest-paying in the United States. Ironically, the people responsible for feeding the country are employed in jobs that often don't pay them enough to feed their own families.[35]

Reflective of the common belief that we live in a post-racial society, many people do not see how race and ethnicity still deeply affect the way people live their lives or what they eat. But these inequalities have always been, and continue to be, a central part of our food dilemma.

Conversations about food ought to include the voices of people who continue to be sidelined by foodie mantras. Today, many of the messages we get about food and family meals come from affluent white men. These foodies sometimes entertain, inform, and inspire us, but they miss important aspects of what is really going on in American kitchens today.

Even though women are still largely responsible for the work of feeding the family and seen as the gatekeepers of their children's health,[36] few researchers have spent time with mothers and their families in their kitchens. Fewer have investigated how being rich or poor, black or white, a recent immigrant or a fourth-generation American, matters in the world of food and eating.

This book represents a five-year journey that we and a team of researchers undertook to understand what it's like to put food on the table in the United States. We interviewed over 150 mothers and a handful of grandmothers who were primary caregivers of young children. Sitting on couches or at dining tables, a recorder between us, we asked women to tell us what they did on a typical day. What do your children eat? Who shops for food? Who cooks it? We asked about food rules, body image, and what they believed to be healthy meals. The majority of participants (138) were from poor or working-class families. Another thirty participants were from middle- and upper-middle-class families.[37] The families in our study lived in or near Raleigh, the capital of North Carolina, and in two adjacent rural counties.[38]

As we spent time talking about food, we began to appreciate the complexities of families' lives and making family meals. Yet that didn't leave us with a complete picture of what families actually did. So we asked if we could watch them in action. We invited twelve lower-income families to participate in extended ethnographic observations.[39] All agreed to participate, and we spent hundreds of hours with them: going grocery shopping with them, tagging along on visits to doctors and social services offices, and hanging out in their homes as they made and ate meals.

We also embedded ourselves in these families' communities, forming partnerships with local churches, farmers, food pantries, and service organizations to better understand their food environments and help address food and health inequalities in their communities. We continued this work over a five-year period, conducting interviews and observations with families multiple times over the course of the project and collaborating with community groups on projects designed to improve access to food and spaces to be active.

As mothers ourselves, we are no strangers to feeding others. But, as we embarked on this study, we were aware that our understanding of this process was limited by our particular experiences as middle-class white female academics. As researchers, we understood the need to see beyond our particular ideas, practices, and contexts to observe the diverse and multifaceted dynamics at play in American homes.

This book takes place in Raleigh, North Carolina, and the region surrounding it. Raleigh is a place of stark contrasts. Home to the late, infamous US senator Jesse Helms, known for his overt racism,[40] Raleigh is also home to the Student Nonviolent Coordinating Committee (SNCC), one of the most influential organizations of the civil rights movement.[41] As one of the fastest-growing[42] and most-educated[43] urban areas in the United States, Raleigh is often hailed as a southern success story. But Raleigh's economic boom has not benefited everyone. In an analysis of economic mobility in the 100 largest counties in the United States, the Raleigh area ranked among the lowest.[44] The rural areas surrounding Raleigh have their own problems; poverty rates in Harnett and Lee counties, the two rural counties where this study took place, are over 16 percent, compared to just over 9 percent in Wake county, which includes Raleigh.[45]

We see these contradictions play out in food. Like many southern cities,[46] Raleigh's food scene has expanded and changed in recent years. For a long time, food in Raleigh was dominated by barbecue restaurants and cafeterias offering "meat and three" specials (essentially a choice of one meat and three vegetable sides).[47] From 1938 until it relocated in 2014, one of the city's best-known barbecue restaurants still had two entrances, relics of the Jim Crow era: one for black customers and one for white customers.[48] Today, craft breweries, hipster food trucks, and artisanal donut shops compete for an increasingly cosmopolitan clientele.

But Raleigh's foodie transformation masks persistent inequalities. Food pantries struggle to keep up with the demand from hungry families.[49] The only large supermarket in Leanne's neighborhood closed in 2012, leading to news reports that a "food desert" had emerged in downtown Raleigh.[50] Raleigh thus exemplifies both the promise and the challenges of transforming the food system from the inside out.

Raleigh and North Carolina are places of rapid transformation and deep injustices, coupled with a long-standing history of resistance. John Edge, director of the Southern Foodways Alliance, writes that the South evokes strong feelings because the United States recognizes "the best and the worst of itself here."[51] The dynamics within the families and communities featured in this book—racism, unequal food access, gendered parenting practices, and everyday acts of defiance and endurance—are not specific to Raleigh or North Carolina. They play out all over the United States. The stories we tell are stories about what it takes to feed a family in the United States today.

The stories in this book are informed by all of the interviews and observations from our research. However, to shine a light on the diverse and complicated dynamics around cooking and feeding families, we focus on nine women and their families. They all live within an hour of Raleigh. They are all raising young children. They all undertake the difficult and, at times, fraught work of making sure their families have food to eat. Yet, despite these similarities, their lives look very different.

Leanne Armstrong can't catch a break, no matter where she turns. She whips up culinary miracles in her cramped, bug-infested kitchen as she plans for better times.

Patricia Washington hopes to get her daughter and two grandchildren out of the hotel room where they've been living for four months. She dreams of a real home, where they can share a meal around a table.

Rae Donahue has positive memories of the Sunday dinners of her childhood. But she is terrified of developing the health problems confronting many in her family and sees the foods she grew up eating as the primary culprits.

Marta Hernández-Boynton goes by the book when it comes to feeding her two sons, taking a different approach from the way her mother raised her in

Mexico. But nutrition advice is always changing, and she questions whether she is getting it right.

Melanie Richards loves food but hates the body she lives in. As she tries to hang on the lowest rung of the middle class, her children's growing waistlines are constant reminders of what she's up against.

Rosario García is determined to be a model immigrant. She grows her own food and makes Mexican dishes from scratch. But her children, born in the United States, prefer pizza and hot dogs.

Greely Janson goes to extreme lengths to shop locally and eat ethically. Food matters to her, but the time and energy she invests in cooking and shopping are wearing her down.

Ashley Taylor strives to raise her daughters to be independent and self-determined, just as her mom and generations of African American women before her did. She works to put food on the table, but food isn't a huge priority in her life.

Tara Foley's childhood was marked by hunger and loneliness. She will do whatever it takes to keep her kids from going through what she went through as a kid, even as circumstances conspire against her.

These nine women gave us extraordinary access into their lives. The book is an intimate journey through their homes and kitchens, as well as their worries and hopes.

We organize the book around seven foodie messages. Some are insightful. Some are misguided. And some are well intentioned but miss the point. We illustrate how these messages resonate and don't resonate in these nine women's lives. By showing the work it takes to feed a family, we demonstrate why it is not enough just to tell mothers they should try harder and care more.

Our research convinced us that the solutions to our collective cooking pressures won't be found in individual kitchens. Families care about what's for dinner. They are doing a lot, and they're trying very hard. It's not enough. Instead, we need to look outside the kitchen.

We hope you will be convinced after reading this book that we won't fix the food system by retreating into our kitchens—a solution that just makes inequality worse, because those with more resources have more options. We need collective solutions that help meet the needs of diverse American families. Some of these solutions involve food. Food should be a basic right, and we should make it easier for families to enjoy a healthy meal at the end of the day, whether they have cooked it themselves or not. Some require broad changes, like policies that better support families and wages people can thrive on. Others require shifts in our collective imagination about what it takes to put food on the table, shifts that recognize the strength and dignity of all people and a commitment to right the injustices that undermine and divide us.

1 YOU ARE WHAT YOU EAT

Tell me what you eat, and I'll tell you what you are.

—JEAN ANTHELME BRILLAT-SAVARIN,
French gastronome, in *The Physiology of Taste* (1825)

Why do people care so much about food? More than just physical sustenance, people's food choices tell others *who* they are. Eating home-cooked food, around the dinner table, has become a symbol of people's commitment to family life and good health. Food can also be a symbol of our cultural roots, of where we come from and where we belong and don't belong. Food is never just food.

2 ROOM 105

"You need to come say grace before dinner," Patricia Washington announces as she removes a sizzling Tony's pepperoni pizza from the microwave. Patricia's age is hard to judge. She keeps her salt-and-pepper hair short, with her bangs pushed back. Given her smooth brown skin, she could be in her late forties. But her two missing front teeth and stooped posture create the appearance of someone beyond her fifty-eight years.

"It's hot," she advises her grandchildren, carefully divvying up slices of pizza between four-year-old Mia and one-year-old Jayden. She puts Jayden's three small slices in a blue plastic bowl. Mia's three slices sit in a black plastic bowl, recycled from last night's TV dinner.

Patricia picks Jayden up from the carpet and expertly situates him on her hip. Without prompting, Mia scrambles onto the bathroom vanity to wash her hands. With her knees on the counter to steady herself, she hunches over the sink basin, trying to grasp the knob of the faucet. She wears skinny jeans and a pink T-shirt. At four, Mia is small for her age. Her petite frame, combined with her broad smile and infectious laugh, seem to have a magical effect on adults, who often comment on how cute she is.

Teetering, Mia manages to turn the faucet on and wash her hands. But getting down presents a dilemma. "I can't get down," Mia tells Patricia, who has her hands full with Jayden. Mia's legs dangle over the side of the counter, searching for a foothold. Eventually, her foot finds the edge of the beige plastic wastebasket under the sink. She steadies herself enough to get down and walks over to where Patricia is sitting with Jayden on her lap. Like his sister, Jayden is petite. At his last doctor's visit, he was in the fifth percentile for height and weight. He has delicate features and dark hair, cut close to his head. He is dressed in a T-shirt and diaper.

Patricia decided it wasn't worth putting his shorts back on after she changed him the last time, since it will be bedtime soon.

Finally, with everyone situated, Patricia begins the dinner prayer. "God is great and God is good," she says in a soft voice. Mia repeats each line after her. "And we thank Him for our food. By His hand we must be fed. Give us Lord, our daily bread."

Steam rises from the slices of pizza. Mia holds her bowl up to her face. Delicately, she blows on it.

"Still hot, Mama," she reports.

Jayden copies her, blowing dramatically into his bowl.

After a minute, Mia bites into the chewy crust, struggling to tear it away from the rest of the slice.

Jayden pops an entire wedge of pizza, half the size of his hand, into his mouth.

Patricia doesn't eat.[1] Saundra, Patricia's daughter and the children's mother, usually joins them for dinner. Today, however, she is still out job hunting and won't be back until later.

An episode of *Family Feud* is playing on the outdated television set. One of the contestants shouts something out.

"Oh, yeah, that's a good answer," Patricia tells the contestant, glancing at the television.

It's a familiar scene, except that Patricia and the kids aren't at a kitchen table, or even in a kitchen. With plates on their laps, they are all crowded into a hotel room, sitting on one of the two full-sized beds that take up most of the space in room 105, where the family has been living for the past four months.

Most people have an idea of what family meals should look like. Maybe they pull it off on a regular basis, maybe they don't, but they hold in mind a similar ideal of what it means for a family to sit down and eat together.

From her cramped hotel room, Patricia looks forward to better times, when her family will have a home, a table, and tableware. "I'd really like to have a kitchen table, you know?" she says in her soft voice. She envisions Mia and Jayden setting the table and everyone gathering around it. "The kids will put the table in order, and everyone will sit down and eat together."

This is how Patricia remembers the mealtimes of her youth. She has good memories of eating with her family growing up. She was born in a small town a few hours from where she is now. "I grew up in the old days and I grew up on beans, you know, so I love beans," Patricia says. She breaks into a broad grin with the memory. It's only as an adult, looking back, that Patricia realizes her family was dirt poor. They rarely ate meat. Instead, a good meal consisted of soul food staples like beans, cornbread, fatback, and greens. Patricia's mom would send her to the little grocery store down the street to get fresh collards and mustard greens. "I still like mustard greens to this day," she says, smiling.[2] She remembers pinto and lima beans simmering on the stove for hours, later served with corn bread. After Patricia's mother died, she moved in with her aunt.[3] She knew her aunt was better off because they regularly ate meat and dessert.

When Patricia thinks of greens and beans, she is transported back in time, to the days when her mom was still alive and they ate simple meals together as a family. Patricia misses those times. Adults and kids would eat dinner together at the table, and afterward, the adults would sit around on the front porch and talk. She worries about how things have changed since then. "Sometimes when I reminisce on my childhood, I just look and think about this generation in comparison to my generation," she says. Things are different today. People have bigger houses, shifting schedules, and everyone is looking at a screen. The effect, Patricia feels, is that people no longer make time to eat together.

"Growing up, there might be two or three kids to a room, and everybody eats at the dinner table together," Patricia says. "Now everybody eats at their own time, whatever they want to eat. You still do have some people who are doing it the old-fashioned way. Some families still eat together, but most of this generation, they just slip through."

Family dinners are deeply symbolic. For Patricia, the past represents a simpler time, when it was easier to gather everyone around the table. Saundra agrees. When Saundra thinks about the past, she remembers the whole family—Patricia, her dad, her brothers, and Saundra—eating together. "As we got older, that's where everything started taking its toll," she reflects. "Back then, we were actually closer as a family."

"Back then" was before Saundra got pregnant at the age of thirteen. Before Patricia's husband left her. Before they got evicted and had to move into the hotel room.

Most people think of the family meal—coming together around a dinner table for the evening meal—as stretching back through the ages, but it's a relatively new phenomenon. As cultural historian Abigail Carroll notes in her history of mealtime rituals in the United States, the family meal as we know it today has only been around for about one hundred and fifty years.[4]

Dinner in the colonial era was a midday activity focused more on physical sustenance than family togetherness. The goal was to get energy to keep
working. It wasn't until the late nineteenth century that families began eating
the main meal in the evening, as family members increasingly began spending
their days working outside the home for pay.

Many people didn't take kindly to the change. In 1870, cookbook author
Jane Cunningham warned, "Six o'clock dinners destroy health." She cautioned
that eating so late in the day was bad for digestion and encouraged idleness.
Freed from the responsibility of preparing and serving a traditional meal in
the late morning and early afternoon, women would surely "give the day to
gossiping and visiting," she speculated.[5]

But Cunningham and other critics of the evening meal were wrong. Rather
than bringing American families to ruin, the evening meal instead became a
symbol of family cohesion. Dinnertime offered a chance for family members
to bond after spending most of the day apart. It was also an opportunity to
socialize children and teach them manners befitting their class position.

In turn, the family meal was mythologized. Dinner came to represent
family, home, middle-class prosperity, and eventually even American-ness.
For example, Norman Rockwell's famous 1943 painting, *Freedom from Want*,
depicts a family gathered around a food-laden Thanksgiving table. The image
blends the relatable concepts of food and domesticity with more abstract
ideas of patriotism and abundance.[6]

Images and messages about the importance of family meals continue to
infuse popular culture. Even though there's good evidence these claims are
overstated, many people fear the family dinner is in danger, including Patricia.[7]

Patricia believes the problem with today's generation is that people refuse
to turn the television off and eat together, like her family did when she was a
child. But this is the very situation Patricia finds herself in these days. Patricia
tries to create a sense of home and routine in the hotel room; they eat meals
together, even if it is on a bed, and they say their prayers beforehand. However,
Patricia often eats later, after she is sure the kids have had enough to eat, or she
doesn't eat at all. And the TV is always on. It's Patricia's lifeline to the outside
world from the dark, curtained hotel room.

Like Patricia, a lot of people feel they are coming up short in realizing the
idealized version of the family meal. Polls find that even though Americans
say they rank family meals as a high priority, getting the family around a
table to eat a meal together doesn't happen as often as many people would
like.[8] When we do eat at home, our meals don't necessarily involve cooking;
many people bring home takeout or heat up a frozen pizza, as Patricia did.[9]

Americans across the income spectrum also eat out quite a bit.[10] In short, there is often a disconnect between what people want and what they are actually able to do. As is true in Patricia's case, ideals are sometimes out of sync with the realities of people's lives.

Married for twenty years, Patricia raised six children, including Saundra, the youngest, and five sons. Saundra dropped out of school when she was pregnant with Mia. A year after Mia was born, Patricia's husband left her. Without his income, they could no longer afford to pay the rent for the house they were living in. Eventually they moved into a cheaper place—a dingy white duplex, just down the street. Saundra's second baby, Jayden, was born shortly after they moved in. The kids' father is in the picture, but it's complicated. He has an older child with another woman and drifts in and out of their lives. When Jayden was just two months old, Saundra went back to school to get her General Equivalency Diploma (GED) while Patricia watched the kids. Just a few months later, the bank foreclosed on their house. They found a new place, but they had to pay an additional $100 in rent and the insulation was bad, so their gas bills went up. They didn't have enough money, so they started paying half the rent and half the utility bills. Their landlord took them to court, and they were evicted.[11] They've been in the hotel ever since. It's a dilapidated hotel just off the exit from a busy highway. The room costs $270 a week, making it one of the cheapest rooms in the city.[12]

Fortunately for Patricia, who has trouble climbing stairs, they secured a room on the ground floor. One drawback is that they have to keep the heavy starched curtains closed if they want any privacy from people passing by. Peeking out of the curtains one day, little Mia, who is wise beyond her years, offers an accurate assessment. "A lot of people stay here," she states plainly. Patricia explains to Mia that sometimes people hit hard times. They are not the only family in this hotel that is in transit. An assortment of items—a grill, a folded-up air mattress, and a swivel chair—is heaped around a dumpster. People come and go, carrying plastic bags and plastic laundry baskets filled with clothes. Hotel lore has it one family stayed there for three years.

Patricia is certain her family won't be living in the hotel for three years. But she didn't imagine they would be here for as long as they have. Their room is cramped. It's a typical roadside hotel room that barely accommodates the two full-sized beds, nightstand, dresser, and plastic chair by the door. The bathroom sink and counter are located just outside the bathroom. Black trash bags, filled with clothes and other possessions, are lined up around the perimeter, making the room seem even smaller than it already is. Some of their things, including the kids' toys, are in storage, but other items and furniture have been lost permanently between the moves. With almost no room to move around, the family uses the beds for just about everything: eating, sleeping, and hanging out. The counter along the wall is stacked with Styrofoam Popeye's cups and 20-ounce plastic soda bottles. A hot plate, currently not in use, is buried under a pile of clothes. There isn't a spare inch of space in the whole room. Clothes sit in piles on the nightstand, shoes are scattered under the chair, and packages of diapers and other odds and ends are stashed underneath the counter.

A sour, musky smell pervades the air, and the hotel is prone to bug infestations. A few weeks ago, they had roaches crawling up and down the walls and into their bags. Unlike some of the landlords Patricia has known in her years of renting, the hotel management promptly called in an exterminator, and the bugs disappeared for the most part. At least for now.

Patricia has gout and asthma, and the bones in her hand are deteriorating. She plans to apply for disability but isn't optimistic. The approval process can be long, and she knows that she might not end up getting any benefits. They have no income besides food stamps, Medicaid, and Women, Infants, and Children (WIC) vouchers. The only way they can afford the hotel room is because Patricia's son Doug, who works for a moving company, helps them pay the rent. He helps as much as he can, but business has been slow lately.

The family is among the one and a half million households in the United States that poverty scholars Kathryn Edin and H. Luke Shaefer (2016) call the "poorest of the poor": households getting by on cash incomes of less than $2 per day per person in any given month, far below the official poverty line set by the federal government.[13]

Patricia and Saundra are pursuing the few viable paths they see. Saundra recently passed her GED exam. She hopes to enroll in classes at the same for-profit technical college as Leanne Armstrong, introduced at the beginning of the book, so that she can get certified as a medical assistant. In the meantime, Patricia watches the kids in the hotel room while Saundra looks for a job. They try their best to support each other.

"Mia is real attached to me, real close," Patricia confides. The kids have lived with Patricia their whole lives. "She was close to my husband, too, but he left, so I got to be the grandma and the granddad—to not let her down, because I feel that he let her down a lot." But at fifty-eight and with mobility issues, Patricia finds it hard to take care of two active children. She tries to get the kids out of the hotel at least a couple of times a week. They go downtown, to the library or the post office. Sometimes they visit friends on their old street. Outings are infinitely more difficult without a car. Patricia has trouble wrangling two kids onto the bus, which often runs behind schedule. And her asthma makes it hard for her to walk long distances. If she had a car she would take the kids "out to see things," or to the park or library more often.

Mostly, they all look forward to getting out of the hotel. Saundra spends a lot of time looking through help wanted ads on the internet and calling people. Patricia tries her best to navigate the complicated rules for securing long-term Section 8 housing, but she finds them difficult to understand.

As it is, they spend most of their time in the hotel room. Mia and Jayden pass the time by making games out of climbing in and out of cardboard boxes. Jayden rolls around on the beds, sometimes hiding his face as if playing peekaboo. Mia likes to mimic the adults around her. Pretending to talk on a cell phone, she feistily tells an imaginary caller, "Oh my God. My mama's at her job. Best leave me alone, girl! Mama call you back. I'm not gonna keep messing with you. Bye, girl."

But without toys or space to run around, the kids get bored and become easily frustrated. Patricia and Saundra spend many days whiling away the afternoon, lying on the bed, half watching TV, half sleeping, as Mia and Jayden climb over them. They spend a significant amount of time dreaming about when they will move on to bigger and better things. But Patricia is also grateful for what she has.

Mia and Jayden finish their pizza slices as the final round of *Family Feud* is starting. The host looks at his oversized index card and reads the question. "Name something one is thankful for at Thanksgiving."

"Life," Patricia says to the TV.

The contestant answers, "Family!" and receives fifty-one points. Out of one hundred people surveyed, fifty-one said that family is something to be thankful for at Thanksgiving. The host asks the next person the same question. Again, Patricia urges him to say "life."

It is a striking moment. Maybe it's because without a job or a house, and with few people she can depend on, there's little for Patricia to be thankful for aside from the fact that she is alive. But it may also be Patricia's way of saying that the small things don't matter. To be alive is to appreciate life.

DEEP ROOTS

Across town, Rae Donahue smiles as she opens the door to her family's home. She and her husband, Kenny, bought the one-story brick ranch, which resembles all the other 1970s-style houses in their neighborhood, five years ago. Large oak trees line Rae's street, providing some relief from the hot North Carolina summers. Rae likes the neighborhood, which is mostly quiet. They have a back-yard where Kenny sometimes throws around a football with their six-year-old son, Tyler, on the weekends.

Rae kicks off her shoes as she closes the door. Her bare feet sink into the white carpet in the living room. She pads to the adjacent dining room, painted a warm shade of olive green, and sits down at a large glass dining table that takes up most of the room. It's where Rae does the books for the salon she bought a year ago.

In her mid-thirties, Rae has a round face, clear brown skin, and soft brown eyes. Other than a subtle application of pale pink lip gloss, her face is free of makeup. She wears faded black skinny jeans and a V-neck black sweater. The sweater is loose but hints at a bulge around her middle.

When she talks, Rae's bright red and orange hoop earrings shake and shimmy, giving her outfit a dash of color and verve that matches her warm, vivacious personality. But when the topic turns to her health, she frowns. "I definitely consider myself overweight," she says matter-of-factly. Rae has been conscious of her weight since elementary school, where she felt big compared to her peers. "Until I went to school, I was around other people who were my size and people in the neighborhood. But when I went to school, I went to a pretty much all-white elementary school and they are very, very small. I wasn't huge, but I was not tiny."

It was in elementary school, Rae remembers, that she and her sister started thinking, "I guess we *are* a little chunky." Track and dance helped Rae slim down in middle school, and she stayed what she calls "a decent size" throughout high school. As an adult, her fears about being overweight have reemerged. It's been six years since she gave birth to her son, and she is disappointed that she still hasn't lost the weight she gained during pregnancy.

Becoming a mom offered Rae little shelter from the harsh judgment women face about their bodies. "After Tyler was born, I realized that he was only eight pounds, and the other forty-two were mine to keep. I was like, 'Wow! Really!?'" she says, poking fun at herself. "So I'm still getting used to having a new body." Around the same time, a family member told her that she was "getting a little chunky," which only reinforced her concerns.

Sometimes, Rae can laugh about her struggles. But she admits it's been "emotional," and she doesn't feel good about her current weight. "I would love *not* to be overweight," she says. "I would love to be back like maybe at 140 [pounds], or something like that, and just healthy."

Rae's story is familiar to many mothers. Pulled in many directions, Rae feels like she doesn't have a minute to focus on her own health. "After Tyler was born, I was so focused on him," she remembers. "And even now, I am still focused on him and my husband and family. So I don't have the time that I had before. I used to go to the gym a lot, and cook a lot. So I tried, but never really got my groove back."

Rae's dilemma is common. It's also tied to shifts in motherhood and family life over the past few decades in the United States. In the mid-1990s, sociologists began documenting how motherhood had become increasingly all-encompassing.[1] Even though many mothers, like Rae, work long hours to earn income for their families, many also believe that children must be their number one priority, even if it means sacrificing other pursuits or goals, including health.[2]

But it's not just motherhood that makes it difficult for Rae to be healthy. It's also her experiences as an upwardly mobile black woman and her taste for southern comfort foods, the foods that she loved as a kid but now thinks are unhealthy.

Rae and Kenny have deep roots in the South. They both grew up in Raleigh, only leaving to attend college. "We moved to go to school—my husband and I—for four years and then we came right back," she says, her pride in her hometown showing through.

Although Rae loved growing up in Raleigh, there were times when she felt isolated. She lived in a predominantly black neighborhood, but the schools she attended were mostly white. There were never more than three black kids in her classes in elementary school, as she remembers it. Her high school was more racially diverse, but the advanced classes she took were still mostly filled with white students. She often felt like everyone was watching her. As she explains, "Like you definitely didn't want to be in an advanced history class, or advanced English or math class, and be the dumbest one in there."[3] She adds, "But definitely if all eyes are on you . . . you just kind of feel like you're kind of being judged a little bit more. So, yeah, I did want to kind of stand out, in a good way."

Rae's experiences—of being a black person in a sea of white faces and feeling judged on the basis of her skin color—are familiar ones for many African Americans, especially those who are upwardly mobile. These situations, along with other forms of discrimination black people encounter as they climb the economic ladder, help explain why upward mobility—for example, an increase in household income—brings health benefits for white people, but not for black people.[4]

Going to a historically black university for college was transformative for Rae. For the first time, her classes were filled with other black students. She met Kenny there, and she also learned a lot about African American history and culture. "I *really* loved it," she recalls, smiling. "I broke out of my shell and started going to different plays and learning about history—really being engulfed in black histories and learning about different parts of the culture that I didn't know about."

At the same time Rae was acquiring a new sense of pride in black history and culture, she began to distance herself from the soul food she grew up eating, defining it as unhealthy.

College is a place where people often discover new ways of eating. Rae already knew there were diverse ways of eating; what she didn't realize was that soul food has such a complex history in black communities.

The term "soul food" emerged in the early twentieth century. It originally referred to the black church and "feeding the soul."[5] However, the term didn't take off until the 1960s, when soul food "became a rallying cry for black solidarity," writes culinary historian Adrian Miller.[6] Civil rights activists and soul food cooks proudly claimed that foods like chitlins, greens, and cornbread, which had been cooked by their ancestors under incredibly adverse circumstances, were symbols of their shared heritage and a banner under which black people could unite politically.[7]

But the uniting power of soul food was short-lived. Long-standing debates and critiques of foods associated with African American culinary traditions reasserted themselves.[8] Echoing arguments made in the early 1900s by Booker T. Washington and W. E. B. Du Bois, who famously called on black people to dethrone the "deceitful pork chop" from its place of prominence in many African Americans' diets, many black people denounced the foods associated with soul food as unhealthy, a scourge on black communities.[9] Another critique focused on the hypocrisy of celebrating a cuisine that descended from slave food.[10] Civil rights activist Dick Gregory argued that contrary to being a source of racial pride, soul food was deadly, a legacy of what white slave owners had forced or allowed black slaves to eat. He stated, "I personally would say that the quickest way to wipe out a group of people is to put them on a soul food diet."[11] Class fissures also emerged, with many upper-class African Americans "snub[bing] the cuisine as poor people's food."[12]

Rae waded into these debates in college and came down on the side of those who see soul food as unhealthy. But these are still the foods she loves to eat.

"My favorite meal [as a child] was fried chicken, potato salad, and sweet potato pie. Collard greens," Rae says with an embarrassed laugh. Before she went to college, Rae didn't think the foods her parents and grandparents made were so bad. "My grandmother and grandfather didn't cook absolutely healthy," she says, in a confessional tone.

The words tumble out as Rae thinks back to her childhood. "It was a lot of fried this and that. My granddaddy had a garden right beside the house. So whatever grew in the garden—beans, peas, you know, string beans—we ate. And a whole bunch of fried fish, fried chicken. Yeah. That's it. Fried meat pretty much every night. Fatback. Stuff like that. A lot of us grew up eating those things, and that's what we learned how to cook. Maybe it's a good thing I wasn't in the kitchen when mom was cooking, I don't know. But those are the things that we learn—it depends on where you grew up and what you could afford to eat. And you just carry that on from one generation to the other generation."

Rae points to the way food traditions are passed from one generation to the next, but rather than viewing this continuity as a celebration of family and community, she sees it as one way African Americans have embraced unhealthy eating practices.

Taking on the perspective of an outsider, she says, "So from the outside looking in, it's like, 'Why don't you just eat more broccoli? Do you know how to eat vegetables and fruit?' It's—I guess it's kind of difficult to explain."

As she struggles to convey how she can simultaneously love the foods of her childhood and consider them unhealthy, Rae channels a collective black "we." "We want to be healthy. We want to know how to cook better, but not at the risk of starving or eating small tiny portions, or eating food that does not taste good. You know, you trying to retrain your whole way that you do things. And there's really not a whole bunch of black folks that can say, 'You know what? If you like fried chicken you should really try this recipe that doesn't consist of your fried chicken.' You know, maybe gear more towards what we like to eat, but healthy."

The foods Rae remembers from her childhood, foods that are beloved by both white and black people across the South—fried chicken, collard greens, sweet potatoes, field peas, string beans—are rooted in the knowledge and practices of enslaved black people.[13] In *The Cooking Gene*, culinary historian Michael Twitty traces the story of African American food "from Africa to America, from slavery to freedom."[14] Slaves were fed corn, rice, and yams on the months-long journey across the Atlantic.[15] Those who survived the brutal passage typically ate corn for their first meal after they arrived. Sweet potatoes in the antebellum South replaced yams.[16] Collard greens were introduced to Africa by Portuguese colonists, then cultivated by slaves in plantation gardens. Chickens were often the only animal slaves were allowed to raise.[17]

Corn mush, field peas, okra, sweet potatoes, and greens were the foods that literally allowed enslaved people—like Rae's ancestors—to survive. In many African American families, fried chicken has long been the centerpiece of the Sunday dinner. In the first half of the twentieth century, fried chicken and biscuits, packed in "shoebox lunches," sustained black travelers when Jim Crow laws prohibited them from buying food at restaurants along their way.[18] In the 1950s, black cooks sold fried chicken and cakes to raise money for the Montgomery Bus Boycott, when Rosa Parks and other blacks took a stand against racial segregation by refusing to move to the back of the bus.[19] Fried chicken, collards, and other emblematic foods of African Americans and of the South are thus sources of pride, sustenance, celebration, entrepreneurship, and protest.

But Rae's conflicted feelings about the foods she associates with black culture and history are rooted in long-standing and complex racial dynamics. The vital contributions made by African American chefs to the evolution of food in the United States, and to the South in particular, have been almost entirely overlooked, argues food writer Toni Tipton-Martin.[20] Moreover, as American Studies scholar Psyche Williams-Forson notes, whites have long used the foods associated with black culture to perpetuate racist stereotypes, as when a Jim Crow–era postcard depicted a black man dressed in stereotypical tribal garb frying a white woman in a caldron, with the copy, "Well Fry Mah Hide! . . . Ah'm Having Chicken for Breakfast!"[21] The postcard associated fried chicken with a primitive and predatory black nature, a stereotype used to discourage black-white relations and justify the violent reign of terror black people were subjected to under Jim Crow segregation laws.[22]

The cuisines associated with African American heritage and black chefs have become more diverse since the 1980s, less tethered to "the narrow perspective that black food meant only pork parts, greens, and cornbread," argues Tipton-Martin.[23] But the debates that have played out throughout the twentieth century—whether soul food is a celebration of resilience or a symbol of oppression, an important link to the past or a way African Americans are killing themselves in the present—keep resurfacing. "The food we have been eating for decades and decades has been killing us," black vegan chef Jenné Claiborne tells the *New York Times*.[24] Rae agrees, but she's conflicted.

Health is critically important to Rae. In fact, one of the main reasons she decided to enroll Tyler in a private school was because it offered a healthier lunch menu. "One of their bigger selling points is their nutrition thing," she says. "Like they don't cook any pork, and they serve vegetables every single day. Healthy snacks and stuff like that. So the nutrition part was huge." Rae also wanted Tyler to have a different school experience from the one she had growing up. His classes are small, and most of the other students are black, she says. "They focus a lot on African American history. So he can tell you about black inventors, he can tell you about, you know, discoveries that were made and a whole bunch of different things like that. He knows he's African American. He knows what that means. He knows about President Obama and, you know, a lot of the history."

Rae is pleased that Tyler is learning about African American history and traditions and getting healthy meals at school. But she personally hasn't found a model of good eating for herself. Rae says the foods touted as healthy don't look anything like those she ate growing up. What she means is that they don't look like the southern comfort foods of her childhood.

"It's nowhere that I can go to and say, 'Okay, this person eats like I eat. And they're healthy. So let me follow this person to see what they are doing 'cause they seem like they know what they are doing. They're not going to tell me to eat mustard on asparagus or something like that.'" Learning to eat other food requires nothing short of "retraining" her southern taste buds, Rae believes. But she keeps trying. She is constantly looking for healthy recipes online, even though she keeps coming up short.

Despite its diverse population, the United States has yet to truly embrace diverse definitions of healthy eating. The foods Rae identifies as healthy, like broccoli and asparagus, are foods stereotypically associated with white diets. They are foreign foods to Rae, a far cry from the foods she loves.

"Do you just eat stuff because it's healthy or do you eat it 'cause it's good to you? Or do you make it good for you or what?" Rae wonders. The only thing she knows for certain is that the foods she enjoyed in childhood aren't healthy. She believes that these foods have contributed to the diabetes that runs in her family. "My aunt on my father's side just got her leg cut off about a month ago. And she still eats the same way even with the leg—oh wait, both of her legs are gone now!" Rae has even lost family members to diabetes. "All the older people, that's what they died of. It's not like they just had it and lost a limb. They *died*." Diabetes isn't an issue on Kenny's side, but high cholesterol is.[25]

Yet, for Rae, eating "healthy" involves replanting her roots in a culture where she is not convinced they will be nourished or thrive.

4 BY THE BOOK

From the road, the birth center doesn't look like anything special. It's a squat brown building with a small parking lot out front. The midwives' offices are on the third floor, above an acupuncture practice. A reverence for women and the art of motherhood permeates the waiting room. A decorative plaster cast, of a woman's breasts and swollen belly, hangs above the reception desk. A corkboard on the wall is cluttered with fliers advertising an array of parenting, birth, and breastfeeding classes and support groups.

When it's time to give birth, women are attended by a midwife in one of the three rooms on the first floor, each painted in soft pastels. On the whole, the birth center clientele tend to follow the creed that the best intervention is no intervention, so they do most of their laboring at home. By the time they show up, some of them have to hold their legs together to prevent the baby from arriving before they make it onto one of the beds.

The birth center has a warm, albeit low-budget, feel. The furniture is quaint but outdated. The examination rooms are cramped and the paint faded. Blood draws are done in the back room, on a padded medical chair with a frayed armrest. Yet many of the birth center's clients are middle-class women who have chosen to give birth here instead of opting for the modern hospital down the road.

Marta Hernández-Boynton is one of those women. Marta is a calm, no-nonsense type of person. Her athletic frame, short bob haircut, and full eyebrows are congruent with an aesthetic that prioritizes function over form. She rarely applies makeup to her light olive skin. On weekends, she prefers to dress casually, in polo shirts, jeans, and sandals.

Marta prides herself on the inside track that her degree in exercise science gives her when it comes to navigating the medical world. After doing a lot of research and talking with friends, Marta concluded that a traditional hospital was the last place she wanted to give birth. Friends had told her the nurses at the hospital didn't know anything about coaching women through a drug-free labor, and that their monitoring policies would prevent her from being able to move around during the birth. Marta wanted to feel free while giving birth, or at least not be forced to lie on her back, "loaded up with drugs." "I wanted a little more of a natural birth," she explains. She felt the birth center would give her the security and control she sought.

Having a baby growing inside her felt fascinating to Marta, and she took the job seriously. In preparation for motherhood, she made every effort to "read the books." Prompted by a deepening sense of maternal responsibility, Marta became more conscious about what she ate.[1] Her burgeoning belief that every bite of food could impact the baby intensified when the midwives instructed her to keep a food diary for three days and bring it to the next check-up. This was routine practice, but it made Marta feel self-conscious. She suddenly felt guilty about the extra desserts she'd been eating. "So I would try to think of the three days that I ate the best," Marta laughs, remembering how worried she was about what the midwives would say.

That was the diary she presented to the midwife: the best-case scenario. Afterward, because Marta wanted her practices to reflect what she had reported, she decided to lay off the desserts altogether. A couple of months later, eyeing her chart, the midwife suggested that Marta wasn't gaining enough weight. She told Marta that it wouldn't hurt for her to indulge in some ice cream, which Marta then dutifully did. Her efforts appeared to pay off. Marta gave birth to a healthy, seven-pound boy, Sebastian.

Five years later, Marta returned to the center to give birth to a second son, Mateo, whose weight (ten pounds, three ounces) shocked even the midwives. Marta proudly tells anyone who asks that not only did she give birth to such a big baby, she did it "completely vaginal. No drugs."

The birth of Sebastian, her first son, marked a new journey for Marta, one characterized by intensive research and monitoring of food. Little did she realize how much effort this would take.

Although nutrition advice is often presented as if it's a simple formula— eat right and in moderation—people today have a vast array of advice to choose from, much of it conflicting and almost all of it susceptible to change. Nutrition advice has always reflected more than just scientific findings, and that's because it is shaped by popular wisdom and current trends, which are also constantly shifting. Following this advice can be hard to pull off, and doing so on behalf of your children can be even more stressful.

Many parents in the United States today are anxious about their children's safety and well-being. Public policies emphasizing individual choice and responsibility over collective protections, and the rise of cultural narratives stressing the importance of parents protecting kids from risk, have led mothers, especially, to "up" their parenting game.[2] And the rising expectations around motherhood include how (and what) we feed our children. It's not sufficient to just get dinner on the table. On billboards and bus stops, on television and in magazines, messages about how to best feed children and protect their health are everywhere. Buy organic. Avoid additives. Build children's food repertoires.[3]

Being a good mother has long involved raising healthy children.[4] The problem is that the bar today has become exasperatingly high. Mothers are expected to be fully invested in protecting their children while also being ethical and informed consumers.[5] The seemingly never-ending job of mothering includes navigating shifting expert advice on how to cultivate children's healthy eating habits while minimizing their contact with harmful food additives and chemicals.[6] In this context, feeding children becomes a high-stakes activity.

Marta moved from Mexico to the United States after college, to get her master's degree. She never intended to stay, but she met James, now her husband, while in graduate school. After they got married, they realized it would be much easier for them to get jobs and live in the United States. It was hard to imagine moving back to Mexico when they had good job prospects here.

After Marta found work as a wellness program manager at a local hospital, and James as a clinical coordinator for a nonprofit health organization, they began looking for a place to raise a family. They took their time before finally selecting the right place: a cream-colored, two-story house in a suburban neighborhood.

"We're lucky," Marta says. "The neighborhood has a lot of trails. That's one of the reasons that we chose it, that there were a lot of walking trails." With its tree-studded lawns and wooded trails, the neighborhood seemed perfect for the nature-loving couple. Marta's suggestion that they were "lucky" to find their home belies the extensive research that went into choosing the house and location, however. They didn't end up in the neighborhood by coincidence.[7] They wanted a house that had easy access to walking trails and was close to a grocery store, so that's what they looked for. "We wanted to be able to walk to the grocery store, or bike," she explains. "We haven't done it yet. But we could if we wanted to."

Marta and James brought Sebastian home the same day he was born. While this was standard practice at the birth center, their friends and family were shocked to learn that the new family of three had come home so quickly. "Everybody was horrified," Marta laughs. "Like, 'Oh my God, I can't believe they let you come home!' But I was glad. We got home and we slept really well, all of us."

Other things didn't go so smoothly. Marta's forehead creases when she recalls the early days of breastfeeding. It was excruciatingly painful. "I was just at a conference and we were talking about working with infants and toddlers and breastfeeding," she says. "And the woman who was giving the conference was saying 'Well, what I always say is that it doesn't hurt.' And I'm just like, 'I'm sorry. I just do not agree with that.' People always told me that!" Marta imitates the dreamy voice of the breastfeeding expert: "It shouldn't hurt; if it's hurting they're not latching on correctly." She rolls her eyes. "That's what they tell you. And that just makes you feel horrible, like obviously I'm not doing this right. 'Cause with both of them I was in *pain*."

To make matters worse, Marta's son Sebastian was not gaining weight at first. Marta tried to stay calm. She had help from James and from her mother, who had come from Mexico to stay with them for six months. Like many middle-class women, Marta was determined to breastfeed her babies.[8] But Marta's mother had old-school beliefs about raising and feeding babies. She didn't breastfeed Marta or any of her other children.

A series of small clashes about feeding ensued. "It was difficult," says Marta, choosing her words carefully. "Because it was like having somebody else who wanted to make the decisions. So it was very hard. And she was always second guessing what we were choosing to do."

Pausing to gather her thoughts, Marta adds, "And we were definitely like—we had read the books. Like with the breastfeeding, she didn't understand that. She was always kind of questioning."

The books did not convince Marta's mom, who saw her daughter taking a very different approach to infant feeding than she had. "My mom did not breastfeed any of us. And she was constantly telling me that I was not giving Sebastian enough food when he was just nursing. She and my aunt—who is a doctor—they kept saying that I wasn't feeding him well. And I was like, 'He's getting everything he needs! He's fine.'"

It was a long six months.

"I was following it whole by-the-book," Marta explains. The books said to wait to introduce solids until the baby could sit up properly, so that's what she did. "I waited until six months. And, of course, my mother was freaking out, like: 'Oh my God! You're waiting so long!' It was difficult . . . We wanted to do it a certain way and she did *not* get it."

Marta believes that, in many ways, her parenting is a radical departure from her own childhood in Mexico. Sometimes she feels good about this, but at other times, she questions the legitimacy of doing things differently.

When Marta's mother was still staying with them, baby Sebastian got a fever. Marta and James preferred to wait and see. "I mean there is nothing the doctor is going to do but send us home and tell us to watch for the signs." Marta reasoned. Her mother disagreed. "My mother is like, 'As soon as they seem like they're sick, take them to the doctor.' And so that was very hard. 'Cause it kind of was a lot of friction. And, of course, I'm stuck in the middle and I always felt like, 'Am I doing the right thing? You know, like she's my mother. She raised three kids. Maybe I should do what she says?' "

Ironically, even when Marta does try to reproduce some aspects of her own childhood, like letting Sebastian play outside by himself, she faces criticism. Playing outside alone, even going to the store down the road on her own, was an everyday part of Marta's life growing up. "You know, we could go out in the street and buy something," she reminisces. "I don't ever remember that being a big deal. It was like, 'Can I go buy some potato chips?' Some adult would say, 'Sure, go.' " With that, Marta would zoom down the street with a fistful of change. "So, I think there was a lot more freedom about that stuff in my house growing up."

She wants the same freedom for her kids. But despite the manicured lawns and nature trails in Marta and James's neighborhood, very few people seem to actually take advantage of the green spaces. When children do go outside, their parents guard them like hawks. One time, seeing one of the neighbor kids outside, Sebastian wandered over and asked if he wanted to play. Minutes later, the child's father walked over to Marta's house, the two kids trailing silently behind him. When Marta opened the door, the man looked her squarely in the eye.

"Is it okay for him to be out here?" he asked, nodding to Sebastian.

Flushing with embarrassment, Marta replied, "Yeah. It's fine."

Before that, Marta had occasionally allowed Sebastian to take their dog for a walk in the neighborhood. But after the incident with the neighbor, she was reluctant to let him do it again, for fear of being judged a reckless mother.[9]

Some of the biggest differences between her own childhood and Sebastian's revolve around food. As a kid, Marta didn't eat junk food around the clock, but she was mostly allowed to have it whenever she wanted it. "One of the things I remember is that my mom always had a candy bar in our lunchbox," she says with disapproval. "So, now, it's one of those things that I'm so careful about, what I put in my son's lunchbox." In the Hernández-Boynton household, candy bars are contraband.

Marta often feels proud of the decisions she and James make around feeding their family, but she sometimes questions herself, and she is sometimes questioned by others, for their hardline approach. When Sebastian was four, he told Marta's sister that she shouldn't eat at McDonald's because "you could have a heart attack if you eat there too much." She was mad, Marta remembers. "My sister, she just thought I was way too healthy. She was like, 'Okay, whatever. You have your four-year-old repeating this mantra.'" To this, Marta shot back: "It's fine. I want him to know the difference." But these moments stay with Marta and add to her ambivalence about whether she is getting it right.

Although she grew up in Mexico, Marta has a lot in common with many middle-class people born in the United States. She feels torn between her memories of a past in which food was tasty and uncomplicated, and a modern reality in which food seems contested and fraught. The places we shop, the food we buy, and the way we prepare it all say something about who we are as parents and citizens. Every food choice carries moral, ethical, and health implications.[10] But it can be hard to know what is good or bad, or right or wrong, in today's shifting food and health landscape.

Marta is constantly reading up about food and nutrition. When her mother was diagnosed with cancer, Marta turned to the research for solace and a sense of control. "I started reading a book about things that you can do to sort of make your body not as prone to cancer," she explains. "Or at least keep it from growing. And so that just kind of opened up things. I was like, 'Well you know, I probably should eat more broccoli. We don't eat that much broccoli.' And then I started being like, 'Well, let's eat more broccoli, even if it's frozen.' It's one step in the right direction."

Marta and James are especially motivated to orient themselves in the right direction since the birth of their children. But it's difficult, sometimes, to know what the right direction is. "I think it's hard to be a parent in general," Marta muses. "Because everything has changed so much with nutrition. Like one day it's good to do this, and one other day, it's good to do that."

When the winds of nutritional science change, Marta tries to change course. During her pregnancy, she ate the healthiest diet possible. But she followed the midwife's advice when she suggested Marta wasn't gaining enough weight and should indulge in some ice cream.

After Sebastian was born, Marta and James went back and forth about whether to buy organic food. As they came across more studies pointing to the benefits of organic food, they decided to start buying it.[11] And when Marta read about the pink slime scandal at McDonald's, she immediately stopped eating there.[12] "Apparently they've now removed it," she says. "But, that's kind of gross. I've never liked the chicken nuggets. I don't think they taste good. My son likes them. But I've always thought it's not even real chicken."

Not that Marta makes a habit of eating fast food. As a rule, they only eat fast food on road trips. It's part of the treat of going on vacation. But ever since the pink slime scare, Marta drives right past the highway exits for McDonald's, despite protests from her family. "My son hates that," she says. "Now we try to do Chick-fil-A, because we sort of feel like that tastes better. And it does look like chicken. But the kids don't like it as much because they don't get a toy. So, there's like always this fight about it. Sebastian wants to go to McDonald's. He says he prefers the food. But we know better."

It's a constant battle, trying to avoid the junk food and sugar that are staples of the US (and Mexican) diet. Marta remains ever vigilant, yet she's not fully confident she's doing enough. "I feel like we've given Sebastian good enough messages," she says. "But I think if we weren't constantly offering good choices, it would be really easy for him to just be like, 'Well, those Doritos taste pretty good. I want that.'" Case in point: Even though Sebastian once chided Marta's sister about the health hazards of eating at McDonald's, he still likes to go there and is mad that Marta has struck it from their list of places to eat on family vacations.

In the face of uncertainty and conflict, Marta goes by the book. But it isn't easy. Following expert advice often requires charting unknown territory, with no guarantee that things will turn out as we hope. Ironically, writes cultural studies scholar Robert Crawford, we live in an age in which individuals are expected to take responsibility for being healthy, and yet our efforts to do so tend to yield less security and more worry.[13]

A rickety white mailbox marks the turn into the dirt driveway leading to the Richards' tan modular home. To the left is a recently plowed field. A makeshift garden, hemmed in by a circle of cinderblocks, struggles to come to fruition in front of the house. The potted plants next to the garden are having more luck, with small tomatoes ripening already and strawberries not far behind. A sign on the back door reads: "We hope you come as friends and leave as family." Melanie Richards and her husband, Kevin, have been renting the home for a little over a year. They live there with their two children, fourteen-year-old Justin and four-year-old Jade, and Melanie's mother, Judy.

Dressed in gray slacks and a hot pink top, Melanie sits straight-backed on the couch, her green eyes offset by her rosy cheeks and bright shirt. A strand of light brown hair has escaped from the plastic clip holding her hair back; as she tucks it behind her ear, Melanie reflects on how rural the area is. Her neighbors on the right have "been there since they were born," she says. She has gradually gotten used to hearing the sound of gun shots piercing the weekend silence. She thinks there's a local gun club that takes advantage of the isolated setting to get in some target practice on Saturdays.

Melanie's family can't really afford to move someplace else, so she tries to make light of it. "Like I said, if there were to be an invasion we'd be A-Okay. It doesn't bother me too terribly bad. My son thinks it's just awesome." For Melanie, the most important thing is that she feels safe. They know their neighbors.[1]

Their modest house accommodates all five of them: Melanie, Kevin, the two kids, and Melanie's mother, Judy. Judy moved in with them a decade ago, after a tray fell on her during a waitressing shift and damaged the bones in her hand. She now works as a home health aide. The work doesn't pay well and the hours are inconsistent, but it's something.

Things got a lot more difficult about five years ago, when Kevin, still in his thirties, was diagnosed with Parkinson's disease. The disease has affected Kevin's muscles, moods, and memory. Within the year, he had to cut back on his hours as a delivery truck driver for a supermarket. Not long after, he was forced to quit his job. He still does the odd delivery run when the family desperately needs the extra income, but this is increasingly rare.

Living with a chronic illness has worn Kevin down. His shoulders hunch over and his rounded belly protrudes from his faded T-shirt, making him seem shorter than his actual six feet. Dark circles under his deep-set brown eyes contribute to an overall air of fatigue and resignation. He is prone to bouts of depression and anger. If someone casually asks Kevin how he's doing, he's apt to answer, "Oh, good, I guess." After a pause, he'll add, "Except for we got a truck that don't run, a car that don't run, and I ain't workin'. So, good if you don't count that!"

Six months after Kevin received his diagnosis, Melanie found out she was pregnant with Jade. Financially, things were the toughest they'd ever been.

"Since we found out about her is pretty much when we started getting food stamps, since he hasn't really been able to work since then," says Melanie matter-of-factly.

Melanie largely supports the family on her paycheck. She earns $21,000 a year as the director of children's education at a local church. When she describes her daily life, Melanie is clear-headed and practical. It's a struggle sometimes, but they get by, with God's help.

"I think we do pretty well with the money we have," she says. "We have a decent house. We have a crappy car. We've had to lose a lot. You have to learn to be humble when you have a disease. We had to let go of both of our vehicles and, you know, we had to give up all of our credit in order to just, just get by. But we get by. We have, you know—the kids have Christmas every year. They have the food they need. . . . We're very blessed to live in this country and—and have what we have."

Melanie's patriotism and faith give her a sense of hope and self-worth. Biblical scripture also orients Melanie's thinking about food and the body. She believes all God's creatures are beautiful and that our bodies are gifts from God. But it's not always easy for Melanie to embody or practice a philosophy of reverence toward her own body.

Melanie would like to lose weight. By clinical standards, she is obese. Like many women, Melanie is unhappy with her body.[2] And, like many women, she's experienced a lot of attention toward her body over her lifetime. She has been ridiculed for her weight ever since she was young.

"In fourth grade, one girl told me that I would be absolutely beautiful if I weren't so heavy," she says, staring at the floor as she recalls the painful memory. Melanie was constantly teased for being overweight and always picked last in gym class.

For as long as Melanie can remember, food has been her "weakness," as she describes it. "You know I could be rigid with everything else, but when it comes to food, that's probably the one place I just don't have enough willpower. I grew up in an Italian home. So when we're lonely, or when we're bored, or when we want to make everybody happy, we find food. Because food makes us happy."

Her parents worked a lot when Melanie was young, leaving the kids to be fed by relatives. Melanie remembers her grandmother giving them chocolate cake for breakfast. For snacks, they would eat donuts or heat up frozen burritos and slather them with sour cream. A lot of the food they ate was what she now calls junk food.

Yet from an early age, she also got the message she shouldn't enjoy food because she was heavy. Her older brother and sister resented having to help care for Melanie and made fun of her weight. Melanie found herself caught in a vicious cycle of self-loathing, restricted eating, overeating, and more self-loathing.[3]

Melanie also blames her mother for her negative relationship with food. "I had a very bad example," she begins, taking a deep breath. "She did the Atkins Diet for a while. She binges. Like for months she'll eat a bunch of junk and she'll go, 'Oh I feel terrible. I look like crap. I look so fat. Blah, blah, blah.' And then she'll decide that she's not eating but once a day. Or she's not eating certain things."

Her mom has an unhealthy view of her body, according to Melanie. "My mom, to this day, when I take pictures of her [she says], 'Oh delete me, I look horrible.' And I'm like, 'Do you realize—I mean when you say that, do you realize what the children hear? They hear that they should care about that too, because that's what I grew up thinking. I learned to be just like her, until I got older and realized how negative that opinion is. And how harmful it is to say negative things about yourself."

But Melanie admits that it's not just Judy she's gotten these messages from. It's all the kids who taunted her in school. Her siblings who teased her. The doctors who have treated her.

"One doctor was so horribly mean," she remembers, thinking back to her first pregnancy. "He said, 'You shouldn't get pregnant when you're this heavy.

It's like asking a little small Toyota pick-up truck to pull a house.' He was hateful. He almost indicated that I should not have the baby, because I'm just going to kill it with being too fat."

In an effort to defend herself from others' thoughtless comments, Melanie built up a wall around herself. "I guess in my mind it was easier to not talk to people and shut them out," she says. "Because my feelings were very tender and I was easily wounded. It was much easier just to stay aloof, so they couldn't hurt me, as opposed to give them a chance, you know?"

But that moment in the doctor's office stayed with Melanie. She wanted desperately for Justin, her firstborn, to start off on the right foot. Trying to get things right, Melanie did a lot of reading during her pregnancy, just like Marta Hernández-Boynton. And like Marta, she committed herself to breastfeeding her children.

"I'm a very knowledge-hungry person," Melanie says with an uncharacteristic hint of pride. "So as soon as you start having a baby you read everything that's available out there. I was in college at the time, so I had already had some child development classes where they talked about it [breastfeeding]. And so I automatically knew that that was much more beneficial than formula. I honestly wonder if a lot of the obesity that we're seeing in our children hasn't come from the fact that bottle feeding was so prevalent for seventy years."

Melanie speculates that maybe parents who bottle feed are unable to recognize when their children are full and end up overfeeding them. She was determined to avoid being one of those parents. She breastfed both of her kids, because that's what the experts recommended.[4]

"Please forgive me, people who bottle feed," Melanie says, raising one hand to signal that what she is about to say might offend someone but needs to be said anyway. "I mean, like I *can't* imagine getting up at night to make a bottle. Like my sister-in-law. I love her. But she's . . ."

Melanie glances around to see if Kevin is within earshot. "I don't have the word for it," she continues in a lowered voice. "I don't want to say she is less educated, because that sounds really awful. But she just doesn't seem to care enough."

Breastfeeding was difficult for Melanie, but now she's glad she persisted. Having done so gives her a sense of being an extra-caring mother.

One of the reasons people care so much about food is because they see a direct connection between what we eat and how we look. Our physical appearance symbolizes the kind of eater we are, and hence the kind of person we are. Are we a person with willpower? Or are we lazy? Are we committed to health or do we not care?

When people are thin, it's assumed that they watch their weight and care about their health. But thin people—especially women—shouldn't be too thin or too vain, and they shouldn't be too controlling or care too much about food or weight, either.[5] On the other hand, fatness—again, particularly for women—is portrayed as a moral and personal failure, as evidence that a person has failed to manage their eating and weight.[6]

Americans have gotten larger over the last three decades, and as our collective waistlines have expanded, the stigma around fat has intensified.[7] In the face of evidence that children have also gotten bigger, attention has turned to their parents. What are they doing wrong?

The message that parents are mostly responsible for their kids' eating habits and body sizes—and to blame for things like childhood obesity, disordered eating, and poor body image—is widespread.[8] Melanie thinks her own up-bringing played a big role in her battles with her weight and body image, and she wants better for her children.

"Having grown up always overweight, I have always tried to be careful with my children, making sure that they're eating properly," Melanie says. "We're really careful with how many vegetables we get and that we don't eat junk."

Melanie tries to avoid buying snacks, ice cream, or soda. She makes fruits and vegetables a high priority in her family's diet. Even though they don't have a lot of money, when they moved into the house last year, she bought a small above-ground swimming pool and playset. She wants the kids to have a fun place to get exercise outside.

Yet Justin is getting chubby. He can't do a sit-up, and although he isn't the very slowest kid running the mile in gym class, most of the boys in his class are well ahead of him. And not long ago, Melanie got the news that Jade had gained more weight than she should have.

Sometimes Melanie feels like her past is destined to haunt her. Justin is being teased at school about his weight just like she was. Prompted by other kids' comments about his body, he recently declared he needs to lose weight.

Melanie is unsure of how to help Justin be healthy, on the one hand, and also maintain his self-esteem, on the other. The self-loathing she's struggled with all her life is something she earnestly wants to help Justin avoid. She acknowledges that he is "probably not as active as he could be" and wishes he would add more vegetables to his diet, so she tries to convey messages about eating better and being active. At the same time, Melanie feels strongly that just because Justin doesn't like vegetables or can't do a sit-up, that "doesn't define who he is." "And it doesn't define what *we can do*," she says, stressing the last three words.

Melanie is caught between the widespread belief that there are universal standards for health that everyone should achieve, and her commitment to seeing her child for all of his positive qualities.

She believes that it is important to take care of our bodies, too, because they are gifts from God. "It's more of a stewardship, a care of the spaceship God has given us to live in until we die," she explains. "We should take care of the body that we have, so it's healthy for as long as possible."

At the same time, her religious faith emphasizes that a person's appearance does not define who that person is. Certainly, she doesn't want Justin to feel ashamed of his body, like she has for much of her life.

Jade's relationship with her body is also a concern. "I hate that girls think they have to be the thinnest or the lightest," Melanie reflects. "They don't realize that most of the pictures they see [in magazines] are of people who are unnaturally thin. We expect a grown woman to look like a twelve-year-old. That's our image of a healthy woman. And it's just not appropriate."

Messages about the ideal female body affected Melanie when she was younger and have stayed with her today. "I should be happy with how I am and how God made me," she says, "but you pick up magazines everyday or look on the TV everyday and we're constantly confronted with these images of very thin . . ." she trails off. It's a topic she is passionate about. So much so, it's sometimes hard for her to express.

At four, Jade's round face, long blonde hair, and impish smile garner positive comments. People are always telling her how beautiful she is.[9] Melanie tries to temper these comments by emphasizing to Jade that it's what's on the inside that counts. She worries about how she'll handle the pressures about her looks that she'll inevitably face as she gets older. Melanie wants Jade to know that her body and appearance aren't all she is.

"I say, 'Jadie, what makes you beautiful?' And she says, 'God makes me beautiful.' And I say, 'Well, what is it about you that makes you beautiful?'" Melanie recounts. "I'm trying to instill in her that her beauty is the kindness and the caring and the gentleness in her spirit. Those are the things that make people attracted to her. And I hope that'll have an impact."

Like many mothers today, Melanie is concerned with maintaining her children's physical health and psychological well-being. Promoting children's self-esteem is increasingly understood to be part of the work involved with raising healthy, happy children.[10] The expectation to raise both emotionally *and* physically healthy kids, though, can sometimes put mothers in a double bind, especially when kids' bodies deviate from the norm. If a child starts to get heavy, does Mom say something? Is it dangerous or unhealthy to put too much emphasis on a child's weight? As Melanie does, many mothers try to find a middle ground, avoiding hurtful words and emphasizing to their children that they are unique and valued, regardless of their size.[11]

When it comes to her own body, however, Melanie hasn't managed to internalize the belief that all of God's creation is beautiful. When she talks about her appearance, she is besieged by memories of being ridiculed for her weight and a lifetime of guilt and shame around food.

Looking at photos of her younger self, Melanie can now say that she *was* beautiful, that she wasn't as heavy as she imagined. But Melanie has a hard time cutting her adult self any slack. "Too bad I'm not beautiful now," she says. "I should be happy with how I am, and how God made me." But she's not.

2 MAKE TIME FOR FOOD

There are now millions of people who spend more time watching
food being cooked on television than they spend actually cooking it
themselves.

—MICHAEL POLLAN, food writer, in *Cooked* (2013)

Food reformers tell us that it's time to return to the kitchen *en
masse*, to restore the health of the nation and the planet. The time is
there to cook, they believe, if only people would get their priorities
straight. But modern-day families juggle many, often competing,
demands on their time. Not everyone has full control over the
rhythm of their day, and even people with predictable schedules
may still feel they're coming up short at the end of the day.

6 TAKING THE TIME

The early summer air is heavy and damp. It's five o'clock in the evening, but the beating sun shows no sign of relenting. Thirteen kids find relief from the heat in an above-ground pool set up in the middle of Rosario García's dirt driveway. Water slops over the sides of the pool as they horse around, splashing and shrieking at each other.

Months ago, as Rosario began to anticipate the hot, humid days that begin in the spring and last into the fall in the South, she tried to convince a handful of her neighbors, all Latina immigrants like herself, to chip in money for a pool. They weren't interested.

"They're stingy," says Rosario. Her usually warm face twists into a scowl. "My husband says to get the kids whatever, because that's what he works for—the kids. But these women, they worry about looking good while their kids look raggedy." Rosario and her family wear mostly second-hand clothing, but she tries to find brand-name clothing for the kids when she can, so they'll fit in at school. She struggles to find clothes for herself that fit, because she is so short. Rosario has a plump midsection, dark brown hair, umber-colored skin, and glossy brown eyes. Her broad, dimpled smile draws people to her.

Rosario and her husband, Samuel, never could have afforded the pool on their own. In the end, they got lucky. Rosario's sister—a legal US resident with more money to spare than Rosario and Samuel—had purchased a pool the previous year. She wasn't using it, so she gave it to Rosario.

It's not the first time her sister has helped them out. When Rosario and Samuel migrated to the United States from Mexico twelve years ago, Rosario's sister, who was already living in North Carolina, arranged everything. She paid a *coyote* $5,000 to take them across the border, and then told Rosario and Samuel to be at a specific place at a certain time.[1] Rosario doesn't like to talk about the trip, but she remembers the experience of crossing the border as dark, scary, and full of uncertainty.[2] They had to wait until late at night to cross, and they could barely see what was in front of them as they walked. They heard strange noises and didn't know if they were coming from animals or something else. Eventually, they made it to southern California, where they stayed with relatives for a week before making their way to Rosario's sister in North Carolina.[3] Having no children and relatively few expenses at the time, Rosario and Samuel managed to pay her sister back in just over a year. Almost as soon as they made the final payment, Rosario got pregnant with her daughter Victoria, who is now ten. Santiago and Gabriela, now six and four respectively, followed soon after.

The Garcías' hopes of achieving financial security have not gone as planned. They're barely getting by in the United States. Samuel works for a landscaping company. The company is slowly recovering from the recession, but things have been tough. He only gets hours when they have work for him. For side cash, Rosario babysits her neighbors' children, resells clothing and toys at the flea market, and sells homemade tamales. But it's not enough. The American Dream looks increasingly distant to Rosario and Samuel, but so is their memory of Mexico. Their three children have never even been there.

When Rosario and Samuel began assembling the pool in the front yard, the neighbors immediately started asking where the money had come from. "I told them I got it for my kids because I was determined to do so," says Rosario, her jaw set firmly. She didn't tell them the pool was a gift from her sister. Although she is friends with the other women in her neighborhood, she wanted them to feel ashamed for being selfish.

She was further vindicated when, upon seeing the pool full of gleaming fresh water, the neighborhood kids started begging their mothers to swim in it. One by one, the women swallowed their pride and asked Rosario if their kids could use the pool. She said she didn't mind, but under one condition: that she and the other families would split her water bill at the end of the month. They agreed.

School is out for the summer. The daytime temperatures have hovered in the eighties all week, and few of the families on Rosario's street have central air conditioning. The small, hot, cramped houses on Anvil Street are the last places anyone wants to be during the day. At least the kids, who have been splashing around in the pool for hours, are getting some relief.

Rosario and the other moms keep an eye on things from under the shade of a small tent, set up next to the pool. They sit in white plastic lawn chairs, trading stories and gripes in rapid Spanish. Julieta and her husband and three children live on the other side of Rosario's duplex. She has an upbeat, jovial personality, and Rosario often hears her boisterous voice booming through the thin walls. Ana and Angie live a few houses down, in duplexes that are almost identical to the one that Rosario and Julieta live in. Ana, a mother of two, has come directly from work and is still in her uniform. Angie has brought her two girls, as well as three nephews.

The women know each other well. No one bats an eye at the fact that Angie is clad in a tight black tank top and shorts that are meant to be worn as shapewear. The conversation meanders and flows, with occasional pauses punctuated by animated conversation.

Abruptly, Ana stands up. "Vámonos. ¡Tengo que cocinar! (Time to go. I have to go cook!)" she hollers to the kids in the pool. The other women shift in their chairs and begin to stand up.

"I have to go cook," Julieta tells her children.

"Not yet!" a chorus of children's voices cry out.

"I have things to do," Ana says sternly. The kids yell in protest.

Ana's two children are the first to comply. They scramble over the side of the pool, dropping down onto a thin piece of plywood on the ground next to the pool. The plywood is Rosario's makeshift attempt to keep the water from creating a muddy pit in the driveway, but her effort is mostly in vain. There is already a patch of muddy dirt next to the pool.

"Can we come back tomorrow?" Ana's daughter asks as she gets out.

"You can come every day, as long as it's not raining," Rosario magnanimously tells her. Ana has already started walking down the driveway. Her children trot after her to catch up.

Rosario's son, Santiago, is the next to get out. He catapults his lithe body over the side of the pool and flashes a happy grin at Rosario as she hands him a towel, showing off the gaps where he recently lost four front baby teeth: two on top and two on the bottom. Quickly patting off a few drops of water, he trots into the house, the screen door slamming behind him. The remaining children continue splashing, tagging each other and then ducking under the water to escape.

"Get on with it!" Angie orders her oldest daughter, Barbara. She turns on her heel and starts walking toward her house, with Barbara and the four other kids she's brought traipsing behind her.

Julieta's three children hop out of the pool when they see their mother head across the yard to her side of the duplex. Rosario's daughter Victoria gets out as well. She spends most of her days playing with Julieta's daughter Jenny and Barbara. Now that her friends are gone, there is no reason to stay in the pool. Victoria jumps out of the pool and lands with a thud on the piece of plywood, tugging at her tankini top to avoid exposing her slightly rounded belly.

With the pool to herself now, Rosario's daughter Gabi swims in slow circles. She flips onto her back as she tries to figure out how to float, to no avail. Within seconds, Gabi's small frame sinks under the water. Rosario smiles as she watches her spirited, carefree daughter. She is tempted to let her stay in a bit longer, since Gabi always sleeps long and hard after a day of playing and swimming. But Rosario needs to start making dinner. She grabs a green towel from one of the chairs and walks to the edge of the pool. Opening her arms wide, she calls for Gabi to come inside.

One of the most common refrains of modern life is that there is never enough time, especially to cook. It's true that Americans spend less time in the kitchen than they did in previous generations. Home chefs spend about thirty minutes a day cooking, compared to around an hour and a half in 1965.[4] Since the 1960s, men have increased their cooking time, while the amount of time women spend cooking has dropped nearly in half: from two hours a day to about one.[5] More women are in the paid workforce than in the 1960s.[6] Many families today work long hours and feel strapped for time.[7]

Despite these challenges, experts say a lack of time is no excuse. "Taking the long route to putting food on the table may not be easy," writes Mark Bittman, a chef and former *New York Times* columnist, "but for almost all Americans it remains a choice."[8] Bittman rejects the notion that people are too busy to cook. "The time is there," he contends, arguing that people would have more time if they didn't watch so much television. Michael Pollan agrees and points out an irony. "At the precise historical moment when Americans were abandoning the kitchen," he notes, "we began spending... much of our time thinking about food and watching other people cook it on television."[9]

Foodies like Pollan imply that the solution is fairly simple: We should step away from Food Network and return to the kitchen. But it's not Rosario they're talking to. She's already in the kitchen.

Rosario and Gabi enter the kitchen through the battered screen door on the side of the house. Gabi scurries off to change her clothes, and Rosario assesses the kitchen. There are only two small cupboards, and the counters are piled high with pots and pans that won't fit in the cupboards. Despite her lack of storage and space, Rosario takes pride in keeping her home neat and tidy, decorated with small touches from Mexico.

In and around the small home lies evidence of a family navigating a double life, with one foot in Mexico and the other in the United States. Rosario's siblings all live in the United States, but her parents are still in Mexico. Rosario and Samuel speak Spanish at home, but the kids speak English at school and with their friends.

Cooking helps connect Rosario's past with her present. Rosario left Mexico in her early twenties. She had known Samuel for just six months and never really cooked for herself. She learned to cook by watching her sisters after she arrived in the United States. But the foods she makes most often are Mexican; they are the same foods she and Samuel ate as children: *pozole*,[10] *chiles rellenos*, broth with chicken or beef, and tacos.

Rosario usually starts preparing dinner almost as soon as she wakes up. Many of her dishes require time to simmer or stew throughout the day. She likes to make her dishes early in the day in case something comes up later to delay her dinner preparations.

Earlier today, Rosario made a tomato broth with tiny alphabet noodles. The soup resembles a *sopa de fideo*, a classic Mexican soup. This time she used alphabet noodles instead of the thin fideo noodles that are usually in the soup. Lifting the lid off the pot, she checks on the chunks of tomatoes swirling in bright red broth, squeezes in a bit of fresh lime juice, and turns on the burner.

With the soup taken care of, Rosario turns her attention to heating up some leftover pork from a few days ago. The pork has been seasoned with fresh herbs: cilantro, *verdolagas*, or "Mexican parsley," and *epazote*, an herb that is considered an essential part of many Mexican dishes.[11]

When they moved to North Carolina more than a decade ago, Rosario was hard-pressed to find many of the ingredients she needed for her dishes. Now she can get most of what she needs at one of the Mexican grocery stores in Raleigh,[12] but they also continue to grow herbs and chiles in their garden. It is important to Rosario to make her dishes the traditional way. When she couldn't find a particular type of chile, Rosario asked a friend returning from a visit to Mexico to bring her the seeds so she could grow them herself.

Pouring a bit of oil into a frying pan, Rosario turns the heat to medium-high and tosses chunks of pork into the pan. Once the pork is heated, she turns the heat down and wipes the beads of sweat from her brow. The kitchen is stifling. Rosario glances at the clock. It is almost six o'clock, and she still needs to make the tortillas.

She gets out the heavy cast-iron griddle and puts it on the stove, where it stretches across two burners. After turning the heat on high, she pours *masa harina*, flour made from corn that has been cooked and soaked in an alkaline solution, into a metal saucepan. She angles the pan into the sink, anchoring the handle against the ledge of the sink to steady it. Turning on the faucet, she allows a small stream of water to flow into the pan. She simultaneously massages and kneads the corn flour in the pan, then turns off the water. Continuing to knead the dough, she adds a sprinkle of salt. She now has a five-inch ball of sticky yellow dough.

Making tortillas is both an art and a science. It's important to add just the right amount of water. Too little, and the dough won't hold together. Too much, and it will be too sticky. You can't add the water too fast, either, or the dough will turn out lumpy.

Bending down and rooting around in the cupboard under the sink, Rosario finds her trusty tortilla press. The cast iron press is heavy, and she has to use both hands to lift it. She sets it on the counter and then fishes two plastic Walmart shopping bags out of the same cupboard. She deftly wraps one around each plate of the press, which keeps the tortillas from sticking to the press.

Rosario is petite, but her strength in the kitchen is impressive. She grabs a small handful of dough, rolls it into a ping-pong-sized ball, and places it in the center of the bottom plate. Pushing down on the handle, she leans forward to get her full weight behind it. Lifting the handle up, she carefully peels off a perfect disk, about five inches across and uniformly thick.

Heat rises off the griddle, making the hot kitchen even warmer. The griddle sizzles when Rosario places the disk on it. After a short time, she flips it over, then waits until it puffs up, indicating that it's almost ready. She uses the press to make additional flat circles of dough, then puts them on the griddle, repeating the process again and again. When the tortillas are done, she gingerly places them in a small foil-lined basket, folding the edges of the foil inward to keep the tortillas warm. Rosario makes it looks easy, but it's not.[13] The ease of her movements reveals how many times she has made tortillas.

While she could just buy premade tortillas from the store, Rosario firmly believes that fresh tortillas, made from scratch, are far superior. She refuses to fall into the rank and file of Mexican immigrants who, she believes, become lazy when they "come north" to the United States and start buying premade tortillas. It's better to take the time to make the tortillas yourself.[14]

While the tortillas cook, Rosario turns off the soup burner and lowers the heat on the pork. Although she is simultaneously preparing three separate dishes, she manages, as always, to be constantly aware of what each dish requires.

She tastes the soup, decides that it's ready, and ladles some into a shallow bowl. Placing the bowl on the table, she immediately turns back to the griddle. Two of the tortillas are ready. With her fingers, she swiftly transfers them to the basket.

"Victoria, come eat!" Rosario bellows out the screen door. Victoria walks in through the front door just a few seconds later. Rosario sticks her head outside and yells for Santiago and Gabi to come and eat.

A next-door neighbor, a tall African American girl about the same age as Victoria, comes to the door instead.

"Victoria, can you come out?" she calls through the screen door in English.

"Qué dijiste? (What did she say?)" Rosario asks Victoria.

"If I could go outside," Victoria explains in Spanish. Rosario instructs Victoria to tell the neighbor that she is getting ready for dinner.

"I'm getting ready to eat," Victoria tells her. The girl wanders away.

Still the only one at the table, Victoria sits quietly, patiently waiting for her food. Santiago shows up a few minutes later. He is sweaty and thirsty. He grabs an open can of Pepsi from the bottom shelf of the refrigerator and takes a long sip before sitting down. Gabi is still outside. She had walked into the kitchen a few minutes ago but ran back out when she saw the food wasn't ready.

"Do you want soup or pork?" Rosario asks Victoria in Spanish.

"Pork," she replies.

Rosario asks Santiago the same question. "Soup," he tells her. Rosario passes him the bowl of soup that is already on the table. She knew he wouldn't go for the pork. Santiago hates spicy food.

Rosario's kids often refuse to eat what she makes. "Sometimes they say, 'Mom, we don't want you to make this because I don't like it,'" she says. "Take Santiago. When I make pozole, he thinks it's spicy. But it's not."

The kids want Rosario to cook "American" food. They were born in the United States. They are surrounded by children who eat pizza and hot dogs, speak English, and play baseball. And they want to fit in. For them, Mexico exists only in their parents' stories.

Rosario doesn't even bother to ask Santiago if he wants hot dogs, because she knows he'll eat them. She removes two hot dogs from a package in the fridge and puts them on the griddle, now free of tortillas. The griddle is still hot, and it only takes a couple of minutes to heat up the hot dogs.

Removing the hot dogs from the griddle, Rosario slices them lengthwise and places them on a small saucer for Santiago. He picks up one of the pieces with his hands and wolfs it down, ignoring the soup in front of him. He devours the other three pieces in the same fashion.

Finally, Gabi appears at the side door. She peers into the kitchen but is unable to open the door, because her hands are covered with mud and she has a doll wedged under her arm. Rosario opens the door for her, and Gabi sprints to the bathroom.

"Will you be eating?" Rosario asks Gabi when she returns to the kitchen. She shakes her head no and goes back outside.

Having eaten the hot dogs and gulped down most of the soda, Santiago finally begins eating his soup. He has only taken about three spoonfuls when he sees a group of kids walk past the kitchen door. They are wearing cleats, and one is holding a soccer ball. Santiago jumps up, runs back to the kids' bedroom to grab his cleats, and run-hops out the door, still squeezing his foot into one of the cleats. He leaves his plate and soup bowl on the table.

Minutes later, Victoria's friend Barbara walks into the kitchen. She has come through the front door without knocking. Sipping from a big red plastic cup of soda, she saunters over to the table.

"You're taking too long to eat," she tells her in English. Victoria puts the remaining half of her second tortilla back in the basket.

"Ya no tengo hambre (I'm not hungry)," she announces, standing up from the table. Like Santiago, she leaves her plate on the table. Half of the pork is still on the plate. She hasn't touched her cup of water.

Samuel emerges from one of the bedrooms as Rosario is clearing the table. A trim man with olive-toned skin and green eyes, he asks Rosario to make his food, then ducks outside to inspect the garden.

While he is outside, Rosario sets about preparing a fresh batch of tortillas, putting the warm tortillas into the foil-lined basket. She puts most of the remaining pork into a shallow bowl, then carries the basket and bowl into the living room. She sets both on a tiny folding table next to the couch, then goes back into the kitchen, where she fills a tall plastic cup with ice. She brings the cup and an unopened bottle of water to the living room.

Samuel always wants to eat dinner in front of the TV. Rosario wishes he wouldn't do this, because she thinks they should all eat together at the kitchen table, but he insists. She is worried that his bad habits are rubbing off on the kids. They often want to eat in front of the TV now, too.

Outside, Samuel surveys the garden that runs alongside the side of the house. The garden is mostly his domain. Four dark rows of soil are planted with red flowers, tomatoes, and hot chiles. On the porch, small pots are filled with mint and wormseed. In a couple of weeks, the tomato plants will rise up, branch out wildly, and cling to the metal stakes in the ground for support. The mint will also fill out, its green hue deepening in the summer sun. In a month, the yellow-orange flowers of the pumpkins planted in the backyard will emerge, and the mint and cilantro will run rampant. The family will have an abundance of chiles.

Their garden is the only one on the street. Samuel shakes his head. It's a shame, he muses to himself. No one is interested in growing their own food anymore. He surmises that the people around here are too lazy. They don't care about anything, he thinks, with a mixture of sadness and resentment.

Samuel smells Rosario's tortillas calling him. He walks back inside, where he plops down on the couch and digs into the spread Rosario has set up for him.

Seeing that her husband is satisfied, Rosario wipes her brow. "Now I can eat, because *el señor* has been served," she says, returning to the kitchen.

"*El señor*" most closely translates as "the master" or "the lord." Rosario's title for Samuel says a lot about their relationship. She talks about him with pride and deference. They both work hard to raise their family, but Rosario believes Samuel is the head of the household and deserves respect. He is older than she is, and more sophisticated, in her opinion. Whereas Rosario grew up in a very rural part of Mexico, Samuel grew up in a big city. He goes out into the world every day, while Rosario mostly sticks close to home. Samuel works for money and Rosario rules the kitchen. Both seem to find their arrangement agreeable, although it is far less common in the United States today than it was a few decades ago.[15] Samuel is proud of his wife's talents. He often brags about her cooking, telling people they need to taste her tortillas because "they're homemade!" And Rosario rarely questions Samuel's authority.

Pouring herself a tall glass of water, Rosario is finally ready to prepare her own plate. She puts two tortillas and a few pieces of pork on a plate, then sits down at the table, alone. The TV blares from the living room. Rosario eats quickly, folding the tortillas around the chunks of pork. She revels in having a moment to herself. She has been cooking for much of the day, and it feels good to be finished, at least for the moment.

In reality, Rosario's work is never done. As she is swallowing the last bite of the second tortilla, she is already getting up to wash the dishes. A few minutes later, Victoria's friend Barbara comes bursting through the front door.

"Are you going to the park?" she asks Rosario in Spanish.

Rosario sighs. "I'm tired," she tells Barbara. "I'll go tomorrow."

A few minutes later, Gabi and Victoria come in through the front door, asking her to please reconsider going to the park. "Por favor!" they beg. Rosario gives in. "Fine," she tells them, "but give me a second to wipe the table down." She wipes the table with a wash cloth, then washes her hands, drying them on her shorts. She goes out through the side door and walks around to the front porch, where a group of kids is waiting to go to the park: Rosario's three kids, Barbara, and a handful of other neighborhood children. Like the Pied Piper, Rosario leads the pack of kids up the street to the park two blocks away.

In many ways, Rosario is the modern version of the classic 1950s housewife, serving her husband and children, prioritizing cooking and housework, and sacrificing her own interests. This system seems to work, for the most part. But it is precarious. Being a stay-at-home mother allows Rosario some flexibility to arrange her day around cooking meals from scratch. Yet doing so requires that she stretch herself thin in other places. Rosario and Samuel have little money, and Rosario is constantly juggling side jobs. With Samuel's low wages and Rosario's lack of a regular income, the family has no extra money when unexpected expenses crop up. Although there are not as many stay-at-home mothers in the United States today as there were in previous generations, they are more likely to resemble Rosario, with low levels of formal education and few job prospects.[16]

Cooking is a way for Rosario to show how much she cares for her family. And preparing traditional dishes is a daily act of remembering and asserting her Mexican roots. Rosario and Samuel are critical of "lazy people"—a category into which they lump both Mexican immigrants and people born in the United States—who don't take the time to grow their own food or make anything from scratch.[17]

But making food this way—from scratch, with the right ingredients, adjusted to the tastes of each family member—takes a lot of time. Rosario spends hours in the kitchen every day. She also spends lots of time shopping to find the right ingredients. This leaves her with little time for herself.[18]

Rosario's favorite time of day is the afternoon, when she can sit outside and watch the kids play, just as she did today. She enjoys the rare occasions when she can take a walk with her sisters or go window-shopping at the mall. But she doesn't have time to do these sorts of things often. She feels it is her job to cook and care for her family and doesn't want to be like those selfish women who put their needs and interests ahead of their children. "I've never liked leaving my children alone. From the time I had Victoria, I've never left her alone," she states proudly.

7 FINDING BALANCE

Sometimes Greely Janson feels like her whole life revolves around food. As the owner of a pay-what-you-can restaurant, she works with food all day.[1] At home, her efforts to provide and prepare good food for her family take on the magnitude of a second job. But she feels very strongly about the importance of eating fresh, ethically produced, and seasonal food and about the value of her family sitting down together to eat. "We basically try to have breakfast and dinner together," she says. "And I would say that 95 percent of the time we're able to do that. Which, I feel, is extremely rare for families today. But it's important to us. And sometimes challenging, for sure."

Greely stands about 5' 8" and has a slim build. She usually wears her light brown hair tied back in a ponytail, accentuating her oval face and blue eyes. She lives with her husband, Matt, and their six-year-old daughter, Adelle, in a tidy two-story house, complete with front porch and rocking chairs. Around them, well-maintained bungalows and stately colonials sit on lawns maintained by landscapers, predominantly Latino, who operate high-powered gas mowers and leaf blowers throughout the week to avoid disrupting the quiet of weekend mornings. On the rare winter days when it snows, families congregate at the park in the center of the neighborhood. Kids take turns sliding down the hill as their parents sip from thermoses of coffee and discuss their upcoming ski vacations.

The neighborhood is full of young families, which Greely loves, and she is very happy with how things are going at Adelle's school, one of the best-rated elementary schools in Raleigh. But Greely has had a hard time connecting with the other parents. The school is "kind of fancy," and the neighborhood codes are somewhat baffling to Greely. "I feel like even though people are friendly, there's some sort of built-in social or cultural code that I don't seem to understand," she says. "There are people who live in much bigger, fancier homes, and there's this whole social aspect of play dates. I don't know—it's just not as comfortable as I would like it to be."

Bucking the neighborhood code of maintaining pristine lawns with carefully cultivated shrubs and flower beds, Greely planted a row of vegetables along the edge of her front porch.

She feels she bucks a lot of norms when it comes to food. Greely has a vision of health that involves slowing down. Being with family. Appreciating food. Living in the moment. And her sense is that other people in her community want the same thing. But she is aware that, like Rosario García, she spends much more time than the average American cooking, shopping, and producing her own food. "We focus so much on our quality of food and our willingness to prepare good food," Greely comments, trying to explain why food plays such an oversized role in her life.

Their days are nothing short of exhausting, Greely feels. The family gets up around 6:45 each morning. Matt, an accountant, makes breakfast and packs everyone's lunches. Adelle is supposed to feed the cat and get herself dressed. Every once in a while, she looks at the laminated chart she made to help remind herself of what she needs to do in the morning. But most days, she drags her feet or wanders off to play with the cat when she should be eating breakfast. "Sometimes it happens more smoothly than others," Greely sighs, reflecting on the daily routine.

Matt could eat the same bowl of cereal every day of the week, Greely says dryly, but she needs more "diversity" in her breakfast routine. So she makes sure they eat a range of things for breakfast, even if that means she has to cook it herself. "We have hot cereals. There's a buckwheat cereal that's gluten-free and it's more savory. And Adelle will eat that. She'll eat scrambled eggs. Last night I made twenty tortillas. So we had tortillas with our dinner, and she can have breakfast burritos. Today, for breakfast Adelle had some Fage yogurt with honey and then she had some dry cereal and then she had an orange. And what did I have? Oh, I had an apple with peanut butter and an orange and then this." Greely uses the spoon she holds in one hand to point to the half-eaten bowl of yogurt in the palm of her other hand.

Like many parents who work full-time outside the home, Greely says she goes full tilt from the minute her feet hit the ground in the morning. And the end of the day is just as hectic. Meetings sometimes run late. Adelle has regular practices for an after-school chess club. To save money, Greely and Matt arrange for a network of family and friends to watch her after school on the days when they can't pick her up themselves.[2]

Most days, Greely is exhausted by the time she enters the house and sets her bag down. But family meals matter to her. Greely is like the many Americans who believe the family meal is in danger of becoming extinct.

Greely, Matt, and Adelle manage to eat together just about every night. Greely's perception is that this makes them unique, but in fact, about half of American families report eating dinner together six to seven nights a week, a number that hasn't changed much in the last three decades.[3]

Even though there is little evidence that the family dinner is disappearing, anxiety over its demise has certainly ramped up in recent years. And it's a particular version of the family dinner that Greely is anxious about pulling off, one that has always been hard to manage in reality and that many families feel they are coming up short in achieving.[4] It's not enough just to eat together, Greely believes. A proper family dinner is one where parents and children sit down around a table at home and eat a healthy meal, made from scratch and preferably from local ingredients. The TV should be off, distractions should be kept to a minimum, meaningful conversations should be made, and the food should be the centerpiece. Given the hectic pace of their days, Greely deeply fears that if she doesn't maintain her current efforts, her family might end up eating fast and unhealthy food.

Family meals are Greely's anchor points in an otherwise chaotic day of work, errands, and other responsibilities. But because of the high standards she attaches to what ideal meals look like, the family meal also becomes another obligation in Greely's packed schedule.

Things came to a head in the Janson household a few months ago. Greely's workload had increased as she tried to get her restaurant off the ground. But Matt was also busy at work, and they were finding it harder and harder to keep cooking meals from scratch every evening. So, after the dust of the winter holidays had settled, they sat down to figure out what to do. They discussed their options and settled on a plan: They would work smarter instead of harder.

"It was one of our New Year's goals, to work on shopping and cooking over the weekend," Greely explains. "So we cook for hours on Sunday and then create a variety of meals from whatever we have during the week. We roast a lot of things. We cook maybe one pot of soup, maybe some rice or whatever. And then during the week we have a pasta dish, a soup dish, a frittata, or some kind of combination of things."

According to a 2015 Gallup poll, 61 percent of working Americans feel that they don't have enough time to do what they want.[5] As people find themselves beleagured by multiple expectations—having a successful career, raising children, eating right, exercising—they are searching for some way to have it all.[6] And entire industries have emerged to provide an answer. Time management books and phone apps offer tips for how we can become more efficient at work, streamline our email, and exercise in just minutes a day.[7]

Dinner is not exempt from the cacophony of advice. Books, magazines, and blogs offer ideas for how parents can cut corners without skimping on quality. For example, *A New Way to Dinner*, which advertises itself as a "playbook of recipes for the week ahead," suggests that being "hunkered down in the kitchen for three hours" on the weekends—washing, chopping, and roasting—can yield an entire week's worth of meals.[8] And the viral marketing success of the Instant Pot, a programmable pressure cooker and slow cooker, is evidence of people's desire to make healthy meals without spending all their time cooking them.

Kitchen "hacks" and time-saving tips resonate with the spirit of American industriousness. Most Americans continue to believe that if we just work hard enough, we can succeed.[9] It's not surprising, then, that the self-help industry, replete with books, workshops, and life coaches that teach us how to be better versions of ourselves, thrives in this country.[10] Much of the advice assumes that parents have nearly full control over the rhythm of their days. Parents are encouraged to try harder. Take responsibility. Plan ahead. You can do it—and you should.

Greely and Matt's plan worked, for a while. Greely loved how making nearly all of the weekly meals in one big batch saved her from having to pull out a cutting board and a knife and pots and do a ton of dishes every night. And for several weeks, she succeeded at prepping most of the week's meals on Sundays.

It might have kept working if everything else in their lives had continued running smoothly. But that wasn't what happened. Matt had agreed to become an official for Adelle's chess club and was scheduled to attend an all-day training one weekend. Adelle had chess club practice and was invited to a classmate's birthday party. Greely's dad was in town.

"And then Adelle had this other thing on Sunday at three o'clock, and I needed to get some work done. So it did not happen," Greely recalls. "I felt really stressed this morning, because I'm like, 'I don't even know what . . .'" she says, staring into her cup of tea.

Prepping the weekly meals on weekends had made Greely feel competent, like superwoman in the kitchen. "You know, it felt nice," she remembers. "I enjoy cooking in big batches. I made two weeks' worth of granola. I made my own tea mixes. I got into it. . . . When I have the time, I enjoy cooking."

But Greely despairs when she thinks of the week ahead and the fact that she has no prepared meals to tide the family over. "When it's so compressed after a stressful day, cooking is kind of horrible," she confesses, in a tone that suggests that she doesn't want to admit it, even to herself. She doesn't feel she gets enough time with Adelle as it is, and she wonders whether spending an hour cooking is just depriving Adelle of attention. "I want to be able to sit down and help her with her homework or help her finish her Valentines for her classmates," she explains.

As she thinks about the Valentines, Greely begins to fret about what they will eat tonight. "I was supposed to soak black-eyed peas last night and I forgot. 'Cause that's pretty easy. They all like black-eyed peas, collards, and sweet potatoes. So we'll have that later during the week. I don't know what we're doing today."

Women today spend less time in the kitchen than women did in 1965, but they have little free time to show for it. The amount of leisure time that parents enjoy has actually declined since the 1960s. This is especially true for mothers, who have twenty-eight fewer minutes of free time per day, on average, than fathers.[11] And much of that free time is chopped into tiny segments, or "time confetti," as Brigid Schulte writes in *Overwhelmed*, a book about the time pressures working people experience.[12] The time crunch is felt acutely by women, who are more likely than men to report being rushed and plagued by the feeling that they can't get everything done.[13]

The sense that our modern lives are like a pressure cooker is compounded by competing messages about what parents should be doing with their time. Cook more, *and* spend more quality time with your children. Lean in at work, but *also* make sure your kids are involved in extracurricular and enrichment activities.[14]

Today's parents actually spend twice as much "quality time" with their kids—helping them with homework, shuttling them to activities, and playing with them—as their parents did with them.[15] Middle-class parents like the Jansons are more likely than poor and working-class parents to buy into the idea that they need to invest intensive time and effort in cultivating their children's talents, sociologist Annette Lareau finds. But the ante around parenting has risen for everyone.[16]

Further, much of this parenting work is simply not acknowledged, because it is literally invisible. No one sees the mental tape loop running in parents' heads—the constant spooling of tasks that need to be done, the deadlines that need to be met, and the family preferences that need to be considered. For Greely, the mental tape loop is playing as she thinks about what to make for dinner. She strategizes about meals her whole family will like, thinks about the ingredients she already has in the fridge, and remembers that Adelle also has Valentines to make for her classmates.

Families benefit from this invisible mental organization, largely performed by women and required to keep the proverbial household ship afloat.[17] Only recently, though, have researchers started to explore how "contaminated time"—a term that refers to the mental pollution of having one's brain stuffed with all the demands of work, family logistics, chores, and what's for dinner—affects women's well-being by contributing to constant feelings of being overwhelmed and pressed for time.[18]

A wave of nostalgia washes over Greely when she thinks about how much better her life would be if she could slow down a bit. Greely spent a semester in Italy when she was in college and longs to return to that pace of life. "There was more of a culture of appreciating food and taking the time to have good food and share it. And community and family were a huge part of that," Greely remembers. "For me that felt very healthy. Also, the culture of walking everywhere. Not like, 'I have to go to the gym.' It was just a part of the life. You walk places, you spend time with family and friends, you take hours to eat if you want hours to eat. You know, work is important but it's not everything. And sometimes you just leave it. And people can say what they want about their economy, but when you're there, it feels healthy and it feels happy and it feels good."

When she got back from Italy, Greely had a hard time re-acclimating to the frantic pace of life in the United States: long hours at work, long commutes, rushed meals, to-do lists a mile long. Her vision of food involves slowing down and taking the time to eat well. Ironically, it takes an inordinate amount of time and work to make that happen. "I'm obsessed with finding balance and I find that it's extremely hard to do. But I feel like it's worth trying for," she says anxiously.

Even with Greely's relative advantages—a fairly flexible work schedule, a spouse who helps around the house, and a network of relatives to help with childcare—achieving balance in her life eludes her. Indeed, her focus on balance seems to take the shape of a new project to manage.

Ashley Taylor adjusts the bill of her Wendy's cap. It's 8:00 AM on a bright summer morning, and she is ready for work. Ashley is wearing black skinny pants and a red polo with an embroidered Wendy's logo over the heart. Pinned to the polo are her nametag and two buttons. One reads "Choose Fresh, Choose Wendy's," while the other invites customers to treat themselves to a bacon-pretzel cheeseburger.[1] The buttons look massive on Ashley's small frame. It's easy to see why the kids at school used to say she was so skinny she could "hula hoop through a Cheerio." Ashley's black hair, tucked under the cap, is combed close to her scalp and pulled back tight, accentuating her teardrop-shaped face and delicate features. She wears black plastic-framed glasses that look child-sized but fit her well.

Her shift starts at ten. She just needs to get the girls out the door within the next forty-five minutes to go to her mom's place. Her brother, Rob, is picking them up. It's a thirty-minute drive to her mom's and then another fifteen minutes to get to work from there.

Ashley's crisp, put-together look stands in stark contrast to the messy trailer, usually very tidy. The carpet is dirty and full of stains. A twenty-four-pack box of Milwaukee's Best sits on top of the kitchen counter. Next to the box, empty beer cans are scattered alongside a family-size pack of frozen chicken drumsticks that Ashley is thawing out for tonight's dinner. Two plastic Wendy's cups and two partially eaten tubs of dipping sauce, left from the night before, are on the coffee table in the living room.

A lot of people are living in the three-bedroom, single-wide trailer at the moment. Anton, who is Ashley's husband Marquan's brother, is renting the back bedroom. Ashley and Marquan sleep in another bedroom, and their two young daughters, Maylee and

Qianah, share the third. The bedrooms are full, so Marquan's cousin Chris has been sleeping on the Taylors' couch for the last few weeks.

Ashley's morning preparations have woken Chris. He sits on the couch, staring into space. A young man in his twenties, Chris was recently released from jail and is estranged from his wife and kids. He had nowhere else to go, so Ashley and Marquan made room for him in their increasingly cramped home.[2] Chris is wearing a red and black striped shirt, baggy black jeans, black sneakers, and a black baseball cap. Although he's fully dressed, his torpid state suggests he just woke up.

Ashley and Marquan have been together for nine years. They got married four years ago, when Ashley was nineteen and Marquan was twenty-one. A year and a half after they got married, Ashley had Maylee, followed by Qianah a year later. Although close in age and often dressed alike, Maylee and Qianah do not really resemble each other. With her upswept eyes, ebony skin, and lean frame, three-year-old Maylee looks just like Ashley. Two-year-old Qianah is the spitting image of Marquan: broad and sturdy with caramel-hued skin and round, brown eyes.

For the first couple of years of their marriage, Marquan and Ashley didn't have their own place. They didn't even live together. Marquan mostly stayed with his great-grandmother, while Ashley and the girls stayed with Ashley's mother. It's only been in the last year and a half that they've been able to move in together. At first they lived in another trailer, even smaller than this one. They moved to the three-bedroom trailer when Anton moved in with them. Living with relatives isn't always a first choice, but it's a way that low-income families pool their money to support each other.[3]

Ashley goes into her bedroom to finish getting the girls ready. Plastic laundry baskets, piled high with clothes, take up much of the floor space. She lays Qianah on the bed and changes her diaper, then pulls on dark pink shorts and a light pink T-shirt that reads "Once Upon a Time" in sparkly letters. Qianah's hair is usually braided, but today it fluffs out around her head, held back from her face with an elastic headband. Ashley kisses her pudgy cheek as she puts mismatched anklets on her feet.

Maylee, in a light green sweatshirt, whizzes out of the adjoining bathroom. She heads straight through the main part of the trailer, where the kitchen and living room are, to the bedroom she shares with her sister. Ashley follows her, with Qianah on her hip. They pass Chris, still sitting bleary-eyed on the living room couch.

Marquan is asleep on the bottom bunk of the girls' bed. His broad frame hangs over the bed's edge, and his feet dangle off the end. Although the girls have their own room with twin bunk beds, most nights they end up sleeping in Mom and Dad's bed. Sometimes, when Marquan comes home late from work or stays up playing video games with Chris, he sleeps on the lower bunk bed to avoid waking up Ashley and the girls.

Silently, Ashley roots around on the closet floor on her hands and knees. She extracts a handful of shoes from the closet and instructs Qianah to sit down on a small bench.

"What do you want to wear?" she asks, reeling off a list of shoe options: tennis shoes, flip-flops, sandals, and "shoes like Lee." Lee is Qianah's nickname for Maylee.

"Yeah," says Qianah.

"You said yeah to all of them! Which one do you want to wear?" Ashley asks, smiling but exasperated. Qianah points to a pink-and-white tennis shoe in the pile. Ashley kneels in front of her to put the shoes on, then tells Maylee to come over.

Qianah walks over to the bed. "Daddy . . ." she says, climbing into the bed and lying on top of Marquan. Marquan says nothing.

"Where's your tennis shoes?" Ashley asks Maylee. She digs a pair of black tennis shoes out of the closet.

"They boys'," says Maylee, scowling at the shoes.

"They're not boys'!" Ashley exclaims. "They're tennis shoes just like Qianah's got on. Just 'cause they aren't pink doesn't mean they're not girls'. Everything can't be pink." Maylee's love of pink, feminine clothes and toys is a source of amusement and exasperation in the family.

Ashley finishes tying Maylee's shoes and they head out of the bedroom. "Daddy, get up," Maylee says as she passes the bed. Marquan doesn't respond. He worked late last night and will sleep until his next shift, later today. Even with two incomes, Marquan and Ashley don't make much. They both work at Wendy's, although they work at different restaurants, and they both try to get in as many shifts as possible. Ashley often works seven days a week, and Marquan volunteers to work two shifts in a row whenever the chance arises.

Ashley heads for the kitchen with the girls trailing behind her. "I don't want to eat," Maylee whines.

"Why not? You on a diet?" Ashley asks her in a joking tone. She repeats the question three times as Maylee stares back at her.

"Uh uh. Not hungry anymore," Maylee finally answers.

"You want to eat at Grandma's house?" Ashley asks. Her mother often looks after the girls when Ashley works. Softening her tone, she adds, "Okay, you can eat at Grandma's house. I'll leave you alone."

"I don't want to eat," Maylee repeats, not understanding that she's off the hook.

"You don't have to eat, baby. You can eat at Grandma's house," Ashley reassures her. "I just told you, you don't have to eat at my house."

Ashley ushers the girls into the bathroom to brush their teeth, and then they all head back out to the living area. The girls go over to their kid-sized Dora the Explorer table, while Ashley goes into the kitchen. She takes two red nylon Chuck E. Cheese bags out of a pantry and puts a Capri Sun and an individual pack of graham crackers in each. She always tries to send the girls with a snack when her mom looks after them.

In the living room, the girls are fighting over crayons. "My crayon broke," cries Maylee, holding up a blue crayon that has snapped in half.

"I got a thousand coloring books," Ashley tells her, trying to defuse the situation. She digs two coloring books out of a kitchen drawer and places them in the middle of the table, then sits down on the couch next to Chris, who is staring blankly at his fingernails.

Maylee hands Qianah a piece of the blue crayon. "Baby, here, here you go," she says sweetly.

Qianah hands her an unbroken orange crayon. "Thank you, baby," Maylee tells her, having successfully tricked her sister into trading an unbroken crayon for a broken one. Opening up a coloring book, Maylee begins slowly coloring the flowers on one page with the orange crayon. Qianah flips over the other coloring book and stares at the Sesame Street characters on the back.

Ashley and Chris begin discussing her work schedule. Today, she is working from 10:00 AM until 2:30 PM. "I told the manager to put me on a schedule," she complains. "They ask me every day if I can stay late." Chris is sympathetic. He also works at Wendy's, as does Marquan's brother Anton, and he is well aware of the scheduling vagaries.

They are interrupted by shrieks from the girls, who are now fighting over the coloring books. Qianah has grabbed Maylee's coloring book. "Are you being mean to Maylee?" Ashley asks her. "You're not supposed to be mean." Ashley gets up from the couch and joins them, sitting cross-legged on the floor next to their table. She begins quizzing them on the names of the characters on the back of Qianah's coloring book: Cookie Monster, Bert, Ernie.

The girls are still riled up.

"Qianah, you're not my friend," Maylee tells her sister in a grumpy voice.

"I love you," Qianah says sweetly.

Ashley jumps up, retrieves something from a kitchen drawer, and rejoins the girls on the floor. In her hands, she holds flashcards and several brightly colored pieces of felt, each cut into the shape of a hand. "Do you want to tell Mommy your colors?" she asks them. The girls turn to face her, their faces eager. Ashley holds out a red felt hand.

"Blue," Maylee tells her.

"Everything ain't blue," Ashley replies dryly.

"Red!" says Maylee.

"Good job!" Ashley congratulates her. Maylee beams.

Ashley continues, first showing them a gray hand, then a purple hand, a blue hand, and a green hand. They identify some of the colors but need Ashley's prodding for others. She begins laying out flashcards on the carpet. Each has a different-colored shape: diamond, cube, cylinder. Ashley points to each card, slowly reading the name of the shape. Maylee and Qianah earnestly repeat the names back to her. "Good job!" says Ashley. Maylee claps and laughs.

Ashley holds up a flashcard with a picture of a banana on it. "What's that?" she asks.

"Banana," says Maylee immediately.

"I like bananas," Qianah chirps happily.

The next card has a star on it. Without warning, the girls launch into a rendition of "Twinkle, Twinkle Little Star." They lift up their hands, opening and closing their fists to make sparkling stars. Everyone claps when the song ends. Ashley does some more flashcards. They are stumped by "xylophone" but easily get "butterfly."[4]

Yawning, Ashley stands up and walks back to her bedroom. The girls start fighting again as soon as she leaves the room. Qianah throws a crayon, then a felt hand. "Hey!" Maylee shouts.

It's just before 9:00 AM. Ashley looks out the front window. Rob should be here by now. It will take them thirty minutes to get to her mother's house and then another fifteen to get to Wendy's. Ashley sits down on a bench in the kitchen to wait.

Many poor and working-class families have little control over their time. As real wages have stagnated, households often depend on every adult family member working, sometimes in multiple jobs, to make ends meet.[5] Nonstandard employment arrangements—part-time and temporary jobs, nonstandard work hours, and unpredictable scheduling—are increasingly common.[6] Like Ashley and Marquan, about one out of six people in the work-force have unstable work schedules, and the lowest-income workers have the most unstable schedules.[7] Low-income families also often rely on a patchwork of relatives and friends to help with transportation and childcare, a necessary dependence that makes it more difficult to schedule things in advance.[8]

In Ashley's household, the logistics of working, taking care of the kids, getting to various appointments, doing household chores, and grocery shopping are a complicated balancing act. If one thing goes wrong, it creates a domino effect in all the other areas of their lives. Recently the washing machine broke and needs replacing, which they can't afford to do, so Ashley has been hauling baskets of laundry back and forth to her mother's house.

To some degree, all parents depend on systems that help them manage their time, take care of their children, and work. And no one has complete control over their time. Kids get sick. Schools close for snow days. Babysitters cancel at the last minute. But low-income families like Ashley's have less control over their time than wealthier families.

Ashley's days are largely governed by decisions made by others. She and Marquan are employed by the same fast-food chain, but they work in different locations, which are forty-five minutes apart. They have to wait until their weekly schedules are posted to know the hours and even days when they'll be working. Sometimes, they don't find out their schedule until the night before, and then they have to scramble to figure out transportation and childcare arrangements. It doesn't help that Ashley and Marquan live in a rural area, where homes and businesses are spread out and there is virtually no public transportation. Their car is not working, and they cannot afford to get it repaired, so they rely on friends and family members for rides. But their friends and relatives also have unpredictable or nonstandard work schedules. If they are running late, Ashley has to wait. When this happens, as it has today, the domino effect is set in motion. Ashley has to then call her mother to tell her she will be late getting there with the kids. She has to readjust her plan to get a load of wash in at her mom's before going to work; it will have to wait till after work. She has to figure out an explanation to give her manager for her lateness, and she knows she'll have to be agreeable when she's asked to work late to make up for the demerit. It's important to her to stay on good terms with management; otherwise her hours might be cut.

It's not just the amount of time people have that matters, but also the control they have over their time. In fact, the degree of control a person has may be more consequential than the actual amount of time.[9] Nonstandard and unpredictable schedules not only make it difficult to plan in advance, they negatively affect people's physical health, emotions and mental health, relationships, and leisurely activity.[10] One study found that workers with unstable schedules reported more stress and work-life conflict than those with more predictable schedules.[11]

A lack of control over time also affects how we eat. Ashley and Marquan's unpredictable schedules mean their kids often end up eating with Ashley's mom. And Ashley herself rarely eats regular meals. Too tired after working all day at the drive-through window to eat, she usually makes something easy, like pasta with butter, for the girls and skips dinner herself. Food isn't a huge priority for Ashley, and she often has to be reminded to eat, even though she says she'd like to gain a few pounds. But her ever-changing schedule, reliance on others, and the constant juggling act of raising two small children don't help.

Qianah and Maylee crowd around Ashley on the bench. Maylee holds an empty plastic SpongeBob cup over her mouth. Removing the cup, she tells her mother in her best grownup voice, "You get on my nerves."

"You want a whooping?" Ashley teases. "Take that cup to the kitchen."

"I want to sit by you," Qianah whines. Ashley pulls her up and sets her down on the bench. Qianah informs Ashley that Maylee is no longer her friend. "I'm your friend, Mommy," she reassures Ashley.

Maylee runs over. "I'm gonna get you a lollipop," she says sweetly, holding out a crayon to Ashley. "Here you go, Momma."

"That's my lollipop?" Ashley asks. Maylee nods, pleased with herself for coming up with the idea. "I'm going to leave it right here for when I get home from work, okay?" Ashley tells her, putting the crayon on the counter. Qianah grabs for the crayon. As Ashley tries to take it back from her, Qianah swipes a big orange streak across Ashley's black work pants.

"Argh," says Ashley, still patient and playful. "You just marked my pants." She rubs at the mark, knowing her manager won't be happy if she shows up at work with what looks like a stain on her pants.

Ashley looks out the window again. Nothing. She absentmindedly picks up the coloring books from the Dora the Explorer table, then takes them to the kitchen, where she puts them back in the drawer. "Mommy, I want gum!" Qianah begs when she spies the open drawer.

"I try to hide it but you always find everything, don't you?" Ashley says ruefully.

Qianah laughs. "Gum, gum, gum!" she shouts, smacking her lips. Maylee joins in. Ashley unwraps a stick of gum and breaks it in half, giving one half to each girl. She unwraps a stick for herself and puts it in her mouth. All chewing their gum, they walk to the front door. Ashley opens it and looks outside, her foot tapping impatiently. The girls crowd under her leg. They stare out at the empty street.

Maylee and Qianah abandon their vigil at the front door a few minutes later and crowd around Chris on the couch. "Can y'all leave Chris alone?" Ashley asks them.

The girls begin squabbling again. As they roll around on the couch, grabbing for each other, they topple onto Chris. "Get off Chris!" Ashley says, laughing. She picks up Qianah by an arm and a leg. Qianah grins.

They continue tussling on the couch. "Me!" says one. "No me!" shouts the other.

"Okay," Ashley tells them, sitting cross-legged on the floor to play with them. She gives Qianah a raspberry, then picks her up and rocks her in her arms. "Rock-a-bye Baby," Ashley sings, gently rocking her back and forth.

"My turn!" exclaims Maylee, scrambling into her mother's arms.

"You a big baby," Ashley tells her as Maylee pretends to sleep. Qianah whispers something and all three laugh. "You a silly baby. Whoa now, you silly," Ashley tells them.

Qianah piles on top of Maylee, who is still on Ashley's lap. There is lots of giggling as Ashley pretends to tickle them. The girls get up and take turns holding each other on their laps, which they both find very amusing.

Returning to the couch, Ashley checks her phone again, then calls Rob. "Where are you?" she asks. "Fifteen or twenty minutes away?!!" she repeats incredulously. She can't believe he is running so late. She hangs up the phone and notices that Maylee is sucking on a battery. She quickly takes the battery from her mouth. "What did I tell you about that?" she asks her, leaning back on the couch.

"I brought you something," Maylee tells Ashley. Her hands are empty.

"What is it?" Ashley asks.

"A dress," says Maylee.

"So beautiful! I love it," Ashley plays along. "What color is it?"

"Pink," Maylee tells her. "Put it on."

Ashley pretends to pull the invisible dress over her head. Maylee tries to take her Wendy's cap off. Her feminine sensibilities are insulted by Ashley's work uniform.

"I have to keep my hat on. I'm going to work," Ashley says, gently batting away Maylee's hand. "Do I have to wear my hat at work?" Ashley asks sternly, straightening the cap's bill.

"Yes," Maylee dutifully replies.

"Thank you for the dress," Ashley says, softening her tone. "It's beautiful, baby. I'm going to wear it every day."

It's after 9:30. Hearing a car approach, Ashley walks to the front door and opens it. Rob is already at the door. A tall, slender man, he's wearing his usual work outfit—khaki pants and a white T-shirt, with his name tag clipped to the shirt's hem. He steps inside, as Ashley swivels around and heads back into her bedroom to get something. Qianah and Maylee come running down the hallway, eager to see Uncle Rob. Ashley emerges from her room with a laundry basket of clothing in her hands. "I don't have room!" Rob jokes. In the end, there is more than enough room for the three baskets of laundry Ashley loads into the trunk. She plans to do the wash at her mom's place since her washing machine is on the fritz.

Rob and Chris talk in hushed tones as Ashley loads the laundry into the car. "You going to work?" Chris asks. Rob nods. Chris informs him he has the day off.

Finally, at 9:45, they make their way to the car: Ashley, Rob, and the two girls. Rob straps the girls into two car seats in the back of the SUV while Ashley calls her mom to let her know they're leaving. They talk briefly. "Do you want me to pick up pancake mix?" she asks. The answer is no; her mom already has pancake mix. Ashley hangs up and gets in the car. They make a plan. Rob will drop Ashley off at work first, then take the girls to Grandma's house. It is 9:50. Rob pulls out of the driveway and speeds down the quiet rural road. Ashley sighs. She is definitely going to be late for work.

Time is precarious for Ashley, as it is for the millions of other families whose lives are ruled by unpredictable and nonstandard work hours. Regular mealtimes are rare in her household. Food isn't that important to Ashley personally, but she takes feeding her children seriously. She is well aware of the cultural code of being a good mother and a good wife. Good mothers cook. And even if she isn't particularly confident in the kitchen, Ashley is the primary cook in her household. She acknowledges using a lot of convenience foods, but aspires to someday cook meals from scratch and maybe even take over hosting Sunday dinners from Marquan's great-grandmother. She knows how much Marquan loves the big Sunday dinners he grew up with. Ashley hopes to carry on the tradition, and someone's going to have to soon. At eighty-nine, his great-grandmother is legally blind and has a failing memory.

But for now, other obligations take precedence. Ashley does flashcards with Maylee in order to help prepare her for the preschool she'll attend in the fall. A firm believer in the power of education, Ashley wants her daughters to have promising futures.[12] She and Marquan are also trying to save enough money to fix the car and buy a new washing machine. They need to get in as many hours at work as they possibly can. Their shifting schedules and heavy reliance on others for transportation make planning meals ahead nearly impossible.

But even families with predictable schedules feel the pressure. Standards for good parenting have increased, and the messages are loud and clear. Parents must endlessly talk to children to develop their vocabulary.[13] Read to children to foster a love of reading. Make sure children have adequate sleep and plenty of outdoor activity.[14] Teach children to behave. Impart lessons about family traditions and moral values. Help children develop relationships with their immediate and extended family. Create memories that children will cherish as adults. And, of course, cook tasty nutritious meals for children and eat together as a family.

3 THE FAMILY THAT EATS TOGETHER, STAYS TOGETHER

Families that share a dinnertime ritual together—regardless of their
stage, class, or race—enjoy innumerable benefits.

—LES AND LESLIE PARROTT,
clinical psychologist and family therapist, in
The Hour that Matters Most: The Surprising Power of the Family Meal (2011)

The most important thing you can do with your kids? Eat dinner with them.

—ANNE FISHEL, CO-FOUNDER,
The Family Dinner Project, headline in the *Washington Post* (2015)

Experts tell us the most important thing people can do to build strong, healthy families is to gather around the table for dinner. But romantic images of the family meal, straight out of a Norman Rockwell painting, are a far cry from the reality of most people's dinner tables: picky kids, unappreciative partners, conflicting schedules, and unmet expectations. The dinner table is also a place where people attempt to reckon with their own food pasts. And the more the family meal becomes a symbol of good parenting and proper family life, the more dinner feels like a pressure cooker.

SPAGHETTI FOR AN ARMY

"I always make enough for an army," Tara Foley explains, dumping a large pot of boiling spaghetti noodles into a plastic colander in the sink. Her spaghetti sauce—made with canned crushed tomatoes, a jar of spaghetti sauce, lightly browned ground beef, and spices from the spice rack—burbles gently in a nonstick electric skillet on the counter. Steam rises around Tara's face as she shakes the colander to get every last drop of water off the pasta.

The microwave whirs with the frozen chicken teriyaki with vegetables and rice she is preparing as a side dish. Tara proudly claims to make a vegetable with every meal, which is how she explains the unique pairing of spaghetti and chicken teriyaki.[1]

Tara's sons, Tyree and Rashan, are ostensibly watching the movie *Preacher's Wife* in the adjacent living room but keep running in and out of the kitchen. They are experts at navigating around the warped vinyl floor tiles. At eight, Tyree is lean and lanky, with deep brown eyes, long eyelashes, and a shy smile. His dark hair is cut close to his head. Four-year-old Rashan is more solid, with sturdy legs and a round face. He is also wilder and more energetic than his brother, with a mischievous sparkle in his eyes. His hair is pulled into a puffy ponytail. The boys' dads aren't regularly involved in their lives, and Tara feels she is mostly raising them on their own.[2]

"Calm down!" Tara yells, as Rashan dashes into the kitchen. She adores her boys' spunky attitudes, but she is also exasperated by them. They never seem to sit still.

Fifteen-year-old Jennifer, a friend's daughter who is staying temporarily with Tara, bounds in the door. Jennifer is wearing black leggings and a blue sweatshirt. Her straight brown hair is piled in a loose bun on top of her head.

"It smells good in here," she says, coming up behind Tara and giving her a hug. Tara grunts in gruff acknowledgment. Under the harsh glow of the bare lightbulb hanging down from the kitchen ceiling, Tara's pale skin looks even paler than usual, making the freckles across her nose and cheeks stand out. Her blonde hair hangs around her shoulders. Pink sweatpants and a tight pink T-shirt hug her thin frame.

The circles under Tara's eyes and the state of her teeth belie the fact that she is only twenty-six. She tries to hide her bad teeth. If she is asked to smile for a picture, she clamps her lips together while tugging up the corners of her mouth. But when she talks, it is impossible not to notice that her front teeth are whittled down to what look like small brown sticks.[3]

Wilson, Jennifer's dad, wanders into the kitchen in search of his Gatorade bottle. His baseball cap obscures his blue eyes and sandy brown hair. The tattoos on his forearms are briefly visible when he pulls up the sleeves of his maroon sweatshirt. Wilson will also be eating at Tara's house tonight. He spends a lot of time at her place, because Jennifer doesn't get along with Wilson's girlfriend. "They're like cats and dogs or two cats fighting! Women, they's all drama," Wilson explains, his raspy, smoker's voice cracking.

He says that Tara is doing him "a huge favor" by letting Jennifer stay with her. This is the story Wilson tells to mask the harsher reality. Wilson and his family were recently evicted and had nowhere else to go. Tara took Jennifer in for the time being. Wilson and his girlfriend are sleeping in his car.

Feeding extra people strains Tara's limited resources, but she enjoys having Wilson over for meals. She likes how he praises her cooking. But she also believes meals should be shared with others. Besides, one good turn deserves another; when her car breaks down, which happens often, Tara knows she can rely on Wilson to help fix it. When she's running low on gas money, she can bum a ride from Wilson or one of the other people she's fed over the months. But beyond this pragmatic arrangement, something deeper is being fulfilled. Tara likes to have people around her table. It makes her feel as though she is creating the kind of family life she always wished for, even if the feeling is fleeting.

Food is deeply tied to our emotions and memories.[4] A favorite dish from childhood can still trigger a sense of comfort and belonging well into adulthood.[5] Making a grandmother's beloved recipe or eating something we used to enjoy at holiday meals might evoke warm feelings of togetherness, of family. Just the smell of certain foods can conjure childhood memories.[6]

A lot of people have positive memories around the food they ate growing up, even if food was in short supply.[7] Women's food memories, in particular, frequently center around their mothers' cooking, and these are often central to their views about food and how they feed their own families.[8]

But many people's memories of food aren't comforting or happy. Experiences of childhood poverty and food insecurity can have negative effects on people's eating habits as adults.[9] Tara remembers being hungry as a child and feeling like her mom wasn't there for her. These memories motivate how she feeds her own children, but they also make it more difficult to know how to do it.

When Tara thinks of her childhood, she can't recall ever eating meals with her mom and siblings. "It was never like 'sit down for a family meal' or nothing like that," she remembers. "It was just like when you ate, you ate. You made your sandwich or something out of the refrigerator. Didn't nobody really cook, 'cause my mom was never there. She worked two jobs and wasn't never there."

Tara's mom cared not only for Tara and her brother and sister, but also sometimes for her sister's three kids. With six kids to feed and two jobs to work, there often wasn't enough time or food to go around. Tara got used to making herself a sandwich or heating up a can of SpaghettiOs in the microwave for dinner. On nights when the cupboards were bare, she went without.

"I done went hungry many nights before I had my kids. My mom wasn't there," she says bitterly. These days, Tara struggles to get by. She doesn't have a job or any cash income. For a while, she worked as a line cook at a fast-food restaurant, cooking on a "big, old grill." Earlier this year, she had a temporary job in a meat packaging plant, but she was laid off after the plant lost their account with a large meat processor. She's applied for other jobs, without luck.

Tara gets by on her food stamps and WIC vouchers, and the boys have Medicaid. Her uncle lets her stay in the house for free, but every month she has to scramble and scrounge to pay her bills.[10] She borrows money from others, goes to Social Services for help with the heating bill,[11] and sometimes gets money from a nearby church to pay the water bill.

"My fear is trying to keep strong and keep these bills paid. So then I know my kids won't sit in the dark. I don't want them to and I shouldn't make them," Tara says adamantly. "And if I can't pay the bills, then that scares me the most."

Even if Tara can't give her kids a lot in terms of material possessions, she can feed them and give them love. "I'm a family-type person but I ain't never had no family structure," she readily admits. Nonetheless, Tara vows to somehow give her boys a better life than she grew up with. She will be there for them, unlike her mother.

"Sitting down, eating together every night—I never got that as a child," Tara says, the bitterness in her voice giving way to longing. Things are "a whole lot different" now, she emphasizes, contrasting the way she feeds her children with the way she was raised. "We're sitting down eating every night, or I'm sitting down even when we eat breakfast with my children. Stuff like that."

Tara's aspirations around doing things differently extend to the food she cooks. She tries to make what she calls a "three-course meal" most nights, meaning a meat, starch, and a vegetable. Occasionally, she'll make something quick, like sandwiches or corndogs. But this is rare, she says. "Why can't I cook three course meals every day?" she asks rhetorically. "I have time for it."

Remembering all of the times when she went hungry as a kid, Tara is also determined not to let this happen to her children. Sometimes, such as when Rashan refuses to eat, her anxiety surfaces.

"I will [hand] feed him to make sure he will get something on his stomach, because he's not going to go to bed hungry," she says firmly. "You can't go to— I mean your stomach will growl all night and I know how that be."

Besides making sure her kids don't go to bed hungry, Tara's only other strict food rule is that they don't waste food, because that's just throwing money down the drain. "I tell my children every day, 'You can't really be picky about what you eat,'" she explains. "I said, 'There's most kids out here that ain't even got that choice to pick. They only get one choice and they have to eat that every day, all day.'" Tara might not have much money, but she tries to vary the meals they eat. She is also strategic, making things she thinks they'll like so as to minimize waste. She strikes her own balance.

Figuring out the "right" way to feed children isn't easy. For example, nutrition experts say pressuring kids to eat can result in picky eaters, but being too restrictive about food can lead to overeating. Parents aren't supposed to coax or cajole. Instead, they are told to offer an array of healthy choices and let kids make the decision.[12]

Experts warn parents that they must strike a balance between being too lax or too strict, between not caring or caring too much. But continually and casually offering children food they may not eat, as the experts advise, is hard for any parent to do. For poor parents like Tara, who scrimp and save and barely get by, worrying that their kids are not getting enough to eat, it can seem nearly impossible. Instead, like Tara, many poor parents serve foods they know their children will eat, because they can't afford to waste food.[13] These kinds of dilemmas, however, don't seem to be on the experts' radar.

Experts also often ignore how food can become a way for children to exert power and control. Clamping a mouth shut and refusing to eat. Surreptitiously passing a few bites to the dog under the table. Picking a particular ingredient out of a dish. The dinner table is not just a place where people consume food; it's a place where people jostle and vie for a bit of power within the family.[14] Dinners at Tara's house aren't exempt from these dynamics. Despite her hopeful embrace of family meals, food fights erupt regularly around the dinner table.

Tara returns the pasta to the cooking pot and stirs in the sauce. She gets a baking sheet full of garlic bread from the oven. Tired of waiting for dinner, Rashan and Tyree come and go, swiping food as they pass through the kitchen. "You already had four. Leave some for everyone else," Tara scolds Rashan as he tries to snatch another piece of garlic bread.

Tara calls everyone to come get their food while she fixes the kids' plates. There are only three chairs at her small kitchen table, not nearly enough for everyone. Wilson fills his plate and sits at the table with Rashan and Tyree, who are waiting for their food. The kids start complaining about the food even before it arrives. Rashan is suspicious of the chicken teriyaki he sees on Wilson's plate.

"You ain't never tried it," Tara says as she sets Rashan's plate of food down in front of him.

"I don't like it. I don't need it. I don't want it," he replies, his arms crossed in protest.

"I eat it," Wilson says. "Chill out. If you want to grow up to be big and strong, you gotta eat somethin.'"

Jennifer and her boyfriend, Artemis, emerge from the back bedroom where they've been playing video games. Artemis is staying for dinner too. They both take full plates, slather the food with butter, and return for seconds. They eat in the back bedroom.

Tara gets her food last. She bypasses the table where the boys and Wilson are sitting, opting for an armchair in the living room. There isn't room for her at the table anyway. She props her plate on her lap and leans forward; her hair drapes across her face, forming a curtain of sorts.

Rashan isn't happy about his spaghetti.

"I don't like this right here," he complains, flicking a piece of tomato with his fork.

"Pick 'em out," Tara barks from the living room.

Rashan moves his food around on the plate.

"You gotta eat all that food, boy," Wilson cajoles. "For your momma. She made it." When that doesn't work, he changes tactic, telling Rashan he will turn Chinese if he eats the chicken teriyaki. "I used to be a Chinese black boy, then the next day, I woke up white! Better watch out or the same thing will happen to you, since you're half and half and already more white than black," he warns.

Tyree and Rashan say nothing.

"Your momma made this for you and you not gonna eat it? Tsk tsk," Wilson persists. Raising his voice to reach Tara in the living room, he says ingratiatingly, "Thank you for the supper, Tar."

"You're welcome," Tara replies, without looking in his direction.

Tyree gets up from the table. He carries his plate, still mostly full of food, to the microwave to heat it up.

"You ain't warming up your food," Tara yells harshly at Tyree. He promptly slides back into his seat, a sullen look on his face.

"Uh huh, uh huh. Yip yip. You don't know nuthin' about cookin'," Wilson goads Tyree.

Tyree protests, but Wilson cuts him off. "No. Huh uh. Whatever."

"You be burnin' it," Tara mocks from the living room.

Tyree sits up straight and replies, "My cookin' good." He adds defiantly, "I might cook some sausage tonight."

"No! You have school in the morning," Tara commands.

Tyree doesn't pursue it further.

Jennifer walks into the kitchen from the back room. She rinses her and Artemis's empty plates, leaving them in the sink. The boys eat a few more bites of their food and declare they are finished. Wilson scrapes Rashan's leftovers—rice, pineapple chunks, and bits of tomato—onto a plate for the dog. Tara calls Tyree over to collect her plate and tells him to give the remainder to the dog; like Rashan, she avoided eating the pineapple and rice. Tyree dumps the plates in the sink with the others. Tara will wash the dishes and clean the kitchen later tonight.

There's much ado about family dinners these days. Experts encourage parents to make time for family meals, citing all the positive outcomes: healthier and smarter kids, a strong family unit, and fond memories.[15] Seemingly backed up by science, these kinds of messages up the ante, increasing the pressure on mothers to make sure that family dinners happen.

Yet it's probably not the family dinners themselves that cause positive outcomes in the lives of families. It's more complicated than that. It's the quality of family relationships and families' resources that matter the most. Families need time to connect. For families with good relationships with one another, the dinner table is often a place where that happens, although families can also connect over breakfast, on walks, or while reading bedtime stories. In families with strong relationships, regular family dinners are linked to some positive outcomes in terms of children's well-being, such as fewer depressive symptoms in teens. But there's evidence that for families that are struggling to get along, family dinners don't make much of a difference in children's lives. And family dinners themselves don't create strong bonds.[16]

Tara has bitter feelings about her own childhood; she resents not having had regular meals with her family. Cooking and family meals are a way she tries to set her childhood straight and a symbol of her determination to do better for her children. But even as Tara's past motivates her efforts to create the family meals she didn't have, these meals aren't a magic elixir that can wipe away her painful memories. Despite her attempts to right the wrongs of her childhood, the dinner hour often turns into a power struggle around food.

FOURTH OF JULY

When it comes to cooking for others, Leanne Armstrong's philosophy is to go big or go home. She puts on quite a spread. So when she sees her neighbor Mercedes bringing a plate of hamburgers to her apartment on the Fourth of July, she mutters under her breath, "We cookin' over here, Mercedes. You don't need to bring food over." Mercedes doesn't hear her and starts handing out burgers to Leanne's husband, mother, and mother's boyfriend, who are all sitting on plastic chairs by Leanne's front door.

Leanne is dressed for the occasion, in a maxi dress with a halter back and wedge sandals. Before she started cooking, she tied her hair back in a messy ponytail. "Don't like hair in my food," she says.

It's nearly six in the evening, and Leanne has been at it since early afternoon. She's preparing potato salad, a rack of beef ribs, stew, and chicken wings. Later she'll make hot dogs for the kids. Although the beef ribs were on sale, she still ended up spending $80 on food for the cookout.

Leanne decides to take her eight-year-old son, Hakeem, to the corner store down the road to pick out a treat. Her husband, Latrell, took seven-year-old Gage to the store earlier and bought him a treat, so it's only fair. Gage tags along with them, as do three other boys from the neighborhood.

On her way out the door, Leanne asks her mother, Renata, to check on the ribs. "You know I don't cook that," Renata replies sharply. A diminutive woman with short gray hair and oval glasses, Renata's unassuming manner belies her strong personality and the force she represents in Leanne's life. Today she is wearing a blue-and-white striped shirt, jeans, white sneakers, and pink lipstick. Leanne implores her to just keep an eye on the ribs while she is gone. Renata grudgingly agrees but takes the opportunity to berate Leanne for indulging Hakeem. "You have got to say no to that boy!" she tells Leanne.

By all accounts, Leanne's relationship with her mother is fraught. They disagree about how Leanne spends her money, the food she eats, and the way she is raising her kids. Leanne defines good mothering as doing pretty much the opposite of what Renata did with her growing up. Renata walked out on the family when Leanne was four, leaving Leanne, her brother, and their dad to figure things out. As the only girl, Leanne stepped up at a young age to cook for her dad and brother. She developed a cooking style that is very different from Renata's, which is another source of friction between them.[1]

Cooking is one of the few aspects of Leanne's life where she feels she has some control. With three young kids in the house—Hakeem, Gage, and one-year-old Gemma—and constant worries about finances, mealtimes for Leanne are an opportunity to please her family. Every meal holds the potential to put a smile on her children's faces or hear an emphatic, "This is good, Mama!" These moments are fleeting, but they help Leanne forget about unpaid bills or how she is going to pay for her sons' school clothes.

Leanne also sees cooking as her escape. "I taught myself to cook to get away from the stress. I used it towards the kitchen," she says. Although Leanne has cookbooks, she never opens them. She likes the creative challenge of making her own dishes. "I don't even measure," she proudly explains. "I just say 'This might taste good with this,' and I throw it together and try it out. I can make beer can rosemary chicken. I just come up with these ideas. I learned how to make my own strawberry salsa."

At its core, cooking is Leanne's way of making a family. It's what she did for her father and brother after her mom left, and it's what she does now to prove her stripes as a good mom and dedicated wife. Whether it's making her kids' favorite chicken drumettes or buying them a bag of chips or a candy bar from the corner store, Leanne uses food to show her family she cares.[2] Yet food and cooking are also regular sources of conflict in her family.

The walk to the store goes slowly, because it seems like everyone wants to stop and chat with Leanne. "Hey beautiful. What're you doing out lookin' so fine on a hot day?" yells a man walking in the opposite direction. Leanne laughs and keeps walking. "They all be wanting to date everybody they see," she comments.

At the corner store, Leanne lets Hakeem and the other boys who tagged along pick out their own treats. Hakeem is tall and stocky, with a big smile and dimples in both cheeks. He wears his hair in a faux-hawk. Even though Latrell bought Gage a treat earlier, Leanne decides to get him a candy bar. Skinny and much shorter than Hakeem, Gage looks younger than his seven years. Like Hakeem, his skin tone is several shades darker than Leanne's, but unlike his brother, his curly black hair is cropped close to his head.

Leanne also gets two packs of Newport cigarettes and a Monster energy drink for herself. "Let me get my helper!" she jokes about the energy drink. Latrell doesn't like it when Leanne drinks coffee or energy drinks, complaining that they make her irritable.

Cracking open the drink back at the apartment, Leanne defends herself. "This just helps me to stay focused," she says. She takes a few deep swigs and then enlists Latrell, who's been sitting outside the front door talking with Renata's boyfriend, to glaze the beef ribs.

Latrell, a tall, lean man with bronze skin and a baby face, follows her into the kitchen. Latrell likes to tell people that Leanne is a terrible cook but then quickly clarifies that he's joking. "Nah, I'm playing. I'd rather eat her food than any other food," he'll say, making Leanne beam. "One time I ate out, and I ate only half a plate so I could save room for my wife's home cooking!" he brags.

Leanne pulls the ribs out of the oven and hands Latrell a bottle of barbecue sauce. He gets a barbecue brush from a drawer and begins alternately pouring and brushing the sauce on the ribs.

As is true in most American households, Leanne is responsible for much of the day-to-day work of cooking and feeding her family. In fact, she does almost all of it. It's a good thing she likes cooking, because she *has* to do it. Latrell rarely cooks. When he looks after the kids, Leanne gives him money for takeout, to make sure the kids are fed.

The percentage of American men who cook, and the amount of time they spend cooking, has increased considerably since the 1960s.[3] But women are still primarily responsible for the daily work of feeding the family.[4] Men are more likely to "help out" or cook for pleasure or as a hobby, whereas women cook when no one else wants to.[5] When women cook meals for special occasions, the work they undertake to get these meals together often goes unnoticed and underappreciated. It is assumed that women will do this work.[6] And on top of doing the bulk of the cooking for the occasion, women may take responsibility for orchestrating moments when men can symbolically step up to, for example, put a special touch on a signature dish, as Leanne does for Latrell.

Leanne's cell phone rings. It's Latrell's brother calling. He asks to speak to Latrell. Latrell is busy "working his magic," Leanne tells the brother, but he persists. Eventually, Leanne concedes. "Your brother wants to talk," she tells Latrell. He responds defensively that he is glazing the ribs, but then puts the brush down and goes to the phone. Leanne has to keep it plugged into an outlet, because the battery no longer holds a charge.

Gage bounces into the house, sweaty from skateboarding with the neighborhood kids. "You want chicken and beef ribs?" Leanne asks him. Scowling, Gage shakes his head no and runs back outside.

Latrell, just now hanging up the phone, informs Leanne that his brother wants him to go with him to Rocky Mount, a city an hour's drive away.

"That's not gonna work," Leanne says.

"Why?" Latrell questions.

"'Cause it's the Fourth of July and I want to spend it with my husband!" she replies indignantly. He rolls his eyes and resumes brushing barbecue sauce on the ribs. Finished with the ribs, Latrell looks around. When he doesn't see a towel or hot pad, he lifts the hem of his shirt and uses it to pick up the pan of ribs and put it back in the oven. His jeans are sagging, and the maneuver puts his underwear on full display.

"Good God, boy. Lord Jesus! Hurt me! Hurt me!" Leanne says, seeing this.

"Craziness. You see what I gotta deal with?" Latrell laughs.

"That's why I married you. All that booty," replies Leanne. Her flattery may be intended to further entice Latrell into sticking around for the Fourth of July party.

Leanne rinses and dries the chicken legs and arranges them on a medium roasting pan with about an inch of water in the bottom. She coats the legs with cayenne pepper and garlic powder and inserts a pat of butter under the skin of each one.

"That makes the skin crispy and the meat tender," she tells Renata, who has just come inside. Renata informs her that three of the people Leanne invited won't be coming to the cookout. Renata also points out that the fridge door is ajar and then pushes it shut.

Leanne is in her own world. She sways to the rhythm-and-blues music playing from her phone as she pours apple cider vinegar in the roasting pan with the chicken, now ready to go in the oven.

Abruptly, Renata announces she is leaving. "But you haven't eaten anything," Leanne implores. She accuses Renata of having eaten one of the hamburgers that Mercedes brought over earlier.

"No, I didn't eat a burger!" Renata snaps back. Toning down her voice, she adds, "You know I like your cooking."

"Aw, you sweet," Leanne says.

But Renata makes no bones that she prefers her own potato salad. She tries to convince Leanne that *she* likes Renata's potato salad better too. "You like mine," she tells Leanne.

"I like *mine*," Leanne corrects.

In fact, Renata ended up mixing the potato salad while Leanne was at the store with the boys, so it's a blend of their two styles. Renata takes some potato salad and a rib to go, then asks Leanne if she has any plastic forks or spoons. Leanne says she bought plastic cups and paper plates but forgot to buy utensils.

"What about the spoons I gave you? What'd you do with those?" Renata asks.

"That was like two months ago. Those are gone," Leanne says. "We throw—I don't reuse them," she adds apologetically.

One-year-old Gemma wakes up from her nap just as Renata is leaving. Leanne says good-bye to Renata and goes upstairs to change Gemma's diaper and get her dressed. Gage asks for something to drink as she is leaving the kitchen. "Can you get Gage somethin' to drink while I get her dressed?" Leanne hollers to Latrell through the front door.

Latrell gets up and comes inside, complaining loudly, "Gage better learn to use the faucet outside!" He heads back outside a few minutes later without getting Gage a drink. When Leanne comes downstairs with Gemma, Gage is wandering aimlessly around.

"Get Gemma's blue Nike sneakers from the TV stand," Leanne tells him. He retrieves the shoes and hands them to Leanne, who is tugging Gemma into a blue and white striped romper with "USA" in red letters on the front. She lays Gemma on the couch and buttons up the outfit. Gemma shares Latrell's and Leanne's tawny beige skin, while the boys have darker skin than their little half-sister. Gemma has dark, curly hair and a perennially inquisitive look on her small face.

Gage crouches down to play with his little sister, then asks if Leanne wants some socks for Gemma. "Why yes, please, thank you!" Leanne says in a teasing, formal voice. Gage bursts out laughing when he unrolls the pair of balled up socks he finds in a small pile of clean clothes on the loveseat. "They're so tiny!" he laughs. "Tiny socks!" He tries to push a sock onto Gemma's right foot, but she kicks and resists.

"She doesn't like socks on her feet. I gotta get her some sandals," Leanne says, taking over. She sniffs Gemma's foot and pretends it is stinky, which makes Gage laugh.

Latrell saunters inside to ask where the sunscreen is. "It's in my purse on the chair," Leanne tells him.

"Dad, where's my drink?" Gage asks.

"I dunno where your drink is!" Latrell replies in an aggrieved voice.

"You didn't make it?" Leanne accuses Latrell.

"I thought that was his drink right there in the blue cup," Latrell says, gesturing toward the kitchen. He walks back outside with the sunscreen.

Leanne sets Gemma down and goes into the kitchen, where she takes a big swig of her energy drink. Her eyes bulge out and she sticks out her tongue at the taste. "Wooo! I definitely gotta brush my teeth like three times after that. Goodness!"

She pours Gage some soda in a plastic cup. He takes a sip and then hands it back to her with a polite "thank you." He tells Leanne he is going upstairs to watch a movie. "Tell me when it gets a bit darker," he calls. Gage is eager to light the sparklers that a neighbor gave Leanne, and he doesn't want to miss the city's fireworks display, visible from their street.

"Yup," says Leanne.

Leanne's phone rings. It's Latrell's brother again. "What's this about going to Rocky Mount?" Leanne asks. "Oh he think he goin' with you. That's what he *think*. But this is the Fourth of July and I want to spend it with my husband. Imma tell him you already hit the interstate," she says. "Imma tell him you had to hurry out there 'cause you got a flat tire, God forbid." She hangs up and pokes her head out the front door. "Your brother's already hit the interstate," she tells Latrell. He doesn't acknowledge her. She goes back inside.

Latrell's sister arrives. She and Leanne commiserate about Latrell's attempts to go to Rocky Mount while they share a cigarette. Leanne explains her position that Latrell should stay home. "This is our day," she says.

Latrell's sister nods deeply. "I know that's right," she says, taking a drag off the cigarette.

Latrell joins them, and then he and his sister head outside to talk.

It's after eight by now, but no one has eaten much of the food Leanne has prepared. Gage is more interested in the fireworks than food. He won't be ready to eat until later, after the medication he takes for attention-deficit/hyperactivity disorder wears off. Although the boys generally like her cooking,

Leanne describes Hakeem and Gage as "not big eaters." She'll make something simple for them later.

Latrell ate a rib earlier but hasn't shown much interest in the rest of the food. He is still talking about taking off with his brother. Leanne hasn't eaten yet. "When we cook, I'm on my feet the whole time—then I don't want to eat!" she laughs.

11 WHERE'S THE GRAVY?

To say that food is a point of contention between Rae and Kenny Donahue is an understatement. Rae does everything in her power to help her family eat healthier, but she worries she's still coming up short. The biggest problem, in her opinion, is Kenny.

"My eating habits have changed *dramatically* from when Kenny and I first got together to now," Rae remembers. "It's like night and day." By saying her eating habits have changed, she means mostly for the worse. Rae says that before she met Kenny, she was more "health-conscious." When they got married, their tastes and ideas about food collided. After ten years of marriage and many attempts to persuade Kenny to change the way *he* eats, Rae has mostly adopted Kenny's bad habits.[1]

To give just one example, Rae never liked cheese or mayonnaise before she met Kenny. "That's just nothing that I wanted to add extra on a sandwich," she says. Kenny, on the other hand, loved cheese. Recalling their early days together, Rae speaks gruffly, imitating Kenny's voice: "Why don't you put cheese on your spaghetti?"

Resuming her normal tone, Rae explains glumly, "Now it's a part of my diet. Like I've completely picked it up and I probably eat cheese way more than he does."

Next was pork. Rae never ate that either. But after Kenny requested she cook it, she realized she kind of liked the smell and decided to try some. It was good, and she now eats it occasionally.

Rae also had to give up trying to make whole grain rice for Kenny and their six-year-old son, Tyler. "If I eat brown rice, Kenny will say, 'Well where is the gravy?'" she complains. "I'm like, 'Gravy on brown rice? Why don't I just cook white rice?' Because gravy on brown rice doesn't taste right."

She has managed to maintain a few of her good habits. She avoids soda—for the most part. "Kenny will have sodas in the refrigerator," Rae says. "But I don't buy soda. That's one thing I *would not* buy from the grocery store, is soda. So he'll buy them and put them in the refrigerator." A wry grin crosses her face as she adds, "Of course, during certain times in the month, I'll drink all the soda. Whereas before it wasn't even here for me to drink. So, things have changed a little bit. I'm trying to adapt to what Kenny likes, what Tyler likes, what I like. It's a bit much on a budget. We have to eat or drink whatever is here."

Making something that everyone will eat is a struggle that requires mental energy, money, and time. "Even now, I eat turkey bacon and Kenny'll request pork bacon," Rae says. "So when I go to the grocery store it's two kinds of bacon. He drinks regular milk, I drink almond milk. So it's two of those. Wheat bread versus white bread. He requests certain things that he's used to. And I buy certain things that I think that we need."

Rae and Kenny's arguments extend not just to what they're going to eat but also to who is going to cook it. They have completely different schedules. Kenny works the third shift, as a tech support supervisor for a credit card company with a round-the-clock helpline. He heads out the door around the time Rae goes to bed, arriving back home just as Rae and Tyler are getting up and ready for their day. Kenny sleeps during the day, which means that Rae is mostly responsible for taking Tyler to and from school and doing household errands.

Rae doesn't have a standard nine to five schedule either. She bought a nail salon a year ago and is trying to get it up and running. For now, this means that she relies a lot on her own labor, working long hours. She stays at the salon until 6:30 PM several days a week. When she stays late at work, her sister-in-law helps out by picking up Tyler from school and watching him until Rae can come get him.

Kenny's schedule makes it possible for them to eat as a family most of the time; he doesn't have to go to work until the late evening. It's getting dinner together that's the problem.

Things go okay on the days when Rae doesn't have to work late. She picks Tyler up from school and starts making dinner as soon as they get home. She and Tyler are usually pretty hungry by then. It's the other days of the week when things fall apart. Kenny is supposed to cook on those days. But Kenny doesn't really do any real cooking.

"Cook? Kenny? No. Maybe a couple of times," says Rae, raising her eyebrows for emphasis. "When I'm working [late] Wednesday, Thursday, Friday, I'm like, 'You know, you can cook.' "

Measuring out ingredients? Chopping up vegetables?

"Not at all." Rae laughs at the absurdity of the idea. It would be nice if he would cook, she reflects. "Sometimes, I come home and I am starving and then I end up snacking and Tyler ends up snacking and then we eat dinner late. So yeah, that would be nice."

In the images of dinnertime we see in magazines or on TV, everyone is smiling. The real stuff gets edited out. The part where kids or adults complain about what is set in front of them. The part where parents fight about who has to make dinner or who has to clean up. The days when parents can't agree on what to eat. The times when kids refuse to eat their food and instead dump it on the floor. The part where parents try to remain calm and eventually lose their cool. The chaos that ensues when kids start throwing each other dirty looks across the table and a shouting match ensues. On many nights, the dinner table is nothing short of a battlefield.[2]

Somehow the struggles of feeding a family are not usually taken seriously. This happens, in part, because feeding families is what sociologist Marjorie DeVault refers to as "invisible labor." Activities like grocery shopping and cutting vegetables are visible, although their importance is often overlooked. But other tasks, like keeping a mental checklist of each family member's preferences and juggling different schedules to make sure that everyone is there for dinner, are something that someone has to do, but that others in the family may not see. Meal planning is a complex calculus that involves acknowledging the competing preferences of different family members, making sure meals can be prepared within a budget and a certain amount of time, and folding variation into the weekly menu so people don't get bored with the same old thing.[3]

This work is still disproportionately performed by women, many of whom are doing it in addition to the paid work they do outside the home.[4] Rae and Kenny both work hard. However, it's up to Rae to make sure the family eats well on a budget. When she can't cook, they go out. The whole project would be easier if Kenny were on board with her ideas about eating healthier. But Kenny has his own ideas.[5]

Rae takes food very seriously, spending hours reading online articles about how to eat healthier, searching for good recipes, and preparing meals. And she gets visibly upset when she imagines that it might not be enough, that Tyler might become an overweight child. As she talks about it, her voice rises an octave. It is the sound of anxiety.

"I was overweight as a child. My husband was very overweight as a child," she says. "So we both know that it's not nice. It's not a pretty thing. It's not fun to go through. Plus, I want Tyler to be healthy. I don't want him to have another problem to worry about. I don't want him to worry about his weight and stuff like that. Pretty much everybody over fifty in my family has diabetes, or they are pre-diabetic. So that's a huge concern for me with Tyler. Because all the older people in my family, that's what they died of." Rae takes a deep breath. Talking about her family's diabetes makes her anxious. In a quiet voice, she adds, "It's very scary, just realizing what they go through, The dialysis and all that stuff. It is kind of scary."[6]

Rae invests a lot of time and effort in trying to make sure Tyler is healthy.[7] They eat dinner as a family. They rarely have dessert. Rae acknowledges her own tendency to indulge in sweets, so she avoids baking them. She is trying to teach Tyler to cook.

Tyler is a pretty flexible eater, Rae generally feels, but if he decides he is not going to eat something, there is no making him. Like a lot of kids, Tyler doesn't like to try anything that looks unfamiliar. For example, one time Rae used cream of mushroom soup in a dish. Tyler took one look at it and balked, saying, "Wait, what is this? I'm not eating that! You can spank me, Mommy." These moments make the challenges of feeding children painfully clear. Rae simply cannot force her child to eat, and if she tried, it would probably only make things worse. Experts say that pushing kids to eat certain foods usually backfires, although this is a common tactic around the dinner table.[8] A survey of college students found that more than half had been forced to eat foods they did not like as children, and that 72 percent now refused to eat those foods.[9]

When she thinks about Tyler's health and his future, Rae sometimes feels optimistic. He attends a good school that provides healthy lunches. He gets exercise there, and sometimes Kenny plays ball with him in the back yard. Rae is also encouraged by the fact that Tyler eats a range of foods, even though he has specific preferences. Still, she feels she could do a lot better. And she worries about how Kenny sneaks food to Tyler behind Rae's back. She wants that to end.

"Tyler does not drink soda with me," Rae emphasizes. "He does when he's with Daddy. He'll say, 'Mommy, Daddy let me drink soda today!' If they go out to eat, Kenny will definitely order him a soda."

It's not that Kenny doesn't care about Tyler's health. But Rae and Kenny do not see eye to eye on the definition of a balanced diet. Kenny accuses Rae of being too controlling when it comes to food. He believes in everything in moderation. Rae thinks Kenny has a skewed understanding of moderation.[10]

"Kenny and I go back and forth," Rae explains. "I am like, 'Do you want him to be big or overweight?' Kenny is like, 'One thing of fries is not gonna make him unhealthy.' I tell him, 'You know fries every other day, or whenever you pick him up, that will add up!' We just see things differently a little bit when it comes to the long-term effect of what you doing and what you teaching him. Kenny is like, 'Well the boy needs some soda! He can't be deprived of everything,' and this, that, and the other. Yeah. Not with me. He never gets soda with me. Kenny feels like I am too strict with Tyler. And I don't think I'm strict at all. I still don't think that Tyler is eating the way he should be eating, or the way that we *can* feed him. I think we can do better. Like, instead of fries, I order apple slices. But when Kenny takes him to McDonald's, he orders the fries. So he doesn't say it, but he kind of acts like, 'I'm gonna give this boy some fries.' So, yeah. He thinks that I could slack up a little bit."

Kenny's mother is also a source of friction. She lives nearby, and she loves to give Tyler treats. She even manages to do so when she can't see him in person. If her son, Tyler's uncle, is swinging by Rae and Kenny's, she will tuck a sugary little present for Tyler under his arm.

"She'll send him a whole bunch of Honey Buns, Skittles," Rae laments. "She'll send that up just for no apparent reason. It really does make me mad. I've never said anything to her. To Kenny, I'm like, 'Can you talk to your mother about not giving him soda or Honey Buns?' He says, 'Well that's not gonna hurt him.' You know, they on the same page. We'll go down to her house and she always have a cabinet of sweets just for Tyler. She told me one time he ate four Honey Buns in one day. She justifies this, saying, 'Well, he's not here a lot.' So, you know, that's just a Grandma thing. It just tickles her to see him eat stuff. I think that they think we are depriving kids [these days]. They say, 'You had it when you were little.' So it's the deprivation thing."

Tyler understands how these food wars work. If Grandma offers him soda when his mother is around, he'll look at Rae and say, in an angelic voice, "Oh Grandma, I don't want any soda." From Rae's point of view, this bothers Tyler's grandmother, who then accuses Rae of unduly influencing Tyler.

"She is like, 'He does not do this when you aren't here. He drinks the soda and he asks for more soda,'" Rae says, mimicking her mother-in-law.

"So if I say, 'Tyler, we're gonna try to be healthy, we're gonna try to drink more water,' he is with it. But if he is with his father, or if somebody suggests something else, he's with that too."

Rae adores her son and can't help but laugh at Tyler's efforts to please the adults around him. But these moments also make her angry. This particular food fight is about more than soda. For Rae, it is about her commitment to Tyler's health and her perception that neither Kenny nor his mother is as committed to the family's health as she is. From both of them, Rae gets a strong message that by rejecting soda and treats, she is denying joy, stealing moments of happiness from her child.

As a self-described overweight child and now an adult who battles her weight, Rae believes that feeding Tyler healthy foods—and eschewing unhealthy ones, like fries and soda—will help her son avoid the weight issues that have plagued her throughout her life. Kenny was also an overweight child, but he doesn't share Rae's concerns about their son's weight and health.

Rae tries to lead by example. She doesn't buy soda. She makes time to cook healthy meals on the evenings when she's not working. And she encourages Tyler to cook with her and try a range of foods. But Rae is not the only adult member of the household, and she's not the only adult in Tyler's life. She simply does not have complete control over the foods Tyler eats or the messages he hears about food. And those conflicting messages, the ones Rae is constantly trying to counter, are not just coming from Kenny and his mother. They are all around us.

TAKIS

It's 9:30 in the morning, and Rosario García is sweeping her living room. Luna, a neighbor's one-year-old, watches from the couch. *Despierta America* (Wake Up, America), one of Rosario's favorite shows, blasts from the TV. Despite the loud volume and the antics of the hosts, Luna is more focused on Rosario.

Rosario often helps Luna's mother, Fina, by babysitting Luna and her older brother. She charges only $10 a day to look after both kids because Fina, who works at a fast-food restaurant, doesn't make much to begin with.

Rosario suddenly jerks her head around to look out the front window. A police car has pulled up to the curb in front of her house. The officer seems to be studying the plates of a white Toyota Matrix with shiny chrome rims and tinted windows. Rosario's kids, who have been playing on the porch with Fina's brother, Bruno, and some other neighbor kids, quickly silence their games as they watch the police officer.

"Behave yourself or that cop is going to take you away!" Rosario yells through the screen door.

She returns to sweeping. The most difficult part of parenting is having to clean up the constant messes kids make, she thinks. Baby Luna begins to chew on a book. Rosario puts the broom down. "You were supposed to be reading, not destroying it," she chides, taking the book.

Rosario reaches into a small diaper bag and pulls out a bag of Ritz crackers and a bottle of milk. Luna grabs a cracker in each hand and shoves one into her mouth. A steady dribble of cracker crumbs lands on the couch with each bite.

Rosario sighs. Fina's kids have been here since 6 o'clock this morning, and Luna refused to go down for her morning nap. Fina can't get back from her shift and pick up the kids soon enough, as far as Rosario is concerned.

Now with the sweeping finished, Rosario heads to the kitchen to tackle the dirty dishes in the sink. Just as she starts, Santiago comes in to show her something. He holds out his palm to reveal a piece of cake, wrapped in a paper towel, that a neighbor has given him. Eyeing the blue-and-green frosting that is mashed into the paper towel, Rosario rhetorically questions why anyone would wrap cake in a paper towel. It barely looks edible. She dips her finger into the frosting and licks it. "Too sweet," she declares. She instructs Santiago to throw it in the trash. He does and then heads back outside.

Rosario goes back to doing the dishes. Because she has a small sink and almost no counter space, she has a precise strategy. First, she washes all the dishes and stacks them in a pile, then she drains the sink and rinses the dishes before leaving them to dry.

Outside on the porch, the kids are bantering roughly back and forth. Four-year-old Gabi tells Bruno that she is going to kill him. She grins, waiting for his reaction.

Bruno responds by throwing a faux punch that lands inches from Gabi's face. Then he brings out another trick. "Look," he says, making a fist and slowly erecting his middle finger at Gabi. "This is the middle finger," he announces.

Not to be outdone, Gabi erects her own grubby middle finger. Victoria, the oldest García child, laughs, putting on full display her apple cheeks and dimples, just like her mom's. She teases Bruno about how he used to stick up his ring finger until he learned that he was using the wrong finger to flip someone off.

The kids' ribbing is interrupted by Fina, who walks up the porch steps and knocks on the front door. They straighten up and smile politely at her.

Rosario is surprised to see Fina; she wasn't expecting her for several more hours. They sent her home early, Fina explains, since business was slow. She asks if it's okay to pay Rosario the ten dollars tomorrow. Rosario nods.

Fina scoops Luna up and calls for Bruno. "We need to get home before it rains," she tells him, looking at the gray sky. Seeing the ominous signs of rain, Santiago decides to come inside. He heads straight to the back bedroom that he shares with his siblings and turns on the television.

"Do you want ham and eggs for lunch?" Rosario calls to him from the kitchen. A barely discernible "yes" emanates from the bedroom. Rosario heads to the bathroom before starting the food. When she looks after Luna, she rarely finds time to pee.

Santiago hops up from the bed where he has been lounging as soon as he hears the bathroom door shut. He strides into the kitchen, climbs up on the counter, and opens the cabinet above the stove. He removes a box of

Cheez-Its, expertly jumps back down to the floor, and returns to the back bedroom with the box.

Moments later, the screen door at the front of the house slams shut. Gabi runs in, heading straight for the back bedroom. When she sees that her big brother has a snack, she marches into the kitchen and follows the same routine. After grabbing a large bag of Takis chips, she jumps down and casually walks out to the front porch to enjoy her snack while waiting for the rain.

Unaware that the children have been helping themselves to snacks, Rosario emerges from the bathroom and goes into the kitchen, where Victoria is already waiting patiently at the table. Rosario hunts for the bag of corn flour and the cast-iron griddle she always uses to make tortillas, then begins making the dough and rolling it into little balls. One by one, she flattens each ball into a flat tortilla and places it on the griddle.

While she waits for the tortillas to cook, Rosario retrieves a small frying pan from a shelf in the refrigerator. Inside the pan is a thick paste made of beans, peppers, onion, and garlic. Rosario places the pan on the kitchen table and gets a carton of eggs out of the fridge. She adds a small amount of corn oil to another pan sitting on the stove. Then she expertly cracks four eggs on the side of the pan, whipping the eggs with a fork. She sprinkles small slices of ham into the eggs, mixes everything together, and turns off the heat to allow the mixture to slowly cook in the hot pan.

At 11:15, everything is ready.

Rosario calls Gabi and Santiago to come to the table. Victoria gets up to grab a glass of water from the refrigerator. "Where are Santiago and Gabriela?" Rosario mutters. "Come eat!" she calls again.

Santiago joins Victoria at the table. A few minutes later, Gabi walks into the kitchen, gripping the large bag of Takis. Her fingers are stained with the red powder from the chips. "I'm not hungry," she announces.

"Hurry up and put the chips away. You're going to eat," Rosario replies curtly.

"No, I'm NOT!" Gabi yells, her face becoming as red as a tomato and her eyes welling up with tears. She hastily grabs Victoria's glass of water, storms out of the kitchen, and plops down on the living room floor in a sort of protest that also conveniently allows her to watch television.

Rosario is furious. "COME EAT," she yells into the living room.

"I'm not eating," Gabi yells back forcefully.

Rosario doubles down. "Yes. You. Are," she yells back, punctuating each word. Gabi ignores her. Moving swiftly, Rosario marches into the living room and snatches the Takis bag out of Gabi's hands. Turning on her heels, she storms back into the kitchen and places the bag on a high shelf in the cabinet.

Food fights are common in the García household, although Rosario usually manages to quash them before they erupt into a full-scale showdown. This is true in many American households. But in Rosario's household, the conflicts usually center around what Rosario refers to as "American food." Rosario and her husband, Samuel, prefer the traditional Mexican dishes they grew up eating. But their kids clamor for chips, pizza, and hot dogs, and they often refuse to eat the traditional dishes. Rosario frequently ends up making two, or even three, different meals on a given night. Something spicy for herself and Samuel and a non-spicy version for the kids. Tripe soup for everyone except Santiago, who gets fried steak. And on it goes.

Like many children, Rosario's kids are fickle about food. One day they tell her they won't eat meat, and the next day they request it. Sometimes they want hot dogs or hamburgers, foods they eat at school.

Researchers find that although immigrants' diets are often healthier than the typical US diet when they arrive, they—and especially their children— often quickly develop a preference for so-called American food.[1] Sociologist Jennifer Van Hook and her colleagues conclude that because US food culture is so ubiquitous, it can feel almost impossible for immigrant parents like Rosario to prevent this from happening. For the children of immigrants, "adopting an American diet may be as likely as [learning] English," they write.[2]

There are many factors that influence how the tastes of children in immigrant families develop. A desire to eat like their friends. Pressure to prove they're really "American."[3] The generic fare—hot dogs, hamburgers, grilled cheese, salads, and pizza—that is routinely served in American school cafeterias.[4] And then there are the food companies that invest a lot of money in producing and marketing food to appeal to children. Gabi's Takis have been chemically crafted to taste good and are designed to ignite pleasure sensors in the mouth and brain. (For example, Takis are high in sodium and contain monosodium glutamate [MSG]).[5] There are few restrictions in the United States around how Takis and other junk food can be marketed to kids.[6] Although new forms of media (for example, online and mobile ad campaigns) account for a growing share of US food manufacturers' advertising budgets, television is still the largest source of media messages that children receive about food.[7] Junk food is advertised to children much more often than other types of food.[8] One study found that four categories accounted for almost 60 percent of food ads viewed by children and youth: breakfast cereals, candy, fast food, and specific restaurants. Fast-food ads accounted for nearly a quarter of these ads.[9] Another study found that children's exposure to ads for candy on television increased 74 percent between 2008 and 2011.[10]

These ads have an impact. Randomized trials show that kids eat more junk food while and immediately after watching junk-food commercials.[11] And there's evidence that some kids are exposed to more advertising than others. This is largely because advertisers target certain groups—for example, by funneling more of their advertising budget to shows and networks viewed by black audiences.[12]

It's not just US food advertising and companies that Rosario has to contend with, though. In fact, Gabi's Takis, the current source of Rosario's ire, are made by a Mexican company: Grupo Bimbo, one of the largest food companies in the world.[13] And while Rosario contrasts the typical Mexican dishes from her childhood with the American junk food that her children crave, Mexico has changed a lot since she left. Soda, processed snacks, and fast food are all much more readily available than they were a decade or two ago.[14] The food we eat, the companies that make it, and the stores and restaurants where we buy it look increasingly similar, whether we are in Mexico or the United States, Ghana or Brazil.[15]

It's not surprising that Rosario and many other parents often feel like they're "swimming upstream" when it comes to helping their kids develop good eating habits.[16]

Gabi storms back into the kitchen. Tears stream down her now blotchy red face. She shrieks at her mother, "I'm not eating that crap! Where did you put the Takis?" she demands.

"SHUT UP!" an outraged Rosario yells at her daughter. Gabi's face turns even redder. She furrows her brow and sets her face in a determined scowl, even as she continues to cry uncontrollably. She is not backing down, and Rosario senses the moment has spun out of control. She knows she cannot force food down Gabi's throat. Victoria and Santiago stare intently at their mother, waiting to see what she will do.

Rosario takes a breath and regains her composure. Looking Gabi squarely in the eyes, she takes a different tack.

"Do you want a soda?" Rosario asks calmly, her voice tight.

Gabi immediately stops crying and regains her composure. "Yes," she responds. It's not a victorious yes. But it's not an apologetic yes, either.

"I bet you do," Rosario says sardonically, handing Gabi a can of Sprite. Gabi returns to the table and sits down.[17]

Santiago and Victoria glance at Gabi as they finish their lunch. Santiago, who also has a soda, plays a game on his iPod with one hand as he uses his other hand to scoop up eggs with his tortillas. He finishes most of his food, which is rare for him. Victoria also eats all of the food on her plate, sopping it up with the warm tortillas. She is not allowed to drink soda. Last year, a doctor told Rosario that Victoria was overweight and recommended she go on a diet. Rosario cut back on buying sodas and snacks. When these items are in the house, Victoria is not permitted to have them.

Rosario puts a few tablespoons of the eggs and ham on a small plate and sets it in front of Gabi. Gabi stares at the plate, refusing to touch it. After a few moments she gets up, goes over to the counter, hops onto it, and grabs a package of cookies. Rosario watches mutely while Gabi defiantly sits back down at the table and proceeds to eat nothing but cookies and a can of Sprite for lunch.

13 SCARCE FOOD

Saundra Washington still isn't home. After searching help-wanted ads for several weeks, she finally found work with a janitorial company and started four days ago. She had to work today but should be back at the hotel room by now. Patricia has delayed dinner as long as she can, but it's almost eight o'clock and the kids are hungry. Time to serve the food.

The trip from the microwave to the beds isn't far, but with four bowls balanced precariously in her arms, Patricia takes it slow. She looks like a server in a diner, except that the dishes are recycled plastic containers rather than actual plates. She is wearing her usual powder-pink Crocs, the contours of her curvy frame discernible beneath her loose paisley dress.

Patricia manages to carry the steaming bowls of food to the side table between the two beds. She sets them down, relieved. Each bowl contains a small pork chop, fried on the hot plate they keep on the dresser next to the TV, and a small scoop of rice, heated up in the microwave.

"You'd better behave while the food cools," Patricia tells Mia, Jayden, and their half-brother Demani, who are all perched on one of the beds. Demani is Mia and Jayden's dad's child with another woman. Patricia and Saundra help out by watching him sometimes. It's late, and Demani and Jayden are already in their pajamas— Demani in an Eagles T-shirt and loose pajama pants with a skull and crossbones print and Jayden in blue footie pajamas. Mia is wearing a black T-shirt and khaki pants.

Sounds from the cartoon on TV fill the room. Demani sings along. "I need to rock, I need to rock," he belts, slightly out of tune. Patricia joins in, bopping her head back and forth with the music.

"Is the food cool yet?" Demani asks.

"It needs to be warmed up," Mia lectures him, sounding very mature but confusing "cooled down" with "warmed up." She launches into a long explanation about how "hot" can mean two different things—temperature hot, or spicy hot. Mia likes her Takis hot, meaning spicy.

Jayden is rubbing his eyes. "It's almost naptime!" Mia proclaims.

"It's almost bedtime," Patricia corrects her. "You had a nap earlier."

"Is it eight yet?" Demani interrupts. He is hoping to watch a wrestling match that starts at 8:00 PM.

Patricia tells him that it is, but Mia is horrified by the idea of watching wrestling. She hops down from the bed and begins jumping up and down in protest. "I wanna watch cartoons!" she whines. She eyes the bowls of food skeptically. "I don't want to share my food with Demani," she tells Patricia.

"You'd better behave yourself," Patricia replies. "You cry for Demani to come, but then you won't be nice when he's here."

To defuse the situation, Patricia says the food is cool enough to eat. She hands a black plastic bowl to Demani and another to Mia. She holds Jayden's bowl for him. The fourth bowl is for Saundra.

Jayden makes a grab for Mia's pork chop, but she manages to push away his hand.

"Can I have some salt?" Demani asks Patricia. She nods and points to a large cardboard canister of salt on the counter next to the sink. He walks over to the counter, with Mia following him.

The salt canister is big and bulky, with a pouring spout at the top. Demani awkwardly tries to maneuver the canister to pour just a bit on his food, but a teaspoon's worth of salt rushes out at once. Determined to get her own salt like her older half-brother, Mia insists on pouring it herself. She manages to spill slightly less than Demani.

"I did the salt myself," she warbles in a sing-song voice.

Sitting back down on the bed, Demani devours his salty rice and pork chop in a few minutes. "Can I have more pork chop?" he asks as soon as he swallows the last bite.

"Wait until Saundra gets back," Patricia tells him, glancing at the fourth bowl she has set aside for her daughter. Under her breath, she mumbles that she had forgotten Demani was spending the night and didn't have enough food. She sits down on the other bed and pokes at her phone, texting someone.

Jayden toddles over to Patricia and jumps up and down, pointing at the bowl in her lap. She is distracted but realizes what he wants after a few minutes. She tears off a piece of pork chop and gives it to him. He gnaws happily.

Transfixed by the cartoon on television, Mia is mostly ignoring her food. She sings along with the cartoon jingle. But when Jayden wanders over and grabs for her pork chop, she angrily snatches it back.

TV remote in hand, Demani finally has the power to change the channel. He switches it to the wrestling program. "I was watching cartoons!" Mia protests. Patricia is texting again, so Jayden goes to Mia for food. He holds out his hand, but Mia refuses to give him anything.

"It's my food!" she tells him.

Jayden grunts in protest.

"I wanna watch cartoons," Mia repeats.

Jayden walks over to Patricia and begins jumping up and down on the floor. She gives him another piece of pork chop. "Stop jumping. Ask," she reprimands him.

Mia is momentarily appeased when one of the wrestlers on TV starts rapping. But as soon as the song is over, she resumes her whining. "I wanna watch cartoons!" she chants, over and over. Her dinner is still mostly untouched.

Patricia gives Jayden another bite of food from his bowl. There is a knock at the door. Patricia walks over to unlock it. It's Saundra. She wears a black polo, inscribed with the logo of the janitorial company.

"What's wrong with you?" she asks Mia, immediately noticing her furrowed brow and grumpy demeanor. Patricia explains that Mia and Demani have been fighting over the television.

Near the refrigerator, Demani is struggling to pour green Hawaiian Punch from a large jug into a cup. Saundra goes over to help him.

"My dad said drink water," Mia says when she sees the juice. Saundra tells Demani that he can have a cup of juice first, but then only water.

"No, you're not getting my food," Mia chastises Jayden, who is trying to grab at her bowl again.

Saundra gets her own bowl from the bedside table and walks over to the counter next to the sink. Looking around the cluttered counter, she finally locates a large bottle of Texas Pete hot sauce. Once she has sufficiently coated her pork chop and rice with the bright red sauce, she sits down at the head of the bed and begins eating.

Mia eats a spoonful of her rice, then another. Looking at her, Jayden starts jumping up and down.

"Ma, I think he's hungry," Saundra tells Patricia, who is still holding Jayden's bowl. Jayden wanders over to Patricia to get more food.

Demani repeats his request for another pork chop. Saundra bargains with him. There aren't enough pork chops for him to have seconds, but he can have a hot dog. Demani agrees but is momentarily distracted by the television. "You been good?" Saundra asks Mia. Mia smiles in response. "Close your mouth when you eat," Saundra tells her, motioning for Patricia to hand her Jayden's bowl. Patricia passes it to Mia, who passes it to Saundra, who feeds Jayden two spoonfuls of rice in quick succession. Patricia stares blankly at the television. It's been a long day, and she is tired.

"Those cheesecake bites look good," Patricia says to no one in particular, looking at a commercial for Sonic's Cheesecake Bites. The dessert features chunks of cheesecake rolled and fried in a graham cracker crust and accompanied by strawberry sauce. One order is $1.99.

Patricia and the kids have no problem coming together at the end of the day. Between not having a car and Patricia's asthma and gout flare-ups, which make it difficult for her to move around, they spend a lot of time in the hotel. Saundra makes it home for dinner most days, although things are more complicated now with her new job. Coming home to Patricia and the kids is Saundra's favorite part of the day. "Since we don't have that many people that we can fall back on, I feel like they're the biggest support system," she says. "So it's like when we're all together, it just makes me feel good."

Food is in short supply, though, in the Washington household. Every bit is precious. When households don't have enough food to meet their needs, they are considered food insecure. By this standard, the Washington family is among the over fifteen million American households experiencing food insecurity. Women-headed households and households with children have higher than average rates of food insecurity.[1] People experiencing food insecurity adopt a range of coping strategies, including eating lower-quality foods or the same thing over and over, eating less at mealtimes, or even skipping meals altogether.[2]

The responsibility for preventing children from being hungry falls most heavily on women in food-insecure households. Women skip meals, eat later than everyone else, or take smaller portions in order to minimize the impact of food shortages on their kids. And there's good evidence that the coping strategies mothers adopt in their efforts to keep children from going hungry are detrimental to their own health, disrupting eating patterns and increasing the risk of obesity, for example.[3]

But despite the fact that Patricia and Saundra do a lot to buffer the kids from hunger, it's clear that the kids understand there's not much food to go around. Mia is astute. She knows she is sharing her limited food supplies with Demani, and she notices that her mom and grandma often don't eat when she does.[4] Mia's not the only kid in food-insecure households who recognizes when food is tight. Studies have found that kids like Mia use their own coping strategies to try to ease the burden of food insecurity on their families, like policing the family's food supply, eating less at meals even when they're hungry, telling siblings not to ask their parents for food, or not requesting foods at the grocery store. Kids aren't necessarily known for being subtle, but many manage to hide their knowledge of their family's food scarcity, even from their parents.[5]

"It's time to start thinking about what to make for Thanksgiving," Saundra says. They had hoped to be out of the hotel, but it is undeniably apparent they'll be cobbling together some sort of Thanksgiving dinner on the hot plate. No one answers. Jayden and Mia have finished their bowls of food.[6] Saundra lets out a heavy sigh. "Go get the grease," she tells her daughter, referring to the product she uses to braid Mia's hair.

"Can I get a cold hot dog?" Demani asks Patricia, realizing he still hasn't gotten the hot dog he was promised.

"Cold hot dogs aren't good for you," Patricia warns.

"Can I get a warm hot dog?"

"You can heat one up in the microwave," Saundra tells him, nodding with her head toward the microwave.

Mia gets a tub of translucent green grease from the counter and brings it to Saundra. She swipes through the grease as Mia clenches her teeth, bracing for the pain of having her hair done.

Going over to the small fridge, Demani retrieves a package of hot dogs. He removes one and places it in a clean plastic bowl. Opening the microwave door to put it in, he hears Saundra behind him.

"Don't put it on too long," she warns. Seeing Demani prepare food reminds her of what she has just eaten. "The pork chops were good," she tells Patricia.

Demani carefully punches the buttons 2-0-0 on the microwave.

Patricia, who is watching from the bed corrects him. "One-oh-five."

"A minute, five seconds?" Saundra asks incredulously. "That's gonna burn," she adds, shaking her head. Turning back to the task at hand, she continues to methodically weave Mia's strands of hair into a pattern.

"How can you braid so fast?" Demani asks her, the microwave whirring behind him, set to a minute and five seconds as per Patricia's recommendation.

"I'm used to it," Saundra tells him.

The microwave dings. Demani removes the steaming hot dog.

"Get out of the trash!" Patricia tells Jayden, who is poking around again. He has already retrieved what he was looking for and hands Patricia a torn candy wrapper.

"I almost froze while waiting for the bus," Saundra says while she puts the final touches on Mia's braids. "And on top of that, the driver was rude. A woman with a baby asked the driver to hold the Number One, her transfer bus, but he refused, telling her the Number One wasn't his bus. He could have held the other bus. He also refused to answer someone's questions about the route, so I had to give her the answer."

Patricia nods. "Wow." Injustices like this are an everyday part of her family's life, but they never cease to be felt strongly. "It's a blessing to have a job. There are plenty of people waiting for that job," she says, referring to the bus driver, who doesn't seem to care enough about his job to do it well.

Saundra heads out to retrieve the laundry from the dryer down the hall.

Patricia hasn't eaten anything yet today and feels lightheaded and tired. Fortunately, at the same time that Saundra gets back from the laundry room with the dry clothing, Patricia's son Doug arrives with a bag of Popeye's chicken. He hands Patricia a small rectangular box and a cup of soda before heading back out the door. Doug tries to chip in when he can.[7] If he hadn't brought the takeout tonight, Patricia likely would have gone without eating. She shares the food with Saundra, who has another long, physically demanding day at work tomorrow.

4 KNOW WHAT'S ON YOUR PLATE

Every time you spend money, you're casting a vote for the kind of
world you want.

—ANNA LAPPÉ,
food activist and writer, in *O Magazine* (2003)

The "eating for change" movement argues that individuals have
the power to change the food system. By paying attention to what
they put on their plates and where they put their money, consumers
can work toward healthier bodies and a healthier planet. But not
everyone has the money to vote with their fork. And even those
with the means to do so may find themselves exhausted and disappointed, swimming against the tide as they try to eat healthfully
and sustainably. When shopping for food is seen as a sign of good
parenting and ethical consumption, it can also become a test of
who is, and who is not, caring and thoughtful.

14 VOTE WITH YOUR FORK

Greely Janson cares a lot about food: where it comes from, how it's produced, and the implications it has for people's health and the environment. Some people probably perceive her as too "controlling and intense," she says, because of how much she cares about food. But Greely believes there is something deeply wrong with our food system. We've gotten very good at producing food that is "cheap and fast," she explains, and this comes with a host of unintended consequences. Mistreated animals, farmworkers who are sick from pesticide exposure, polluted environments, and ingredients that leave people chronically undernourished are at the top of Greely's list of concerns.

"I know more than most people care to know about the [problems in the food system]," Greely says, matter-of-factly. "And it's hard for that *not* to influence how you eat, and how you frame food for your family."

Like many mothers, Greely is skeptical that the government is adequately looking out for the safety and well-being of her family or anyone else's, for that matter.[1] If she wants to achieve her goals of fostering a healthy family and a healthier planet, she feels she has to take charge and make good choices.

Greely's food philosophy involves making meals from scratch, using mostly organic ingredients, on a daily basis. She primarily shops at her local farmers' market and the "health food giant" Whole Foods.[2] She also sources food from other venues, like Trader Joe's and conventional supermarkets, on occasion. "We get meat at the farmers' market," Greely explains, referring to one of the biggest farmers' markets in the area. "They have more vendors who have sustainably raised meats. We usually get our eggs and meats and some of our produce from there, and then Whole Foods as well. When the farmers' markets are in season, we try to get more produce from there. We used to know someone who had a CSA (community-supported agriculture) that we could pick up in the parking lot at a store in [the neighborhood]. We did that for a while, but I don't think we are gonna do it again. Those are the primary places. Sometimes Trader Joe's [and] very occasionally other places."

Greely puts a lot of thought into her shopping decisions. She tries to buy organic as often as she can, although she wishes she had even more options. "Especially for Adelle, I try to do as much organic as possible," she says. She takes other considerations into account when making decisions about what foods she will buy, she explains. "As an adult, I've been more focused on local, just in supporting our local food culture here and being able to, over time, influence practices. There are plenty of great, small farms who have good farming practices."

Greely is part of a growing movement of conscientious consumers striving to create a better food system, one purchase at a time, by supporting local, sustainable, and ethically-produced foods and the farmers who grow them.[3]

Greely "votes with her fork" by eschewing conventional supermarkets, buying from local farmers, and choosing organic. She is the first to admit that this strategy is expensive and time-consuming. But like many others, she thinks it's one of the best ways to change the food system.

At the end of one of Greely's favorite documentaries, the Oscar-nominated *Food Inc.*, a series of words scroll across the screen.

> You can vote to change this system.
> Three meals a day.
> Buy from companies that treat workers, animals, and the environment
>   with respect.
> When you go to the supermarket, choose foods that are in season.
> Buy foods that are organic.
> Know what's in your food.

Especially over the last two decades, the alternative food, or "eating for change," movement has blossomed as a means of allowing consumers to use their food purchases to challenge or bypass what they see as the dangers and problems inherent in the industrial food system. As sociologist Norah MacKendrick notes, the message espoused is one of "consumer citizenship": that we can engage in political action through our shopping decisions.[4]

Early iterations of the movement centered largely around farmers' markets and other venues that brought consumers and producers into direct contact with each other. Farmers' markets and CSAs are places where people not only can buy sustainably-raised meat, milk from nearby dairies, and seasonal vegetables, but also can get the chance to "know their farmer." Organic, fair trade, and place-based labels aim to provide consumers with transparency about how and where their food is produced, even when it comes from far away.[5]

The vote-with-your-fork maxim has been picked up by high-end supermarkets like Whole Foods,[6] niche food companies like Hampton Creek and Annie's HomeGrown, and even conventional food retailers like Walmart.[7] There is ample evidence that consumers have embraced the idea of voting with their forks. Sales of organic food doubled between 1994 and 2014.[8] The United States now has more than 8,600 farmers' markets, scattered in tiny towns and big cities all over the country.[9] Seventy-three percent of people surveyed in 2016 said they had purchased locally grown fruits or vegetables in the past month, and 68 percent reported buying organic food.[10]

The idea that people have a right to eat clean and healthy food from local and sustainable sources resonates with many consumers. However, critics point out the limitations of enacting change through our shopping decisions. One is that many of the most visible advocates of "voting with our forks" are male chefs, farmers, and activists, even though it is usually women who do the bulk of the shopping and cooking for their families. This creates a gendered solution to the problems in our food system, whereby female foodies like Greely are the ones doing the actual work—shopping at multiple stores, searching for new recipes to make use of seasonal produce, spending extra time chopping vegetables—required to make the movement successful.[11] Moreover, because people can only vote with their forks through their food purchases, it's the people with the most money who have the most votes.[12]

Even Greely cannot always cast as big a vote as she would like. Eating ethically and sustainably is expensive. Greely and Matt have a combined yearly income of $80,000, putting them above the median in the United States.[13] They spend $150 dollars each week on groceries to feed their family of three, but it isn't enough. "I would like $250 a week to spend on groceries," Greely says with an embarrassed laugh. "For sure. That would be awesome. But that's not going to happen anytime soon. We kind of put ourselves on a stricter budget in January. We're trying to use more things from our pantry more creatively."

Meat is the biggest strain on their budget, because sustainably-produced meat is a lot more expensive. "It's just not fitting into our budget super well," says Greely. "Like one week we spent $200 between the farmers' market and

Whole Foods. We got a London broil and we got a sausage and we got a whole chicken to roast. We made really good chicken soup. We definitely made the chicken go far at least. The steak doesn't. It was like one dinner and then it's like, 'Really?'"

Greely wishes she could incorporate more meat into her diet. But it has to be the right kind of meat. "I generally feel better if I have like a very high protein and vegetable kind of diet," she reflects. "That's hard for me right now. Right now, I'm not able to do that. We eat plenty of beans and rice and those things. The meat is certainly more filling, but a lot more expensive."

People who believe in the promise of voting with your fork are often frustrated when they cannot fully see it through.[14] Even Greely—with a relatively high family income, knowledge of the best local deals, and steely resolve to devote time to cooking and sourcing food—can't eat the way she thinks she should.

Many reasons motivate Greely's decision to vote with her fork, but motherhood is one of the most important. Of her efforts to make sure Adelle eats well, she says, "It's something that we're constantly working on, just trying to give her the knowledge and the opportunities to make good choices for herself and exposing her to a range options on the higher end of the spectrum."

Helping Adelle develop the right outlook, so that she can eventually vote with her own fork, requires big investments of time and energy, such as when Greely and Matt took Adelle to a local farm in order to show her what "a positive experience" on a farm looks like for animals. For the most part, Adelle is a receptive audience. In fact, when she found out that the all-beef hot dog she ate at Greely's pay-what-you-can restaurant didn't come from a small local farm, she was horrified. "She's like, 'Mom! Why did you not tell me?' and I was like, 'Oh my gosh.' I didn't realize how serious she was about it."[15]

Greely hopes that when it comes time for Adelle to make her own food choices, all of these efforts will pay off. "I would just like to set her up for the most success possible, healthwise. And I think that's just exposure, and developing a palate that appreciates healthy food," she concludes.

Enacting these ideals is important to Greely, but it requires ongoing resilience and adaptation in the face of a food environment that in many ways seems to constantly threaten her mission. It also sometimes causes tensions between Greely and Adelle. Most recently, as with the hot dog incident, the tensions come from Adelle's embrace of Greely's ideals and her disappointment with her mother for not always living up to them. But in the past, it had more to do with Adelle questioning Greely's food ideals and practices.

When Adelle started kindergarten last year, Greely packed almost all her lunches. She made sure they were healthy, tasty, and fun. She even sent sushi in Adelle's lunch. But Greely soon discovered that Adelle didn't appreciate all of her efforts. One day, Adelle informed Greely that some of the kids at school were making fun of her for bringing sushi for lunch. Toward the end of the school year, Adelle decided she wanted to try something different.

"She came to us and said, 'I want to buy the school lunch. I want to be like everyone else,'" Greely says, with a hint of wounded pride. "So finally we looked at the menu together. And yes, we're kind of controlling and intense, but I just said, 'I would prefer if you're gonna eat the school lunch for it not to include meat, because in general we feel this way about the meat.' And so she looked at things. And then she ended up deciding that nothing really sounded good. And, you know, I think she was also paying more attention to what people were getting and looking at it more carefully and realizing that it wasn't as interesting as it seemed." The crisis was averted, and these days Adelle seems to be on board with Greely's food philosophy. But Greely gets flak from friends and family for the ways she shields Adelle from certain foods. Like the time she took Adelle to a birthday party and other mothers stared at Greely, mouths agape, when Adelle pointed to a bowl of M&Ms and asked, "What are those?" These moments make Greely feel like a cultural outsider. They highlight how food can signify belonging or exacerbate feelings of deviance or difference.[16]

The school lunch and M&Ms incidents prompted Greely to reevaluate whether she was being too intense about food. Was she doing Adelle a disservice? Would Adelle grow up to feel like an outcast or like she doesn't belong, as Greely did? But not long after the back-and-forth about school lunch, Adelle's teacher asked the kids to write a list of reasons they loved their moms. One of Adelle's reasons was that her mom "made special lunches" for her.

In that moment, Greely felt like she was winning at parenting. It's a moment she comes back to again and again when she starts to question herself. "I think Adelle's gotten to the point where she realizes we take the time and we care and we put energy into making something that's maybe different but has some thought put into it," she reflects. "And I think at this point she is more proud than concerned about it."

It's critical not to dismiss the power many women exercise through their food practices, argue sociologists Kate Cairns and Josée Johnston. Women have long used their household purchases as a way to assert political power. Although critics sometimes characterize "voting with your fork" as a poor substitute for actual voting or political action, shopping has led to political activism in some cases, rather than distracting from it.[17] Consumer movements can lead to broader, long-lasting changes.[18] But "eating for change" can also be exclusionary; not everyone has the time or the money to vote with their fork. Even Greely has to make tradeoffs.[19]

Voting with her fork gives Greely a sense of power in a food context she thinks is unhealthy and unsustainable.[20] And more often than not, it feels like her efforts are paying off. People are often "surprised and impressed" with Adelle's appetite and the range of healthy foods she happily eats. "She'll go to the farmers' market with us and be like, 'Can we get collards this week?' And people are like, 'What?!'" Greely says, smiling. But these moments of pride are always tempered by Greely's fear that her beliefs and choices are alienating Adelle from mainstream culture. And although Greely is fine paying the price for her own food beliefs, she's never certain about the extent to which she should be making these decisions on behalf of her daughter.

15 THE REPERTOIRE

"I've been trying to introduce new things to the repertoire, but they're not kind of taking with the kids," sighs Marta Hernández-Boynton. "Like quinoa. They were like, 'I don't know what this is. I'm not eating this.' I've done a barley risotto, and they were like, 'Okay, I'll eat it,' but they weren't super excited."

Marta laughs. The furrow between her brow softens for a moment as she tries to make light of just how hard it is to convince her boys to try new things. She's particularly worried about the diet of her older son, Sebastian. "He's *really* skinny. Based on his BMI, he's underweight," she says. The pediatrician assures Marta that Sebastian's weight is fairly normal, despite consistently hovering in the underweight category. "She's like, 'As long as he's eating a variety of foods, he'll be fine.' So, we try." Marta agrees with this approach. She works in the health field and has read a lot about the importance of making sure children have a diverse diet starting at a young age.[1]

It sounds simple and worthwhile, but getting seven-year-old Sebastian and his three-year-old brother to eat "a variety of foods," as the doctor recommends, is easier said than done. Marta puts a lot of intensive time and energy into feeding the kids—buying and preparing meals from scratch, staying up on the latest nutrition research, and teaching the children about food.[2] She plans their weekly menus in advance. She tries to get the boys involved in cooking, hoping they will learn some new skills and become more excited about food. But despite Marta's efforts, Sebastian still wants to eat the same things over and over again.

Marta and James enjoy eating a wide range of foods. When it was just the two of them, they tried different things all the time. "I like things that are kind of spicy," says Marta. "We used to make a lot of spicy Thai recipes." With the arrival of the kids, they cut all of that out. Now stir-fry is a novelty dish. "We recently started doing stir-fries, but we have to remember that we can't put anything really exotic or spicy or anything in it," says Marta. "And exotic is like, mushrooms. Sebastian won't eat a mushroom. We used to put the little canned corns in. Yeah, they won't eat that. So, I gotta be very thoughtful. Like there has to be broccoli and carrots in it, and then I know that they'll eat."

The window of opportunity to expand her kids' palates is closing, Marta worries. This is the period when she has the best chance of influencing her children's tastes for healthy foods. Marta always has an eye to the future. If she can instill good eating habits now, the kids will make good choices for themselves when they are older, she thinks. But for now, they aren't buying it.

Parents are expected to do whatever it takes to help their kids develop healthy eating habits, but they must walk a fine line. Modern feeding advice is full of mind-boggling, and often contradictory, dos and don'ts. Feeding kids can often become a power struggle, but it doesn't have to be, the experts tell us.[3] Be upbeat and smile; your efforts to feed your kids should seem, well, effortless. Don't deprive your children of food, but don't restrict it either, which can lead to food fights and disordered eating down the road. In order to help kids develop a taste for a variety of healthy foods, you should present them with many different kinds of foods. If they don't want it, that's okay. Keep trying. One day they just might eat it. You may need to try eight to fifteen times before this will happen, but just keep offering it.[4]

Yet most parents struggle with feeding their kids, and advice like this can leave parents feeling like they're doing it all wrong.

Marta is determined to get it right. And the stakes are high. Even though she is concerned that Sebastian is too thin, she also worries about kids who seem to be getting bigger and bigger these days. Childhood obesity rates in the United States are among the highest in the world.[5] There are also more obese adults in the United States than in any other industrialized country in the world. Mexico, the country where Marta was born, comes in second.[6] Marta is concerned about statistics like these. "It seems like we're always getting some sort of flier at school or something about studies [about childhood obesity], or it's just something I read for work, or in a magazine," she says. "And, I mean, I do notice. Like we go to the mall to the play area when it's raining. And I do find myself noticing when there are kids that are obese . . . and I think, 'Oh, wow! That little kid should not be that big for that age.'"

Marta attributes the good health of her own children—notwithstanding the fact that Sebastian is thinner than she'd like him to be—largely to her efforts. She has worked hard to teach Sebastian to make good choices and resents parents who, in her opinion, are uninformed or oblivious to the consequences of their decisions. For example, she's critical of parents who send their kids to school with lunch boxes loaded with Lunchables and chips. "I think most people don't think about what their kids eat, you know?" she says, unapologetically. Marta is proud of the lunches she packs for Sebastian, which she sees as another example of her thoughtfulness as a parent.[7]

But recently, Marta learned that Sebastian isn't such a fan of them. "Sebastian tells me that his friends have made fun of him because he has carrots or fruit or something," she says. "And they tend to have Cheetos or Doritos. He used to ask for Doritos in his lunchbox.[8] And I was like, 'No. I'm sorry.'" Sebastian has also lobbied Marta to pack Lunchables in his lunchbox. She stood firm. "I haven't even looked at Lunchables to see whether they're good or bad, but I just—the idea of somebody packaging lunch meat and cheese into something that's more attractive . . ."

Marta assesses Lunchables using the same criteria she applies to most food decisions. Fresh food, prepared in your own kitchen, is good. Food made in a factory, packaged in plastic containers, is bad.[9]

Marta feels strongly that people need to know what's on their plate. Too many people don't. When she imagines a stereotypical unhealthy or overweight child, Marta pictures a kid with poor, uneducated parents. She explains, "I know nutritionists who work with low-income families who get very frustrated that they don't seem to make a dent into . . ." She trails off, perhaps wondering how this portrayal might sound. "I don't know," she backtracks. "I think part of it is that if you are surrounded by—you know, your surroundings don't help you make the better choices. You might be getting food from WIC and they are telling you the kinds of things you should buy, the kinds of cereals [that are healthy]. But, you know, if anybody else in your house is probably eating sugary cereals, or potato chips . . . it's like a contradiction."

For some people, Marta acknowledges, money is an issue. "I think I usually spend $30 or $40 [a week] on fruits and vegetables," she says. "So I'm sure it's hard for [low-income] people to justify [spending so much]. You know, my husband and I always comment that you can buy a big bag of potato chips for the amount of a little bag of carrots."[10]

It's not just about knowledge or resources, though. Marta suspects that some parents are simply unwilling to put in the effort to get their kids to eat better. "I mean, it's harder sometimes to think about," she acknowledges. "When you've got to coax your child to eat it, it's a lot more effort. Since

I work in the health field, I feel like it's worth it. Because later on, I don't want to have to be fighting back those habits."

Marta is vexed by parents whom she considers uninformed or unmotivated. And it's not just because she's worried about the health of the next generation; these parents' lax policies make it even harder for Marta to get her kids to eat right. When Sebastian sees other kids eating foods that Marta has banned, it just supports his perception that Marta's food policies are unfair and increases the already onerous work she undertakes to feed him well. It would be so much easier if everyone were on board with healthy eating and cared about what was on their plate, she reflects. It would also be easier if Sebastian didn't think of mushrooms as an exotic ingredient.

Nutritionists argue that eating a wide range of foods is important because it's healthier. And parents want their children to be healthy. But that's not all there is to feeding children.[11] What we eat and how we look signify our social status. People's diets, and the size of their bodies, are seen as a reflection of their education, values, and morals.[12] A child's good or bad eating practices are taken as evidence of their parents', and especially their mother's, ability to convey the right values and habits.[13] In short, what we eat is about more than being healthy. It is also about being seen as smart, motivated, and sophisticated.

In today's foodie landscape, being an omnivorous eater carries cachet.[14] Adults should feel equally at ease eating ramen noodles from a food truck as enjoying a four-course tasting menu at a Michelin-starred restaurant. Similarly, having a child with a "refined and global palate" is a sign of prestige, while having a child who only eats plain pasta or refuses to eat vegetables reflects poorly on the parents.[15] Upper-class parents derive pride and prestige when their children display self-restraint and control around food, argues sociologist Priya Fielding-Singh.[16] When kids are willing to eat diverse foods and say no to junk food, it says something about how well their parents have raised them.

Both of these objectives—health and status—are on Marta's mind. She is committed. She has the know-how. She's got the money. Marta and her husband make a combined $100,000 a year. And she's willing to invest a lot in healthy food.

But it's tricky, she finds. Given her concerns about Sebastian's weight, she wants to make sure he eats *something*. So she has pared back their staple meals to be centered around ingredients that Sebastian will tolerate. But because she wants Sebastian and his brother to eventually eat a range of foods, she continues to introduce new foods and repeatedly serve foods they've rejected in the past in an effort to win over her sons' taste buds.

"We've been eating sweet potatoes," she says. "And [Mateo], the little one, never, never eats them. We have made mashed sweet potatoes. I've tried sprinkling brown sugar on it. I have tried different presentations for him. Nothing. And last night, he ate it! And I didn't even ask him to eat it."

While Marta feels encouraged by the modicum of success she's had with Mateo, it has been even harder with Sebastian. The more Marta tries to make him branch out and try new foods, the more he rebels. With mounting anxiety, Marta has resorted to tactics that, she admits, only seem to backfire.

She recently introduced a timer at the dinner table. The mealtime antics that prompted this strategy will sound familiar to many parents. Night after night, it was the same thing. Sebastian would dawdle over his dinner, refusing the food on his plate. Marta first tried cajoling him to eat, to no avail. Then she adopted a harsher tone. Sebastian would try to negotiate with her, saying things like, 'How many more bites do I have to take?' Marta would grow increasingly frustrated. By the end of the meal, everyone would be cranky, and Sebastian's plate would still be mostly untouched. So Marta brought out the timer.

"We used to say, 'Well whatever you eat until the timer goes off,'" Marta recalls. She hoped the timer would help to resolve the nightly battles over food. Some nutrition experts recommend timers for exactly this reason. "Timers work because they do the nagging for you!" says Dina Rose, author of a book on helping children develop healthy eating habits. "And they're consistent."[17]

But the timer didn't work for Sebastian. Instead, it made him more anxious. "He was just tense about eating," Marta remembers. "So we were like, 'Forget it.'"

Exhausted and out of ideas, Marta resorted to a timeless negotiation strategy: bribery. "I would say, 'I need you to try a little bit of everything, and there's really not going to be any dessert if I feel like you're not really trying,'" she explains. "So, he's gotten a lot better."

Marta sounds both relieved and defeated as she recounts what finally worked. In general, Marta thinks her expertise about nutrition and health is a boon. But it also has its drawbacks, such as when she employs tactics that go against the experts' recommendations. As one of the experts, she knows some of the strategies she's tried aren't ideal.

Marta has read that turning food into a power struggle should be avoided at all costs. So it is to her relief, but also a bit to her dismay, that threats and bribery have worked better than all the recommended tips she's tried to follow.

Despite having to resort to what she views as an undesirable method to get Sebastian to eat, Marta achieved her goal in the end. But it wasn't easy.

And she wonders if this is actually hindering Sebastian from developing future good eating habits—like actually *wanting* to try new foods.

SOUR GRAPES

Late on a Thursday afternoon, Melanie and Kevin Richards and their two children pile into Melanie's old PT Cruiser to head to the grocery store. Melanie and Kevin recently sank a bunch of money into repairing the car. "Thank the Lord it's fixed," Melanie exhaled when it came back from the shop. Their other car, an old Honda, has major transmission problems. They usually manage to "coax the car to run," Kevin says, but they don't know how long this solution will hold and haven't been able to come up with the $700 or $800 it will cost to fix it.

Melanie pulls into a space in the Food Lion parking lot, and they all pile out. As they approach the sliding glass doors, Melanie's eye is drawn to the in-store specials that are plastered on the store's front windows. "Oh, watermelon's on sale," she remarks.

"Ice cream!" fourteen-year-old Justin says gleefully, pointing to a poster advertising a sale for Breyers ice cream. Justin has braces and the gangly appearance of a teenage boy in the midst of a growth spurt. His big feet and long arms suggest he will be tall like his dad, and his slightly protruding belly is a miniature version of his dad's. Justin has sandy blond hair and deep-set brown eyes. Today he is wearing a red polo shirt tucked into dark cargo pants and gray Fila toe shoes that look like gloves for feet.

Sweet Baby Ray's barbecue sauce is also on sale this week, Melanie sees. She's making a mental note to look for it in the store when Jade interrupts her train of thought.

"I want to ride it!" four-year-old Jade exclaims, pointing excitedly to the corral of carts just inside the store entrance. She is wearing khaki shorts, a pink T-shirt that says "Perfect Princess," and pink Crocs adorned with Disney princesses. Jade is eyeing a cart that has been retrofitted as a fire truck cab, complete with a steering wheel. Before Melanie has a chance to answer, she intensifies her request. "Can I ride it?" she begs, clasping her hands together in mock prayer.

Melanie sighs but nods in agreement. She knows the cart will be difficult to navigate around the store. Taking Jade by the hand, she walks her over to the cart. Jade situates herself inside the fire truck and begins playing with the steering wheel.

Melanie promptly pushes the cart into the store. Justin and Kevin follow. Steering the cart to a kiosk, Melanie scans her loyalty card. A minute later, the machine spits out a page of coupons. Digging around in his pocket for their plastic EBT card, Kevin hands it to Melanie. "Bye," he calls over his shoulder as he ambles back toward the sliding glass doors. He smooths a few mussed strands of hair over his receding hairline and pulls a box of cigarettes out of his pocket as he goes outside.

Melanie grabs the coupons from the machine and sifts through them. "Why aren't we leaving?" whines Jade.

"I'm reading," Melanie tells her brusquely, but then puts the coupons away. She steers the cart toward the produce section and glances at a large cardboard bin brimming with watermelons. "One watermelon per customer," reads a paper sign affixed to the box. The text below explains that they are being rationed because of a watermelon shortage this season. "They look small," Melanie says, her excitement waning when she realizes the sale price is not a great deal given the size of the watermelons. She moves on.

Next, she stops at a display of corn. "Ten for $3—how much is that each?" she quizzes Justin. He glances at the sign and shrugs.

"No. How much each?" Melanie presses him.

"I don't know!" Justin protests. Melanie calmly walks Justin through the math. She asks him to put ten ears into a bag and then turns to look at the grapes.

"They're on sale—do you want some?" she asks the kids.

"I want grapes!" Jade exclaims.

"Yeah. Not green ones," Justin adds, prompting Melanie to reach for a bag of red grapes.

"I want green ones! Green grapes!" Jade protests. Melanie sighs. She has worked all day, and now she has to referee a grape dispute.

"You don't like the green ones," Justin tries to convince Jade.

"Yes, I want green," Jade says stubbornly.

Justin is often annoyed by his sister, who is nine and a half years younger than he is. Rolling his eyes and sighing, he appeals to Melanie, "Can we just get red?"

"Green grapes! Green grapes!" Jade chants.

"I can't get both, you have to pick one," Melanie replies.

"I don't like the green ones, I just want red this time," Justin whines.

"Green grapes! Green grapes!" Jade shows no signs of relenting.

"Stop Jade," Melanie says firmly. "Listen. I'm thinking of a number from one to five—."

"Nooooo!" Justin moans.

"It's fair. I'm thinking of a number from—."

"Just—fine! Get green. Whatever," Justin cuts in, ending the dispute. Ready to move on, Melanie selects a bag of green grapes and puts them in the cart. Justin scowls and shoves his hands into his pockets. "You win," he says, sneering at Jade.

A puzzled look crosses Jade's face. She doesn't understand what she has won, so Melanie explains that Justin is letting her have green grapes.

"I win!" Jade shouts, throwing her hands up in the air. Her triumph is followed immediately by an announcement that she needs to go to the bathroom. It's urgent, she says.

Melanie quickly takes her to the bathroom in the back of the store. After helping Jade wash her hands, Melanie takes a few grapes out of the container and washes them.

She hands them to Jade once she's back in the cart. Jade pops a grape into her mouth. "I'm eating green grapes and they're sour!" she announces to another customer. He smiles at her and comments that her fire truck looks pretty cool.

"Green grapes good for you?" Jade asks Melanie.

"Grapes in general are good for you," Melanie tells her.

The federal government estimates that it would cost at least $550 a month to feed a family of four and meet nutrition recommendations, even when making the thriftiest choices.[1] Melanie spends much less than this, budgeting $300 a month for groceries. "How do you do it?" she asks rhetorically. "You shop cheaply. You buy the store brands—well, there are some things you can't buy cheaply. I mean sausage is one. The cheap sausage is terrible. We don't buy a lot of sausage. We don't buy a lot of bacon. We buy necessities. We buy meat for each meal. We buy a starch—so whether it's noodles or potatoes, some kind of starch. And then we buy vegetables. And—and we buy fresh fruit. . . . But you don't buy extra stuff. You don't buy ice cream and candy and junk."

Money is especially tight in Melanie's household right now. There are five people to feed: Melanie, her husband, her mother, and the two kids.

Occasionally, Kevin will do a delivery or two for his former company, but this has become increasingly rare in the five years since his Parkinson's diagnosis. Their main source of income is from Melanie's job as director of children's education at a church. The church doesn't have a lot of work for her during the summer, so Melanie is employed only nine months out of the year. Melanie's mom gives them $100 a month in rent, but that's about it.

Food stamp allocations are calculated according to a formula that takes into account the number of people living in the household, their assets, and their total household income.[2] Melanie's household has an annual income of around $21,000.[3] But this income is not evenly distributed throughout the year, because Melanie doesn't work during the summer. Melanie's food stamps are certified every six months. For the period that includes the summer, when she is unemployed, they get around $400 a month in food stamps. The rest of the year, they receive about $200 a month.[4]

To manage the fluctuations in their food stamps, Melanie tries to spend no more than $300 a month on groceries. If she doesn't spend all of the money in one month, it rolls over to the next. She reserves some of the food stamps that she saves during the "plentiful" months to use during the lean months. But feeding a family of five on $75 a week is difficult. It involves making a lot of tradeoffs.

Melanie would like to buy more organic food, for example. And she's not alone. Poor, middle-class, and wealthy Americans express similar levels of interest in eating organic food, but people with higher incomes are more likely to actually buy it.[5] Melanie would also love to buy more fresh produce and, ideally, join a CSA to get it from local sources. But she can't do any of those things on a budget of $75 a week.

Always on the lookout for opportunities to use her background in education, Melanie imparts lessons about health and eating to her children. If she can't practice what she preaches, she can at least preach the message of good food and hope it sinks in.

"I hate this cart. It's like driving a tractor trailer," Melanie complains, struggling to maneuver the heavy cart around a display. Bringing it to a halt in the condiment aisle, she consults with Justin about his preferences before selecting two bottles of brown mustard. She hopes the mustard will add a bit of excitement to the sandwiches they eat regularly for lunch. In the same aisle, she grabs two bottles of Sweet Baby Ray's barbecue sauce.

Heading toward the meat aisle, Melanie hopes she will find some good deals. They eat meat with nearly every meal. She picks up a package of $5 steak with a pink sticker on the plastic wrapper. "Value priced! I think we're going to have steak for dinner," she tells the kids cheerily.

"Steak? I don't—" Jade starts to complain, her legs hanging out of the fire truck window.

Melanie cuts her off. "You can have something else. I know you don't like steak."

"Yay!" says Jade, happy about the victories she is racking up today.

Melanie continues to peruse the deals, selecting a package of cube steak for $6.97 and two packs of value-priced chicken breast tenderloins, at $5.04 each. She smiles and waves at a teenager who is stocking the dairy shelves, then pushes the fire truck to the deli meats. "Lunch meat on sale!" she exclaims incredulously. But after inspecting the package more closely, she concludes, "Oh, that's only six ounces, that's not a good deal. That's ridiculous." She puts it back.

Justin, who has been lagging behind, catches up with Melanie just as she is assessing the bacon selection. He is holding a tub of hummus in his hand. Melanie selects a package of bacon and a package of Bob Evans sausage and puts them in the cart. Justin holds up the container of hummus and grins hopefully.

"You can get hummus," Melanie tells him.

"Yesssss!" says Justin, pumping his fist in the air. She smiles. She has to say no more often than she would like, so it makes her happy to say yes every once in a while.

"Did you get pita to eat with it?"

"I saw a deal on crackers," he suggests.

"Pita is whole grain. Crackers are just flour and butter, and we don't need that," Melanie instructs, imparting another nutritional lesson.

"Okay. I saw like, a deal on these small pitas, like eight pieces." Justin holds up his thumb and pointer finger to approximate the size. "Do you think that's better than the big ones?"

"Whichever you prefer," Melanie answers. Justin leaves in search of the pita.

In the dairy section, Melanie grabs sour cream and then ponders the cheese shelf. Justin returns with the whole wheat pitas. Because there are six in the package, it's a good deal, he explains.

"Okay," Melanie replies, turning back to the dairy case. "Ooh look, Muenster. Daddy likes Muenster," Melanie says, putting the cheese in the cart. Scanning the rows a second time, she looks perplexed. "I can't find the other one he likes."

"Aged Swiss?" Justin suggests. Carefully scanning the rows of cheese, Justin spots a package of Sargento sliced Aged Swiss cheese. "Oh, it's Sargento. It's expensive," he tells Melanie.

"Yeah, it's okay," she says over her shoulder. "Oh—butter!" She heads toward a stack of rectangular boxes of butter.

"Brrr, it's cold! Good thing I'm in the car!" Jade exclaims. Melanie laughs. Her children have a knack for driving her nuts one minute and providing a joyful moment the next.

As they walk toward the registers at the front of the store, Jade spots a display.

"Cookies?" she asks her mother hopefully.

"We don't need cookies," Melanie tells her.

"They're junk?" Jade confirms, using the same words she's heard Melanie use many times before.

"Yes, they're junk. We already had chips this week," Melanie answers. "Get those popsicles," she instructs Justin as they pass a freezer case filled with frozen tubes of flavored ice.

"Popsicles!" both kids cheer, united by their love for the freezer pops.

"Wait," says Justin, holding the freezer door open. "Which kind? Not the sugar free?"

"Not the sugar free. They don't taste good," Melanie tells him.

"I'm getting out!" Jades announces, scrambling out of the fire truck. She runs over to a giant plastic display of Pepperidge Farm Goldfish. Digging around inside the display, she extracts a small cardboard carton of multicolored baked cheddar crackers.

"Jade, we can't—," Justin starts to say.

"Okay, you can have it," Melanie interrupts.

Jade squeals with delight. "I got Goldfish, I got Goldfish," she chants triumphantly.

Not far from the display are the normal-sized bags of Goldfish crackers, which are the same price as the smaller cartons. Melanie suggests that Jade get one of these bags instead. Jade frowns, telling Melanie she wants the multicolored ones in the small milk carton-sized box. She clutches it to her chest. Melanie finds a large bag of the multicolored Goldfish and swaps it out for Jade's small one, explaining that this way she gets more for the same price.

On her way to the checkout line, Melanie sees an endcap holding rows of sodas, conveniently located near the cash registers. "I guess Kevin's probably gonna want a soda," she says. She walks over to the endcap, selects a two-liter bottle of Mountain Dew, and puts it in the cart.[6]

Melanie dreams of a better day—a day when she can eat as healthily as she would like. She and Kevin struggle to pay their bills and feed the kids, and they don't see themselves getting out of this financial hole anytime soon. There is a lot that she can't give her kids right now, but one thing she can do is offer them the occasional treat, even when it's not as healthy as she would prefer.

Food can offer a moment of relief from the day-to-day grind of living on the margins. Treating kids, who know money is tight and food is scarce, can make parents feel good about being able to do something to ease the hardships their kids face.[7] By saying yes to Goldfish and freezer pops, but also to grapes and hummus, Melanie puts a smile on her kids' faces and reduces the number of times she has to say no. She tries to find a balance, offering healthy options alongside occasional treats and a steady drumbeat of messages about eating well.

Melanie is informed about nutrition; she knows about the health implications of what's on her plate. But the food on her plate is not always the food she considers ideal or the healthiest. If her family had more money, Melanie is unequivocal that they would eat differently. "If we could afford to buy things that were organic, with less hormones, absolutely [we would]," she says. "If you think about the fact that a chicken is born and in two months they're killing it and it's full grown—that's got to worry you a little bit. So, you know, free range—I'd love to have chickens of our own. And we would buy a lot more fruits and vegetables. It's really expensive to buy fruits. I could go buy junk food cheaper than [fruits]. The cheapest stuff is the stuff in the boxes, as opposed to fresh fruits and vegetables, and things that have come right out of the farm. We've thought about joining a co-op where they deliver you a box every week, but it's like $90 a month. That's a lot of money—it's too much."

Her children, like all children, deserve a healthy future, Melanie believes. And she wants to do as much as she can to ensure that they consume safe and nutritious foods. Research finds that mothers with diverse class, racial, and ethnic backgrounds share a common goal of keeping their children healthy.[8]

Melanie's food beliefs aren't actually that different from Greely Janson's, despite the vast differences in their economic situations. Melanie would prefer to buy hormone-free chicken and fresh produce from local farms. Like Greely, she sees value in eating local, farm-raised meat. "Fresher meats would be good, you know, things that aren't in a package at the grocery store but that you actually bought from a butcher who actually got the animal from a farm would be something that we'd do [if we could afford it]." Unlike Greely, though, Melanie almost never buys organic.

Kevin reappears just as Melanie is navigating the large cart into the narrow checkout lane. She says nothing about his absence. "Gotcha a soda!" she tells him cheerfully.

Kevin raises his eyebrows. He looks like he's about to say something snarky, but then changes his mind. "Thank you," he says sincerely. "That'll last me about a day," he adds, making light of the copious amount of soda he drinks.

The cashier's outfit is accentuated by large silver hoop earrings, and her neon green nail polish shimmers as she deftly moves the items across the scanner. After scanning the last item, she punches a number on the keyboard. The total comes to nearly $80.

"Debit or credit?" she asks.

"EBT," Melanie replies. She hands the plastic card to the cashier. "There's $71 on here," she tells her. The cashier swipes the EBT card and then taps some buttons on the keypad. The total drops to $8.56.

"We've gone over budget," Melanie mutters to Justin, who wants to know why she is digging around in her bag for her debit card. She swipes her debit card and punches the PIN code into the keypad to pay for the remainder.

"What'd you buy that requires cash?" Justin asks. (Food stamps can't be used for hot food, vitamins or medicines, or nonfood items like toilet paper and toothpaste.[9])

"We went over budget," Melanie repeats curtly, taking the receipt from the cashier. She pushes the cart toward the sliding glass doors. As they cross the parking lot, Justin asks his mother when their food stamps will be replenished.

"On the fifteenth. We got butter, a couple weeks of meat, so it should last us two weeks."

5 SHOP SMARTER, EAT BETTER

I'm not judgmental, but I've spent a lot of time in poor communities, and I find it quite hard to talk about modern-day poverty. You might remember that scene in [a previous TV series], with the mom and the kid eating chips and cheese out of Styrofoam containers, and behind them is a massive fucking TV. It just didn't weigh up.

—JAMIE OLIVER,
celebrity chef and restaurateur, in the *Guardian* (2013)

Celebrity chefs and nutrition experts offer tips and recipes for "eating well on a budget." Poor people can eat healthfully, they suggest, if only they'd shop and cook smarter. But poor people already know a lot about getting by on a budget. For many poor mothers, trips to the grocery store are complicated by complex calculations about what they can and can't buy, judgment about the food in their carts, and constant reminders that they don't deserve to treat themselves or their children.

SMART SHOPPER

"I want one!" cries two-year-old Qianah Taylor from the front of the grocery shopping cart. She points at the kid-sized cart her three-year-old sister, Maylee, is pushing.

"Oh boy, here we go," says Marquan Taylor, pushing the big cart with Qianah in it. Baggy black jeans with checkered patterns on the back pockets and an oversized white T-shirt magnify his broad frame. "Hey, hey," he murmurs to Qianah. He has to hunch over slightly to be able to push the cart. He bends down further to try to get Qianah's attention, but she keeps crying. She begins kicking her feet. A shoe falls off.

Ashley Taylor walks on ahead of them, focused.

If there were a competition for smartest shopper, Ashley would be a contender. She never goes to the grocery store without her black three-ring binder, stocked with coupons, arranged carefully by store section. When it comes to grocery shopping, Ashley means business.

The open binder rests on Ashley's forearm as she travels up and down the store aisles. Occasionally she flips through it to check on a deal, but truthfully, she hardly needs to check at all. She has looked at the binder so many times that she knows most of the prices by heart. She has already calculated what her total should be at the end of the shopping trip.

Marquan hates grocery shopping, but he usually comes anyway. Ashley insists on it. Otherwise, the girls are too distracting and she ends up missing a deal. To make it easier on Marquan, Ashley organizes the coupons so she can efficiently select each item as they cruise up and down the aisles. She used to figure it out in the store, as she shopped, but Marquan got annoyed with how long it took. So now she clips coupons and organizes the binder at home. This system seems to be working better, at least from Marquan's point of view.

The family usually shops once a month, right after their food stamps come in. Ashley gets her list together a few days before it's time to go shopping. "I think, what do we need? What's different from last month, you know? And that's how I do it," she explains. Her matter-of-fact tone belies the complex calculations that go into each shopping trip.

There is a long-standing myth in the United States that better money management is the solution to many people's problems. Ashley tries to follow the money-saving tips she reads and hears about.[1] She budgets how much money she can spend. She goes in with a game plan and a shopping list. She compares prices for different items and tries to avoid buying things that aren't on sale. When she finds a particularly good deal on something, she buys extra so she won't have to buy it again next month.[2]

For a long time, experts have told women they can overcome meager budgets and hectic schedules by being more efficient household managers. At the turn of the twentieth century, advocates of "rational eating" calculated the "calories per dollar" for different foods, in order to show shoppers how to get the most nourishment for the least money. Economical eating became so popular that middle-class women hosted "poverty luncheons," competing to see who could host the most elaborate meal on the smallest budget.[3]

Prices of food and other consumer goods rose sharply due to inflation during and after World War I. The costs of rent, food, clothing, and other living expenses doubled between 1913 and 1920.[4] Rather than focusing on the political and economic conditions that were pushing prices up, people blamed shoppers for not managing their resources wisely. In 1914, the president of the National Housewives' League argued that "wasted food dollars" were due to women's ignorance of market conditions, naïve trust of grocers, and laziness. She declared, "With the high cost of living one of the most pressing questions of the day, the average American housewife is sitting complacently by, absolutely indifferent to the situation that confronts her."[5] In short, women were expected to solve the problem of rising food costs by being better, wiser, more efficient shoppers.

Today, as back then, shoppers are expected to successfully economize while still maintaining a healthy diet, even as the standards for what constitutes healthy continue to ramp up.[6] The image of the "efficient housewife" is alive and well, argues sociologist Shelly Koch; consumers must be rational and efficient with their time and money and adopt strategies like clipping coupons, shopping sales, and even leaving their children at home or shopping on a full stomach in order to avoid unnecessary purchases.[7]

But while shoppers like Ashley try to get the food they need at the lowest possible prices, supermarkets are busy figuring out how to get us to stay longer and buy more.[8] And they want us to enjoy the experience, so we'll come back and spend more money the next time. For example, most stores are designed so that shoppers enter through the produce section, where fresh, tasty-looking fruits and vegetables create a positive first impression. Bakeries and floral sections are often also located near the store entrance, because good smells stimulate appetites, and hungry shoppers buy more food. The dairy case is usually in the back corner, so that people will have to travel through the entire store if they come in to pick up a carton of milk. The most expensive options are stocked at eye level or just below, forcing consumers to make an effort to locate cheaper versions. Impulse purchases like candy and magazines are conveniently located near the checkout. Store promotions—for example, "ten for $10" or "buy two, get one free" offers—make customers feel as though they're getting a deal, but these can also lead them to buy more than they'd planned.[9]

Indeed, supermarket design is a science. "Outside an intensive care unit, there are few environments so obsessively monitored and reconfigured as supermarkets," writes food writer and activist Raj Patel.[10] Music, paint colors, and lighting are all carefully chosen to prime people to spend more time and money in the store.[11] Stores regularly rearrange the layout, hoping that shoppers will find products they weren't looking for and hadn't anticipated buying. And supermarket chains use loyalty cards to closely track consumers' buying habits, link them to their demographic profile, and target their stocking and marketing efforts accordingly.[12]

None of these tactics would work very well if consumers were purely rational. But grocery shopping is anything but rational, researchers conclude.[13] Buying decisions are even affected by something as small as whether a person remembers to bring their cloth bags to the store. A Harvard study finds that shoppers who use cloth bags are, not surprisingly, more likely to buy organic foods. But they are also more likely to purchase high-fat and high-calorie foods like ice cream, cookies, candy bars, and chips. It isn't simply that people who use cloth bags buy these items, the study concludes; the bags themselves prompt the behavior. People feel good about themselves for using cloth bags, and as a result, they think they deserve a treat.[14]

Ashley usually has a precise idea of how much her groceries will cost. So when the total on the cash register reads $160.53, she is puzzled. This is more than she anticipated. Not wanting to hold up the line, she swipes her plastic EBT card through the reader. As they make their way toward the sliding glass doors, she asks Marquan to pull the cart to the side while she carefully scans the long receipt.

Marquan stares at the receipt over Ashley's shoulder. They confer for a minute, and then he begins rummaging through the grocery bags. Eventually, he finds the bag containing four bottles of Neuro Sonic drinks. The bottles are beautifully packaged, with curved shapes and bright colors. Each one promises a different "neurological effect": increasing energy, promoting relaxation, or improving mental performance.[15] But at $2.99 a bottle, Neuro Sonic doesn't come cheap. Frustrated, Ashely remembers that the store circular advertised that all drinks in the store were discounted. As it turns out, Neuro Sonic was excluded from the special offer.

Unwilling to pay such a high price for the drinks, Ashley walks over to the customer service desk while Marquan and the girls head to the car with the groceries. She places the drinks on the counter and looks around for someone to help her. Minutes drag by and no one appears. Determined to get her money back, Ashley waits patiently for over ten minutes, watching other shoppers come and go, until a customer service representative finally appears.

"Was there something wrong with them?" the representative asks in a bored voice.

"My husband wanted to try them, but we thought they were on sale," Ashley explains.

"So you don't want them?"

Ashley takes a deep breath. "No," she says.

18 BLOOD FROM A TURNIP

Standing on the pavement outside her apartment, Leanne Armstrong assesses the situation. Her food stamps should have been replenished this morning, but there was some kind of glitch in the computer system. The food stamps were not transferred to her EBT card.[1] She'll have to figure out what happened later. They're out of food, and she needs a plan B.

Leanne has $30 in her bank account, which won't be enough to tide her over until she can get the mess with her food stamps figured out. Fortunately, today is payday. The paycheck plus the $30 in her account might just be enough. The checks are cut at 2:00 PM.

With Latrell looking on, Leanne and her mother, Renata, make a plan. They will drive to McDonald's, get Leanne's check, cash it at the bank, and drive to the store.[2] Renata almost always goes grocery shopping with Leanne, both because she manages Leanne's money and because she owns a car and Leanne and Latrell do not.

Hakeem and Gage bound over to Renata's green Ford station wagon. "Can we go?" they clamor.

"No! We don't have room!" Renata tells them curtly. The heat is making everyone agitated.

"Go play!" Latrell tells the kids. He hands Gemma to Leanne, then goes into the house and returns with Gemma's plastic car seat. With some effort, he installs it in the back seat of the station wagon and starts to buckle Gemma in.

Gage runs off, but Hakeem hesitates. His lip quivers at the thought of being left out. Leanne leans her arm out of the passenger window. Hakeem's sad, puppy-dog look tugs at her heartstrings. "We will get you some candy, baby. Is there anything in particular that you want?" she asks. Hakeem is inconsolable. He stares forlornly at the ground.

"What you want? A Pepsi? Chocolate?" Leanne prods.

No answer.

"I'll surprise you!" Leanne says cheerfully. Latrell finishes buckling Gemma into the car seat.

From the driver's seat, Renata adjusts the rearview mirror. She catches Gemma's eye. "Take that pacifier out your mouth! You gonna get a whoopin' today!" she tells her, cackling at the hollow threat. Gemma continues to suck on the pacifier.

Renata shifts the car into gear and is backing out of the driveway when a young boy suddenly appears out of nowhere at the driver's side window. Renata stomps on the brakes.

"Will you buy me a drink?" he asks hopefully.

"Mercy!" Renata replies exasperated. "Where's your dad?"

The boy sheepishly backs away from the car. With a "tsk, tsk," Renata continues reversing out of the driveway. It's 1:30 PM.

The first stop is McDonald's, where Leanne will pick up her paycheck. The old Ford lurches as Renata speeds down the road, occasionally and unpredictably swerving to miss potholes or change lanes. Even with the windows down, it is boiling hot inside the car.

Renata and Leanne discuss what to buy at the Food Lion across the street from McDonald's. Renata knows the deals by heart. She remarks that chicken leg quarters are on sale for approximately $6.90. "I'm sick of all the shit I make from them old school recipe books," she tells Leanne.

"I want some Shake 'n Bake," says Leanne, changing the subject. Renata remembers that she wants to look for some boxed dinners that are also on sale.

"Like those Banquet dinners?" Leanne asks, scrunching up her nose.

"No, no! They are not Banquet. They're $3. Hold on. I can't think." Renata puts her hand to her forehead. "It's all in one box. For $3. A $3 meal. That's a good deal. Meat already in the box!"

"Meat and everything?" Leanne questions.

"Everything!" Renata says jubilantly, her hands gripping the wheel. While stopped at a red light, she informs Leanne that she recently bought some fresh ears of corn on sale. "I got four for a dollar. Then I went back and it was two for a dollar and I was like, 'What? Really?'" For Renata and Leanne, sales are worth showing up for and never last long enough.

When the light turns green, Renata steps on the gas and makes a sharp left into the shopping complex entrance. She makes a beeline for the Food Lion at the far end of the parking lot. Pulling into the loading zone, she slams the car into park and turns to Leanne.

"Run in there and get one of them papers, baby," she orders her. Leanne dutifully climbs out of the car and heads to a small rack of fliers just inside the store entrance. On her way back to the car, she stops to talk briefly to a man with short dreads and a red shirt. Leanne and her mother know a lot of people in this neighborhood.

Leanne gets back in the car and peruses the flier as Renata drives across the street to the McDonald's, where she finds a shaded parking spot right in front of the restaurant. She puts the car in park. Almost immediately, heat descends like a heavy blanket.

"They have a good deal on cereal—buy one, get one for free," Leanne remarks. "And coffee is only $6.99." Looking up from the flier, she stares out the windshield across the parking lot. "Gosh. This sucks that I have to pay for groceries," she says.

"I know. Right?" Renata replies, snatching the flier out of Leanne's hands.

Leanne gets out of the car and comes around to Gemma's side to check on her. Leaning against the side of the car, she lights a Newport and takes a long drag. Surveying the parking lot, she sees a man in the distance. He is wearing a McDonald's shirt and is headed in Leanne's direction. A smile spreads across her face. "Hellooo!" she yells to get his attention.

The man looks up, smiles, and walks over to the car. After a short exchange, he peers into the back seat. Seeing Gemma, he says, "How you doin'?" Gemma beams back. "You are simply gorgeous!" the man tells her. She smiles again. Her brown eyes sparkle. Leanne takes another drag of her cigarette.

They say goodbye, and Leanne gets back into the car. Even with the windows down, the car is sweltering. Beads of sweat form along Gemma's hairline. Renata turns the key in the ignition and reads the dashboard clock. It's 1:51 PM.

"We only have nine more minutes," Leanne says optimistically. Renata bides her time by scanning the flier. She points out that Pop Tarts are on sale: two for $4.

"That's what I'm gettin'," Leanne says enthusiastically, looking over Renata's shoulder. "That and the fruit snacks that are two for $4. Why they put Rice Krispies treats under the breakfast section?" she ponders aloud.

"I don't know. They nasty! I wouldn't pay two cents for those. But you can get tomatoes three for a dollar or the plum tomatoes for $1.49 a pound. Those are the small Roma tomatoes," Renata explains. She demonstrates by forming her right thumb and index finger into an oval. "And you can slice them long and put them on a sandwich. You save like that."

Nine minutes slowly pass. When the dashboard clock finally reads 2:00 PM, Leanne opens the creaky car door, gets Gemma out, and heads for the McDonald's entrance. A refreshing blast of cool air greets them inside. The restaurant is almost empty, the lunch crowd gone. A woman with a McDonald's visor sits alone in a booth, eating a burger.

Leanne walks over to the woman. "Heyyyyy," she says in a syrupy voice. The woman, in her early sixties, looks up. Brown permed hair sticks out of her visor at odd angles. She smiles at Gemma, then appraises Leanne. Her gaze comes to rest on Leanne's slightly protruding stomach. She reaches out and touches it.

"You aren't fixin' to have *another* baby are you?" she asks.

Leanne looks down at her belly and says good-naturedly, "Naw. I'm just fat." "This is my last one," she adds, nodding to Gemma.

The woman eyes Leanne disapprovingly.

"Well, two people just got fired today," she says.

"Who?" Leanne asks, looking surprised. The woman explains that one employee texted the manager that she quit, so technically she wasn't fired. The other employee never showed up, so they let him go. Leanne seems unfazed by this turn of events.

"What you doin' here anyways?" the woman demands.

"I am here to get my check," Leanne replies.

The woman folds her arms across her chest. "Well, they don't come in until three o'clock," she informs Leanne, as if she should have known this already.

Leanne's jaw drops. "Not until three o'clock?! I thought they were ready at two?"

"They changed the rule. It's now three," the woman says. As an afterthought, she adds, "But you could go ask the manager anyways."

Leanne swivels abruptly and heads toward the counter. She says hello to a young woman behind the register and asks if the checks come in at three o'clock. Just as she gets confirmation, the manager, a burly man in his early thirties, appears from the back. Leanne asks him about the checks, explaining that she thought they came in at two o'clock. He listens with a deadpan stare.

"They come in at three o'clock," he says flatly.

Leanne doesn't protest. "Well, I'll be back then," she says, already heading toward the door.

On her way back to the car, Leanne looks up when she hears a voice say, "Heyyy!" Turning around, she stares blankly at a woman about her age.

"You don't know who I am, do you?" the woman laughs. Leanne admits she doesn't.

"It's me, Tiffany!"

Leanne smiles, now recognizing her. "Oh hey!" she says. She visually scans Tiffany, who is wearing skin-tight pants.

"You look good!" Leanne exclaims. Tiffany laughs. The two women quickly fill each other in on the last couple of years. It turns out Tiffany's boyfriend lives down the street from Leanne.

"You work at McDonald's?" Tiffany asks.

"Yup."

"I should come to McDonald's sometime. We can do lunch," she suggests.

"Sure," says Leanne, politely but without conviction.

Renata watches the exchange like a hawk. She barely waits for Leanne to get back in the station wagon and close the door before she begins interrogating her.

"Who was that?"

"Tiffany."

The name doesn't ring any bells for Renata.

"Remember? She's that girl that you didn't want me to hang out with because you thought she was fast."

"Well, she still looks fast."

"She's got five kids, too," Leanne says. Leanne's three youngest children live with her, but her first two children, both born when she was in her teens, were removed from her custody at a young age. They live with relatives, and she sees them only occasionally.[3]

"I don't understand your generation!" Renata says forcefully. "Y'all got all these children you can't feed, and no education, no nothing!" After a silent pause, she adds, "And you smell like grease!"

Renata suddenly realizes Leanne is empty-handed. "Where's your check?" she asks incredulously.

"They aren't ready until three."

"What?!"

"And two people got fired today," Leanne adds glumly.

"Well, I don't care about that," Renata retorts. "Somebody needs to fire McDonald's for not telling their employees when the damn checks come out! What are we supposed to do now?" she asks in an accusatory voice, as if this is Leanne's doing.

Gemma, content until now, begins to whimper from the back seat.

"Hush up! Quit your whining!" Renata tells her.

"What you want to do? Go look around?" Leanne suggests half-heartedly.

Renata gazes in the direction of the Food Lion. "We can go get groceries in the cart, ask them to hold them for us, and then come back here and get your check," she proposes. Leanne seems ambivalent and remains silent. A few quiet minutes pass. The heat is staggering.

Renata decides to go through the drive-through to get Gemma some water and an ice cream. She pulls out of the parking space and navigates the car up to the ordering station, where she hollers into the speaker, "Hey. Can I get a fifty-cent ice cream and a water?" A garbled voice on the other end informs Renata that the water will cost twenty-five cents.

"Aw, shit!" Renata exclaims. She digs through her change purse and retrieves a quarter. "Okay!" she yells into the speaker and puts the car in gear. As they pull up to the window, Leanne recognizes the cashier and leans across Renata to talk to her.

Renata interrupts their chit-chat. "I can't believe they charge a quarter for water!" she admonishes the cashier. The young woman smiles noncommittally and takes Renata's money.

As they pull away from the drive-through, Leanne says softly, "Not like she can do anything about it."

Renata finds a shady spot in the parking lot and shuts off the engine. She gets out, surveys the shimmery heat rising from the pavement, and opens Gemma's door. Squeezing her narrow hips into the space between the car seat and the door, Renata smiles at Gemma.

"Look what Grandma got you!"

Gemma smiles eagerly as she watches Renata put a bit of ice cream into a plastic spoon. Gemma takes a bite and smiles some more.

"Look. She loves it! Give me some of that water," Renata tells Leanne. Leanne hands the small plastic cup to her mother, who seizes the opportunity to tell Leanne that small kids should always drink water with ice cream, to rinse the sugar off their teeth. In the middle of her lesson, a dollop of ice cream falls on Renata's shirt, but she doesn't notice. She feeds Gemma more of the ice cream, alternating it with the water. When Gemma seems to have had enough, Renata passes the half-eaten cup of ice cream up to Leanne and gives Gemma another sip of water.

"You don't know how much your check is, do you?" she questions Leanne.

"No," Leanne responds glumly.

"Well how many hours do you have?" Renata snaps.

"Forty-four."

Renata takes out her cell phone and punches the numbers into the screen. At that exact moment, the phone rings.

Renata puts the phone to her ear. After listening for a minute, she tells the person on the other end, "Boy! You need to take your happy pill or something! Just 'cause you talkin' doesn't mean you are up. Bye, boy!" But instead of hanging up, she continues to talk, "No! We haven't started! We're handling it!" She pauses and then yells into the phone, "Because we need something to do but sit in this hot-assed sun!"

Renata hangs up the phone and looks at Leanne. "He can't call me no damn word. F'n piece of shit! He should have come up here with me!" The person on the other end of the phone is Renata's boyfriend. By all evidence and according to Leanne, they have a tumultuous relationship.

Renata looks at Leanne and again proposes they start shopping without the check. "Do you think this is a good idea?"

"No," Leanne quickly replies, as if she has been waiting for Renata to ask her that question.

"Well, I don't know what else to do, Leanne!"

"Do you think they'll let us do that?"

"Sure they will! We know people who work at Food Lion."

"I don't know any of the faces in there," Leanne says, distancing herself from the ways this plan could go wrong. "You wanna go back to my house?" she suggests.

"No! I ain't got gas like that!" Renata says, giving Leanne a look that says she should know better.

"This sucks," Leanne says drearily. "And I gotta be to work at five o'clock."

"You gotta be at work at five?" This steels Renata's resolve. "We're going inside and we will just have to go to customer service and tell them our plan. There's no sense wasting time!" Without waiting for Leanne's reply, she puts the car in gear.

Walking through the sliding glass doors of Food Lion,[4] Renata and Leanne are welcomed by a blast of cool air. Renata heads straight to the customer service desk, while Leanne selects a cart and buckles Gemma in. Renata knows the young woman behind the counter and asks how her mother is doing before explaining their situation. She outlines her plan: shop first, leave the cart, go across the street to pick up Leanne's check, and then come back. The customer service representative listens patiently and assures Renata this is not a problem.

Renata heads toward the produce section. "Do you want to start over here?" she calls to Leanne.

"Yeah," Leanne replies perfunctorily.

Renata waves to a woman in the deli area and veers over to the counter. Leanne follows her, pushing Gemma in the cart. As they approach the counter, the woman notices Gemma.

"When did this happen?!" she asks, her eyes bright with curiosity and excitement.

"Last year," Leanne smiles. Renata continues talking while Leanne meanders toward a bread display. She selects a loaf of white bread and places it in the cart. She then bends over to kiss Gemma, who playfully slaps her mother in the face. Leanne pretends to slap her back, and Gemma throws her head back and laughs.

"You love Mommy?" Leanne asks sweetly, putting her face close to Gemma's. Gemma smiles. Leanne turns her attention back to the task at hand. She contemplates a display of honey peanut butter but decides against buying it, because it is not a necessity.

Leanne is grabbing a can of canned green beans from the shelf when Renata asserts that she prefers the French-cut style. Shopping with Renata involves constant negotiations. Leanne puts back the ones she has in her hand and selects four cans of French-cut beans.

As Leanne makes her way around the store, she periodically records her selections in a steno pad. In aisle three, she picks out different types of Oodles of Noodles, which are twelve for $3. Renata spots the boxed dinners she had mentioned earlier. "*This* is what I was talking about," she exclaims, pointing to a row of Banquet Wholestyle Bakes on the bottom shelf.

"Eww! I don't like stuff like that," Leanne says, glancing at them.

"Well I haven't tried it yet, but's it's cheap," Renata says defensively. "Banquet *is* nasty, but I will try it." She throws the box in the cart.

Leanne gives her mother a dubious look and keeps walking. She selects Velveeta whole grain pasta, a twelve-pack of Pepsi, and a twelve-pack of grape Sunkist. A box of premade pasta salad, a small bag of sugar, and several packages of meat also make it into the cart. Leanne finds a small bag of Cheetos and presents this to Gemma, whose eyes light up as she grabs for it.

Renata's phone rings. She answers it and saunters off to have a private conversation. Leanne selects a bottle of store brand vegetable oil.

When Renata returns, she immediately spies the bottle of oil in the cart. Picking it up, she scrutinizes the label. "I believe the proceeds from this will help kids in the United States," she comments approvingly.

Leanne stares at the contents of her cart. "This is the least groceries that I've ever bought," she says.

Renata nods in agreement and throws in a package of pork chops for herself. Leanne finds a package of turkey wings for $5.90. "We are going cheap now!" she says, attempting to muster some enthusiasm. "Let's go look at hamburgers and hot dogs."

Leanne discovers that bacon is on sale, for $1.59. She calls Renata over to look.

"Shut up! I want one too. I hate to spend my money on this. They don't never mark down daggone sausage!" Renata exclaims.

Leanne finishes up, adding packaged deli meat, coffee, and a few energy drinks to the cart. The energy drinks and coffee are what keep her going when she has to stay up late. Between studying for her classes, working shifts at McDonald's, and caring for the kids, Leanne has been pulling a lot of late nights.

"I'm ready to leave," Leanne tells Renata. She apprehensively wheels the cart over to customer service and apologetically explains their situation again. The women behind the counter assure her it's fine to leave the cart there.

Leanne secures Gemma in her car seat as Renata gets behind the wheel. Once Leanne is in her seat, they slowly drive back across the street to the McDonald's. Renata parks and Leanne opens the door. "I'll be right back!" she calls out.

Renata yells to Leanne out the window. "Pull your dress down! In the back!"

Leanne smiles and tugs at the back of her cotton dress.

"She doesn't hear nothin', she's so focused on other people," Renata mutters. After a few minutes, Leanne reappears, check in hand. She gets back in the car.

Renata peers over Leanne's shoulder as she opens the check. They stare at it for a moment. Finally, Renata nods approvingly at the amount: $246.[5] Without saying a word, she puts the car in gear and heads to the bank down the street.

Leanne deliberates out loud about what she should do with the money as they drive to the bank. The choices are stark. She is delinquent on a bill, but they need to eat.

"It's pay this bill or else let them take me to court. I should let them to take me to court, right?" Leanne asks her mother. "'Cause I really need groceries."

"Let 'em take you to court!" Renata urges. "Tell the judge you have three children to feed. Girl! Do you know how many medical bills I'm behind on? You can't get blood out of a turnip!"

Every day in the United States, families are forced to make hard decisions like whether to fall behind on rent, ignore medical bills, or let the cupboard go empty.[6] Many, like Leanne, make the choice to buy food, reasoning that the alternatives can't be worse than going hungry. One of every eight American households lacked sufficient food at some point during 2016. Between 2008 and 2014, as a result of the Great Recession, the number was higher: one out of every seven households.[7] Food insecurity—not having enough food to live a healthy, active life—is often associated with economic shocks and constraints, such as losing a job, having unexpected expenses, losing food stamps, or having a very limited financial cushion.[8]

Few resources mean families are forced to make hard choices. A number of studies have shown that food insecurity often goes hand in hand with other forms of hardship, including being unable to meet housing or medical expenses, "doubling up" and living with others to save money on housing, or being evicted.[9] According to sociologist Matthew Desmond, many poor families spend most of their income on housing, with little left over to pay for things like healthcare, transportation, and even food. "The rent eats first," he argues.[10]

But families prioritize their needs in different ways; sometimes the kids eat first. In this case, Leanne Armstrong decided to buy food instead of paying a bill. People make these decisions knowing they face the possibility of going to court, being evicted, having the electricity turned off, or skipping medical care and other expenses.

For the final time that day, Renata, Leanne, and Gemma cross the street in Renata's beat-up Ford. To Leanne's relief, they find the grocery cart right where she left it, in front of the customer service desk. Leanne wheels it into the checkout lane. She begins unloading the groceries onto the belt but then remembers she promised the boys some candy. Contemplating the display, she selects a Twix for each of the boys and a package of Starburst candy for Gemma. While the cost of little treats like this adds up, straining her limited budget, the tradeoff of seeing her kids happy sometimes matters more to Leanne.[11]

Leanne asks the cashier if she knows her brother, Marvin, who used to work at this same Food Lion a long time ago.

The cashier smiles politely but doesn't answer. "That'll be $118.90."

Leanne had estimated that the bill would not be over $100, but she feels pleased anyway. "I just saved a bunch of money shopping at Food Lion!" she says, looking at Renata.

"I *always* shop at Food Lion," Renata responds confidently.

"I'll push the cart if you take Gemma," Leanne proposes. Renata sighs and reluctantly hoists Gemma out of the cart and onto her hip.

"Thank you, baby!" Renata tells the cashier.

Renata, Leanne, and Gemma are greeted by a wall of heat as the glass doors slide open. On the way to the car, Leanne sees a man she knows and stops to chat while Renata buckles Gemma in. Leanne unloads the groceries into the station wagon, already filled with odds and ends. As Renata slowly backs the car out of the parking lot, Gemma whines from the back seat. She is tired and it has been a long, hot afternoon.

"What?" yells Renata, glancing anxiously in the rearview mirror. "Quit being a cry baby!"

Gemma clutches her pack of Starbursts and quiets down. Leanne lights a Newport and holds her arm out the window as she exhales.

At 3:45 PM, more than two hours after they set off, Renata eases the car into a spot in front of the apartment. She puts the car in park and turns to Leanne.

"He better not come on out here and cuss me. He wants to!" Renata says, referring to Latrell. He often complains about how long Leanne has been gone or what she has bought. Renata wants Latrell to help with the groceries, but he's nowhere in sight. Impatient, she walks to the front door and knocks. There is no answer.

"Where's Trell!" she shouts to Leanne, who is opening the back of the car.

"He upstairs," Leanne replies, looking up at the second story.

Renata knocks again, to no avail. She fishes her cell phone out of her pocket and dials Latrell's number. He picks up on the second ring and tells Renata he's on his way, adding that the back door is already open.

"I am not lugging a bunch of groceries around the back!" Renata huffs into the phone.

Moments later, the door swings open.

"Back door service!" Latrell jokes as he darts past a still-fuming Renata and walks to the back of the car. His eyes narrow as he looks into the car.

"I know you ain't get more coffee!" he says to Leanne disapprovingly. He doesn't like it when she drinks coffee.

Leanne silently takes an armload of grocery bags and heads into the house. Latrell follows with more bags. Renata releases Gemma from her car seat and brings her inside.

Unpacking the bags, Leanne tells Latrell she decided to spend her paycheck on the groceries. "I'm going to let them take me to court," she says firmly.

Latrell raises an eyebrow but doesn't comment. "Where did you shop?" he asks.

"Food Lion," says Renata.

"In that case you could have gotten me some frog legs!" Latrell says.

"Food Lion doesn't carry that kind of thing. You would need to go to the Mexican store for that," Renata says irritably.

Latrell throws two packs of bacon into the open freezer door, as if shooting hoops. He picks up a bag of groceries and peers inside. Seeing the Oodles of Noodles, he frowns. He looks at Leanne angrily.

"You didn't get no chicken?" he accuses.

"You *like* shrimp," Leanne replies softly.

"That's why you should have called the phone back. I could have told you not to get those!" Latrell says, his voice growing louder.

"Sorry," Leanne says quietly.

"You always tell me that *after* you get back from the grocery store! The kids gonna have to eat the shrimp!" He looks at Renata with a stern look. His upper lip is trembling with growing indignation. "The kids gonna have to eat the shrimp!" he repeats. "YOU want the shrimp?" he asks Renata.

She deadpans back at him. He fumes. "Seriously? I really don't eat shrimp! I don't! I DO NOT like shrimp Oodles of Noodles."

With Renata and Leanne studiously ignoring him, Latrell's rant against Oodles of Noodles burgeons into a food manifesto. "I eat the chicken, and I like the ones in the cup. And I got the boys into the cup too, with the little spices. I WILL NOT eat the shrimp. Somebody else can eat that. I'm a picky eater. I don't like anything healthy. No veggies. I'm a junk food person."

Renata says nothing. Leanne is quiet as well; she's used to Latrell's outbursts. She finishes putting away the remaining groceries and heads to the bedroom to get ready for her five o'clock shift. Latrell will be "babysitting" again. Renata heads home to deal with her bad-tempered boyfriend. Leanne will take a cab to work, spending a few more dollars from her paycheck.

THE CHECKOUT LINE

On the way to the grocery store, Tara Foley makes a mental list of the things she needs. Last month, the state of North Carolina announced that families would see a reduction in their food stamps. Tara's food stamps were cut, and now she is fretting about having enough to buy groceries today and being able to save some for the upcoming holiday meal.[1]

Tara's game plan is to buy her meat at Save-A-Lot, because they have the best prices. Then she will go to Lowes Foods to take advantage of their ten for $10 sale.

Inside Save-A-Lot, Tara grabs a cart and briskly heads to the meat section in the back. A large banner advertises five packs of meat for $19.99. Tara usually buys in bulk and quickly selects ten packs of chicken drumsticks, five packs of chicken thighs, and five packs of pork loin chops. But she slows her pace when she reaches the ground beef, furrowing her brow. There is only one package left, and she's going to need more than that. Looking around for help, Tara spots a door with a glass window. A sign on the door reads: "Employees Only."

Standing on her tiptoes, Tara lifts her small frame to look inside. Not seeing anyone, she knocks on the door. A tall man with a white apron eventually pushes the door open. Getting right to the point, Tara asks if he has more ground beef and cube steak in the back.

"Wait here," he tells her, heading back through the door. Several minutes later the man reappears with packages of ground beef and cube steak in his hands. Tara places them in her cart. To round things out, she selects several boxes of frozen French fries, a package of corndogs, and a box of frozen breakfast sandwiches.

She wheels the cart to the register. The total comes to $125. Tara's EBT card is falling apart and heavily taped together. She knits her lips tightly together as she repeatedly swipes the card through the card reader. Finally, the swipe is successful. Tara puts the groceries in the car and heads to the next store. She has $135 left on her card.

At Lowes Foods, she gets out her phone as she snakes through the aisles, systematically deducting the cost of every item she puts in the cart. Seven loaves of generic white bread. Bologna, turkey breast, and breakfast sausage. Two gallons of milk and a dozen eggs. A bag of clementines. Three tubes of biscuits, on sale. A container of vegetable oil spread. Three boxes of cereal and two gallons of Hawaiian Punch. A large bag of potatoes and a small one of salad mix. Some reduced-price tomatoes.

Finally, Tara reaches the section that enticed her to shop at this store in the first place: the ten for $10 sale. She scans the shelves, her anticipation quickly shifting to frustration and disappointment. "They showed more items in the ad than are actually on sale," she comments. Her shoulders slump as she stares at the shelves indecisively. Finally, she settles on two boxes of Hamburger Helper, two boxes of spaghetti, and two boxes of macaroni and cheese.

Between the two stores, Tara has now been shopping for nearly two hours. It's a rainy, miserable day, and she is tired. She plans to throw something in the oven for the kids when she gets home, so that she can relax for a minute. She circles back to the frozen section and picks out a party-size package of Stouffer's Lasagna, a bag of garlic bread, and a box of breadsticks. She tosses a few frozen dinners into the cart as an afterthought. After grabbing a few two-liter bottles of soda from a sale display, she heads to the checkout aisle.

Taxpayers are "sick and tired of watching their hard-earned money going down the drain" to buy candy and soda, wrote Paul LePage, the governor of Maine, in a 2016 letter to the US Department of Agriculture justifying a proposal to prohibit food stamps from being used to purchase candy or soda. A year later, a controversial and widely read *New York Times* article featured the headline: "In the Shopping Cart of a Food Stamp Household: Lots of Soda." The article reported that sweetened beverages, including soda and sugary drinks like Kool-Aid, account for almost 10 percent of the money that SNAP households spend on food. As critics quickly pointed out, the article neglected to mention the fact that non–food stamp households spend similar amounts of money on sweetened beverages as those who pay with food stamps.[2] The damage had been done, though. The article lent credence to the common (mis)perception that people using food stamps consume more sugary junk food than those spending their "own" money on groceries.[3]

Since the 1980s, steep cuts have been made to the programs that historically provided a safety net for American families. With traditional "welfare" programs now decimated, food stamps and Medicaid are the only forms of public assistance available to many struggling families.[4] One in seven Americans participated in the food stamp program in 2016.[5] And almost one in five people in the United States has received food stamps at some point in their lives.[6] But the stigma of using public assistance is still there.

People who use food stamps are criticized and shamed for needing help in the first place and for the specific items they buy.[7] And the judgment extends beyond soda and candy. In 2016, Patty Ritchie, a state senator from New York, introduced a bill to ban the use of food stamps for so-called "luxury items" like "high-end steaks and lobster" and "decorated cakes."[8] Similar bills have been proposed in other states. In Missouri, state representative Rick Brattin told the *Washington Post*, "I have seen people purchasing filet mignons and crab legs with their EBT cards. When I can't afford it on my pay, I don't want people on the taxpayer's dime to."[9]

In this climate, people who use food stamps can't win. An experiment finds that if poor people use governmental assistance to purchase organic food, they are perceived as making a bad choice. Yet when wealthier consumers buy organic food using their own money, they are perceived as making a good choice, a moral choice. As the study authors succinctly point out, "People are judged differently for making identical choices, depending on where their money comes from."[10]

Many Americans are skeptical of the very idea of federal dollars being funneled into food assistance programs. A deep-rooted belief that the best way to help the poor is via "self-reliant communities of neighbors, taking care of their own" characterizes the general sentiment in the United States, writes sociologist Janet Poppendieck.[11] However, the Great Depression revealed the limits of relying on neighbors for a charitable hand, illustrating in graphic detail the vital need for a federal response to hunger. After the 1929 stock market crash, people took extraordinary and desperate measures to feed their families, staying alive by begging and foraging in garbage cans or subsisting on what they could find in the woods: dandelions, wild onions, and wild lettuce. Some families sent their children out to ring strangers' doorbells asking for food, while others sent their children to steal milk from front porches in affluent neighborhoods.[12]

By 1931, the situation had reached a crisis. In the absence of federal food assistance programs, people were literally dying of hunger. Ironically, at this time, the United States was also suffering from crop surpluses.[13] Corn was so cheap, it was burned for fuel in the Midwest, and dairies poured down the sewers milk they couldn't sell. And yet people were starving. For many

Americans, this juxtaposition of hunger and abundance became a symbol of the irrationality of the economic system. "A breadline knee-deep in wheat is obviously the handiwork of foolish men," wrote commentator James Crowther.[14]

Our current food assistance programs are a legacy of Franklin D. Roosevelt's attempt, under the New Deal, to solve both of these problems by sending surplus agricultural products to the poor.[15] Although many of the New Deal regulations were eventually dismantled, their legacies remain. For example, SNAP (the Supplemental Nutrition Assistance Program) and WIC (the Special Supplemental Nutrition Program for Women, Infants, and Children) are both administered by the US Department of Agriculture (USDA), even though they aren't tied to farming in the same way as other USDA programs, like farm loans or soil conservation programs. The legislation authorizing SNAP is included in the Farm Bill, which also oversees agricultural subsidy and crop insurance programs.[16]

Many Americans depend on food stamps to get by. Forty-four million people received SNAP benefits, or food stamps, in 2016.[17] Yet we continue to debate whether poor people deserve to get help from the government. The SNAP program is perennially under attack.[18] "Long-term dependency has never been part of the American dream. [The] USDA's goal is to move individuals and families from SNAP back to the workforce as the best long-term solution to poverty,"[19] proclaimed Secretary of Agriculture Sonny Perdue, explaining the need to tighten the work requirements associated with SNAP. The draft of the Farm Bill released by the House Committee on Agriculture in April 2018 included a proposal requiring that most "able-bodied adults," including those with school-age children, work or enroll in twenty hours of workforce training per week in order to be eligible to receive food stamps.[20] Supporters framed the proposal as reducing dependency and ensuring that food stamps go to those who are truly in need. "We believe that breaking the cycle of poverty is really important," said Michael Conway, a Republican representative from Texas and chair of the committee.[21]

What arguments like these ignore is that most food stamp recipients who can work are already.[22] And research shows that food stamps work; they lift families out of poverty, improve the long-term health of children and adults, and help boost spending during economic downturns.[23]

When it comes down to it, political debates about who is worthy of food stamps serve to maintain the stigma around receiving public assistance. Studies find that far from motivating people to make positive changes, stigma actually makes people's lives more difficult.[24]

The checkout lines aren't long today, but Tara wheels her cart to the self-checkout anyway. Even though it takes longer, this way allows Tara to check the price of each item and track the total. She begins scanning each item in her cart in order of priority, looking carefully at the total on the screen before choosing another item. If she runs out of food stamps, at least she'll have the necessities.

The bagging area soon becomes overcrowded. Tara tries putting some of the bags in her cart, but the machine beeps, commanding her to put them back in the bagging area. She can't continue because the machine locks up, and she has to call the attendant to override it.

This happens again and again. After putting a bag of grapes with no bar code on the scanner, Tara is perplexed about what to do next. She calls the attendant over.

"How am I 'spose to pay this?" she asks.

"Tap the button for produce and put in the four-digit code," the attendant explains.

Tara nods and dutifully enters the code, then places the grapes in a bag in the bagging area. To her dismay, the automated voice asks her to remove the item from the bagging area. Tara sucks her teeth in frustration and looks over her shoulder.

The attendant, now standing right behind her, watches closely. Tara has to repeat the entire process, this time leaving the grapes on the scale long enough for them to be weighed and added to the bill.

"Is this the regular price or the food stamp price?" Tara asks anxiously, looking at the total at the bottom of the screen. The total on the screen includes sales tax, but tax is discounted when groceries are paid for with food stamps. Tara isn't sure how much money she has left for the remaining items in her cart.[25]

The attendant ignores Tara's question about the total and continues to observe Tara as she scans each item, making it clear she's watching so that Tara doesn't sneak something into one of the shopping bags without paying for it.

Tara finishes scanning the last item in her cart and is relieved to see that the total has come to $130.77, slightly less than the remaining balance on her EBT card. She has to swipe the battered card twice before it works, with the attendant still hovering behind her. She loads the bags into the cart and heads for the exit, straining to push the heavy cart.

Back in the car, Tara takes a deep breath. She's pleased because she has $5 left on the card. "But DAMN," she thinks to herself, feeling tired and wounded. "Did she have to eyeball me the whole time?"

BRING GOOD FOOD TO OTHERS

It is a disgrace and an outrage that this country of ours, with an
overabundance of [food], should permit millions of our own to
continue to be under-nourished and hungry.

—HAMILTON FISH,
Republican congressman from New York (1932)

There has never been a fair, just, or healthy food system in the United States
of America.

—LADONNA REDMOND,
food justice activist and founder of the Campaign for
Food Justice Now, in a TEDxManhattan talk (2013)

Not everyone in the United States has enough food, especially
not nutritious food. In response, a vast network of initiatives has
emerged, all aiming to bring good food to others. Nonprofits
have brought community gardens and farmers' markets to poor
neighborhoods. Food charities have mushroomed to meet the
needs of hungry families. And government programs like WIC try
to help improve families' access to healthy foods. These efforts reflect Americans' collective sense of altruism and care for others. But
paying attention to where these efforts originate and how they are
administered is important for understanding why they are sometimes met with disinterest or dismay by those they're meant to help.

Growing up, Greely Janson "often had a feeling" of being different from most of the people in her small North Carolina town. "Like I didn't belong there," she says. "There was nothing that made sense to me."

Worrying that her statement is too strong, Greely backtracks a bit. "Okay, that's an exaggeration, but I didn't feel like I fit in, or that people understood me in general."

She still feels this way. One of the things that sets Greely apart is her passion for food. Most people don't really understand why Greely and her family eat the way they do. The Jansons buy all of their meat from small local farmers. When they eat out, they opt for restaurants that offer mostly local and seasonal food. It's more expensive, but Greely is willing to pay a bit extra for what she believes in. They never eat at McDonald's or any other fast-food restaurants, though Greely is acutely aware of how this marks their family as different, and perhaps even as snobby.

"I have to be very careful," she says hesitantly. "Because lots of people go to these places [fast-food restaurants]. And that's fine." She is especially careful about teaching six-year-old Adelle not to judge other people's food choices. "Because, I mean, there is just nothing to be gained from that, right?" Greely says. "Basically, my message to Adelle is: 'If it's important to you how the animals are treated and how the food is made, those are the reasons that *we* don't go to McDonald's. And not everyone knows all of the stuff behind that.' It's not that people are saying like, 'I don't care.' It's just that some people aren't as in tune."

Greely wasn't always "in tune" with what she now sees as the ethical and ecological problems associated with the modern food system. "I certainly didn't grow up eating that kind of food," she says, referring to the fresh, local, sustainably produced food she now prioritizes. "My mom was a single mom, and she felt very strongly about dinner. You know, we had meals together. But she was working and they were quick meals." Greely's childhood meals consisted of chicken tenders, fish sticks, pot pies, and casseroles with canned cream of mushroom soup as a base.

Moving to New York State after college marked the beginning of Greely's food awakening. She first got a job doing prep work for a catering company, and then another as a pastry chef at a restaurant. The jobs helped Greely develop an appreciation for cooking and food, but it didn't take long for her relationship with these establishments to sour. "I got sick of working in restaurants and with sugar," she states matter-of-factly. "It was like a birthday present to myself. I was like, 'I'm out of this business, I'm not doing this anymore.'"

Increasingly distrustful of the food industry and fascinated by the links between food and health, Greely decided to go back to school for an interdisciplinary master's degree in food studies. She also started volunteering at a community garden in a low-income neighborhood. After finishing her master's program, she made a case to the city council to create a full-time job for Greely to develop a garden program. They agreed, and the garden grew.

In fact, it grew into something much bigger than Greely had initially imagined. Together with some folks Greely had met who were as committed to food justice as she was, Greely founded "Food for All," a nonprofit organization dedicated to working with farmers and gardeners to improve access to fresh food in low-income communities.

Looking back, Greely's entrée into food justice was the logical result of a number of experiences, each one reinforcing her growing sense that something was very wrong with the food system. "When I was in college I taught English language classes to migrant farm workers," she says. "And I remember just being horrified at how sick the workers got after things had been sprayed [with pesticides]."

Ongoing health battles have also fueled Greely's passion for reforming the food system. Since Adelle's birth, Greely has suffered from bouts of stomach pain, which she eventually identified as a gluten intolerance. She has eliminated gluten from her diet and is feeling better. But some symptoms still linger. Greely can't help wondering if her health issues are at least partially related to the unhealthy food she ate growing up. Greely's mother also smoked while she was pregnant with her and "took her prenatal vitamins with a gin and tonic." Greely theorizes that all of these things must somehow be related to her current health problems.

Like many people, Greely believes that the foods we eat have a cumulative effect. Eating the right foods can keep us healthy and possibly prevent disease or illness from taking root. Eating the wrong foods can make us sick or even kill us. Her uncle died of cancer at a relatively young age, and Greely believes that his poor diet exacerbated his health issues and may have even shortened his life. "He did not agree with my feelings about food," she recalls somberly. "When he was extremely sick [with cancer], and he had months [left], his doctors told him all of the same things I had been telling him. They were like, 'Well, you should only eat this and this and this.'"

That the doctors had waited so long to advise her uncle to modify his eating habits angered Greely. It was one more sign of a general dismissal among the medical community of the healing power of food. "I was like, 'If they know that, then why aren't people being told this?' I mean, you have to wait till you're super sick to eat things that aren't compromising your health? That's crazy!"

Greely's history of health problems and her personal experiences with food's healing powers have opened her eyes. She cares a great deal about the food she feeds herself and her family. Greely also cares deeply about making sure others have access to safe, healthy food. She wants to "make good food accessible and affordable" to everyone, she says, whether that means teaching people to grow their own food or making sure that farmers' markets accept food stamps. And she has dedicated her life to this mission, first in New York and now in North Carolina.

The "eating for change" movement is one that advocates changing the food system by thinking carefully about the food we put on our plates.[1] The basic principle behind the movement is that if we make the right decisions when it comes to food, we have the power to fundamentally overhaul our unhealthy, unsustainable, and dangerous food system.

Many consumers have enthusiastically embraced efforts that fall under the umbrella of "eating for change": farmers' markets, community-supported agriculture, and organic and fair-trade labels.

But the movement doesn't appeal to everyone. It has been dominated by people who are mostly white and middle class. The people buying organic produce and milk at farmers' markets are largely white, affluent consumers. Many of the farmers associated with the movement are white. The chefs in the farm-to-table restaurants, but not the kitchen staff, are predominantly white and disproportionately male.[2]

In response, a growing chorus of voices calls on people who care about changing the food system to move beyond just voting with their forks, instead working toward "food justice."[3]

The food justice movement has roots in the environmental justice movement, which showed how poor communities and communities of color were disproportionately exposed to toxic waste dumps and other environmental problems.[4] As such, food justice advocates are fundamentally concerned with inequality—in particular, with disparities in the kinds of foods people eat and can afford. Many of the initiatives under the food justice umbrella have taken the form of promoting "equal access to healthy food."[5] But food justice involves more than just having access to fresh produce. Food justice is also about addressing deeper structural inequalities in the food system.[6] Not only this, it prioritizes protecting the rights of marginalized people to "lead the movement to provide food for their community."[7]

Community-led food justice efforts span the nation.[8] One of the largest inner-city urban farms in the country, for example, was established in Los Angeles by a group of indigenous people from Mexico and other Latin American countries. By cultivating heirloom varieties of crops grown in their home countries, farmers are preserving both the biodiversity of crops in the United States and their own cultural identities, Teresa Mares and Devon Peña, both anthropologists, argue.[9] Similarly, black female community gardeners in Detroit "transform vacant land into a community-based, healthy food source that allows them to be able to feed themselves," writes environmental justice scholar Monica White. Instead of petitioning the city to improve access to food or lobbying supermarkets to locate in Detroit, these women took up gardening as "an exercise of political agency and empowerment."[10]

Self-reliance and self-determination characterize these food justice efforts, which are part of a long history of marginalized groups carving out spaces of community solidarity through food. Yet many food justice initiatives come from outside the communities they are targeting. And all too often, "justice" has been defined in narrow, market-based terms.

Even though the food justice movement is "more race- and class-conscious" than the "eating for change" movement, argues geographer Julie Guthman, much of its on-the-ground work is the same: educating people about where their food comes from and making it available in poor neighborhoods.[11] These efforts are fundamentally oriented around "bringing good food to others," says Guthman.[12] By starting community gardens and encouraging farmers' markets to open in poor neighborhoods, many food justice efforts operate under the assumption that "if you build it, they will come."[13]

These initiatives might resonate with the food preferences and beliefs of white middle-class consumers and volunteers. But what happens when these values and beliefs are not shared by members of the communities they're intended to serve?[14]

Greely and Matt lived in New York for eight years, but after Adelle was born, they decided it was time to move back to North Carolina, where they had both grown up. They've been in Raleigh for a bit over four years. Inspired by what "Food for All" had achieved back in New York, Greely set her sights on a new project in North Carolina. She imagined opening a small café that would offer healthy, local, and sustainably grown food, priced on a sliding scale. Those who could pay full price for the food would do so. Those with fewer means would pay what they could afford. Greely found partners who shared her food philosophy and a building she could lease in a city not far from Raleigh. Matt agreed to use their family savings as capital. Combined with the money from her partners, that was enough to get her up and running. Greely forged partnerships with local food growers and designed a menu that reflected what she hoped was an inviting feel and organic ethos. Lotus Café has been open for three months now.

So far, Greely feels her vision for making local and organic produce more accessible is coming to fruition. "We did the numbers and 48 percent of our ingredients currently are from local producers, whether that be a farmer or local baker," Greely beams. "Our goal is for it to be over 75 percent." Greely is a realistic and pragmatic person. She knows the business is still young and that it will take some time—and more capital—to reach their target.

In the meantime, she and her partners are trying to tackle a more pressing stumbling block. Before it became Lotus Café, the space was home to Lucinda's, a mom-and-pop restaurant that served bland coffee, grilled lunches, and rich homemade sweets. The business was moderately profitable, and it was popular with its customers, mostly working- and middle-class families from the neighborhood. After the site re-opened as Lotus Café, Greely soon learned that not everyone was as excited about the revamped menu as she was.

Ironically, Greely and her partners have had to tone down the very feature they believe in most: locally produced organic food. "We don't advertise the organic as much because we don't necessarily want to come across being super—we're not fancy," she explains. "The concept [we] envisioned is to kind of, have really high-quality food and a casual setting that's family friendly and affordable." Nonetheless, the café has gotten mixed reactions. Initially, the menu highlighted the café's organic coffee, supplied from a local roaster. "Some people were like, 'that's awesome'," Greely recounts. However, not everyone felt that way.

Greely had expected the new coffee to appeal to people. But some customers were confused by the organic label and complained that they were being sold on something too foreign. "People would come and be like, 'Well, I just want regular coffee. I don't want—what is the organic?' And it's hard to know what to do with that. I mean, on one hand, it's opening that door for conversation. But when you need to move lines quickly, and people are already complaining about the wait times, then we can't have the conversations there."

Greely shrugs, as if to say, "What choice did we have?" She adds with resignation, "So we took [the word] organic off the second menu."

Part of the problem is that Greely and her fellow food justice advocates are confronting a clientele for whom food might hold different meanings than it does for them. For Greely, an organic label is a good thing, something worth paying extra money for. But while organic and local foods are produced, packaged, and sold in a way that is generally appealing to white, middle-class consumers, these same products—and the places where they are sold—may seem unfamiliar or unwelcoming to others.[15]

It's not necessarily a lack of knowledge or even a lack of money that prevents some of Greely's customers from eating the way Greely does, it's also a lack of fit: a sense that this food is not for regular folk. Food reformers have long made claims about the moral superiority of particular foods and sought to convert poor people, people of color, and immigrants to new ways of eating.[16] Though these may be well-intentioned efforts, they can affirm the beliefs and knowledge of privileged groups with no recognition of how they may be alienating others—in particular, marginalized communities that are already doing things like growing their own food and eating seasonally.[17]

Greely bristles when parents steer their children away from the fruit basket she purposely places near the register and instead encourage them to buy a Rice Krispies treat. Most people haven't complained that soda isn't on the menu, but some resent not having more options. "Basically," Greely explains in a somewhat defeated tone, "people are kind of like, 'Well who are you to decide what I can and cannot have?' Basically. I mean that's the heart of the comments. Like the majority of people have either been positive, like, 'That's great,' or they've been neutral in that 'I wanted that but okay, I'll have a lemonade or okay I'll have a sweet tea.' But there have been a few people that have been like, 'I should be able to have whatever I want.' I try to be as diplomatic as possible. Not all of the owners feel the same way." Greely enacts her well-rehearsed response to these customers: "I'm sorry you feel that way, but we do offer plenty of other options, and we felt that this was the best bet for this space."

Just as she does in her kitchen at home, Greely tries to find a balance at the café between pleasing others, keeping the menu affordable, and maintaining her own sense of integrity. One of her strategies has been to omit information that she anticipates might cause tension. The café offers Rice Krispies treats but doesn't tell customers they're made with brown rice and are gluten free. "We're trying to find that balance between not being too in-your-face, but just kind of offering healthy options," Greely explains.

Greely has made other compromises at the café as well. She has to keep her costs down. She needs to serve food that doesn't require too much time to prepare. She's kept some of the traditional items—the same ones the Lucinda's lunch crowd loved, like hot dogs and hamburgers—on the menu. Greely accepts these tradeoffs because she gets organic hot dogs and uses locally sourced beef for the hamburgers. And customers are excited about the vegetarian chili on the menu. Greely is happy about this. "It's very simple. It's very healthy," she says. "But it's also like a comfort food."

Some of the newer stuff, which Greely wasn't convinced would sell, is also taking off, like a spinach frittata and a pizza with Brussels sprouts and blue cheese. "We're trying to basically give people the comfort foods that they'd expect but with—like at a higher quality and with a little bit of a twist," she says.

Greely's emphasis on keeping "comfort" foods on the menu is a nod to the popularity of rich, warming foods that invoke soothing memories.[18] She wants the people who loved Lucinda's to know they can still feel at home at Lotus Café and "find some familiar things" that are much healthier than the fare offered by the previous owners.

But despite Greely's good intentions and the compromises she has made, the café has received its share of negative feedback. Greely is quick to point out that lots of people do like the café. But the negative responses are what she dwells on. "I tend to want to make everyone happy, which is next to impossible. It *is* impossible. Someone wrote something about how crazy it was that we didn't have snow cones, and that she has memories of going [to Lucinda's] with her grandfather and her father and all these memories of sitting in a booth eating a snow cone." Greely pauses and scrunches up her face, "I thought that was interesting. Like, does it have to be something that is sweet and unhealthy to make it memorable?"

21 A SMALL FRIDGE

The curtains are drawn, and everything is peaceful inside room 105. Saundra Washington is taking a shower while her mother, Patricia Washington, gets ready to go grocery shopping. Dressed in a pink caftan dress with paisley edging and black sandals, Patricia gathers up her plastic hotel "key," her EBT card, her cell phone, and a blue inhaler for her asthma.

"What do you want?" she asks her granddaughter Mia.

"Pizza," Mia says decisively.

"I'm headed out!" Patricia yells to Saundra. She opens the front door and turns to Mia and Jayden, who are sitting on the bed. "Love you," she tells them, closing the hotel door gently behind her. Patricia can hear Jayden's muffled cries on the other side of the door as she walks down the sidewalk toward the lobby.

The woman at the lobby desk greets Patricia with a smile. A monitor behind the desk is split into twelve screens, offering simultaneous views of the hotel stairwells and other areas. Five of the screens are blacked out, with "Video Loss" stamped across the bottom of each.

Standing in the lobby near the front desk is Patricia's son Doug. A tall man in his late thirties with broad shoulders, close-cropped hair, and a neatly trimmed beard, Doug wears a T-shirt printed with the logo of the moving company where he works. Even though Doug has little money to spare, he spends what he has to help Patricia and Saundra. He is holding several plastic bags. Explaining to Patricia that he's going to unload them in the hotel room, he says he'll meet her at the store.

Patricia hands her room card to the woman behind the desk, who smiles at her in return.[1] After a brief exchange, the woman asks Patricia if she can bring her back a Mountain Dew.

Patricia sets out on foot, first cutting through an alley permeated by the sharp, tangy smell of urine. At least it's an overcast fall day and a comfortable 60 degrees, Patricia muses. Walmart would have been her first choice for today's shopping trip, because the prices are lower there, but she didn't have a ride. So today she will buy only what she and Doug can carry back.

Crossing the street, careful not to step in the big piles of goose droppings coating the sidewalk and road, Patricia makes her way to the entrance of a Food Lion located in the middle of a largely boarded-up shopping center. She pauses as she reaches the entrance, scanning the empty storefronts in the complex. She is winded after the short walk.

Pushing a cart with one hand and holding her EBT card, inhaler, and cell phone with the other, Patricia heads straight for the middle of the store. In the cereal aisle, she selects two boxes of Cinnamon Toast Crunch and tosses them into the cart. Just as she is reaching for two boxes of Kool-Aid Jammers, which are a couple of cents cheaper than Capri Sun drinks, Doug appears beside her.

"Can you go and find frozen hot wings, Hot Pockets, and a cheese pizza for Mia?" she asks Doug. He nods and heads toward the frozen section. Patricia slowly makes her way to the baking aisle, where she selects a box of seedless raisins from one shelf and a package of self-rising flour from the other.[2]

Moments later, Doug returns.

"I found Buffalo-style wings, but not hot wings," he explains, putting the cheese pizza and Hot Pockets in the cart. Patricia frowns, unsatisfied with his answer.

Reading the disappointment on his mother's face, Doug knows he's got to try again. "I'll double check," he reassures Patricia. "Maybe there are hot wings," he adds hopefully, heading back in the same direction. He returns a few minutes later and confirms that they're out of hot wings.

"They must've changed it. I guess I'll hafta deal with it," Patricia says with stoic resignation.

Patricia picks out several more items from the frozen food aisle, including a package of chicken wing drummettes and three Michelina's macaroni and cheese dinners, on sale for ten for $10. Living in the hotel limits Patricia's ability to cook. The refrigerator is small, and cooking is restricted to what can be done in the microwave or on the electric skillet.

At the last minute, another frozen dinner entrée catches Patricia's eye: Marie Callender's Herb Roasted Chicken dinners. At $2.59 each, they're more expensive than the Michelina's brand, but Patricia decides to try them.

She puts two in the cart. Her last stop is the produce section, where she selects a three-pound bag of tangerines.

Maneuvering her cart toward one of the two open checkout lanes, Patricia remembers that she promised to get the hotel clerk a soda. She grabs a 20-ounce bottle of Mountain Dew from the cooler at the end of the lane.

Doug puts the items on the belt. When he finishes, he hustles to the end of the belt to bag them, while Patricia stands watching the register monitor. The cashier continues chatting with a co-worker as she scans each item. Behind her is a locked glass cabinet with shelves of cigarettes and baby formula.[3] The total comes to $74.17. Patricia swipes her plastic EBT card.

Finished loading the plastic bags into the cart, Doug wheels it toward the door.

"I wish we could just push it all the way down," he says to Patricia, referring to how some of the people staying at the hotel routinely push their grocery carts from the store to the hotel parking lot.

Patricia pauses as she considers their options. "As long as you bring it back," she tells Doug reluctantly. "That cost to the store gets passed to the consumer," she warns. When carts are left in the hotel parking lot, the store either has to send someone out to collect them or buy new ones.

As he sets off, pushing the grocery cart in front of him, Patricia yells out, "Watch out for the geese mess!" But Doug is already too far away to hear her warning over the clanging of the grocery cart wheels as they bounce along the rough surface of the parking lot.

The issue of food access—in particular, whether people live near stores selling healthy and affordable food—has gotten a lot of attention in recent years. In late 2012, the problem of unequal food access came to the forefront of Raleigh politics, when the only supermarket in one of Raleigh's poorest neighborhoods announced that it would soon be closing its doors.[4] With the loss of the neighborhood's sole grocery store, a Kroger supermarket, the community would officially become a food desert, according to the USDA definition.

Although there are debates about how to best define the term, the USDA defines a food desert as a low-income neighborhood in an urban area where a significant proportion of the population lives more than a mile from a supermarket or large grocery store, or a low-income neighborhood in a rural area where the distance is more than ten miles.[5]

Much of Raleigh's southeast quadrant, where Leanne Armstrong and Rosario García live, and where Patricia lived until she was evicted, qualifies as a food desert.[6] After the Kroger in southeast Raleigh closed, the remaining choices were a handful of Food Lions, including the one near Patricia's hotel. But these stores aren't very handy for many people in the neighborhood, like Leanne and Rosario, who both live near the now shuttered Kroger. Residents in that neighborhood have to cross a major highway to get to a grocery store now—making it a dangerous, if not impossible, trip. The city bus system is an option but a notoriously impractical one for many people. It always seems to be running behind schedule, and some routes take almost an hour when they should require half this time. People in Raleigh use the bus less than residents in other, similar-sized cities, and most in Raleigh avoid buses altogether if they can.[7] There are lots of corner and convenience stores in the neighborhood, but local residents find their prices exorbitant, and they typically specialize in chips, soda, beer, and cigarettes, with very few carrying fresh fruit and vegetables.[8]

The closing of the Kroger generated headlines. Residents without cars wondered how they were going to get to the grocery store. "This is a necessity for this area," said a city council member. "The seniors . . . depend on the groceries here and the medicine here. People in this area [will] have to go five miles to get food for their house, and it doesn't make sense."[9]

In February 2013, soon after the Kroger closed, forty people gathered in the fellowship hall of a historically African American church nearby.[10] The meeting was an opportunity for people to discuss their concerns and brainstorm solutions for improving food access in southeast Raleigh in general. But the conversation kept circling back to the Kroger.

People expressed outrage at the way a newspaper article had reported the Kroger closing. The article said Kroger had closed because it couldn't make a profit in the neighborhood, since the customers were too poor. "But food is a need," declared a young black woman who was employed at a local nonprofit organization. "Food is not a way to make money. Until we remember that, we're going to continue to struggle with access issues."

Not everyone agreed with her. A middle-aged woman stood up to speak. After acknowledging to the room that, as a "white girl from the suburbs," she was in a different position than the residents of the neighborhood, she stressed her background on issues related to food access. "I understand what you're saying," she said. "But at the same time, they [Kroger] had infrastructure. They had workers they had to pay."

The appeal to consider the grocery chain's bottom line was overshadowed by another woman who stood to talk. "As a resident, I had complaints about Kroger," the woman said, her strong voice commanding attention. "But it's a hardship that it's not there. When we think about food as medicine, then for someone to not have access [to a supermarket] at all..." She trailed off to calm her voice. "Then your next choice is to walk to a convenience store."

Reportedly first used by Scottish public housing residents over two decades ago to describe their food situation, the term "food desert" quickly gained traction among researchers and lawmakers who sought to understand how living in poverty makes people sick.[11] Food deserts seemed to be one of the links. Researchers reasoned that being poor meant living in neighborhoods without many grocery stores and thus not having easy access to fresh and affordable food, which in turn could affect eating habits and long-term health.

Over the last twenty-five years, geographers and public health researchers have documented the presence of food deserts in a variety of contexts. Researchers in the United States find that poor and predominantly minority neighborhoods have fewer supermarkets than other areas and are subject to higher food prices.[12] In some regions, wealthier neighborhoods have three or even four times as many supermarkets as poor neighborhoods.[13] Moreover, black neighborhoods, like southeast Raleigh, are usually farther away from supermarkets than white neighborhoods.[14]

Attributing people's food decisions to a lack of supermarkets in their neighborhood appeals to people's liberal sensibilities.[15] Instead of accusing poor people of causing their own health problems, people can point to structural inequalities, like the uneven distribution of food, as the culprit.

Research on food deserts also paves the way for a relatively easy fix that almost everyone can get behind: getting more stores and farmers' markets into poor neighborhoods. This solution follows the "if you build it, they will come" model of solving the problem of unequal food access.[16]

The early phase of food desert "fixes" seemed promising. Starting with Pennsylvania in 2004, states began passing laws to incentivize grocery stores and supermarkets to invest in low-income neighborhoods.[17] In 2010, the Obama administration announced the federal Healthy Food Financing Initiative, which offered grants, loans, and tax breaks to grocery stores and other "healthy food retailers" willing to move into poor urban and rural communities.[18] Former First Lady Michelle Obama stated that the goal was to "eliminate food deserts completely."[19] Private retailers jumped on board, with Walmart committing to opening new stores in areas that serve food desert residents.[20]

But despite the recent flurry of attention to food deserts, it's unclear how living in a food desert actually affects people's health. Some studies find that people who live closer to supermarkets eat more fruits or vegetables,[21] while others find no relationship between distance to supermarkets and what people eat.[22] There's some evidence that people living in food deserts are more likely to be overweight or obese,[23] but other studies conclude that the link between living in a food desert and being overweight or obese simply doesn't exist once other factors are taken into consideration.[24]

Research on food environments typically relies on surveys that look at people's behavior or health outcomes at only one point in time, which makes it difficult to figure out what is causing what.[25] However, the opening of two supermarkets in food deserts—one in Pittsburgh and one in Philadelphia—provided a unique natural experiment. Researchers surveyed people in these neighborhoods before and after the supermarkets opened. In both cases, they found that people were happy about the new stores, but the presence of the stores didn't increase consumption of fruits or vegetables.[26]

The availability of supermarkets undoubtedly matters, but access to grocery stores in and of itself is not a magic bullet to improving health. Increasing the number of supermarkets or farmers' markets in poor neighborhoods can stimulate competition with corner stores, potentially lowering food prices.[27] Yet as Patricia's grocery shopping outing shows, food access is about more than whether there is a supermarket nearby.

Patricia is not currently one of the people in Raleigh experiencing "low food access," generally defined in terms of proximity to a supermarket.[28] The Food Lion is just across the street from her hotel. But to get there, she has to walk along a foul-smelling and busy road. And, in her opinion, Food Lion doesn't give her the range of options or deals she could get at Walmart. Having to lug everything back on foot also limits what she can buy.

To make matters more difficult, Patricia has no room to store, cook, or eat food in the hotel room. She doesn't have any sharp knives or other kitchen tools, and the microwave and hot plate are the only appliances they have to make a warm meal. Cooking in the poorly ventilated hotel room also makes it stink. It is next to impossible to wash dishes in the small bathroom sink, and doing so in the bathtub is awkward and messy. Processed and microwavable foods are more expensive than raw ingredients, so Patricia's food stamps—which, with no cash income at the moment, are all she has to buy food—don't go as far as they might otherwise.

Everyone deserves to have access to stores and farmers' markets. Patricia's life is a little easier because she has a supermarket nearby. But she is dealing with other pressing issues that need to be addressed, like homelessness, lack of money, and a range of health conditions, from gout to asthma. And the store across the street isn't her first choice.[29]

During her slow walk back to the hotel, Patricia ponders how she might be able to take the kids to the state fair, held at the fairgrounds on the outskirts of Raleigh, the following week. She decides that her best option might be to go on Thursday, when you get free admission if you bring five cans of food. The fair donates the canned food to the food bank. Ironically, Patricia's only chance of going to the fair is to go on the day when they are raising money to help hungry families like hers.[30]

By the time Patricia gets back to the room, Doug has placed the plastic grocery bags on one of the beds. The light above the bathroom sink gives off a small glow in the dark room. Saundra has gotten the Kool-Aid Jammers out of the bag and is pouring some into a plastic cup for Jayden.

Patricia puts the boxes of Cinnamon Toast Crunch on top of the microwave.

"You got two?" Mia asks.

"They were two for $5," Patricia explains.

"Five dollars? That's too high," four-year-old Mia says indignantly.

"Two for $5? That's cheap!" says Patricia, keeping a straight face but silently amused by her adult-like granddaughter.

Seeing Patricia move to put the Jammers away, Mia springs into action to help. "They're not heavy," she reassures her grandmother, hoisting up the box of drinks and expertly placing it behind Saundra's bed.

"Good girl," Patricia praises. "No lazy little girl." Patricia continues to wedge things into the mini-fridge, but it's full and the door won't stay shut.

Out of the corner of her eye, Patricia sees Doug head toward the door to go back outside.

"Just leave it across the street where the other carts are," she says, referring to the corner of the Food Lion parking lot. She takes a step back to survey her work. The bottles of ketchup and vegetable oil and the bag of flour are neatly stowed to the right of the bathroom vanity counter. Oatmeal packages, microwavable soups, applesauce, cereal, and Krispy Kreme honey buns are skillfully stacked on top of the small fridge.

After carefully rearranging the contents, Patricia finally manages to jam the fridge door shut.

DAILY BREAD

At ten on the dot, Renata pulls her green station wagon into the parking lot of Daily Bread, a food pantry located in an industrial area on the edge of the city, just a few miles from Leanne's house. Leanne Armstrong is in the passenger seat, and two of her kids, Hakeem and Gemma, are in the back. Their cupboards are dangerously low, and their food stamps won't be renewed for two more weeks.[1] Looking at the building, Leanne sighs. They haven't opened the doors yet, and there is a line of twenty people waiting.

Renata parks the car, and Leanne gets out to unbuckle Gemma from her car seat in the back. She takes a closer look at the people in line. Reflecting the demographics of the neighborhood, they are predominantly black and Latino/a, along with a few white people. There are more women than men. Many of the women have children with them.[2]

"She should walk herself, because she's a fat girl," Renata clucks at Leanne, who is carrying Gemma on her hip as they walk across the parking lot.

"She's too slow to walk the whole way," Leanne responds, but she puts Gemma down anyway. Slowly, they make their way toward the food pantry, a boxy white building with a large loading dock to the left of the entrance.

A few minutes after ten, a cheerful woman with curly hair unlocks the front door and enthusiastically greets the crowd. People begin to slowly file in.

Daily Bread is part of a network of more than 200 food banks and 61,000 food pantries and soup kitchens that distribute more than three million meals every year in the United States.[3] As anti-hunger activist and author Andrew Fisher notes, these meals are an important part of how many low-income families survive. Food pantries help supplement paychecks or governmental benefits that aren't sufficient to get people through the month. They also serve people, like undocumented immigrants, who are ineligible for food stamps or other government benefits. They allow families to use their scarce cash to heat their homes or buy medicine, knowing they'll still have something to eat.[4]

Although soup kitchens and food pantries in the United States can be traced back to the Great Depression, the modern "charitable food system" really began in the 1980s. The first food bank—a center that collected surplus food from supermarkets and food manufacturers and distributed it to poor people—was established in Phoenix in 1967. By 1977, a national organization had been established in Chicago, to guide the replication of food banks across the country. In the 1980s, in the wake of a deep recession and steep cuts to the federal safety net, the charitable food system exploded: from thirteen food banks in 1979 to 180 in 1989.[5]

Today, there are food banks across the United States. And there are food pantries in schools, churches, and volunteer associations, sustained by a wide range of donors, from supermarket chains and food manufacturers to food drives at schools and churches.[6] There are mobile food pantries that go where the need is and food pantries in elementary, middle, and high schools and on college campuses.[7]

Food charities are evidence of the "astonishing ingenuity of the American spirit."[8] "Literally millions of Americans support these programs with contributions of food, money, time, and effort," writes sociologist Janet Poppendieck. "It is an outpouring of compassion, both organized and individual . . . a 'kinder, gentler nation.'"[9]

But the charitable food system has also snowballed out of control, argue Fisher and Poppendieck. Originally intended as a temporary stopgap to relieve suffering from relatively short-term setbacks, it has grown into "a seemingly permanent feature of the country's landscape."[10]

Yet, we might ask, if these food charities are serving a need, and clearly they are, is there really a problem?

The simple answer is yes. The entrenchment of this vast system of food charities, critics point out, has negative implications: for the people who rely on food pantries and food banks, and for our ability to adequately resolve the problem of hunger in the United States.

Charitable efforts work at the individual level, by serving as a "moral safety valve," reducing people's discomfort with seeing visible inequality and destitution. At the governmental level, these efforts "work" by making it easier for policymakers to shed responsibility for the poor.[11] But although they fill an important need, food pantries don't always work well for the people using them.

"Welcome!" bubbles the cheerful woman at the door, smiling widely at each person who crosses the threshold into the building. Her name tag reads "Kathy." Leanne and her family are the last ones inside. The door closes behind them, and Kathy follows them in.

Two older white women sit in folding chairs at a collapsible table just inside the door. Leanne tells them her name and collects a wooden token with the number twenty-nine on it while Kathy waits off to the side. Seeing that Leanne has her token, she escorts the family into a room behind double glass doors.

"I like her dress," she tells Leanne, nodding approvingly at Gemma's green dress.

"Thank you!" exclaims Leanne. "I think I got it here, actually."

"Really?" says Kathy. "It's so pretty. And it matches her shoes. She's so coordinated!"

"I hate them shoes," grumbles Renata under her breath. She has been complaining about Gemma's Sesame Street shoes all morning.

They push through the glass doors and enter a large room, divided into two separate areas by gray partition walls. The walls are decorated with inspirational posters. Large fluorescent lights make the windowless room feel artificially bright. It smells like bleach.

Two rows of gray plastic chairs are lined up in front of the partition in the center of the room. Leanne leads everyone to a group of empty chairs in the second row. Hakeem makes sure he gets to sit next to Leanne. He nestles his head into her shoulder.

"We the last ones here?" he asks.

"No," Leanne says, explaining that the last people will be the ones who come at one o'clock, when the food pantry closes.

Tall shelves with bins of clothes are visible behind the partition wall. Every few minutes, someone emerges from behind the partition and calls out a number and a first name. "Number eleven. Jennifer."

Less frequently, a voice over the loudspeaker announces that an order is ready. "Number two, your order is ready. Please meet us out front."

Seeing that Hakeem is bored, Leanne tries to distract him. "How many are left before our number, twenty-nine?" Leanne quizzes him.

Hakeem pauses, and Leanne starts to give him a clue. "Wait, wait!" he says, furrowing his brow in concentration. "Twenty-seven!" he announces proudly.

A voice on the loudspeaker announces that number six's order is ready. A staff member calls for number fifteen to go back behind the partition walls. They still have a long way to go. Hakeem plays a game with Gemma to pass the time. He beats his chest with his fist. "Ooh," he says, imitating a caveman. Gemma laughs and copies him.

Number eight's order is ready.

"They going fast, that's good," Leanne says to Renata.

Thirty minutes after they sat down, a woman with a nametag that reads "Mandy" emerges from the back. "Number twenty-nine, Leanne," she calls out. Renata tells Leanne that she will stay in the waiting room. Leanne gathers up the kids and follows Mandy down a narrow hallway and into a cramped room with bright green paint.

Mandy wedges herself into a chair behind a small table. An old computer monitor sits on top of the table. Leanne sits in a plastic chair on the other side of the table, holding Gemma in her lap. Hakeem sits in the plastic chair next to her.

"I brought my ID," Leanne informs Mandy, who is entering information into the computer.

"Okay," Mandy murmurs. She looks up. "Hi," she says to Gemma. She turns back to her screen.

"This is Gemma, the baby," Leanne says brightly, but Mandy is preoccupied with the form and doesn't respond.

"What are the last four digits of your social security number?"

Leanne recites the four numbers.

"And there are five people living in the house?"

Leanne confirms this is accurate.

Gemma grabs for a box with the word "Sample" scrawled across it.

"No, no. Stop it!" Leanne tells Gemma, as Hakeem giggles. It's a box of tampons.

"And she didn't put down that I needed baby clothes, but I do need those—and wipes," Leanne tells Mandy.

"Okay. Okay, we don't have any wipes, but did you need diapers, too?"

"No, we're fine on diapers," Leanne says.

Hakeem tugs on Leanne's sleeve.

"I have my football game on July first."

"Really? I'll see if I have to go to work," Leanne replies distractedly.

"You have to pay $75 for me to play my football game," Hakeem tells her.

"We'll talk about that later. Right now Mommy's trying to take care of business."

Mandy hands her a dark green card that says "clothes" and has Gemma's size written on it.

"Do you need some?" Mandy asks Leanne, pointing to the box of tampons. Leanne nods, and Mandy adds tampons to the order.

"You're all set," she tells Leanne.

Leanne picks up Gemma and returns to the main office, with Hakeem following behind her. She greets Renata, who is still waiting in the plastic chairs, then walks behind one of the gray dividers to an open area. Two volunteers, both older women with graying hair and pale skin mottled by the southern sun, are sorting through bins of clothing. A sign on the wall behind them reads: "No One Can Enter without a Clothing Ticket."

Hakeem immediately makes his way to a table piled with stuffed animals and small toys. "One Toy Per Child," instructs a sign on the wall behind the table. Leanne sets Gemma on the floor. She toddles toward her brother. "Come back!" Leanne calls, but then decides to let Gemma go.

Leanne hands her green ticket to one of the women, who pulls down two bins in Gemma's size—one with shirts and one with pants. Leanne sifts slowly through the bin of shirts. She pulls out a long white shirt with a pink overlay.

"That's adorable," Leanne murmurs. She folds the top and puts it next to the bin on the table. "One?" she asks the woman helping her.

"One from here, and one from here," the woman clarifies, touching each of the two bins. Leanne digs through the items in the other bin, eventually selecting a pair of white pants with colorful flowers embroidered on the pockets. It's a good match for the top she just chose.

Leanne gives the pants to the woman, who grabs a white plastic grocery bag and shakes it open. She puts the pants and the shirt in the bag. "You can pick out a dress too," she tells Leanne, pointing to two garment racks.

Sliding dresses along the rack, Leanne checks the tags for sizes. She chooses a blue gingham dress with a Peter Pan collar, then pauses, reconsidering. "You know, I'd rather get this one," she says, holding up a white dress with red flowers. "Sorry."

"That's okay!" says the woman, folding the dress into the bag and handing it to Leanne.

Leanne turns to Hakeem, who is clutching a stuffed Clifford the Big Red Dog.

"This is the toy Gemma wants," he tells Leanne eagerly.

"Hakeem, let her pick. Let her do this, not you," Leanne insists. Scowling, Hakeem puts Clifford back on the table.

"What can I get?" he asks in a hurt voice.

"Nothing!" Leanne tells him. "Toys are for babies, not eight-year-olds." She holds up several plush toys for Gemma, who shows no interest. Leanne reluctantly picks up the Clifford doll.

"Oh ho!" Gemma exclaims happily.

Leanne laughs and concedes.

With slumped shoulders, Hakeem shuffles slowly behind Leanne as she prods him to keep moving. They return to the waiting area.

"He picked out Clifford for Gemma, and now he's mad 'cause he can't get a toy," Leanne tells Renata, who wants to know what's wrong with Hakeem.

"I picked it out for me!" Hakeem protests.

Leanne is frustrated. "We'll get you a toy. Later."

They sit down to wait to be called again.

Hakeem slumps in his chair, staring at the floor while they wait. He's in a deep funk about the toy.

Fifteen minutes pass.

Finally, the loudspeaker says, "Order twenty-nine is ready." Leanne scoops Gemma up and everyone walks out to the loading ramp.

A man in his late twenties is pushing a large metal cart piled high with food. His sandy brown hair clings to his damp forehead.

"That's a lot of food," Hakeem says, his eyes wide.

"Twenty-nine?" the man asks, confirming Leanne's number.

"Yes, sir," Leanne confirms.

The man pushes the cart down the ramp and follows Leanne and her family across the parking lot to the station wagon. He begins unloading boxes and bags from the cart into the back of the car.

"See, this is a good place," Leanne comments, watching him.

Food pantries like Daily Bread and the food banks that supply them were invented as a solution to an ironic problem in the United States: the fact that we have a surplus of food, but also many hungry people.[12] Food banks get their food from a number of sources, including food purchased by the federal government to bolster US farms; donations of products that supermarkets are not allowed to sell, like expired baked goods; surplus food from food manufacturers; blemished or undersized produce; leftovers from caterers and restaurants; and donations from canned food drives. In turn, they distribute food to food pantries and soup kitchens, the "frontline" institutions that interact directly with people seeking food.[13]

Food pantries and food banks exist, in theory, to feed hungry families. But because the charitable food system is also a convenient solution to waste in the food chain, it isn't always set up in a way that adequately meets the needs of the people who rely on it. Food pantry recipients are frequently subject to long waits and humiliating rules to make sure they qualify and don't take more than their fair share of food. Although Leanne is used to this and likes the service at Daily Bread, the food she gets is another matter. Because food pantries rely on donations, the foods they distribute are often a random assortment. The quality of the food varies widely, too.[14] The pantries themselves are strapped, with many relying entirely on volunteer labor. Most are severely constrained in their ability to distribute healthy food.[15]

Latrell is outside playing basketball when Renata pulls into the driveway. He saunters over and begins unloading food from the car. It takes several trips to get the food inside. Leanne and Latrell poke through the bags, taking inventory.

"Spinach artichoke dip! Why they keep giving me this?" Leanne exclaims, making a face. She removes three cans of Dr. Pepper from another bag.

"This is my dinner, right here," Latrell says, chuckling to himself. He cracks open a can and takes a big gulp. Leanne pulls several small packages of crackers out of a bag.

"Chocolatey peanut butter!" she yells, howling with laughter as she reads the label.

"Chocolatey!" Latrell repeats, laughing. Leanne starts dividing the food into categories on the table.

"Can I eat these?" asks Hakeem, holding up a pint of strawberries.

"Wash them first," Leanne instructs. Latrell takes another sip of soda, puts the can on the counter, and walks out the front door. Realizing he's disappeared, Leanne mutters to herself, "I wish somebody would help me put this stuff up."

Gemma shoves a strawberry into her mouth and drops the hull on the floor. Leanne picks up two small cans featuring homemade "pasta sauce" labels. When she opens the pantry door to put them away, a dozen cockroaches scatter.

"Ugh!" she shrieks, stomping on the floor, annoyed but not surprised. Seeing the front door cracked open, she walks over to shut it.

"Gemma, where's Daddy? Tell him he needs to help me put these groceries up," she says, loud enough for Latrell to hear outside.

She pauses.

"I'm not joking," she announces firmly out the door before closing it and returning to sorting. Moments later Latrell appears in the living room.

"Are you going to help me put this stuff up? It's for both of us!" Leanne exclaims. Latrell looks around, surveying the food.

"You eat most of this stuff anyway!" he says. He half-heartedly moves a few things around, puts the eggs away, and sits down at the dining room table.

"There's a lot of strawberries, and we're not gonna eat all these strawberries," Leanne tells Renata, who's been sitting at the table watching Leanne unpack the food.

"I'll sure take 'em. You know that child will eat 'em," she says. Hakeem spends a lot of time with Renata, and he loves strawberries.

Leanne pulls a loaf of bread from a bag. "I got rye bread!" she announces happily.

"Shut. Up. No you didn't!" Renata says, her mouth wide open.

"Well, it's marbled." Leanne puts the package close to her face and inhales. "Mmm." Renata makes to grab it. "You're not gettin' the whole thing, Momma!" Leanne says, pulling the loaf out of her mother's reach. She picks up a frozen mushroom pizza and inspects the packaging.

"I don't like mushrooms," Latrell complains.

"I'll take it," volunteers Renata.

"I am still going to fix the pizza," Leanne says.

"Why you gonna fix it if you're not gonna eat all of it?" Renata asks.

"I'm gonna eat it, just not all of it maybe." Leanne opens the freezer door and shoves the pizza in.

"That bread's pretty fresh," Renata says, returning to the loaf of marbled bread.

"*This* time," Latrell scoffs.

"That's what I'm saying, *this time*," Renata agrees.

"The last few times it was molded," Latrell reminds everyone.

Leanne separates the loaf of rye bread into equal halves. She puts one of the halves in a white plastic grocery bag and gives it to Renata.

Latrell retrieves his can of Dr. Pepper from the kitchen counter. "Yuck!" he exclaims dramatically as he walks past the spinach and artichoke dip. "They don't got no pineapple cake?" he asks Leanne, staring at a boxed lemon cake.

"Baby, we don't go in there and look! They give us what they give us," Leanne says in a clipped voice, as Latrell pushes open the door and goes back outside.

Rifling through her cabinets to find a Tupperware container, Leanne sighs. She feels fed up with Latrell.

"I cannot believe he gave all my Tupperware away." She tells Renata that Latrell took food to someone once and never got the Tupperware back.

"You don't need to give him anything of yours. Anything," Renata tells her in a stern voice. "You a single parent, basically. You out working and going to school and raising these babies. I just want you to keep your stuff for yourself, okay?"

Leanne nods and lights a cigarette. She sits down at the table. Gemma toddles over and pats her knee.

"I'm burned out. Really burned out. I'm totally burned out," Leanne says. She slouches at the table, her head in her hands, collecting her thoughts before she rallies. She has classes to attend and homework to do, and she plans to make fajitas for dinner.

23 STOP CRYING

A thin woman in her mid-forties sits behind the intake window of the WIC (Special Supplemental Nutrition Program for Women, Infants, and Children) office. She has tan skin, long black hair, and a French manicure. Her name tag says "Patti."

Patti staples a sheaf of papers together and begins the standard intake procedure for Melanie Richards. She barely looks at Melanie as she mechanically asks each question.

"Is the phone number still the same?"

"We only really use that number for the internet," Melanie answers, sitting up straight.

Patti raises her head. With her pen poised, she gives Melanie a deadpan stare.

"Okay. What's your other number?"

Melanie's cheeks flush as she recites her cell phone number to Patti. She tugs self-consciously at her shirt, which is tight around her stomach. Her hair is pulled back and fastened with a barrette at the top of her head, and her bright green eyes are accented with a hint of eye shadow and mascara. Melanie has come straight from work.

Patti writes the number on a piece of paper. "Okay, have a seat and you will be called soon," she tells Melanie.

The WIC office resembles a cross between a doctor's office and a typical government agency, like the Department of Motor Vehicles. Rows of hard plastic chairs, all facing the television, line the perimeter of the room. Melanie chooses a seat. Her four-year-old daughter, Jade, makes her way over to an area with a small table and children's toys. Today, she is wearing a striped blue and white T-shirt, a short blue skirt, and pink Crocs.

The posters on the walls of the waiting area are filled with health promotion messages. "Health care starts with breastfeeding," reads one. Another, taped to the door of someone's office, assures mothers: "Breastfeeding works around any schedule." A third poster features a smiling white woman with her hand on her pregnant belly. The words above the picture declare: "You quit, two quit," referring to a state campaign to help pregnant and new mothers stop smoking cigarettes.

The staff at this WIC office is a lot friendlier than at other offices, Melanie feels. When Jade was a baby, she went to another office that was especially bad, in her opinion. There were always long lines, and the staff neglected to return phone calls. Melanie was particularly frustrated when they "practically tried to force her" to give Jade formula. Melanie remembers them asking her, "Don't you want some formula? It's free!" Melanie thought this was odd, given WIC's official policy of promoting breastfeeding.[1] She ignored the advice and breastfed instead.

Jade is already bored with the toys, which are geared to much younger children. Jade will turn five soon and age out of the WIC program. "Are we going to see a doctor?" she asks her mother seriously. Jade hates going to the doctor.

"No, honey," Melanie explains patiently. "They are not doctors. They are nutrition counselors. They just want to check and make sure that you are healthy and that Mommy is feeding you the right food."

Never one to pass up a teaching moment, Melanie explains to Jade that WIC gives food to kids so they can grow and be healthy.

"Where is the food?" Jade asks earnestly.

"We won't get food right now," Melanie explains. "But we get coupons," she says, referring to the vouchers that can be redeemed for specific types of food, including whole-grain bread, milk, cheese, peanut butter, eggs, and fruits and vegetables.[2] WIC is a government program that provides low-income pregnant and postpartum women and their young children (under age five) with "nutritious foods," nutrition education, and screening and referrals for other services. Established in 1972, WIC is an important program for many mothers and young children; the USDA reports that 53 percent of babies born in the United States participate in WIC.[3]

"What's a coupon?" Jade inquires, her brown eyes wide.

"A piece of paper," Melanie tells her. Jade stares at her mother with a confused look. She starts to ask another question, but she is cut off when a door at the back of the room opens. A woman in a bright green T-shirt holds the door open with her foot and looks down at her clipboard. "Jade Richards?" she calls into the waiting room.

Melanie stands and ushers Jade toward the door. The tag on the woman's shirt says her name is Debbie. In her sixties, Debbie is short and plump, with gray hair. She leads the way into a small room and gets right down to business.

"Mom, what is your height and weight?"

"I am 5' 2" and . . ." Melanie pauses. "I weigh way too much," she adds sheepishly.

Debbie looks up from her paperwork. She is not feeling patient today. "I'm gonna need a number," she tells Melanie.

Melanie looks at Debbie. Jade is staring at Melanie. "I weigh 245 pounds," she mumbles, her voice barely audible. Debbie notes this in her paperwork. She instructs Jade to step on a square scale in the middle of the floor so that she can record her weight. Jade dutifully does as told, standing ramrod straight and perfectly still.

"Forty-two point six pounds," declares Debbie. She tells Jade to stand against the wall so that she can measure her height. The measuring device consists of a tall board affixed to the wall. Numbers along the edge of the board mark off inches and feet. A piece of sliding Plexiglas is attached to the board.

"Put your heels against the board," Debbie instructs Jade. Jade quickly complies, and Debbie slides the Plexiglas to rest just on top of Jade's head.

"Forty inches," Debbie reads, making a note in her chart.

"Well, hopefully that's it!" Melanie says in a peppy voice.

"It's been three months since she came in," Debbie says, eyeing the chart. "We are going to have to do a test."

Melanie stares at her. This is not what she was hoping for.

Jade doesn't immediately realize what this means. She stands there, blissfully unaware of what the adults are talking about.

Debbie gets out a pair of purple gloves. In a monotone, I-do-this-every-day-let's-get-this-show-on-the-road voice, she instructs Jade to sit in the hard plastic chair in front of her. Jade clambers onto the chair. A cloud crosses her face when she sees Debbie putting on the gloves.

"What are those gloves for?" she asks Debbie, wide-eyed.

Debbie is a WIC veteran and never stops moving. Ignoring Jade's question, she quickly grabs her finger. Alarmed, Jades tries to jerk her finger back, but Debbie has a pincer grip on it.

"What a pretty finger that is," Debbie says in a flat voice, as if she's been instructed to say this to settle children down. She takes a cotton ball, dabs it with alcohol, and begins cleaning Jade's finger.

"Why are you rubbing that on me?!" Jade asks in alarm, her voice growing louder. Melanie gets up and stands behind her.

Debbie silently and efficiently rubs Jade's small finger with the cotton ball.

"No! Don't do that to my finger," Jade pleads, staring at the tip of her finger poking out from Debbie's hold on it. The finger is turning bright red from Debbie's grip.

"It's okay. They are just cleaning your finger," Melanie tells Jade in a soothing voice.

But the charade can continue no longer. With her other hand, Debbie grabs a small plastic rectangle.

"No! I don't want that!" Jade says and begins to cry.

Without breaking stride, Debbie presses the plastic rectangle to the tip of Jade's finger and pushes the lever, releasing the needle inside to prick Jade's finger.

Jade starts to wail, and Melanie holds on to her shoulders, telling her softly that she is okay.

Still holding Jade's finger in a pincer grip, Debbie collects the blood sample, then covers the pricked area with a plain Band-Aid. She reaches for a Hello Kitty Band-Aid, which she expertly wraps around Jade's finger to keep the other Band-Aid in place.

Large tears roll down Jade's blotchy cheeks. Her shoulders heave as she sobs. Debbie puts the blood sample into an instrument, slips off the purple gloves, and opens a drawer next to her. She takes her time thumbing through a tray of stickers. Theatrically fingering a Batman sticker, she decides against it. Instead she stands up, turns around, opens a cupboard above her head, and pulls out another box of stickers.

With her back still turned to Jade, Debbie says, "Are you going to stop crying? You get two stickers if you stop crying. If you keep crying, you only get one."

Jade continues crying.

"I thought you was a big girl," Debbie chastises. "Aren't you fixin' to go to school?"

Hiding behind Melanie, Jade lifts her face. It contorts as she tries to stop crying. A single tear rolls down her cheek, and she accidentally lets out a whimper.

"Are you going to stop crying?" Debbie repeats. She turns around and fixes Jade with a steely look, then looks into the sticker box in front of her, slowly reaching her hand in for dramatic effect, an ear cocked to detect any cries coming from Jade.

Realizing what's on the line, Jade grimaces while tightly holding her finger, trying to trap her cries from escaping.

Slowly Debbie rips off a Dora the Explorer sticker and hands it to Jade, who takes it, still battling to calm herself down.

A machine beeps, breaking the silence. Debbie glances at it. "Twelve," she reports to Melanie, referring to Jade's iron level. It's in the normal range. Debbie then puts her hands on the sticker box again, moving slowly. Jade looks at her with anticipation, her eyes still watery. Finally, without looking at her, Debbie hands a second sticker to Jade.

"She didn't cry one bit last time!" Debbie tells Melanie, implying that Jade's reaction signifies a major regression.

"Actually, she screamed last time," Melanie says softly, but with a detectable hint of defiance in her voice.

"Oh. She did?" replies Debbie. She quickly switches gears. "The next time she goes to the pediatrician, you can tell them that we already took Jade's iron so that they don't have to do it again. You can tell them since I won't be here, because I am retiring."

"Oh! Well, congratulations!" Melanie says graciously. "Now you can enjoy some freedom."

Debbie reaches up to put the box of stickers back in the cupboard.

"I don't know how much freedom it will be, but I'm retiring," she replies dryly.

Back in the waiting room, Melanie consoles Jade about "getting pinched." Jade wants to know "why Debbie did that." Melanie gives her a hug and tells her that it was to check her iron. Jade asks what iron is, and Melanie gives her a complex explanation about iron carrying oxygen to the blood.

Suddenly, Jade looks at her finger and says, "My teacher is going to be so impressed!" She flashes her characteristic impish smile. Melanie looks at her endearingly.

"I love you," Melanie says.

The next twenty minutes pass slowly. Jade plays an alphabet game on Melanie's phone. Finally, another woman calls them to come back into another office. This woman, Pamela, is all smiles and seems friendlier than Debbie. She tells Melanie and Jade to sit down in the chairs in front of her desk.

The room is cramped. Melanie's knees are practically touching Pamela's desk. Looking at Jade sympathetically, Pamela asks, "Did you get your finger pricked?"

Jade frowns and nods yes.

"Aw," Pamela offers.

"How is Jade?" Pamela asks Melanie.

"She is fine," Melanie beams with pride.

"Is Dad still giving her soda?" Pamela's tone is kind but pointed.

Melanie purses her lips. "Less," she says.

"So about how much would you say that he is giving her?" Pamela presses.

Melanie pauses. "Um, I don't know really. But I know we're giving her less because I've made a big stink about it."

"Oh, okay. What is she drinking now?"

"Mostly water and milk, and the sugar-free Kool-Aid."

Pamela makes a note of this in her chart. "Okay. That's fine."

"About how often does she eat fruits and vegetables?"

Melanie perks up with the confidence of a mother who knows she's got this one. "Every day!" she says.

"Do you have any concerns about what she's doin'?" Pamela asks.

"Nope. I think she's doin' great," Melanie says, looking affectionately at Jade.

"Okay, because she gained a little more weight than we want her to. She has gained three pounds," Pamela says with a concerned tone.

Pamela places Jade's growth chart on the desk in front of Melanie as evidence.[4] Using her pen, she points to the dot on the curve from their last visit. She then points to the one from this visit. As Melanie inspects the chart, Pamela explains that Jade's height has not increased, just her weight. This means her weight gain can't be explained by a growth spurt.

"This is why I was asking about soda," she says. Her voice is soft, perhaps to ease the blow of her words. Melanie is silent.

"What about Jade's activity?" Pamela inquires.

"She plays at school and does ballet. At home she is probably not as active as I would like her to be," Melanie says, her confidence waning.

"What sorts of things does she like to do at home?" Pamela is trying to make this casual, but it's hard to accomplish. Both she and Melanie are aware of who is sitting on what side of the desk. Jade's chart has triggered a red flag for Pamela, and now Melanie has to account for it.

"Um, she watches TV. We sort of have to turn it off."

"It's getting really pretty outside," Pamela says in an encouraging voice. "It is a great time to go outside and play." It might be fun for Jade to play water games, she says. She suggests Jade's big brother might even want to play and recommends a game called Duck Duck Splash, which involves kids pouring cups of water from a bucket, pool, or large bowl onto each other's heads. It's fun for everyone, she says.

"It helps keep them cool in the heat too," Pamela adds, trying to squeeze in one last selling point.

Melanie listens attentively. "Yeah, that sounds like fun," she offers in a limp voice.

Pamela hands Melanie a pamphlet with recommended servings of the food groups and says that if Jade has days when she wants more snacks, Melanie should make sure she gets extra exercise too.

"Turning the TV off early would be a good idea," she adds with a smile. Melanie nods and remains silent.

Sensing this moment has reached its limit, Pamela glances at the paperwork on the desk. "Do you want cheese again?" she asks, referring to the food vouchers the office will now dispense. Melanie nods. Pamela circles a box.

"Do you have any questions?" Pamela asks.

"No," Melanie says, gathering up Jade. "Thank you," she tells Pamela.

"You're welcome," Pamela says warmly, standing up in front of her desk. She looks at Jade. "She's so cute," she tells Melanie as they turn to the door.

Melanie relies on WIC to get staple foods. She doesn't like getting public assistance, but she feels a deep responsibility to ensure that her children have the food they need to grow and be healthy. WIC helps her do that. WIC also helps Melanie in her ongoing efforts to get Kevin to stop giving Jade soda and other unhealthy foods. She can say it's not just her idea, but that WIC also thinks this is important. But getting this help requires a grueling, and at times humiliating, ninety-minute office visit. Sometimes it takes even longer.

The message that is dispensed at WIC along with the vouchers is clear: Melanie is responsible for Jade's health, which they can easily and objectively evaluate by measuring her height and weight each visit. When Jade gains weight, the WIC counselor tries to figure out what Melanie is doing wrong at home.

Assessing children's body sizes and tracking the rate at which they grow is an important way for doctors to monitor children's development. Babies are frequently weighed in their first few weeks of life, and healthcare appointments for older kids also typically include checking a child's height and weight and comparing them to a "normal" growth curve, as the WIC counselor did for Jade.[5] Children's bodies serve as an important source of feedback about their health and well-being.

In reality, though, there's still a lot we don't know about why people gain weight and how bodies grow. Weight gain is often framed as a simple matter of "calorie balance" (the number of calories we consume as food or drink minus the number of calories we expend through physical activity), yet researchers know that body sizes are also affected by a wide range of other factors, including stress, environmental contaminants, and genetics.[6] But despite this uncertainty, people routinely assume that body size is a choice, something that people have control over. With children, mothers are assumed to be primarily responsible or irresponsible. Children's bodies thus become visible metrics not just of their health but also of their mothers' ability to feed and care for them properly.[7]

This is not something that only happens at the WIC office. Children's bodies are assessed and scrutinized in a variety of contexts: at school, at doctors' offices, and even by friends and relatives who comment on a child's appearance.[8] But lower-income families like Melanie's experience additional surveillance over their children's bodies and the ways they feed their children, as a result of the social assistance programs they participate in.

In order to qualify for these programs, people have to jump through lots of hoops: regularly reporting their income and changes in life circumstances, for example, or proving that they are employed or actively looking for a job.[9] To receive WIC, people must participate in regular weigh-ins and nutrition education sessions. These requirements increase both the administrative burden on the agencies collecting the information and the risk that recipients will land in the crosshairs of an agency, sometimes by mistake, for failing to comply with the rules. In some US states, for example, mothers receiving welfare benefits who don't keep their children fully up-to-date on their vaccinations, risk being sanctioned by losing a month of welfare support.[10] The decisions made by the government employees who administer social assistance programs—typically overworked, inadequately trained, and poorly paid themselves—often seem arbitrary. Even worse, researchers find patterns of racial bias in how sanctions are applied. [11]

Shuttling back and forth to different offices—to get vouchers at the WIC office, for example, and then to another office for Medicaid—also takes time. It is stressful. When people's life circumstances change, even just a little bit— for example, if someone takes on a temporary job or picks up some additional hours at work—it can mean losing their benefits. Sanctions are often interconnected; violating the rules of one program may mean losing benefits associated with other programs.[12] And the process can be demoralizing. In a study of Medicaid, the single largest public health insurer in the United States, for example, political scientist Jamila Michener found that recipients reported feeling stigmatized for using Medicaid and being "treated like stupid animals" and "looked down upon" for needing help.[13]

Obtaining social services also generally requires submitting to the prevalent American ethos that individuals are solely responsible for their fate, whether it is by actively seeking employment to receive welfare payments (called Work First in North Carolina to emphasize that employment should be the priority), working for free to show your willingness to work, or bowing to dominant narratives about individual accountability for health and nutrition.

The WIC office doesn't withhold Melanie's vouchers, but they do subject Melanie to a grilling about her family's food habits and make her feel as though she is failing at food and health.[14] With this notion of personal responsibility comes a great deal of judgment. According to this mindset, poor health is a consequence when people fail to care enough to take responsibility for their health.[15] Melanie cares a lot about her family's health, and the implication that she doesn't do enough, or care enough, stings.

Back in the waiting area, Melanie is deflated. She and Jade wait for the food vouchers to be ready. Jade is tired, and they're both hungry. Melanie becomes more and more incensed about the episode with Pamela as she waits. In fact, she is sure Jade did not gain three pounds since her last visit. She does some calculations in her head and concludes that the scales at this office must be off, or that they are rounding up the numbers. Melanie thinks about a recent visit to the pediatrician. Jade was weighed at that appointment, and the pediatrician didn't say anything about Jade being overweight. Melanie takes nutrition and health seriously. But she is skeptical that a standardized, one-size-fits-all system is appropriate for assessing all children's weight and growth. "No kid is going to be the perfect weight. You're not going to see them gain evenly all the time," she says.[16]

Studying the pamphlet that Pamela gave her, Melanie informs Jade, "Four teaspoons equals one serving of vegetables, Jadie." Melanie is back in teacher mode.

"What's taking so long?" Jade whines. "We're the last ones."

Melanie nods.

"I always wanted to be the last one!" Jade says happily.

Melanie chuckles.

"Did you?" Jade inquires.

"Not really," Melanie replies. "You're awfully cute."

"What's taking sooo long?"

Melanie doesn't answer. She continues reading the pamphlet. "I think you're not getting enough servings of milk during the day," she says.

Finally, after fifteen minutes, Patti calls Melanie to the counter to collect her food vouchers. Before she gets them, Patti reminds her to make her next appointment, for three months from now. She tears Melanie's vouchers along the perforated lines, stacks them, and stuffs them into an envelope she distractedly hands to Melanie. "Thank you. Have a nice day," she says without looking up.

7 FOOD BRINGS PEOPLE TOGETHER

The seated dinner, with its minuet of invitation and acceptance,
its formalities and protocols, its culinary and dietary challenges,
its inherent requirements of guest and host, alike is under threat,
many say.

—GUY TREBAY, *New York Times* journalist,
"Guess Who Isn't Coming to Dinner" (2012)

If you really want to make a friend, go to someone's house and eat with
him. . . . The people who give you their food give you their heart.

—CÉSAR CHÁVEZ, Mexican American farm worker,
labor leader, and civil rights activist

There's a lot of handwringing about the demise of the dinner party. Why don't people invite others over for dinner anymore? In fact, Americans *are* still eating together, but in ways that may not resemble the sit-down dinners of our collective imagination. Food remains an important way people celebrate one another, affirm identities, resist oppression, and experience and negotiate networks of care and community.

24 SUNDAY DINNER

As a kid, Rae Donahue remembers her extended family getting together almost every Sunday. "The old people made everybody go to church and they cooked for everybody," she recalls. "Like, you know, you just go to Grandma's house and she'd have a big pot of this and a big pot of that."

They always went to church first. If someone didn't go, Rae reminisces, "they would just get slammed, like, 'How dare you skip church and come to dinner?'" She laughs. "So that made everybody go to church. And that was pretty much—that's all we did. We ate and we talked and talked and ate."

Food was at the center of Rae's childhood. "Food is what brought everybody together," she says. "It played a huge role. *The* role. There was no gathering that we came together for that food was not important." Continuing to enumerate the central role of food in her childhood, Rae notes, "You know, food got us up in the morning without fussing. Breakfast was ready; come and eat. You smelled the biscuits, you smelled the fatback, and there was no question that this is what got us up. We sat down at the table, everybody, and we ate every single night together. And Sundays were the big church gatherings."

The Sunday table was always loaded with typical southern dishes: fried chicken or fried fish, biscuits, greens or string beans cooked with fatback, sweet potato pie. These are the foods that Rae's grandma and aunts made every week, and these are the foods that she still finds comforting.[1]

But Rae's family no longer gets together for Sunday dinner. At six, Tyler has not been to a single one. "We got busy," Rae says, trying to explain how such an important tradition could end so abruptly. "We started having families, but that's no excuse. They did it forever when we were little. I think the old people paid more attention to it."

Rae's generation took the dinners for granted. "We didn't really think about it," she acknowledges. They didn't think about the time that went into preparing those big meals, or what a financial strain it must have been for her grandma, who was on a fixed income, to feed so many people, she says. Today, it's hard to imagine anyone being willing to pick up the mantle. "I don't think that anybody will be like, 'Y'all come over *every single* Sunday, bring your family and bring your kids, and we'll just eat," Rae laughs. "Selfish. I don't know."

Rae's trying to avoid eating fried food and biscuits these days, and she wouldn't want the responsibility of cooking for so many people. But she yearns for those Sunday dinners. "It was huge," she says. "I do miss it."

Tyler probably wouldn't even know what she was talking about if she started telling him about those big family meals, with everyone gathered around platters of fried chicken and sweet potato pie, Rae imagines. She laughs as she says this but then becomes more serious. The ritual of the Sunday dinners brought everyone together, rain or shine. But those days are gone. "It's a really bad thing," she says. "Everyone's still in Raleigh, but we never get together to eat. I was just telling Kenny this morning that I need to go see my aunt and my older relatives. And Tyler is missing out."

Rae is proud of the fact that she and Kenny are making a good living and are successful at their careers, but it seems as though her family's prosperity has come at a price. Sacrificing Sunday meals means she feels less connected to the rest of her family. Tyler hasn't experienced these gatherings, so he doesn't know what he's missing. But Rae worries he's losing out on the opportunity to have the close bonds she remembers from her childhood, with everyone together around the Sunday dinner table.

It's not just Rae's extended family that has stopped getting together for meals. Americans today are less likely to invite people over for dinner than we were in previous generations. In *Bowling Alone*, Robert Putnam cites a decline in entertaining at home as evidence of our growing social isolation. In the 1970s, the average American "entertained friends at home" between fourteen and fifteen times a year—hosting dinner parties, organizing card games, and inviting people over for coffee. By the late 1990s, people hosted friends only eight times a year. "Visits with friends are now on the social capital endangered list," Putnam writes, warning that if these declines continue at the same pace, our "centuries-old practice of entertaining friends at home might entirely disappear from American life in less than a generation."[2]

Bowling Alone was published almost twenty years ago, but the trend that Putnam identified has persisted. The proportion of people who said they had entertained in their home at least twelve times in the past year dropped from two in five people in the 1970s to fewer than one in five in 2003. Over the same period, the share of people who reported "frequently" or even "ever" hosting dinner parties declined just as much.[3]

Why have we stopped having people over for dinner?[4] Some people attribute the death of the dinner party to changes in our family and work lives. People are working longer hours and commuting farther and don't have as much time to socialize.[5] Others blame technological innovations like social media and the internet, which may have "privatized" our leisure time, making it more tempting to stay home and watch Netflix or play video games than go to a friend's house to play cards.[6] Finally, as occurred in Rae's family when her grandmother and older relatives were no longer able to organize and make those large meals, "generational shifts" play a role, as the older generation is replaced by their less-engaged children and grandchildren.[7]

Studies confirm that Americans are more socially isolated than they were in the past.[8] Our social networks—the friends, neighbors, and relatives with whom we can discuss important issues—have shrunk. But although people are less likely to have others over for dinner, they are also dedicating more time to their nuclear family. Married couples spend more time hanging out with each other than they did in the 1960s, and there has been a large increase in "family time" among married couples with children. People spent, on average, about two hours per day with their spouse and child(ren) in 1965; this had jumped to almost three hours a day by 2012.[9] Quality time with children has also increased.[10] And some researchers argue that Americans do still get together with friends; it's just that the location has changed. When we get together with people, we're now more likely to meet at a park for a playdate or a bar for happy hour than someone's home.[11]

In other words, the simplest explanation—that we don't have people over for dinner because we work too much and then collapse on the couch to play around on our smartphones—doesn't really hold up. Part of the answer is that we are spending more time with our partners and children.

Even if Rae did manage to get her family together on Sundays again, there would still be the question of what to serve. Rae has fond memories of eating fried fish, fried chicken, and fresh vegetables from the garden. It was tasty, but "it was a lot of fried this and fried that," she says ruefully. Nowadays people are focused as much on what's *in* the food as who's around the table eating it. And it's gotten pretty complicated.

Many members of Rae's family are dealing with chronic health issues. Rae wants Tyler to eat differently from how she ate growing up, in part because she worries about him developing the same health problems that run in her family. But it's hard to imagine some of her older relatives agreeing to a dramatically different menu from the typical southern fare of her childhood.

For others, hosting dinner may be complicated by guests' food allergies or the specialized diets they've adopted—gluten-free, vegetarian, vegan, or Paleo—in the name of health.[12]

No wonder having people over for dinner seems so daunting.

25 CUPCAKES FOR COUSIN

It's Saturday night, and Ashley Taylor has just finished a long shift at Wendy's. The day is not over, though. She has plans to make cupcakes with her two young daughters as a treat for Marquan's cousin Chris, who is staying with them as he gets back on his feet. Chris is in his mid-twenties and got out of prison not long ago. Wanting to see him repair things with his wife and kids and get his life on track again, Ashley and Marquan Taylor are doing what they can to help. Marquan vouched for Chris to get a job at Wendy's, where he and Ashley and Marquan's nineteen-year-old brother, Anton, all work. They're already renting their only spare bedroom to Anton, but Ashley and Marquan told Chris he could sleep on their couch for as long as he needs.

The Taylors have a full house, but they are committed to bringing Chris back into the family fold after his time in prison. Making cupcakes in his honor is part of that effort.

For decades, African Americans have been heavily targeted by heightened criminal justice surveillance and punishment. Racial profiling, stop-and-frisk policing, and mandatory sentencing policies have contributed to an era of mass incarceration. Young black men like Chris are especially likely to be imprisoned and have to figure out how to pick up the pieces of their lives afterwards.[1]

Marquan and Ashley's efforts—offering up a couch, making special meals, and helping track down employment and other opportunities—are part of the everyday work black families undertake to help reintegrate formerly incarcerated black men into their communities and resist having their criminal records define them.[2] Food plays an important role in these efforts and has long been an important way African Americans have resisted oppression.[3] Making cupcakes for Chris seems like a small act, but it holds great significance. And like so many women who have taken care to manage the seemingly everyday and mundane aspects of family life, such as remembering birthdays and anniversaries, Ashley Taylor shoulders much of the responsibility for making the evening a memorable one.

Tonight, everyone is home for a change. Chris, Anton, and Anton's girlfriend, Shontay, are playing video games in the living room. Chris is still in his Wendy's uniform, his shirt untucked. He sits on the couch where he sleeps every night. Shontay and Anton have only recently started dating, and she doesn't know the family well. She sits shyly next to Anton, her attention directed at the TV. Anton's smudged glasses slip down his nose as he leans forward, holding the game controller. He has to regularly prod them back up with his index finger.

Ashley and Marquan confer in the kitchen about the cupcakes. Like Chris, Marquan still hasn't changed out of his work outfit. Ashley changed as soon as she got home, into a blue T-shirt and black basketball shorts. She doesn't like the way the smell of cooking grease clings to her uniform.

Maylee and Qianah kneel on a bench at the kitchen table, their hands folded in front of them, eagerly waiting to start making the cupcakes. They are wearing matching gauzy teal skorts and gray T-shirts. Their shirts are adorned with a life-size head of a blonde Barbie and the words "Sweet Dreams" written below it. Turning to the girls, Ashley tells them to go wash their hands in the bathroom while she gets everything ready.

Marquan pulls a box out of the top cupboard. "Chocolate chip?" he asks.

"No, we're making cupcakes, not cookies," Ashley gently chides. She reaches for a box of Betty Crocker Rainbow Chip Cake Mix. Rummaging around in the lower cupboards for a bowl, she eventually produces a battered plastic ice cream tub. She places the tub on the table in front of the girls, who managed to wash their hands in record time.

Marquan tears open the bag of cake mix and hands it to Maylee "Me do it!" she clamors, dumping most of the cake mix into the bowl in a big plop. A puff of the cake mix powder rises from the bowl and settles on the table. When the bag is almost empty, Marquan takes it from Maylee and gives it to Qianah, who earnestly shakes the remnants into the bowl.

There's barely room on the small kitchen counter for the large cardboard box of five-dozen eggs Ashley has pulled out of the fridge. The box teeters perilously on the edge as she gets an egg out.

"How many?" she asks the girls. She takes the egg and cracks it on the side of the counter near the sink; the plastic bowl she's using to make the cupcakes is too flimsy to crack an egg on.

"One," Maylee says dutifully.

Ashley cracks another egg in the bowl.

"Two," Maylee says.

A third egg is cracked.

"One," Maylee says again.

"No," Ashley corrects her. "What come after two?"

"Five?" Maylee tentatively suggests.

"No," Ashley says. She prods, "One, two, . . . ?" After a pause she answers herself. "Three." Maylee, who has just turned three, repeats the number reverently.

Next, Ashley gets a one-gallon jug of store brand vegetable oil from an upper cabinet. Muttering to herself, she digs through a lower cabinet and eventually produces a plastic measuring cup. In goes a third of a cup of oil and a cup of water.

It's time to mix the batter and, after a quick search, Ashley realizes she must have loaned the electric mixer to someone. Marquan looks at her, concerned. "It's okay. We'll just mix it with our hands," she quickly reassures him. She tells the girls they will have to stir fast to mix the batter by hand. "Stir it up real good," she says.

The girls zealously and clumsily mix the batter with their small forks. "Do it. Do it!" says Qianah excitedly. She flicks the fork as if she is splatter painting. Batter flies across the kitchen.

Ashley is momentarily distracted by the TV in the adjacent living room. Marquan has joined Chris, Anton, and Shontay, who have switched from playing video games to watching the horror film *Jeepers Creepers*. Maylee and Qianah take surreptitious bites of the cupcake batter, thinking their mom's attention is elsewhere.

Ashley is making cupcakes because she wants to show Chris, a family member going through a difficult time, that he is loved. She is also teaching her daughters the importance of doing things for and with family. This is a key principle in Ashley's life.

Like most Americans, especially those in low-income families, Ashley and Marquan live relatively close to their extended families.[4] Ashley and Marquan both grew up in North Carolina and have deep family roots in their rural county. Marquan's great-grandmother still lives in the home she bought with her husband in 1969, the same house where Marquan was raised. It's just ten minutes down the road. A number of Marquan's cousins live nearby, as well as Ashley's six half-siblings—a brother and five sisters. (Ashley never calls them "half" though, simply referring to them as her brother and sisters.) One of her sisters rents the trailer next door.

Relatives constantly come and go from the Taylors' place, giving Ashley or Marquan a ride to or from work, stopping by to borrow something or play video games, or dropping off the girls from a playdate.

Spending time with family is very important to Ashley and Marquan. Qianah is so close to Ashley's brother Rob that she gets jealous when he is around other kids. Rob recently started dating a woman with a baby, inflaming Qianah. Upset to see Uncle Rob with a baby on his lap, she clambered onto him, and he had to quickly pass the baby off to prevent her from climbing on top of them both. Ashley describes her relatives as "family-oriented" and relishes the times when they all get together. As it is for many families, food is an important aspect of such gatherings.

Making cupcakes in Chris's honor is an affirmation of his place in the Taylor family. It also recruits Chris into the web of family and kin-like ties that the Taylors, and many families, depend on to survive.[5] Work and family policies in the United States make it hard for parents to juggle the demands of raising children on their own.[6] Most families get help from their "networks of care": the family members and friends who pitch in and help out, forming a safety net that catches and cushions them and helps them bounce back from everyday challenges.[7]

These ties are reciprocal, based on the idea that people will give help when they can, and in turn, they will receive help when they need it. These days, Ashley and Marquan are in the position to lend things out, like their electric mixer, and provide a place for family members to stay. But not that long ago, they relied on their families to house them. And they still depend heavily on family networks for things like childcare, transportation, and emotional support. When Chris gets back on his feet, he may be in a position to help them if the need arises.

Networks of care and family ties do not magically appear and sustain themselves, however. They require cultivation and maintenance. It takes time, it takes intention, and it takes skill to create and preserve a sense of family. By declaring that the cupcake evening is for Chris, Ashley is engaging in a very deliberate process that helps to form the feelings of closeness and intimacy people associate with families.[8] Food preparation and feeding others are so strongly associated with family that they shape and define family life in many ways.[9] And because historically the work of making food and caring for family members have been understood as women's work, women are more likely to take on the invisible labor of using food to sustain family relationships.[10]

Marquan checks on the cupcake progress in the kitchen. Maylee and Qianah are treating the batter like edible finger paint. They have their hands in the bowl, and batter is going everywhere. A fair amount is making it to their mouths.

Observing this, Marquan turns to Ashley. "You know they're eating?" he asks.

"I know they're eating," Ashley replies dryly.

The girls look euphoric. It's not every day they get to eat cupcake batter, and they bask in the delight of the stolen pleasure.

"I caught you!" Ashley says teasingly when she spots Qianah taking a bite.

"Mom, it's finished," declares Maylee.

"Finished?" Ashley asks. She tests the batter, gives it a few vigorous stirs and proclaims that yes, it is done.

Ashley sticks pale yellow cupcake liners in a muffin tin, then places the tin on the counter. She starts to spoon batter into the liners using a shallow dinner spoon. It is slow going.

Her hands still covered in batter, Maylee talks excitedly about the pink sprinkles she has picked out to decorate the cupcakes.

"Of course, she chose pink," Ashley says to Marquan. Ashley and Marquan often describe Maylee as their "girly-girl." Ashley's mom once bought Maylee a car seat that she refused to sit in because it was brown and thus not girly. The story gets told often, and Maylee always puffs up when she hears it, proud of her commitment to all things feminine.

Ashley asks Marquan to wash the girls' hands. He takes them into the bathroom. While they are gone, a short, wiry man comes into the trailer. He's wearing a white T-shirt and baggy jeans. One eye is very bloodshot. He and Chris talk quietly.

Ashley gets the cupcakes into the oven and then turns to Chris and the man. "Oh no, you got to go," she tells the man. He ducks his head abashedly, making no effort defend himself. Chris worriedly ushers the man to the door.

After he leaves, Ashley says indignantly to Chris, "I don't know [if] he intoxicated. You should see what he did to my floor the other day! I don't even know what he did. It was something. French fries everywhere. I came out and I thought he was dead." The furrow between Chris's eyes deepens as he apologizes to Ashley, promising it won't happen again.

Ashley is doing her best to help Chris, but he runs with a crowd that's rough around the edges, and she's not happy about his friends coming around drunk and making a mess in her home. She is firm throughout the conversation but keeps a smile on her face. She doesn't want Chris to feel unwelcome, but she needs to establish some boundaries. She wants Chris to be a family man, not to spend his time partying with his friends.

Marquan and the girls return from the bathroom, oblivious to the tense scene that has just unfolded. They settle in the living room, where the horror movie is now reaching a climax. "Is she going to die?" Maylee asks, referring to a female character in the movie.

"No, she's smart," someone answers. Maylee repeats the question two more times, as is her habit, and gets the same response. Mollified, her face relaxes, and she watches the movie. On the screen, a bat-like creature is wreaking havoc on a small town while a psychic makes ominous predictions.

Ashley goes into the kitchen to check on the cupcakes. Qianah dashes in to hover behind her.

"Back up," Ashley says to Qianah four times, sounding more exasperated each time. Finally, Qianah backs up ever so slightly. She eagerly watches the cupcakes as they come out of the oven.

Steam rises off the cupcakes, and Ashley places the hot tin on the stovetop. She presses the cupcakes. They bounce back. They are done.

Seeing the cupcakes coming out of the oven, Maylee asks Marquan to wash her hands, even though he washed them not long ago. He picks her up and holds her over the kitchen sink. He squirts dishwashing liquid into her hands, and she rubs them together vigorously under the running water. Marquan repeats this process with Qianah, who is not as effective as her big sister at getting the soap off herself. Marquan gently rubs her palms with his spare hand, helping her clear away the soap bubbles.

The children's hands now clean, Marquan gets two disposable plastic spoons from a bag in the pantry and a container of Betty Crocker vanilla icing from the fridge. The icing has already been opened, and about a quarter of it is gone. Ashley says quietly that the cupcakes will be too hot to ice, but nevertheless starts to take them out of the tin and place them in front of the girls, who are once again kneeling on the bench.

"I want to do it. I want to make a cake," Maylee demands.

Marquan scoops out a small spoonful of icing for each girl, then walks away to joining Anton and Chris, who are now playing a loud video game. They crouch on the coffee table, game controllers in their hands, staring intently at the screen.

Ashley's back is turned as she prepares the next batch of cupcakes at the counter. Qianah immediately eats the spoonful of icing her dad gave her. Seeing this, Maylee tentatively licks at hers. She then dabs a small amount of icing on each of the six cupcakes lined up in front of her.

"Mom, I'm finished," she announces.

"You finished?" Ashley asks. "Doing what, Baby?"

"Icing the cake."

"Huh?" Ashley asks distractedly.

"Icing the cake," Maylee repeats.

Ashley turns around and says, "What you doing with it? You just eating the icing!" Qianah has an icing moustache and looks deliriously happy.

Ashley takes the icing from the girls just as Marquan comes back into the kitchen. Maylee scoots into the living room to offer Shontay one of the cupcakes she has iced, but she shakes her head no. Ashley says teasingly, "Chris gonna be sick today," implying that if no one else wants to eat the cupcakes, Chris may have to eat them all.

Still kneeling on the bench, Qianah is happy to help eat the cupcakes. She digs her fingers into one of the six lined up in front of her.

Using two spoons, Marquan artfully sculpts dollops of icing onto a few of the cupcakes. They look almost like store-bought cupcakes when he's done.

Maylee comes running back.

"What's that, Daddy? That yours?" she asks.

Marquan doesn't answer.

Qianah jumps in and asks, "That Maylee's, Daddy?"

"Yep," Marquan replies.

"That Chris's," Maylee sternly corrects him. She swivels around on the bench and calls into the living room, "Chris, come get your cake." She holds up the plastic jar of pink sprinkles as enticement.

Chris doesn't respond. The cupcake making is in his honor, but he isn't exactly playing along. Maylee shrugs and returns to decorating her cupcakes. Marquan bends awkwardly over the girls as he tries to contain the mess. Qianah, who has a sweet tooth, is chowing down. She takes the cupcake Marquan has just iced and eats the entire dollop of icing off the top. Then she uses her icing spoon to dig into the cupcake, eating big bites. She now has an icing beard to match her moustache.

Marquan sits down heavily on the bench between the girls. Still in his Wendy's uniform, he looks tired and hot. He had a long, busy shift today. He helps Maylee open the jar of sprinkles, telling her she can put some on the cupcakes lined up in front of her. The small dabs of icing she applied earlier have mostly dissolved into the still warm cupcakes.

Having put the next batch of cupcakes in the oven, Ashley sits on the coffee table next to Anton and grabs one of the game controllers. She laughs and eggs him on as they battle each other in the video game.

Qianah peels the liner off yet another cupcake and smushes it into her mouth.

Delicately, but with great intensity, Maylee shakes pink sprinkles onto the cupcakes in front of her. She puts only a small amount on each cupcake. Most don't stick, because the icing has melted.

Icing is dripping down the corners of Qianah's mouth. She reaches for the sprinkles. There's a bit of a struggle.

"Mine!" Maylee says firmly three times.

Marquan intervenes and gives the sprinkles to Qianah. "Let Qia do this one," he says softly.

Maylee relents. Qianah shakes the jar recklessly over her cupcakes. Marquan lets her shake sprinkles over Maylee's too, until Maylee says indignantly, "Dad they're already on," and Marquan redirects Qianah to her own cupcakes. The tops of Qianah's cupcakes are thoroughly covered in pink sprinkles, whereas Maylee's cupcakes are only sparsely sprinkled.

Finished with her round, Ashley comes into the kitchen while Marquan takes her place at the video game.

"I put it on there," Qianah says.

"Huh?" Ashley asks.

Qianah repeats herself.

"I see! Those are beautiful cupcakes," Ashley praises the girls.

There are five cupcakes in front of Maylee and six in front of Qianah. Maylee's are untouched, whereas Qianah's are in a state of disarray, with the icing either completely licked off or the cupcake partially eaten. Qianah is now sneakily eating the sprinkles off the top of one of Maylee's cupcakes. Ashley laughs when she sees the cupcakes and says she is going to take a picture for Grandma. "Those are beautiful cupcakes," she repeats as she takes a picture with her smartphone. By taking pictures to share with Grandma, praising the girls for their concoctions, and letting them sneak bites behind her back, Ashley engages in the invisible labor that helps the girls form positive memories of the cupcake-making evening.

Qianah digs another hunk of icing off a cupcake to eat. Maylee selects a cupcake that isn't iced and peels the liner off. She pulls the cupcake apart and eats a small piece, no thicker than a slice of bread, and then runs into the living room to join the adults, leaving the majority of the cupcake uneaten.

Ashley says to Qianah, "Look at your face. It's full of icing!"

Maylee sits on the coffee table between Marquan and Anton. They are both leaning forward, the controllers in their hands, concentrating on the game. Maylee's feet are crossed at the ankle and dangle cutely.

"Damn," mumbles Marquan, as the sound of gunfire from the video game ricochets around the trailer. Shontay is still sitting quietly in the corner of the love seat.

Chris has gone outside to smoke. He doesn't come back inside. The man with the bloodshot eye who came in the trailer earlier, only to be evicted by Ashley, is still outside. He and Chris talk animatedly, beer cans in their hands. Cupcakes aren't really Chris's thing, but he appreciates the gesture. Separated from his own family and going through a difficult time after his incarceration, he knows that being included in the cupcake-making evening was meant to make him feel like an important part of the family. Ashley hopes he will eventually step up and become an uncle-like figure to the girls, leaving behind friends who may derail him, like the guy with the bloodshot eye.

Cupcakes may leave Chris feeling nonplused, but they will likely hold fond memories for Maylee and Qianah.

26 THANKSGIVING

"What should I do with the yams?" Tara Foley calls across the kitchen to her mother, Vicky. A large foil pan of yams, roasted and mashed and then mixed with brown sugar and maple syrup, sits on the counter. Tara puts her hands on her hips as she waits for Vicky's answer. She is wearing pink sweatpants and a T-shirt, and her dirty blonde hair is pulled back into a messy ponytail.

"Add butter, put it in the oven, and then take it out and add the marshmallows," Vicky instructs. Vicky's hair is also pulled back in a ponytail. She is dressed comfortably in an oversized gray T-shirt and pajama pants. The deep grooves around her eyes and mouth are telltale signs of her many years of smoking.

Tara uses a metal spoon to scoop margarine out of a plastic tub and plops two generous spoonfuls on top of the yams. "Is that enough?" she asks expectantly.

"You need several spoonfuls more," Vickie tells her, glancing at the pan. Tara dutifully spoons margarine into each corner of the pan.

It's a little after 9:00 AM on Thanksgiving morning, and Tara and Vicky are both tired. Around midnight the night before, Tara got a flat tire on her way home from Walmart. She had gone there to buy food for the big Thanksgiving meal, which they had decided to hold at Vicky's house. She couldn't call anyone, because her cell service has been temporarily disconnected. Fortunately, Tara wasn't that far from home. She managed to walk to the house, get the spare tire, walk back to the car, take the flat tire off the car, replace it with the spare, and drive home. She is proud to have done this on her own, without asking for help. But it was very late by the time she got to bed, and she had to wake up early to get to Vicky's house to cook.

Vicky is exhausted as well. "I've been up since 2:00 this morning cookin' the turkey and pies," she informs her daughter. Vicky likes to have Thanksgiving dinner early and aims to have everything done by 11:00 AM. But this means she had to start cooking in the middle of the night. Three pies—apple, blueberry, and chocolate—beckon temptingly from the counter. The turkey, also done, is covered with foil and sitting on the counter.

Tara's two young sons, Tyree and Rashan, wander in from the living room where they slept the night before. It was easier to have them sleep at Vicky's since Tara knew the Thanksgiving preparations would start early.

"Good morning, baby," Tara says to Tyree, who is still moving slowly, having just gotten up a few minutes ago. He takes the earbuds out of his ears.

"Good morning," he mumbles, blinking his eyes.

Rashan isn't as groggy as his older brother and eagerly scans the food on the kitchen counter. His thick hair has been braided into long cornrows that dangle around his shoulders. They have gotten frizzy and need to be redone.

Now finished putting butter on the yams, Tara reaches for the bag of jumbo marshmallows on the counter. She tears open the bag, preparing to sprinkle them on top of the yams. "The marshmallows come later, baby," Vicky reminds her.

"Okay," Tara replies, putting the bag back on the counter. Tara takes pride in her cooking skills, but she has never made this dish. Her relationship with her mother is also perennially strained, and today, it seems she is willing to take cues from Vicky to avoid conflict.

"Can I have some?" asks Rashan, who has been closely tracking everything Tara is doing. She hands him a marshmallow. Satisfied, he pads back into the living room, where the TV is tuned to a Thanksgiving Day parade.

"Can I see the turkey?" asks Tyree, pulling back the foil that covers the turkey. He reaches in and pinches the turkey.

"You need to wait," Vicky tells him firmly, quickly putting the foil back. Tyree shrugs and puts his earbuds back in. "You better not break those like you did the last pair," she warns as he leaves the kitchen.

Perhaps no other holiday in the United States better symbolizes the relationship between food and family than Thanksgiving. The national story of Thanksgiving dates back to 1621, in Plymouth, Massachusetts, when white colonists held a festival attended by Native Americans to celebrate the corn harvest; this led to the story of Pilgrim and native people coming together to give thanks for the harvest. In 1789, President George Washington named November 26 a day of national thanksgiving. But Thanksgiving didn't really take off until 1863, when, prompted by intense lobbying by magazine editor Sarah Josepha Hale, President Abraham Lincoln declared the fourth Thursday in November a national holiday. Deemed a "holiday of family homecoming," Thanksgiving was meant to reassert the primacy of the family at a time when many believed that changes brought about by industrialization and urbanization posed a threat to American family unity.[1] In 1941, Congress made Thanksgiving Day a federal legal holiday, further solidifying Thanksgiving's place in the pantheon of American holidays.[2]

Today, most Americans spend Thanksgiving cooking and eating, and some go shopping.[3] Americans consistently identify Thanksgiving as the happiest day of the year, a day traditionally spent with family and friends. And the percentage of Americans who say they are most grateful for family at Thanksgiving has risen over time, suggesting that Thanksgiving offers families a treasured time to connect with one another.[4]

But there is also discontent. A lot of people say there is family conflict during Thanksgiving, a holiday that arrives just a few weeks after Election Day. Polls find that many families grapple with the issue of how to keep politics off the Thanksgiving menu.[5] Large gatherings like Thanksgiving are also stressful because people usually have high hopes for creating idyllic memories. We hope nothing will go wrong, and it's easy to end up feeling disappointed by the realities of getting a group of people together, all with their own opinions, and feeding them a large meal that takes hours or even days to prepare. The stress and tension people feel at Thanksgiving is so common and relatable that it is routinely the topic of Hollywood films, TV, and memoirs.[6]

Moreover, as was true in 1621, women do far more of the cooking at Thanksgiving than men, and, not surprisingly, they report greater levels of stress during the holidays.[7] Lincoln proclaimed Thanksgiving a national holiday during the Victorian era, and the holiday exemplified that period's efforts to anchor women to the realm of home and family, according to historian Elizabeth Pleck. "Thanksgiving was a day of intensified patriarchy," she writes, "when the differences between male and female responsibilities was pronounced."[8] For many women, the Thanksgiving meal still revolves around cooking food for others and serving them, in the name of the family.

The meal is also supposed to be an opulent display of abundance and even excess. Vicky hasn't prepared just one or two pies; she's made three. But expectations of plenty on the Thanksgiving table can be hard for families to achieve, leaving lots of people feeling like they aren't measuring up and poor families wondering how they're going to pay for it all.[9]

In fact, among the many things keeping Tara up at night is figuring out how she is going to pay her bills and get through Christmas next month.[10] Having two major holidays—Thanksgiving and Christmas—so near one another, both with expectations of bountifulness, creates major financial strain for many low-income families.[11] Tara has no cash income and no idea how she is going to get the boys Christmas presents and make sure there is food on the table next month. But she is determined to make the holidays special. It's part of her mission to give her sons the childhood she wishes she had known.

It's after ten o'clock. Vicky sets a pot of water on the stove to boil for the macaroni. All that is left to make are some side dishes, including macaroni and cheese.[12] She sits down at the kitchen table to smoke a cigarette, feeling fatigue setting in. Tara waits until the water is boiling and then empties a large bag of elbow noodles into the pot.

"I already salted the water, so you don't have to," Vicky says, smoke curling around her head.

Tara puts another pot of water on the stove to boil and adds several pieces of fatback to the water. "Where's the can opener?" she asks, holding up an industrial-sized can of green beans. Vicky puts her cigarette in the ashtray and searches the kitchen drawers, but she is unable to find it.

"Do you know where it is?" Vicky asks Phillip, Tara's stepfather, who has just finished washing dishes. A quiet man in his mid-fifties, Phillip is wearing faded boot-cut jeans and a black shirt. His stomach fills out his shirt. He doesn't know where the opener is but volunteers to use a knife to open the can.

"No," Vicky tells him curtly. "It's too dangerous." She digs around in the kitchen, eventually finding an older metal can opener that everyone avoids using because it gets stuck easily.

Tara dubiously takes the old can opener from Vicky's outstretched hand. Her concerns about its inadequacy are almost immediately confirmed as she struggles to latch it onto the can. "Keep at it. You can do it," Phillip teases. Tara eventually gets the opener latched on, then starts to turn the crank. As it slowly grinds around the can, she complains that it is hurting her thumb because she has to push so hard.

"Are you sure you don't have another can opener?" she asks plaintively.

When Vicky says no, Tara quietly but audibly says, "You suck." She doesn't say it in a mean way, exactly, but neither is it completely playful or joking.

Vicky doesn't respond.

Tara finally succeeds at opening the jumbo-sized can of beans. She drains and rinses the beans and adds them to the pot of boiling water and fatback. Vicky opens, drains, and rinses two smaller cans of green beans and adds them to the pot.

Tara glances at the macaroni, still boiling on the stove. "How do you know when the macaroni is cooked?" she asks Vicky.

"You could figure it out the old school way and throw the pasta at the wall or the cabinets," Vicky laughs. "Or you could see if it looks white."

Tara peers into the pot. Satisfied the noodles are cooked, she gets a metal strainer ready in the sink and then grabs the pot by the handle. It's too heavy for her to pour one-handed, but she can't hold the other side without burning her hand. "Help, help, help!" she calls frantically. Vicky grabs a dish towel and uses it to anchor the other side of the pot. Together, they dump the noodles and boiling water into the strainer.

Tara and Vicky have a complicated relationship. Tara feels she didn't have much of a childhood. At thirteen, she moved in with a friend because she and her stepfather weren't getting along. She got pregnant with Tyree at seventeen and gave birth to him just a few months after turning eighteen. "I had to grow up fast," she says wearily. Her brother's death, when Tara was twenty, was a tough time for the entire family.

Committed to giving her kids the kind of life she didn't have growing up, Tara is adamant she will do what it takes to raise them properly.

"I would never put men above my children," she says, her jaw set. Her mom was married and divorced several times. It bothers Tara that when she quarreled with her mom's partners, Vicky often didn't take her side.

"The only thing that's worth anything in this world to me is my children. That's the only thing I have. That's the only thing that's going to love me for the rest of my life," Tara says.[13]

She is determined that history will not repeat itself. She is going to be a different kind of mother than Vicky was to her. She will put her children first.

Tara pulls the bubbling pan of macaroni and cheese out of the oven and sets it next to the yam casserole, now covered with marshmallows and golden brown from the oven. The turkey is sliced. The collards and green beans, seasoned with fatback, and the mashed potatoes, made from a box, are ready to serve.

"Come eat!" calls Tara, getting plates down from an upper cabinet and stacking them on the counter.

Fifteen-year-old Jennifer and her boyfriend Artemis, who have been dozing on the two bare mattresses scattered on the floor of the guest bedroom, make their way to the kitchen. Jennifer has been temporarily living with Tara since her family was evicted from their house a few months ago. For the last few days, Artemis has been staying with her too.

Tyree and Rashan need no calling. They have been hovering in the kitchen for most of the morning and are now seated at the kitchen table, patiently waiting. Tara scoops a bit of everything onto two kid-sized plates. Of the three seats at the table, Tyree and Rashan take two, and Artemis occupies the third.

Tara serves Artemis a heaping plateful of food and then offers to fill Jennifer's plate for her. A picky eater, Jennifer opts to get her own food. She hovers around the food, deliberating over each item. Tara, Vicky, and Phillip get their food last. It's just after 11:30, only a few minutes behind Vicky's schedule.

COMMUNION

By six o'clock in the evening, fifteen cars are parked alongside Ana and Tomas Rivera's house. The party, in honor of their daughter Julia's First Communion, has just started. Julia is Rosario García's niece, and most of the guests are her relatives and close friends.

It's humid and hot, still in the eighties. People fan themselves to get some relief from the heat. Many make a beeline for the house, where the tantalizing smell of food that's been cooking for hours draws them in.

Rosario, Ana, and Julia's godmother, Teresa, started cooking large batches of food at 7 AM, finishing by 3 PM so they could turn their attention to other matters, like setting up for the party.

Along with Tomas and Rosario's husband, Samuel, they unfurl and hoist a large blue tent in one corner of the yard and set up an inflatable castle, rented just for the party, in the other corner.

Once everything is ready, they stand back to see how it looks. Four long tables—covered with red, white, and blue tablecloths—are arranged under the tent. Plastic forks and spoons and napkins have been placed on each table. Four coolers are filled with drinks: Pepsi and Sunkist, Bud Light, and Little Hugs fruit drinks for the kids.

Everyone is wearing their party clothes. Rosario has on an orange T-shirt and white skinny pants with a flowery motif and black sandals. Her hair, usually pulled back in a tight ponytail, is loose and wavy for the party. She has applied black eye liner and eye shadow as a finishing touch. Ana is wearing Capri jeans, a black T-shirt with purple flowers, and black flip-flops. Samuel and Tomas are dressed very similarly, in plaid shirts tucked into Wrangler blue jeans.

Rosario and the other women started heating up the food thirty minutes before the first guests arrived. "It should be eaten hot,"

Rosario comments, although this is no small task. The food, which has been cooked in large aluminum pots, must go back on the stove to be warmed. There are more pots than stove burners, so a portable electric range with two burners has been set up to allow all six pots of food to be heated at once. Timing is key. All of the dishes need to be served hot at the same time. Once the food is sufficiently hot, each pot is placed on a trivet on the kitchen table, to prevent leaving permanent marks. The stove has been on for most of the day, and the kitchen is sweltering.

Rosario's three children run around the yard with their cousins and friends as the adults work. They arrived at seven this morning with Rosario. Santiago and Victoria are wearing their usual outfits of T-shirts and shorts, but Gabi decided to dress up for the party, in a denim dress and patent-leather shoes. Their cousin Julia, the one who is being celebrated today, is dressed in a shimmering white dress. Her long brown hair trails behind her as she chases her cousins around the yard. All of the kids are hot and sweaty, their hair plastered to their foreheads.

In the kitchen, Rosario glances around, taking inventory of the food. Ana splurged and purchased a whole pig for the party. The pork has been seasoned with fresh herbs and slow roasted. It turned out tender, juicy, and absolutely delicious, Rosario thinks.

Along with the pork, they have *frijoles puercos*, beans cooked in the northern Mexico style, with chorizo, chiles, and cheese; *chicharrones*, crispy pieces of pork skin; and red and green salsa.[1] Rosario prepared the chicharrón using her own recipe. She fried it with banana leaves, which she often uses in her cooking, to "give it flavor."[2] She also made the salsas. The red salsa, she explains, is made with *guajillo* chiles. Rosario sautéed the chiles in one pan and the onions in another, then combined the chiles and onions with red tomatoes and garlic before puréeing the mixture. The green salsa, deceptively spicy, is made of puréed green tomatoes, jalapeño peppers, cilantro, avocado, and garlic.

"And of course, we made rice," notes Rosario, peering into a big pot of rice to make sure they have enough. They decided to buy the tortillas, even though Rosario often makes her own. It will be hard enough to keep the tortillas warm for so many people. They are expecting a big crowd.

The party is in honor of Julia's First Communion. Communion is one of seven sacraments within the Catholic church. In its modern iteration, stemming from a 1910 papal decree, it's intended to represent the early stages of a child's religious education.[3]

Mexican identity and Catholic identity are tightly intertwined. Eighty-one percent of people in Mexico and 61 percent of Mexican Americans identify as Catholic.[4] Originating with the sixteenth-century spiritual (and military) conquest of indigenous people by Spanish colonists, Mexican Catholicism (as practiced both by people in Mexico and by Mexican Americans) is distinct from other forms of Catholicism; it is more centered on oral tradition, celebrations, and festivities.[5] In Mexico, fiestas and celebrations commemorate religious holidays, such as the feast day of Our Lady of Guadalupe, Mexico's most beloved saint. They also honor individual sacraments and milestones, including a baby's baptism, a child's First Communion, and a young woman's *quinceañera* (fifteenth birthday).[6]

These celebrations have deep religious significance,[7] but they go beyond that. For Mexican American families like Rosario's, they are a way of maintaining ties to their communities in Mexico and the United States. By recreating traditions and customs that they associate with Mexico or remember from their own childhoods, Mexican Americans express their identity as Mexican. Celebrations like Julia's First Communion also serve as collective reminders for Mexican Americans "of the importance of memory and tradition in their adjustment to life *en el otro lado*, on the other side" of the US-Mexico border, writes Chicano/a studies professor Mario García.[8]

By seven, the party is in full swing. Rosario and Ana run back and forth between the kitchen and the tables, busy with all of the jobs they have to do. They serve food as people arrive and warm it back up as the hours pass. New batches of tortillas are heated on the stove and placed in small baskets on the tables. Bowls of salsa are replenished. Drink cups are refilled. As one wave of people leaves, the women quickly clear the tables to make room for the next guests.

Samuel and Tomas greet the male guests as they arrive. With a hug and a slap on the back, they invite them to come around to the back of the house, where several generations, dressed in plaid shirts and cowboy hats, congregate over cans of Bud Light.

The women's outfits vary. Some wear dresses and high heels, while others are dressed more casually, in jeans and blouses. Every family has brought a gift for Julia. Ana collects the gifts, placing them on a table inside the house. Some families have also brought bottles of tequila for Tomas.

The adults pay little mind to the children, who know how to amuse themselves. A soccer game is underway at the edge of the yard. Another group of kids jumps, laughing and screeching with delight, inside the inflatable castle. Still others opt for a good old-fashioned game of chase, running through the yard and darting between the cars parked alongside it.

Rosario's nephew acts as the DJ, loudly blasting *narcocorridos* from a laptop connected to two speakers in the corner of the yard. With their upbeat guitar and accordion melodies, the songs sound like old-time Mexican folk ballads. The lyrics are another story; they tell of drug lords, their glitzy lifestyles, and the violent exploits of Mexico's drug wars.[9] The teenagers dance to the music, creating their own dance floor in the space between the inflatable castle and the tent where everyone is eating.

The music is so loud that it's hard for people to talk, so they focus on their food instead. Some use tortillas to scoop up their food, while others use forks. As soon as people have finished eating, Rosario and Ana and the other women swoop down to clean away the plates. They swat at the flies. Even though no plate is ever left unattended, the flies are everywhere.

Rosario sits down at one of the tables to take a short break. Victoria and Gabi run over to her. Gabi scrambles into her mother's lap. Breathing hard, Victoria collapses into the chair next to Rosario. "Now she wants to sleep," Rosario tells the woman who is sitting across the table, gesturing at Victoria's limp form. "All morning since 7:00 AM . . . now she is exhausted."

Rosario begins chatting with the woman and her husband. This is the first time they've met. Rosario admits she's relieved that so many people have come to the party. "I was afraid this morning," she tells them, "because the weather wasn't very good."

The woman nods her head in understanding. The weather turned out to be bright and sunny, but earlier in the day the sky was gray. It looked like they might have rain. They got lucky with the weather. "But a lot of people have come, right?" asks the woman, looking around.

"Yes!" replies Rosario, relieved. Her face clouds over as she remembers the last party she and Ana hosted. "We killed a calf, and we had a lot of leftovers. People never came," she says mournfully. "The day was ugly and rainy and nobody came to the party. My sister and I spent a month eating the meat."

"Here sometimes, the weather spoils everything," the man agrees, referring to the common but unpredictable thunderstorms in North Carolina in the spring and summer. "It's different than Veracruz."

"Are you both from Veracruz?" Rosario asks the couple. Veracruz is a state in eastern Mexico. They nod. Rosario looks at the man's light skin. "And you, sometimes do people confuse you with an American?" she asks.

He laughs. "Yes, all the time! They speak to me in English. The other day I overheard a couple of Mexican men saying, 'Look at this *pinche gringo* who speaks such good Spanish!'"[10]

"Then I turned to them," he continues, "and I said, 'I am Mexican!'" He breaks into a loud laugh, and Rosario and his wife join him.

"It's because you are *güero*,"[11] Rosario replies, referring to his light skin. "The same thing happens to my husband, because he has green eyes. You know my husband, right?"

The man nods. "Yes."

"People confuse him with an American," Rosario tells them, "and they think: look at that Mexican girl who married an American!"[12] They all laugh.

"Have you taken your children to visit Mexico?" the woman asks Rosario.

"No, I haven't," Rosario says with a sigh. "I want to go back someday. We built a house there."

"You rent the house out to someone?"

"No, it's empty. If I have to go back, I don't want to go live in my mom's house," Rosario answers. Rosario and Samuel want the house to be ready for them if they have to move back. They know that going back would be hard on the kids, though. "My kids want to stay here," Rosario reflects. "They were born here, and they don't know what it's like in Mexico. I have lived here for twelve years."

The woman empathizes. "The same thing happened with my kids," she tells Rosario.

"We'll probably go back," Rosario tells her, her voice resigned.[13] "Not my sister. She has papers. She is a resident."

Out of the corner of her eye, Rosario sees Samuel trying to catch her attention. He comes over to the table. "We have to put out more tables," he tells her. More people have arrived, and they need more space.

Rosario excuses herself and goes to consult with Samuel about the organization of the tables. He retrieves two small card tables, which he sets up at the edge of the tent. Rosario covers them with birthday tablecloths, the only ones she can find.

There are so many people at the party that a short line has formed for entering and leaving the house. Six people get out of one car, and eight people tumble out of another. Several cars are trying to park, but they are blocked by a white SUV trying to turn around in the tight space. People start to park their cars near the tables, taking up more space in the front yard. The handful of kids who have been playing soccer in the front yard move their activity to the back.

Even as she worries that they are running out of space, Rosario is pleased. The party is a hit.

There is a long history of people complaining about the "extravagance" of Mexican Americans' religious festivities. The people who host the celebrations are criticized for being overly status conscious, wasting their money, and straying too far from the religious origins of the events.[14] The critiques are not unlike critiques that have also been made of poor people in the United States. When policymakers propose to ban food stamps from being used for "luxury items," or people complain that people are using their food stamps to buy seafood or steak, they are saying that poor people don't deserve to splurge once in a while, that they don't deserve to celebrate.[15]

But critiques of the way that Mexican Americans celebrate First Communions and quinceañeras also reflect long-standing accusations that Mexican Americans have been slow to assimilate into US culture. By pointing to things like speaking Spanish or maintaining certain traditions, critics raise alarms that Mexican Americans are not properly embracing American ways.[16] The United States is often depicted as "a nation of immigrants," but persistent and ongoing criticisms like these highlight the concerted efforts—mostly by white elites—to craft a white, Protestant American national identity.

The party *is* a big investment of time and money. Rosario and Samuel have spent the entire day at Ana's house, helping them get ready. Ana has purchased a ton of food. She and Tomas are better-off than Rosario and Samuel, but they don't have a lot of money to spare.[17]

But being at the party makes it clear why events like these matter. It's a celebration of a milestone for Rosario's niece. It's a commemoration of an important religious sacrament. But it's about more than that. For Rosario and Ana and their families, the party is also about maintaining ties to Mexico. It's about making sure their children know where their family comes from. It's about building a community in the United States and sharing the experience of being on the other side of the border. And it's about gathering together and having fun, with food as an important centerpiece.

Later in the evening, a boisterous group of teenagers abruptly stops dancing and troops inside the inflatable castle. Their gleeful shrieks nearly drown out the loud music. Suddenly, the castle starts to tip over from the weight of all of the people, and the mother of a small child in the castle shouts at the older kids to get out. They run out, laughing exuberantly, and resume dancing.

Inside the house, an older woman enters the kitchen and picks up a tupperware dish from the pile stacked near the table. She asks Rosario where the "*chicharrón*" is. Chicharrón loosely translates to crackling or pork rind and usually includes layers of meat, fat, and skin. Rosario points with her finger to a cooler near the door. The woman fills the tupperware with chicharrón pieces. All of the food is well-received, but the chicharrón is especially popular; several people take some for later or leave chewing on pieces, wiping their greasy hands on napkins.

It's 8:15 in the evening, and another wave of guests is pulling in. Overwhelmed, Rosario wipes her brow, watching as someone attempts to park a car close to one of the tables at the edge of the lawn. Samuel approaches to discuss the situation. If more people keep pouring in, they may need to move some of the tables to make room for the cars. Despite worrying about the parking situation, Rosario and Samuel are happy with the turnout. The guests seem to be enjoying themselves, and everyone is eating plenty.

These events are special, giving Rosario an opportunity to showcase her cooking and remember Mexico. It has taken a lot of time, work, and money, but it feels worth it. As guests wave goodbye, plastic containers of chicharrón in hand, new ones arrive. They are greeted by a remake of a classic Mexican song. The adults prefer the old version, but the kids, shaking their hips to the beat, love the remake.

28 CONCLUSIONS

THINKING OUTSIDE THE KITCHEN

The stories of the nine families featured in this book are a testament to the complex, messy, joyful, creative, fraught process of putting food on the table. And these families are not alone. Americans are increasingly strapped for money and time, contending with rising costs of education, healthcare, and housing; longer commutes to work; and growing uncertainty about the safety of our food system. In this context, sustaining the determination to put a decent meal on the table can feel like a meaningful act, undertaken by those who want to demonstrate care for their families and the environment.

In fact, many see family meals as a way parents can combat our fast-paced, technologically saturated, consumer-driven world. The dinner table is positioned by everyone from social workers to nutritionists as a modern-day refuge, a place where families come together, with the hope of staying together.

Increasingly, foodies also see cooking as a political act. Spending the time and energy to make a home-cooked meal, some argue, constitutes a vote against mass-produced, processed food. It's a way to resist the standardization and industrialization of our food and keep our children safe. Home cooking is a way to demonstrate our commitment to being good parents and our nostalgia for another time, a time that we imagine as simpler.

Family meals have long been symbolically laden with lofty aspirations. The valorization of family meals sprang up during the industrial era, coinciding with the new idea, and ideal, of the nuclear family as a retreat from the public realm. With more men (and many women) leaving the home each day to go to work in factories and businesses, the home and motherhood became sentimentalized, as something pure and untouched by the barbarism of commerce, a place where family members could seek respite. But of course, this public-private divide was one that only the most affluent households could ever hope to achieve, usually by employing poor women to do the bulk of the housework and childcare.[1] The family has never been a private, inner sanctum, separate from the external world. Whether it is by shopping for food, looking after children or doing other work at home for pay, or negotiating the complex rules and requirements of public assistance, women and families are entrenched in and tied to the world outside the home.

Moreover, family dinners are often left to women to figure out. Some women find it deeply satisfying to make food and feed others. And their efforts are important, forming webs of care and commitment that sustain us all. But those webs are profoundly gendered; for the most part, it is women who are expected to take on the work of feeding families.[2]

Leanne Armstrong describes feeding her family as tremendously rewarding. It is one of the few areas where she and her husband, Latrell, find unconditional common ground. Leanne's cooking is a point of pride for Latrell, who praises her efforts in the kitchen. This puts Leanne at the center of her family; she is key to their care and well-being. This role, in turn, is a profoundly important component of Leanne's identity as a good mom.[3] Yet even as cooking provides a creative outlet and serves as a source of pride, there is a downside. Latrell is proud of Leanne's cooking, but he offers no help in procuring or preparing food. She has to do all of the work of feeding their family herself.

Leanne's arrangement is not uncommon. According to national surveys that track how Americans spend their time, women spend more than twice as much time as men do preparing food and drinks, cleaning, and doing laundry.[4]

Typical of Leanne, she makes the best of it. And certainly, the joy she finds in cooking and her can-do spirit are commendable. But her striving and sacrifices also wear her down. Like Patricia Washington, she goes without food when there's not enough to go around. And there are times when she can't get out of bed because she's exhausted, stressed, and overwhelmed by the unrelenting demands of her life.

Most mothers today work outside the home.[5] They have less leisure time than they did in previous generations.[6] We can't keep asking women to juggle more. A long-term solution is to shift household dynamics, with both parents doing their fair share in the home. Women are fatigued from trying to balance being good mothers with being successful in their jobs, notes Anne-Marie Slaughter in her widely read *Atlantic* article, "Why Women Still Can't Have It All." Something's got to give.

Men have stepped up, to some extent. American men cook much more than they used to, and they spend more time doing housework and taking care of children than they did in the 1960s. Many men say that parenting is a positive and important part of their identity. Yet, tellingly, men are also increasingly experiencing a problem women have been reporting for decades— they're having a hard time balancing the demands of work and family.[7]

Working toward greater household equality is important, and we are moving in that direction.[8] But there are limits to how far this solution will go toward solving the challenges of feeding families. For one, many children are being raised by single parents.[9] Single mothers like Tara Foley may not have the option of recruiting another adult to help with the work of feeding the family. Even families with two adults present to help care for children often struggle to meet the unending demands of modern life.[10] The central problem is that families are being asked to do more, with less. Since the 1970s, there has been a steady erosion of the social safety net and regulatory protections in the United States.[11] Real wages have stagnated.[12] And unlike other wealthy nations, the United States lacks policies to help offset the cost of raising children (for example, by offering paid leave to care for children and other family members, childcare subsidies, or universal child or family allowances).[13] If feeding children is more vital than ever before, then families should not have the sole responsibility thrust on them.

A Growing Divide

Food matters. It's a central part of our daily lives. It's vital to our health and our social lives. It's deeply ingrained in our memories.

Food, and our bodies, are also bellwethers of inequality. There is growing evidence of a widening gap in how rich and poor Americans eat. We see this in national dietary surveys,[14] and we see it in our own communities, where foodie restaurants bloom alongside food pantries that don't have enough food to feed the people they serve. Gaps in what we eat are tied to economic inequality, which has increased in the United States over the past several decades. Although money doesn't determine what we eat, it has a lot to do with it. In general, the more money a person spends on food, the healthier their diet is.[15]

And many people in the United States simply do not have more money to spend on food (not to mention on housing or healthcare). Poor families in the United States spend a lot less money on food than rich households: $3,767 a year, compared to $12,340 for the wealthiest households. Poor families also spend less money at restaurants,[16] and they devote more time to cooking at home.[17] But when you calculate how much poor households spend on food as a proportion of their income, they are spending much more than the rich—33 percent of poor households' incomes goes to food, compared to just 9 percent for wealthy households.[18]

There is less and less common ground, so it seems, between families like Greely Janson's, who can afford fresh, seasonal, nutritious fare, and families like Ashley Taylor's, who search for the cheapest deals—ten for $10—to keep everyone fed on the smallest possible budget; between families like Marta Hernández-Boynton's, who have ample resources to safeguard and cultivate their children's tastes, and families like Melanie Richards', who make do with few resources and rely on stigmatizing forms of public assistance that put them at the mercy of bureaucratic glitches and procedures that are often humiliating.

At the same time, these families have much in common. All of the mothers in our study want their children to thrive, to be as healthy and happy as possible. They share similar ideas about what this would require. All of them are taking on the lion's share of shopping, cooking, and meal planning for their families. They all like at least some aspects of cooking, yet all regularly experience some degree of ambivalence, frustration, exhaustion, or failure about the food they are able to put on the table.

Moving Beyond the Kitchen

Most people would agree: it's nice to slow down, eat healthfully, and enjoy a home-cooked meal. But should the kitchen be the front line in reforming the food system?

Food reformers' advice is inviting. It draws on popular notions about individual responsibility and hard work that resonate with the belief that the United States is a meritocracy, a place where individuals can get ahead if they prioritize education and make the right choices. The idea that people have a responsibility to buy sustainably produced food, cook from scratch, and sit down for dinner makes sense. It is something we can do, today.

All of the women in this book, and many families in the United States, do some of those things. Most people would enjoy the chance to sit down and enjoy a meal at the end of the day, and many manage to pull it off. Lots of people are doing their best, every day, to get meals on the table that their kids will eat and that will nourish them and help them grow. Lots of people are "voting with their forks" to support the small farmers in their areas, many of whom struggle to get by themselves.

These are all good things. But they all rely on individual people managing to work better, try harder, commit more. And when people can't—whether it's because they lack the money, the time, or just the space in their lives for it—they hear that they're failing. In 2014, after we wrote the article that led to this book, a mom wrote to thank us. Her husband had died a few years earlier, leaving her with two young children. Even at such a stressful point in her life, she felt she should be doing a better job of feeding her children. "I was mad at myself," she wrote, "for not providing the same standard of healthy eating as my friends. Literally, I would have nightmares about feeding my children chicken nuggets."

We can't keep asking people to do better. Doing so ignores the challenges facing families. Whether it's a family member's illness or death or the grinding demands of paying the bills, many parents are experiencing chronic stress. The way we eat is also inextricably linked to social inequality. Patricia Washington and her family eat sitting on beds in the hotel where they are temporarily living. They heat food in a microwave or on a hotplate.

Trying to solve the environmental and social ills of our food system by demanding that we return to our kitchens en masse is unrealistic. At best, it is a weight of responsibility that will most likely be felt by the women who tend to occupy this space already.

We need to change the way we think about food, family meals, and inequality. Fortunately, there are multiple levels at which we can enact change: in our homes, communities, and nation.

Home
Keep Food in Perspective

We need to uncouple the "package deal" that links good mothering with preparing wholesome family dinners from scratch.[19] This standard is difficult to achieve, especially when few families have ever resembled the iconic *Leave It to Beaver* family of the 1950s.[20] Families in the United States still spend quite a bit of time cooking, with many cooking almost every day.[21] The most recent surveys suggest that Americans are actually cooking slightly more than they were a decade ago.[22] Yet women, in particular, often feel a sense of inadequacy and anxiety around cooking, a sense that there is never enough time in the day to do it "right."

Cooking matters, but we should avoid falling into the trap of believing that dinnertime alone can cause, or prevent, children from being healthy or happy. As sociologists Kelly Musick and Ann Meier find in their research on the impacts of family dinners, eating meals together offers natural opportunities for interacting. But these are not always positive experiences. What seems to matter most is that children get quality time to connect with their parents,[23] whether that happens while driving to soccer practice, taking a walk, or playing a pickup game of basketball. A large body of research shows that parents often feel especially anxious and worried about food. But families need to decide for themselves which tradeoffs they would like to make.[24]

Allow Food to Mean Different Things to Different People

We can celebrate food's meaning in our families and our cultures while acknowledging that the process of getting dinner on the table is time-consuming and not always very rewarding. We can try to make sure our children eat their vegetables without demonizing certain foods. We can work hard to master our grandma's recipe for enchiladas or chicken pot pie and also appreciate the convenience of being able to put a frozen pizza in the oven and have it ready in fifteen minutes.

Food means different things to different people, and we should celebrate this. Even among nutrition scientists, there is little consensus around which foods are the healthiest or the degree to which our diets are linked to our weight or overall health.[25] Instead of insisting on a universal definition of what it means to eat healthy or eat well, we should recognize that our beliefs about food are rooted in our family histories and our particular social contexts and intertwined with inequalities linked to gender, race, ethnicity, and class. Food is incredibly complex for Rae Donahue, who is still figuring out what food means to her as a black middle-class woman raised in the South. For Rosario García, deciding what's for dinner involves constantly feeling pulled between the Mexican food traditions she wants to preserve and the American foods her children have embraced.

Recognizing the diversity of our food experiences also means listening to others and challenging dominant narratives about food. Our current food discourse is still dominated by white men. While white men can and should certainly be advocates for food reform, addressing long-standing food inequalities requires insights from people of diverse backgrounds and experiences, particularly immigrants, people of color, poor and working-class people, and women—groups whose voices, preferences, and practices have long been excluded from public conversations about food.

Community
Share the Work

It takes a great deal of labor to get dinner on the table. People are already feeling the pressure, and asking them to somehow make it all happen seems like wishful thinking. It's time to consider other ways to make it possible for families to enjoy a meal at the end of the day without expecting the work of creating this meal to happen solely in the home.

For families that can afford it, the market has answers. Upscale supermarkets have expanded their lines of prepared foods, including weekday meal plans, with all foods made in-house. Companies like Blue Apron will send recipes and pre-portioned ingredients for complete meals every week. Grocery stores and AmazonFresh will even deliver food to your door, depending on where you live. But these options do little to address the inequalities in our food system.

We need collective solutions that will benefit people across the income spectrum. Some of these would need to come from the federal government. School lunch does not have to be a source of inequality and stress for parents. Universal school lunches, made with fresh foods and according to diverse recipes, would go a long way toward nourishing kids in the middle of the day. It would cost more to provide lunches for all students, but not necessarily a lot more, and better school lunches are an investment in our kids' health and in the environment.[26]

Local governments and businesses can also contribute to collective solutions. Schools, daycares, and churches could share their commercial kitchens to help fill the cooking gap. Institutions like these are capable of producing healthy, tasty food, especially when they link up with local farmers. Buying in bulk and having the space to store and prepare food on a large scale saves money and could provide families with hearty, affordable dinners, such as lasagna or soup, to reheat at the end of the day. Making these meals available on a sliding scale would also help share the expense of feeding families and equalize people's access to food.

Finally, we don't have to reinvent the wheel. Collective solutions are already in motion, in small towns and big cities across the country. Community suppers—hosted in churches, community centers, and private houses—bring people together not just to share food but also to share stories.[27] They're often funded by a system that allows wealthier people to pay a little extra so that others can eat for free. Participating in these dinners is about more than having an excuse not to have to cook, although that's a good reason to go in itself. It's also a chance to meet and interact with people from outside a person's usual circles, whether this means people from a different generation, people from another neighborhood, or people with different backgrounds.

With a little creative thinking and some economic support, communities can work together, investing in the health of all.

Listen

We know that fundamental inequalities shape the food we put on our plate. These range from the types of stores in our neighborhoods to the tools in our kitchens. In recognition of these disparities, neighborhood groups and nonprofits are trying to ensure that everyone in their communities has access to good food to eat. Many of these organizations are doing exceptional work. But in a context where funding is tight and people want to see immediate results, food justice advocates often implement solutions without considering the needs and values of the people who they are trying to help. And as cities like Raleigh continue to grow, people end up evaluating food systems according to how many artisanal donut shops, craft breweries, or even farmers' markets there are, instead of asking who gets to define what good food looks like.

Working to bring about true food justice starts by trying to understand people and communities and building on their ideas.[28] What works for one neighborhood may not work for another. After the Kroger in southeast Raleigh closed, one man started a mobile market that brings fresh produce, dairy, and meats to food-insecure residents. In some ways, the mobile market is similar to other mobile vendors springing up all over the country. But it is different in key ways. It allows people to pay with food stamps, and it accepts credit, often on an informal basis. It offers the foods that many of Raleigh's older residents remember from growing up: mustard greens and turnip greens, for example. In the end, the mobile market looks quite different from AmazonFresh. It not only delivers food but also helps form a network of community ties, showing that someone cares. The key to the success of food justice efforts is close attention to the particular needs of a community.

Nation
Make Food a Human Right

One out of every eight Americans does not have enough food to eat,[29] and many more do not have enough money to regularly afford healthy foods. The gap in the quality of the food that rich and poor people in the United States eat is growing.[30]

Food pantries and other charities cannot keep up with the demand. Our federal food assistance programs—food stamps, WIC, and school breakfast and lunch—were founded in part on the belief that it is our duty as a nation to make sure that our citizens don't go hungry.[31] But these programs are increasingly subject to debates over whether the people who use them are deserving or dependent and morally suspect. When the government says that food stamps should be only available to working adults, as was proposed in the draft of the Farm Bill released just as we were finishing these conclusions, they are saying that not everyone—not even every child—in this country deserves to be free from hunger.[32]

We need to reframe the way we think of food: not as a privilege to be dispensed by charities to people who deserve it, but as a fundamental human right, for everyone.[33] The right to food is included in the Universal Declaration of Human Rights, adopted by the United Nations in 1948. The United States is one of the only industrialized countries in the world that has not endorsed a right to food.[34] Public health researchers Mariana Chilton and Don Rose argue that fulfilling the right to food must happen at two levels. First, we must fix structural inequalities in order to stem the tide of hunger at its source. At the same time, we must have a way of feeding people during times of crisis and emergencies.[35]

Recognizing food as a human right would mean evaluating policies based on the degree to which they successfully reduce food insecurity. The United States has measured the prevalence of food insecurity in the nation since 1995. In more than twenty years, there has been no measurable improvement.[36]

To reduce food insecurity, we must tackle the underlying conditions that cause poverty while also strengthening our existing food assistance programs, ensuring that they are available to everyone who needs them. This will require raising the minimum wage, so that working families are able to feed themselves,[37] and investing in affordable housing, given the strong links between housing insecurity and food insecurity. Instead of passing laws that make food assistance programs more restrictive, we should bolster existing programs to make sure that everyone who needs help is eligible and can get it.

More broadly, the most effective way we can reduce hunger in the United States is by reducing poverty. Poverty rates are higher here than in other industrialized countries, mostly because we lack policies to support the people who are most at risk of being poor (for example, single parents or people with low levels of formal education).[38] Other countries' approaches to reducing poverty vary, but research suggests that universal policies—those that are available to everyone—may be more effective than policies that are targeted to families under a certain income level.[39] Some countries and communities have considered trying to raise living standards by implementing Universal Basic Income, premised on the idea that everyone deserves a minimum level of resources, regardless of whether they are working.[40] To give an idea of another proposal, a recent article by a multidisciplinary team of researchers suggests that by converting the Child Tax Credit and child tax exemption into a universal, monthly child allowance, we could reduce child poverty by 40 percent in the United States.[41]

In any case, it's clear our current system is not working. Compared to other wealthy countries, the United States invests very little in families. There is good evidence that not only does this negatively impact families' health and well-being, it also costs the government directly, generating costs that result from children growing up poor and disadvantaged.[42]

Support the Workers Who Feed Us

The food on Americans' tables would not be there if not for the many workers who do the invisible work of planting and picking fruits and vegetables, bagging and ringing up groceries, and cooking and serving food at restaurants. Many of these workers are women of color. Ironically, working to get other people's food on the table often leaves them without enough money or time to feed their own families as they would like to.[43]

It is fundamentally unfair that the restaurants that serve the Instagram-worthy meals are staffed by people who could never afford to eat there, and that the fruits and vegetables that middle-class consumers buy to ensure the health of their children are picked by farmworkers who suffer from chronic health problems because of their jobs.[44]

So what do we do? Consumers and retailers have an important role to play. For example, the Campaign for Fair Food, an initiative of the Coalition for Immokalee Workers, has forged alliances between tomato farmworkers in Florida and consumers around the country. They have succeeded in getting major food retailers, including Walmart, McDonald's, and Burger King, to commit to paying an extra penny per pound of tomatoes. Retailers also commit to ensuring that a human-rights-based Code of Conduct is implemented on the farms that grow their tomatoes. The Campaign for Fair Food has succeeded in confronting and addressing injustices in the food system by linking farmworkers with consumers. Farmworkers determine the priorities that matter most for them, while consumers carry out creative actions—marches, hunger strikes, and concerts—to raise awareness.[45]

The Restaurant Opportunities Center (ROC) is another successful model. Founded in 2008, ROC has gone from "a small, determined group of low-wage [restaurant] workers" to a national organization of over 25,000 workers, 200 "high road" employers, and thousands of diners, all of them "united to raise restaurant wages, benefits, and industry standards." ROC publishes an annual diners' guide that grades restaurants nationwide on how they treat workers, giving consumers the opportunity to choose to support restaurants that not only have good food but also treat their workers well.[46]

Consumer-based campaigns can produce important changes in a relatively short period of time. However, because they often target specific retailers or implicate particular groups of workers, they are somewhat limited in scope. To improve workers' labor and living conditions, we must simultaneously push to change ineffective and harmful laws and regulations. For example, in cities across the United States, workers and activists have begun to demand that all workers be paid a living wage.[47]

Support Families

Caring for others is a vital part of what families do; it's also vital to society. Countries that recognize and value carework intentionally create public policies to support it. This looks different in different places, but countries with strong family policies generally offer paid family leave, paid sick and vacation leave, subsidized preschool, and universal healthcare coverage. A recent cross-national study found that in general, parents are less happy than non-parents, but the "happiness" gap between parents and non-parents is larger in the United States than in other wealthy countries. And this difference is largely explained by variations in social policies.[48] One of the study authors, sociologist Jennifer Glass, explained the findings as follows:

> What we found was astonishing. The negative effects of parenthood on happiness were *entirely* explained by the presence or absence of social

policies allowing parents to better combine paid work with family obligations. And this was true for both mothers *and fathers*. Countries with better family policy "packages" had no happiness gap between parents and non-parents.[49]

The benefits of living in a country that truly invests in its families' and citizens' well-being are astounding.[50] In contrast, American parents often feel alone and isolated in their efforts to raise happy, healthy children. And these feelings are compounded by messages—from TV, schools, social services, and social media—that tell parents they need to do even better and take on even more personal responsibility for their family's well-being. As a society, we must recognize that people can't do the important work of raising the next generation alone. Advocating social policies that support all families is one step toward creating a society in which it is possible for families to feel connected, sustained, and healthy. What happens in families may feel private and personal, but the fact that families struggle with similar issues—time deficits, money woes, picky eaters, and health concerns—means these are not just private troubles, but public issues that demand collective responses.

NOTES ON METHODS

Between February 2012 and March 2013, we conducted semi-structured interviews with 168 black (n = 68), white (n = 56), Latina (n = 41), and biracial (n = 3) mothers and grandmothers of young children in three North Carolina counties.[1] All women received a small honorarium, between $20 and $25, for participating in an interview.[2] All were primary caregivers of at least one child between the ages of two and nine at the time of the interview. One hundred thirty-eight of the families lived in households near or below 200 percent of the federal poverty line. These families were part of Voices into Action, a USDA-funded research and participatory outreach project.[3] They lived in predominantly low-income neighborhoods in two rural counties (Harnett and Lee) and one urban city (Raleigh) in North Carolina. When recruiting the Voices into Action participants, we aimed to ensure that the racial and ethnic composition of our sample was roughly proportional to the composition of the low-income population in the research sites.[4] Interview participants were recruited from a range of places, including churches, health fairs and other community events, daycares and schools, and personal contacts.

To develop community partnerships and recruit research participants, we took a slow, community-based approach in Voices into Action. First, we built inroads into each community by discussing the project with a variety of community members and stakeholders. Eventually, we hired local community residents to serve as mentors (two per research area). The community mentors provided feedback on project design to help shape the contours of the research and participatory outreach activities, shared their perspectives on the communities that were part of the project, and helped us reach out to a broad, diverse group of community members to tell them about our work and recruit research participants. We hired an outreach coordinator, who worked directly with the mentors to recruit participants and connect with communities. She also recruited participants directly—for example, by attending local events. The community mentors played a crucial role in the project, but this strategy was not without its challenges. Because we wanted mentors who were part of the low-income communities in the study, most did not have experience doing anything even closely resembling what we were asking them to do. This, coupled with the fact that we gave them a great deal of autonomy, meant that there was not much overlap in terms of how individual mentors went about fulfilling their mentoring roles. This lack of institutional blueprint also allowed for flexibility and, occasionally, serendipity. It also helped us to reach participants who might not otherwise have found out about or volunteered to be a part of the research project.

We took measures to ensure that interview participants came from diverse networks, recruiting no more than five people from any institution or location and accepting no more than two referrals from an interview participant or another individual person. (This is a common research practice called "snowballing."[5]) In our recruitment materials (e.g., announcements, fliers), we said that we wanted to talk with female caregivers of small children about what it meant to feed their family.

We aimed to include a range of lower-income families in the study. Seventy-seven percent of Voices into Action participants had household incomes under 100 percent of the federal poverty line ($23,050 for a family of four in 2012, when the project started). Nineteen percent had incomes between 100 and 200 percent of the poverty line, and 4 percent had incomes slightly above 200 percent of the poverty line.

Although Sarah Bowen and Sinikka Elliott conducted some of the Voices into Action interviews, we also recruited female researchers—from diverse racial and class backgrounds, many of them graduate students, to interview participants. At the time, Joslyn Brenton was a graduate student and member of the research team. We met weekly, and the team of researchers was involved in all stages of the research process, including developing interview questions, conducting interviews, writing fieldnotes, and participating in data coding and analysis.

Some of the research in this book comes from Joslyn's dissertation. Joslyn used thirty of the interviews with Voices into Action participants for her doctoral study. She conducted all of these interviews herself. She also recruited and interviewed an additional thirty middle- and upper-middle-class participants: ten black, ten white, and ten Latina mothers. All of these women had household incomes above 200 percent of the poverty line. The interviews with middle-class families were not part of Voices into Action. In defining families as middle or upper class, Joslyn took into account not only income, but also level of education and type of occupation.[6] (This is also how we defined poor and working-class families in the Voices into Action sample.) The median household income among this group of thirty families was $100,000. Families were recruited through personal contacts, advertisements on neighborhood listservs, and snowball sampling.[7]

We used the same interview guide for all participants. Interviews generally lasted between one and a half to two hours, and almost all took place in participants' homes. (A handful of interviews were conducted in parks, libraries, workplace offices, or other public places, at the request of participants.) Interviews were conducted in English or Spanish. All interviews with middle-class participants were conducted in English.

Nearly all of the Voices into Action interviews with Latina participants were conducted in Spanish, by a native Spanish speaker, at the request of participants. The interviews focused on beliefs, decisions, and practices related to food and feeding. We asked broad questions ("Tell me what it's like to live here" and "Describe a typical day in your household"), as well as more specific questions about eating habits, food shopping, cooking, and cleaning up after meals. We also asked participants how they fed their children, asking them to describe food rules and routines and children's food preferences. Finally, we asked about participants' broader experiences related to food, including food memories and traditions and beliefs about health and nutrition.

Following the logic of grounded theory,[8] the interview guide was modified as new themes emerged during the course of the interviews. Detailed summaries of each interview were written within twenty-four hours and captured important first impressions and themes, which later facilitated early stages of analysis. An initial round of line-by-line coding was conducted by hand. In order to develop the codes, we read multiple transcripts and hand coded individually. We then met to discuss our codes. We followed an iterative process of coding, memoing, and discussing until we established a codebook, which we used to code all the transcripts. We purposefully kept the codes broad, so that we could conduct focused coding of these more general concepts. Several rounds of focused coding and memoing, which involved analyzing and elaborating upon patterns observed in the first several rounds of coding, helped us develop the analysis that forms the basis of this book.

The research team included black, white, and Latina researchers, as well as one Asian American researcher. Our analysis of the data as a whole indicates that white participants were more likely to express racist sentiments (however cloaked) with white interviewers and that black participants were more likely to discuss their fears and experiences of racism with black interviewers.[9] Social class also infused research relationships, although these dynamics were sometimes difficult to entangle.[10] Researchers also varied in their backgrounds and experiences, including those in parenting; some researchers were child-free by choice, others had small children, and others had decades of experience with parenting. Researchers' different perspectives shaped everything from the development of the interview questions to discussions of what we were finding in the field and our analysis of the data.

The second phase of the research used in this book took place in 2013. Between April and December 2013, Sarah, Joslyn, and Sinikka, along with the other members of the research team, conducted over 250 hours of ethnographic observations in the homes of 12 of the 138 low-income families in Voices into Action.[11] The twelve families were chosen to represent a range of family types and experiences, as well as illustrate some of the key themes we had identified during the interviewing phase. We identified four families from each of the three research sites and asked them if they would allow us to spend time hanging out with them over a period of approximately one month. We organized our "visits" (the observations) with families around particular events, such as a meal or naptime.[12] We explained that we would be writing notes and occasionally recording brief conversations during our time with the families. We told them that they could ask us to exclude any events or snippets of conversation we observed. All of the families agreed to participate in this part of the study; only once were we asked to omit details from our fieldnotes. This occurred during a large gathering and involved information not fully relevant to the project's focus on food and families.

For the ethnographic observations, the team of eight researchers included five graduate students (Joslyn Brenton among them), one part-time research staff member, and two professors (Sinikka Elliott and Sarah Bowen). To help families develop stronger relationships with researchers, we assigned one lead researcher and two secondary researchers to each family. The lead researchers generally conducted eight of the twelve observations, while the two secondary researchers typically conducted two observations each. For the three families that spoke predominantly Spanish, only a lead and one secondary researcher were assigned because there were only two native Spanish-speakers on the research team. Our intent was primarily to observe but also to interact with families, although our level of interaction varied according to the families and the fieldworkers. In some instances, researchers became quite involved in families' routines, playing with children or giving people rides. It often took time for these relationships to develop, however, and secondary fieldworkers had fewer opportunities to cultivate these connections.

Each set of observations started with an initial intake visit. For the intake, the lead researcher met the family in their home, introduced the research project, and asked about upcoming planned events, such as children's doctor's appointments or birthday celebrations. We scheduled observations to include these events, requesting that if participants had medical or social services appointments coming up, they would allow us to accompany them. We also asked if we could tag along to special occasions, like Leanne Armstrong's Fourth of July celebration and Rosario García's niece's First Communion party. The majority of the observations centered on everyday life, such as families' morning, afterschool, and evening routines, which, given our research interest in food, were timed to include breakfast, lunch, and dinner. We accompanied participants on their first big shopping trip after receiving food stamps, for participants who received food stamps; or another big shopping trip, for participants who did not receive food stamps. When possible, we also attended Women, Infants, and Children (WIC) and doctor's appointments and children's school lunches. We conducted an interview during an "appreciation party," held at each family's home for the twelfth observation. We provided the food for the party and ate with each family; this marked the end of our time with them.

Observations lasted between one and four hours, with an average of two and a half hours per observation. We strove to make two to three visits per week for five weeks. Our goal was to finish all twelve families' observations over the course of a nine-month period. Once we scheduled the observations, we gave families a calendar with the dates and times we had discussed together, a checklist of events we wanted to observe, and researchers' contact information. Fieldworkers also called or texted families to confirm the appointment twenty-four hours prior to each observation and ended each observation with a verbal reminder of the next visit.

During the observations, we took notes and sometimes discreetly used a digital recorder to record specific conversations. We wrote detailed fieldnotes within forty-eight hours of each observation, trying to capture in as much detail as possible the setting, participants, dialogue, and interactions.[13] Each set of fieldnotes ranged from five to twenty-five single-spaced pages, with an average of eleven single-spaced pages of fieldnotes per observation.[14] The observations allowed us to witness some of the events and dynamics around food and feeding the family that participants discussed during the interviews—sometimes corroborating, sometimes contradicting, and always contextualizing and enriching the accounts participants had provided.[15]

We also wrote notes-on-notes—essentially reflections and ideas that researchers had after writing or reading any given set of fieldnotes—and met weekly to discuss the observations. Along with giving us an opportunity to discuss what we were learning and troubleshoot problems as they emerged, these weekly meetings helped team members express and work through the complex emotions we experienced in the field. Fieldwork can be emotionally taxing and complex. Researchers can come to feel tightly aligned with participants and take on as our own the perspectives and worries of those we study, but researchers can also feel angry and annoyed with participants, rejecting their points of view and distancing ourselves from those we study. And sometimes—likely more often than not—these feelings of identification and disidentification can occur simultaneously. Paying attention to emotions is important because our emotional responses in the field—including boredom, anxiety, excitement, and fear—not only offer insight into larger dynamics at play, but because fieldworkers may also perceive and characterize the field in ways that correspond with their emotions.[16] Being able to talk openly about the feelings we were having while in the field helped us, as a group of researchers, to be more aware of those feelings and think critically about how they might be informing our fieldwork. While writing this book, we have tried to maintain this critical practice of self-reflection, asking ourselves often whether we have done justice to the complex lives of the families in the book.

We have tried to honor the families by sharing their stories in rich detail and as accurately as we possibly could, changing details only to protect the confidentiality of the families. All of the people in the book—the family members, their friends and extended families, staff at stores and social service institutions, and anyone else they interacted with—are named using pseudonyms. Descriptions of the physical appearance of people and places are as accurate as possible and are based on our fieldnotes. In most cases, proper nouns, such as street names or the names of employers, were replaced with a pseudonym or a different but equivalent name. We did not change the names of supermarkets. In some cases, we changed identifying details—for example, job titles or health conditions—to protect people's identities. Whenever we had to change a proper noun or an identifying detail, we chose a replacement that closely reflected the "spirit" of the original. For example, if someone actually worked as a nanny, we might make that person a daycare teacher, as these positions are often similar in terms of educational background, pay, and job duties; if someone had previously lived in Atlanta, we might change it to Houston, because Atlanta and Houston are both large, diverse cities in the South. In general, we changed details only when absolutely necessary to protect the families' identities.

The only other way in which the book diverges from the fieldnotes is that the order of the chapters does not necessarily correspond with the order in which the events occurred. (For example, as noted in the endnotes, Tara Foley celebrated Thanksgiving before she went grocery shopping.) Instead, we organized the book based on how these women's lives resonated with seven key foodie maxims.

One strength of our project is that we had the opportunity to revisit the families in the Voices into Action study multiple times. Although the specific quotes, stories, and details in this book come from the first round of interviews and observations, the research we conducted in subsequent years informs our analysis and the conclusions we draw.

In the third and fifth years of the project, we conducted semi-structured interviews with all of the families in the study. Throughout the project, we worked hard to stay in touch with participants and build durable relationships with them. These efforts included sending monthly newsletters, engaging participants via social media, and hosting community events, for which we offered transportation and childcare services. Keeping up with the families and remaining active in their communities throughout the project helped us maintain a high retention rate. Ninety percent of the Voices into Action families participated in the third year of the project, and 73 percent participated in the fifth and final year of the project. In the fourth year of the project, we conducted a second round of ethnographic observations with the same twelve families who had participated in the second year of the project. All of them agreed to allow us back into their lives. The second round of fieldwork allowed us to implement the lessons learned from our initial time in the field.[17]

One limitation of the data is that we did not conduct ethnographic observations with any of the middle- and upper-middle-class families and thus have fewer observational details to share about their lives. Almost all of these interviews took place in the women's homes, and Joslyn Brenton was therefore able to see their living spaces and occasionally their interactions with children and other adults in the home. She wrote up her observations about the families' surroundings, appearances, and mannerisms after each interview. Nevertheless, these data are not comparable to the immersive fieldwork we conducted with the families that participated in Voices into Action.

We direct readers interested in learning more about the day-to-day dynamics in middle-class families to the book *Fast-Forward Family*, edited by anthropologists Elinor Ochs and Tamar Kremer-Sadlik. The book's analysis is based on week-long video recordings in the homes of thirty-two middle-class households in the mid-2000s, along with in-depth interviewing.[18] In terms of food and mealtimes, Ochs and Kremer-Sadlik's research team found that the harried families relied heavily on processed and convenience foods, even though these foods sometimes became a point of contention, such as when a child objected to a specific ingredient in a prepackaged meal or refused to eat the meal at all, and parents had to prepare a different meal. Food, overall, was a source of contention in these homes, and getting people together around the dinner table was a rare event. In some households, the authors note, "family members were *never* all together in the same space at the same time."[19]

We hold a deep respect and admiration for the women who invited us into their lives and whose stories form the basis of *Pressure Cooker*. Our experiences as women and mothers informed and shaped our interest in this project, and our training as sociologists pushed us to pay attention to how women's experiences were uniquely theirs but also connected to broader issues and dynamics in society. We did what every well-trained researcher does: we prioritized participants, respecting their rights and their stories. We hope that the expertise, diligence, and compassion we each brought to this project has done justice to the lives of the nine women, and their families, that we present in this book. And we hope that our findings will contribute to further efforts to make sure everyone has the food, respect, and time they deserve.

NOTES

CHAPTER 1

1. Kalleberg and von Wachter (2017) note that poor people, people of color, and people with less formal education were hit the hardest by the recession.
2. See Bailey (2017) for a discussion of the "mommy internet" and how it has changed over the years.
3. Johnston and Baumann (2010).
4. DeSoucey (2016: 201) argues that "food politics are about power, control, and conflict."
5. Coleman-Jensen, Rabbitt, Gregory, and Singh (2017).
6. Jackson (2015).
7. Thomson (2017).
8. Guthman and Brown (2015).
9. Rates of obesity have doubled among adults and tripled among children since the 1980s (Segal et al. 2017). Rates of diabetes have tripled over the same period (CDC 2017a).
10. Salatin (2014).
11. Oliver (2010).
12. One of Michael Pollan's key pieces of advice is "Don't eat anything your grandma wouldn't recognize as food" (Pollan 2009). But of course, the food our grandmothers and great-grandmothers would most recognize is the food they found on their tables, which could include the milk, often contaminated, consumed by nineteenth-century urban dwellers (Dupuis 2002); the stale bread and wild greens that sustained miners during the Depression (Poppendieck [1986] 2014); or the meat, potatoes, and farm-fresh produce of the foodie imagination.
13. Wilk (2010: 428).
14. DeVault (1991).
15. Hays (1996); Lareau (2011).

16. To give one example, dietary reformer Sylvester Graham wrote that home-baked wheat bread—in contrast to white bread, produced by professional bakers—could restore not only the "physical and moral condition" of families, but the values of the nation itself (Veit 2013).

17. DeVault (1991); Sayer (2005); Smith et al. (2013); Tailie (2018); Zick and Stevens (2010).

18. Cairns and Johnston (2015).

19. Between 1880 and 1940, almost all American upper- and middle-class families employed at least one domestic servant (Levenstein 2003). One in every 25.1 households in 1960 had a domestic servant; this had dropped to one in 116.7 by 1980. The rapid decline partly reflects the greater opportunities that women had in the labor market, making domestic service a last resort. Only one in 161.8 households had a domestic servant in 2000 (Kornrich 2012).

20. Trubek (2017: 82).

21. Rehm et al. (2016); Wang et al. (2014).

22. DeVault (1991); Daniel (2016).

23. Haws, Reczek, and Sample (2017).

24. The headline comes from Zagorsky and Smith (2017a). The original study is Zagorsky and Smith (2017b).

25. Williams-Forson (2006). These critiques come from both within and outside black communities. Many black people worry that the foods their ancestors ate are unhealthy and responsible for the health issues that disproportionately affect African Americans, as we discuss in more detail in Chapter 3.

26. Native to sub-Saharan Africa, watermelons were grown by slaves in their gardens. African Americans continued to grow, eat, and sell watermelons after emancipation. Images of black people eating watermelon proliferated at the turn of the twentieth century depicting black people as childish, no more deserving of freedom than children (Black 2014).

27. Williams-Forson (2006).

28. Levenstein (2003: 103).

29. Levenstein (2003: 105).

30. Whitten (2016).

31. CHD Expert (2017).

32. Johnston and Baumann (2010); Ray (2016).

33. Ray (2016) argues consumers might be willing to pay $40 for French or Italian food, but they expect to find Indian, Chinese, or Mexican food for under $10 a plate.

34. Ray (2016) notes that new immigrants have long occupied restaurant kitchens. In 2000, 75 percent of restaurant cooks were foreign born. Most farmworkers and many workers in the meatpacking industry are also immigrants. According to the National Agricultural Workers Survey (2014), 75 percent of farmworkers were born outside the United States, most coming from Mexico.

35. In another example of irony, many of these workers are prompted to migrate to the United States because of US agricultural trade policies. As Wise (2010) explains, as a condition of the 1994 NAFTA Agreement, the Mexican government eliminated tariffs and quotas that protected Mexican farmers from competition from foreign producers. Agricultural subsidies remained, and US farm subsidies since NAFTA have dwarfed Mexico's. According to an analysis of eight heavily subsidized agricultural commodities, the increase in US exports to Mexico ranged from 159 percent to 707 percent since the early 1990s, depending on the commodity (Wise 2010). Decreases in real prices paid to Mexican producers ranged from 44 percent to 67 percent (Wise 2010). The result was the widespread displacement of rural Mexicans, who migrated to cities within Mexico and to the United States as agricultural employment in Mexico dried up. See Polaski (2004).

36. Bowen, Elliott, and Brenton (2014); Cairns and Johnston (2015); Cairns, Johnston, and MacKendrick (2013); Elliott and Bowen (2018); MacKendrick (2018); Reich (2016); Waggoner (2017); Wright, Maher, and Tanner (2015).

37. The interviews with lower-income families were conducted as part of a study on families, food, and health funded by the US Department of Agriculture (USDA). At least one interview was completed by 138 women; 124 women completed the full slate of data collection in Year 1, including an interview, a survey, and at least two dietary recalls.

38. Only one mother in our sample identified as nonheterosexual. We didn't exclude lesbian, gay, bisexual, and transgender (LGBT) families but we also didn't make a point to recruit these families into the study. Studies that do not reach out to marginalized groups, like LGBT families, are unlikely to end up with much, if any, representation of these groups in their sample because they are harder to locate and may be less inclined to participate in research out of privacy concerns or fears of mistreatment by insensitive researchers. As such, LGBT families are often absent from research on families. Indeed, Mignon Moore (2011) titled her book on black lesbian mothers *Invisible Families*. We regret that our sampling procedure reproduced the tendency in family scholarship to underrepresent the experiences of nonheterosexual families (Pfeffer 2016).

39. The interviews with middle-class mothers were conducted by Joslyn for her dissertation. The observations were beyond the scope of the dissertation, and thus, middle-class families were not included in the observations.

40. Helms was not born in Raleigh but he lived there for most of his life. Helms described civil rights activists as "moral degenerates" and infamously filibustered a 1983 Senate bill commemorating the birthday of Martin Luther King Jr. (Snider 1985).

41. The SNCC was established in April 1960 on the campus of Shaw University, the first historically black college in the South. Established in the wake of the student-led sit-ins that started in North Carolina in early 1960, the SNCC, a self-described "beloved community" where white and black young people could meet as equals

and practice nonviolence, became one of the most influential organizations of the civil rights movement (Gosse 2005).

42. The US Census Bureau (2017a) listed Raleigh as the fourteenth-fastest growing region in the United States in 2016.

43. Moody (2017).

44. The study forecasted how growing up in different counties would affect the future incomes of children from low-income families. Children who are born poor are more likely to stay poor in Raleigh and in Wake County, where Raleigh is located, compared to other places (Chetty and Hendren 2018). Moreover, concentrated poverty has increased in Raleigh (and in many other parts of the United States) since 2000 (Kneebone 2014).

45. Poverty statistics come from the US Census (2017b). North Carolina is characterized by a rural-urban divide; a 2015 report found that out of the state's 100 counties in 2013, the 45 highest county-level poverty rates were all in rural counties, up from 31 in 2012 (Mitchell 2015).

46. Edge (2017).

47. Murray (2016) defines a "meat and three" restaurant as a casual, cafeteria-style joint, usually family-owned and operated.

48. The restaurant was Clyde Cooper's barbecue, established in 1938 in a building built in 1884 (Porter 2015). Raleigh was the site of early student sit-ins over lunch counter segregation in the 1960s.

49. Hardison-Moody et al. (2015).

50. See discussion in Chapter 21.

51. Edge (2017: 10).

CHAPTER 2

1. Skipping meals or substituting sugary drinks like sodas for meals is a common strategy low-income women use to try to mitigate the negative impact of food shortages on other family members (Chen 2016; Elliott and Bowen 2018; Martin and Lippert 2012; Olson 2005). See Chapter 13 for a more in-depth discussion of how families facing food insecurity cope.

2. A wide variety of greens are eaten in the South, but the most typical soul food greens include cabbage, collards, kale, mustard greens, and turnip greens (Miller 2013).

3. A substantial body of research demonstrates that the death of a loved one during childhood and adolescence is traumatic and can have lasting effects on a person's physical health and emotional well-being. African Americans are more likely to experience early and more frequent exposure to death than other racial-ethnic groups (see Umberson 2017 for a review of this literature).

4. The history here comes from Carroll (2013).

5. Carroll (2013: 57). Fears around changes in family eating patterns expressed by Cunningham and others in the 1800s point to a common process whereby individuals

in positions to influence others, sometimes known as moral entrepreneurs, use changes in how people live to decry the modern world, warn of wrack and ruin to come, and harken back to a better, simpler time (on moral entrepreneurs, see Becker 1963; on romanticizing the "traditional" family, see Coontz 1992).

6. Carroll (2013: 77).

7. As summarized by Musick and Meier (2012), a large body of literature finds that children who share meals with their parents score better on a range of indicators of well-being. Similarly, Musick and Meier find "strong bivariate associations" between frequency of family meals and several indicators of well-being among adolescents. However, after controlling for other factors (e.g., quality of family relationships, mothers' employment status), the associations between family meals and well-being weakened significantly. See also discussion in Chapter 9.

8. A nationally representative National Public Radio (NPR) poll of US households with children finds that even though families rank the family meal "as a high priority, about half of children live in a home where, on a given night, families don't sit down together to eat or share the same food." When families do eat together, the meals last on average eight minutes. Moreover, "about a quarter of children surveyed live in homes where—on a given night—the TV is on, or someone is using an electronic device" (Aubrey 2013: n.p.).

9. On types of home cooking, see Wolfson and Bleich (2015). Although Americans may not eat together as much as they'd like, when asked how often they eat dinner together as a family, slightly more than half report doing so at least six nights a week (Saad 2013; see also Newman et al. 2015). Analyzing data from the US National Health and Nutrition Examination Survey 2007–2010, Newman and colleagues (2015) find that low-income households are most likely to report eating frequent family meals. The American Community Survey also reveals that lower income households eat together at home more often than higher income ones (as reported in Best 2017).

10. On how often American families eat out, see Zagorsky and Smith (2017b). Although glossy media images of families gathering around the table often depict middle-class families, a study that videoed thirty-two middle-class households for a week concluded that coming together around the dinner table was a rare event in these homes (Ochs and Kremer-Sadlik 2013). Middle-class families feel pressed for time amid the competing obligations of work, extracurricular activities, and home (Best 2017; Hochschild 1997, 2012; Ochs and Kremer-Sadlik 2013) while working-class and poor families are more likely to center their time around family (Edin and Lein 1997; Lareau 2011; Roy and Burton 2007; Stack 1974).

11. With the majority of the poor spending over half their income on housing, foreclosures and evictions are much more common today than they used to be, and evictions are profitable for landlords (Desmond 2016). In 2018, sociologist Matt Desmond and his team launched the Eviction Lab, a national database of eviction records. They found that 3.79 out of every 100 renter homes in Raleigh are evicted

each year, compared to 11.44 out of every 100 renter homes in nearby Richmond, Virginia, one of the top evicting cities. But even with this comparably low rate, there were 3,322 evictions in Raleigh in 2016, or 9.1 households evicted every day. See https://evictionlab.org/.

12. The Washingtons' combined monthly rent for the $270/week room is over $1,000, which isn't cheap and is close to what they would pay to rent a home. But renting a home requires money up front, money they don't have. Being evicted has also hurt their rental prospects, by limiting the number of landlords willing to rent to them (Desmond 2016). There are many hidden costs of being poor (Ehrenreich 2001). Paying weekly rent for a hotel room that adds up to about what the family would pay to rent a home with a kitchen and separate bedrooms is one of those costs.

13. Edin and Shaefer (2016) note that in 2011, about one out of every twenty-five households with children in the United States reported a cash income of less than $2 per person per day. The number has more than doubled since the 1996 welfare reform.

CHAPTER 3

1. Since Hays (1996) coined the term "intensive mothering," researchers have documented the ramping-up of mothering in the modern era (see, for example, Blair-Loy 2003; Blum 2016; MacKendrick 2018; Nelson 2010; Reich 2016). Parents today invest more money in and spend more active time with their children than did parents in previous decades (Currid-Halkett, 2017; Kornrich and Furstenberg, 2013; Sayer, Bianchi, and Robinson, 2004). Dow (2016), however, argues that middle-class black mothers do not privilege intensive forms of mothering. Instead, they create an alternative form of mothering that integrates motherhood with employment, financial self-reliance, and kin and community help with childcare. Rae Donahue's description of mothering as an all-encompassing priority is reflective of dominant cultural messages around mothering, but different cultural expectations about motherhood hold prominence in some black communities.

2. Some research suggests that parents in the United States experience the intensive pressures of parenthood to an even greater degree than do parents in similar nations, like Canada or the United Kingdom. Sociologist Jennifer Glass and her colleagues (2016) argue that this is because parents in the United States don't have the same kinds of "family policy packages" found in other countries, which make it easier to balance the demands of parenthood. See Chapter 28.

3. In many public schools in the United States, excelling academically is associated with middle-class white students, not black or Latino/a students (Downey 2008; Fordham and Ogbu 1986). By saying she stood out by taking advanced, college-track coursework, Rae, a black woman, hints at these racialized dynamics and stereotypes.

4. African Americans who experience upward mobility are *more* likely, compared to nonmobile African Americans, to report "acute and chronic discrimination"

(Colen et al. 2018: 167). In contrast, upwardly mobile whites report less discrimination than nonmobile white people. Colen et al. (2018) find that differential exposure to unfair treatment helps explain a substantial proportion of the black-white gap in self-reported health among their sample of upwardly mobile adults.

5. African American cuisine has gone by several names since West Africans arrived in what is now the southern United States, including "slave food, the master's leftovers, southern food, country cooking, down home cooking, Negro food," and soul food (Miller 2013: 9).

6. Miller (2013: 51).

7. Miller (2013: 51). As an example of the soul food ethos, Miller cites *The African American Cookbook* author Helen Mendes, who wrote: "Soul food unites African Americans not only with their people's history, but with their contemporary Black brothers and sisters around the world. Food is a symbol of love" (as cited in Miller 2013: 51). Miller attributes the political legacy of soul food to a position paper published by the SNCC in 1966. See also Jensen Wallach (2014); Sharpless (2003); Witt (2004).

8. Miller (2013).

9. In 1907, Booker T. Washington criticized people who subsisted primarily on "grits, meat [meaning pork], corn bread." He urged black southerners to "throw off the old habit and not grow into the slavery of using a certain thing on the table because it has been used that way generation after generation" (as cited in Jensen Wallach and Sharpless 2015: 169). Du Bois wrote in 1918 that the "deceitful pork chop must be dethroned in the South and yield a part of its sway to vegetables, fruits, and fish" (as cited in Jensen Wallach and Sharpless 2015: 169).

10. Black nationalists argued "that eating soul food internalizes notions of white superiority that the master purposefully foisted upon the enslaved" (Miller 2013: 52). Elijah Muhammad, leader of the Nation of Islam (NOI), was an outspoken advocate of a "regimented, cultural nationalist diet" that forbade the consumption of pork, collard and turnip greens, cornbread, and sweet potatoes (Jensen Wallach 2014; see also Witt 2004). NOI teachings had an influence beyond active members (Jensen Wallach 2014). A 1979 survey of white and black southerners found that they had similar diets, but that black respondents were more likely than white respondents to label pork an unhealthy food (Fitzgerald 1979, as cited in Jensen Wallach 2014).

11. Gregory (1973, as cited in Jensen Wallach 2014). Gregory advocated a fruitarian, raw-foods diet.

12. Miller (2013: 53). To the contrary, however, some activists decried soul food as a fad being pushed by the black middle class. In 1965, Black Panther activist Eldridge Cleaver wrote that "the emphasis on soul food is counter-revolutionary black bourgeois ideology" (as cited in Miller 2013: 53).

13. Tipton-Martin (2015); Twitty (2017); Williams-Forson (2006).

14. Twitty (2017).

15. Harris (2011).

16. Yams are native to Africa. Once in the United States, some slaves used the term "yams" to refer to the sweet potatoes that were grown in the US South because they reminded them of yams. Today, people in the South still refer to making "candied yams"—in reality, sweet potatoes—at Thanksgiving (Twitty 2017). North Carolina is the top producer of sweet potatoes in the nation.

17. Twitty (2017) notes that by 1692, it was illegal for an enslaved person to own his or her own cow or hog. Laws did not prohibit slaves from raising chickens, and many slaves had a poultry yard with hutches for hens. According to Miller (2013), some slaves were given special privileges to sell chickens and eggs in nearby towns, once they were no longer able to work in the fields.

18. Williams-Forson (2006) argues that narratives about chicken and African American people in the United States have often been loaded with racist stereotypes, but that chicken is also an object of self-expression and resistance for black women, throughout history.

19. Edge (2017).

20. Referring to advertisements for Aunt Jemima pancake mix and the mythical mammy figure in southern literature, "the Jemima code," says Tipton-Martin (2015), was a subtle message that conveyed the idea that "if slaves can cook, you can, too." Tipton-Martin's analysis of 160 cookbooks authored by African American chefs from 1827 to 2010 aims to "break the Jemima code," highlighting the skill, sophistication, artistry, and diversity exemplified by these chefs and their dishes.

21. Williams-Forson (2006). The postcard discussed in the text and others like it can be found online at https://www.historyonthenet.com/authentichistory/diversity/african/4-brute/index.html (retrieved November 29, 2017).

22. Collins (2000); Williams-Forson (2006).

23. Tipton-Martin (2015) states that in the 1970s, black cookbook authors tried to weaken the association between soul food and poverty food by "embracing the confidence and cultural pride of the black power movement, embellishing and deepening it with African foods, celebrations, and practices."

24. Severson (2017).

25. A common refrain among the African Americans we interviewed was that soul food is a scourge on black people's health. While diet certainly matters to health, it's not the only thing that matters. For example, racism and income inequality also affect health outcomes. Black people historically and still today encounter income and wealth disenfranchisement (Branch 2011; Kochhar, Fry, and Taylor 2011), discrimination in healthcare and other institutional settings (Bridges 2011; Matthew 2015), and interpersonal forms of discrimination (sometimes called microaggressions [Sue et al. 2007]). All of these contribute to poorer health outcomes, although there is some evidence that blacks have, over time, adopted coping mechanisms that lessen the impact of discrimination on health (Sullivan 2015). Blaming poor health outcomes on the diets of marginalized groups is a way of shifting blame away from structural and interpersonal inequality. In a similar fashion, attributing high rates

of certain diseases, such as diabetes, to a race-based genetic predisposition ignores the social causes of health problems (Gómez and López 2013; Montoya 2011; Roberts 2010).

CHAPTER 4

1. Like Marta, many women intensify their self-monitoring practices around food during pregnancy (MacKendrick 2010, 2014; Warin et al. 2012). And these expectations are growing. Public health messages in the United States increasingly pressure women to prepare their bodies for motherhood and a healthy gestation far in advance of an actual pregnancy (Waggoner 2017).

2. Cooper (2014) argues that economic, political, and social shifts that started in the 1970s have transformed the way Americans go about creating security in their lives. In a context of economic insecurity, parents worry that their children will not be better off than they were (Pugh 2015). Inadequate regulation of the environment and food system, fears about bad parenting, and the rise of a "cottage industry" of advice books for anxious parents, have fostered the sense that children are constantly at risk and in need of adult supervision (Rutherford 2011) and protection (MacKendrick 2018; Waggoner 2017).

3. Pregnant women are encouraged to take individual responsibility over managing the risk of ingesting harmful substances by making safe purchases and avoiding chemicals, according to MacKendrick (2010, 2018), which she calls "precautionary consumption."

4. Cairns and Johnston (2015); Lupton (1996).

5. Apple (2006) argues in *Perfect Motherhood* that mothers are tasked with becoming the experts on their own children, a job that involves sifting through conflicting advice about how best to raise children, trying out different strategies, and managing the inevitable anxiety that comes along with attempting to get it right. See also Cairns et al. (2013); MacKendrick (2018); Reich (2016).

6. See MacKendrick (2018) for a discussion of how middle- and upper-class mothers, in particular, engage in "precautionary consumption" in order to gain a sense of control in a context in which they do not trust the way their food is produced or how it is regulated. See Waggoner (2017) for an analysis of public health campaigns around risk and health that target pre-pregnant women.

7. Lareau (2014) found that middle-class parents had "mental maps" that shaped the neighborhoods they considered. They eliminated lower-income areas and relied on social networks to share information about communities, limiting the scope of their search.

8. Breastfeeding rates are higher among middle-class mothers than among poor and working-class mothers. In general, as income and education increase, so do breastfeeding rates. While a high percentage (72.9%) of mothers with a high school degree report having breastfed, the percentage is much higher (92%) for college

graduates. Mothers with higher levels of education also tend to breastfeed longer. For example, while 40.9 percent of mothers with a high school degree report breastfeeding until the 6-month mark, this number is markedly higher (72.5%) for mothers who graduated from college. On the pressures and challenges middle-class women experience related to breastfeeding, see Afflerback et al. (2013) and Avishai (2007).

9. Rutherford (2011) argues that as middle-class children have gained more private freedoms within their nuclear families (for example, by being given choices and having their viewpoints taken into consideration), their public freedoms have eroded. Fewer children are allowed to roam neighborhood streets, catch the school bus on their own, or run down to the corner store to buy milk for the family. See also Lareau (2011) on the ways middle-class children are heavily supervised by adults.

10. Cairns et al. (2013); Cairns and Johnston (2015); MacKendrick (2018); Waggoner (2017); Warin et al. (2012).

11. Organic food sales totaled around $47 billion in 2016, more than doubling since 2007 (OTA 2017). Despite the rising popularity of organic foods, a review article finds that while consuming organic foods may reduce exposure to pesticide residues and antibiotic-resistant bacteria, evidence that they are more nutritious than conventional foods is lacking (Smith-Spangler et al. 2012).

12. "Pink slime" is a meat-based product derived from beef trimmings heated and then treated with ammonium hydroxide or citric acid to kill bacteria. It is used as a food additive or to reduce the fat content of meat. McDonald's removed pink slime from its burgers in January 2012 after the British chef Jamie Oliver led a campaign against it (Annable 2012) and a few months before ABC aired an exposé about its use in the beef industry.

13. Crawford (2006).

CHAPTER 5

1. Melanie also checked online before they moved to the area to confirm that no one nearby was a sex offender. On parents' fears about sex offenders and efforts to protect their children from sexual hazards, see Elliott (2012).

2. Body dissatisfaction is present in women of all ages, and across the life span, although there's some evidence that body dissatisfaction decreases as women age; but middle-aged women and obese women are most likely to report dissatisfaction with their bodies, preferring a body that is leaner/slimmer (Runfola et al. 2013).

3. In a study that followed people over a fifteen-year period, Puhl and colleagues (2017) found that people who experience weight-based teasing (i.e., who were fat-shamed) as children are more likely to be obese as adults, especially women. Further studies are needed to examine how individuals internalize shame around weight and what the consequences are for future weight-related outcomes and body image

(see also Lupton 2012; Puhl and Heuer 2009, 2010; Throop et al. 2014). Fat stigma has long existed in the United States, but fatness has only been linked to ideas about health fairly recently (Farrell 2011).

4. The World Health Organization and the American Academy of Pediatrics recommend that women exclusively breastfeed for at least six months. See http://www.who.int/topics/breastfeeding/en/ and https://www2.aap.org/breastfeeding/faqsbreastfeeding.html. For a discussion of the breastfeeding challenges faced by the poor and working-class mothers in our study, see Hardison-Moody et al. (2018).

5. Cairns and Johnston (2015) use the term "calibration" to refer to the process by which women position themselves as "reasonable, informed, and moderate" in terms of how they eat, shop, and feed children.

6. Saguy (2013) argues that similar frames are often used to describe poor people and overweight people. In both cases, individuals are blamed for their failure to take control or responsibility for their situation. Given that rates of obesity are higher among the poor and people of color, individual blame serves to reinforce existing race and class hierarchies. See also Boero (2012); Guthman (2011); Kwan and Graves (2013); Strings (2015).

7. According to the Centers for Disease Control and Prevention, 37.9 percent of US adults are obese (a body-mass index [BMI] of 30 or above) and 20.6 percent of US children ages 12–19 are obese (CDC 2017b). As noted in Chapter 1, rates of obesity have doubled among adults and tripled among children since the 1980s (Segal et al. 2017). Regarding the social construction of the "obesity epidemic," see Boero (2012); Guthman (2011); and Saguy (2013).

8. Mothers are often blamed for childhood obesity (Boero 2007; Saguy 2013; Wright et al. 2015). A 2011 anti-childhood obesity campaign in Georgia, for example, created billboards and public service announcement videos implying that mothers made children fat by feeding them big meals and that mothers were accepting of children's bigger body sizes.

9. A common theme in our interviews and observations was the attention people pay to girls' and women's appearances. From catcalls to casual comments, the female body is routinely subject to appraisal (Bordo 2004; Evans and Riley 2014), conveying the message that women's value lies in their looks (Young 2005).

10. See Hays (1996) on how protecting children's self-esteem has become an imperative of mothering.

11. Elliott and Bowen (2018).

CHAPTER 6

1. A *coyote* is a border-crossing guide, a person hired to transport people over the border into the United States. Crossing the border is expensive and risky, and it has become riskier in recent years, as a result of the terrorist attacks of September 11, 2001, and the increased militarization of the border (Holmes 2013).

2. The Border Patrol documented 6,023 deaths in California, Arizona, New Mexico, and Texas between 2000 and 2016 (Fernández 2017). There are likely many more undocumented deaths.

3. See Holmes's (2013) and De León's (2015) vivid accounts of the physical and emotional suffering and deaths that occur as migrants try to cross the border.

4. Smith, Ng, and Popkin (2013) find that for people who cooked, time spent cooking decreased from around an hour and a half per day to just over thirty minutes per day between 1965 and 2007. Notably, a more recent analysis (Tailie 2018) finds that overall cooking *increased* in the United States between 2003 and 2016.

5. Among people who cook, men increased their cooking time from 37 to 45 minutes per day between 1965 and 2007, while women decreased their cooking time from 112 to 66 minutes per day over the same period (Smith et al. 2013). See also Sayer (2005) and Zick and Stevens (2010). Tailie (2018) finds that between 2003 and 2016, both men and women increased their cooking time: by five minutes per day, on average, for men, and by three minutes per day for women. However, these patterns vary substantially by race, ethnicity, and education level.

6. In the United States, 39.3 percent of women were in the paid labor force in 1965, compared to 56.8 percent in 2016 (United States Department of Labor 2018).

7. On the time pressures facing modern families, see Hochschild (1997); Schulte (2014); Thistle (2006); and Wajcman (2015).

8. Bittman (2011).

9. Pollan (2013: 3).

10. *Pozole* is a stew made from hominy, broth, chiles, herbs, and chicken and/or pork, usually garnished with diced raw onion, shredded cabbage, sliced radishes, lime wedges, cilantro, and oregano. Styles of pozole vary between regions in Mexico. Rosario made a red pozole, with guajillo peppers and chicken thighs. The history of pozole in Mexico dates to the Aztecs, for whom it had a ritual significance (Castañón 2010).

11. For example, *chilaquiles* are a typical Mexican dish, made from fried corn tortillas and tomato-chile sauce. Abarca (2006) writes that people often add their own twist, but "if they are going to be authentic, one must add a few leaves of *epazote*."

12. It is easier for Rosario to find what she needs because of the many Mexican immigrants who have recently moved to North Carolina, prompting the opening of grocery stores catering to Latino/a customers. North Carolina has one of the fastest-growing Latino/a populations in the United States (Stepler and López 2016). In addition, as American food preferences have become more varied over time, chiles and other specific ingredients are increasingly available at mainstream supermarkets (Johnston and Baumann 2010).

13. Patting the tortillas into shape requires "as much finesse as grinding require[s] strength," and cooking the tortillas also requires "a practiced hand and a careful eye" (Pilcher 1998: 101).

14. Rosario's beliefs about the importance of fresh tortillas illustrate how definitions of "processed" and "from scratch" change over time and across places and are tied to moral ideals about women's labor. For centuries, tortillas were basically made the way the Aztecs had made them (Pilcher 1998; Rodríguez-Alegría 2012). Corn was simmered overnight in a mineral lime solution, to make *nixtamal*; and then ground by hand, using a stone *metate*, to make the dough for the tortillas (Pilcher 1998). Grinding corn was a labor-intensive process that took four to six hours per day or longer. The mechanical mill, which replaced the metate in the early twentieth century, fundamentally changed tortilla-making. The mechanization of the entire process in the mid-twentieth century was the next step, followed by the invention of masa harina, the flour that Rosario uses. Taking off in the 1970s, masa harina "revolutionized tortilla production" because it only requires the addition of water to make the dough, which can then be used for tortillas (Bank Muñoz 2008). Scholars have debated the gendered implications of these shifts. While the mechanical mills were framed as freeing women from servitude (Abarca 2006; Pilcher 1998), some note that mechanization removed women from the production of tortillas, making them marginalized workers in a male-dominated industry (Keremitsis 1983), while others show how women workers enacted forms of collective resistance (Fernández-Aceves 2003).

15. In 1960, most white women and nearly half of black women in the United States depended on their husbands' income for support (Thistle 2006: 172). By the mid-2000s, less than one-third of white women and barely over one-tenth of black women relied mainly on men's income for support. To learn how public policies that supported women's—especially white women's—work in the home were dismantled in the late twentieth century, see Gordon (1994); Gustafson (2009); Hays (2003); and Thistle (2006).

16. Cohn, Livingston, and Wang (2014).

17. As we discuss in Chapter 12, although Rosario often contrasts the fast food of the United States with the more traditional food of Mexico, food practices in Mexico have also changed rapidly in the last few decades. Processed foods and fast-food restaurants are increasingly available in Mexico. Even so, one way racialized immigrants situate themselves as worthy in a white-dominant society such as that of the United States can be to assert their moral superiority. This strategy often relies on women and men performing highly unequal gender roles, with the burden of demonstrating moral worthiness falling especially heavily on women and girls (Espiritu 2001). Migration to the United States can reinforce but also challenge and transform heterosexual married couples' gender-differentiated roles (Hamal Gurung 2015).

18. Latina mothers have, on average, forty-four fewer minutes of leisure time than other US mothers (Kimmel and Connelly 2007), perhaps because of their gendered labor.

CHAPTER 7

1. Greely does not actually own a pay-what-you-can café. We altered the description to protect her identity, but her real business is food-oriented and combines a market orientation with a social justice orientation.

2. Hansen (2005) refers to the relatives and friends who help with childcare as families' "networks of care." Networks of care are vital to helping many families meet care-based needs.

3. According to a 2013 Gallup Poll, 53 percent of adults with kids eighteen and younger report eating dinner together at least six nights a week, a number that has remained fairly consistent since 1990 (Saad 2013). An analysis of nationally-representative data similarly found that half (49.6%) of participants reported eating family meals frequently (seven or more times per week) (Newman et al. 2015). High-income families are the least likely to share frequent family meals, compared to poor and middle-class families.

4. With the partial exception of the 1950s, only a minority of families have been able to meet the ideal of a "proper family meal" (Cinotto 2006), many by employing domestic servants (Kornrich 2012; Levenstein 2003; Trubek 2017). Although many families today make time to eat together (Newman et al. 2015), these meals may not look like the idealized version that Greely envisions and strives for (Aubrey 2013, NPR 2013).

5. Newport (2015).

6. Slaughter (2012), in an *Atlantic Monthly* article that went viral, argued that women who continue to work full-time often feel haunted by guilt that they are bad mothers and daunted by too many expectations.

7. For examples of time-saving advice, see Feriss (2007) and Reynolds (2013). For those who can afford it, a plethora of market-based options exist to help individuals connect with others, meet mates, throw children's parties, care for aging parents, plan vacations, get fit, and on and on (Hochschild 2012).

8. See Avins's (2017) review of *A New Way to Dinner* (Hesser and Stubbs 2016).

9. Kraus and Tan's (2015) experimental research found that Americans exhibited "substantial and consistent" overestimations of the extent that people can move up or down the social class hierarchy. Social mobility is actually lower in the United States than in other industrialized countries (Mishel et al. 2012), and it shows no signs of improving. Income inequality has increased in the last four decades (Burkhauser et al. 2009; Piketty and Saez 2003). Two recent studies (Chetty et al. 2014; Chetty et al. 2017) suggest that social mobility in the United States has decreased or remained the same, depending on the measure.

10. Hochschild (2012).

11. Between 1965 and 1998, mothers' free time decreased by 41 minutes, while fathers' free time decreased by 15 minutes (Sayer 2005). In 1998, mothers reported having 28 fewer minutes of free time than fathers (Sayer 2005). Mattingly and Bianchi

(2003) find that marriage, the presence of preschoolers, and more hours of paid employment inhibit free time for women. For men, the number of children and hours of employment inhibit free time, but marriage. See also Kimmel and Connelly (2007).

12. Schulte (2014). Time-use scholars call this "fragmented time" (Bittman and Wajcman 2000; Mattingly and Bianchi 2003). Beck and Arnold's (2009) qualitative study of thirty-two middle-class families found that only about 15 percent of parents' time at home was dedicated to leisure. Mothers and fathers often experienced leisure time in "very short, fragmented episodes," although fathers had some longer periods of leisure time.

13. In addition to finding that women are more likely than men to report "always" feeling rushed, Mattingly and Sayer (2006) find that women's time pressure increased significantly between 1975 and 1998, but men's did not.

14. See Sandberg (2013). Lareau (2011) finds that middle-class parents engage in a form of concerted cultivation, which involves spending money and time cultivating children's vocabularies, interests, and talents. See also Currid-Halkett (2017).

15. Time spent "teaching and playing" with children—what many people consider "quality time"—increased for both mothers and fathers between 1965 and 1998: from 13 minutes to 28 minutes per day for mothers, and from 10 minutes to 22 minutes per day for fathers. Total time spent taking care of children has also increased (Sayer et al. 2004; Sayer 2005). Increases in time spent with children are especially likely among more affluent parents (Dotti Sani and Treas 2016).

16. Lareau (2011). Not only do poor and working-class families have fewer resources to perform this kind of parenting, notes Lareau, they are often skeptical of its unintended consequences, such as hurried kids and frazzled parents.

17. DeVault (1991).

18. See Schulte (2014). Craig and Brown (2017: 225) found that "mothers averaged more contaminated leisure and less pure leisure and did much more unpaid work multitasking than fathers."

CHAPTER 8

1. We have replaced the real fast-food restaurant where Ashley and other members of her family work with "Wendy's" to protect the Taylors' identity. Wendy's is a well-known and popular fast-food restaurant that shares characteristics with the real company they work for.

2. Surveys find that many formerly incarcerated individuals experience "housing insecurity" upon release, including homelessness, eviction, and living with others temporarily without paying rent (Fragile Families 2011).

3. Nearly half of the low-income mothers surveyed by the Fragile Families and Child Wellbeing Study reported doubling up at least once by the time their child was nine

years old (Pilkauskas, Garfinkel, and McLanahan 2014). See also Edin and Lein (1997).

4. Ashley hopes that working with Maylee on her colors and shapes will help prepare her for the Head Start preschool program, which she qualifies for in the fall.

5. In 1960, 25 percent of married couples with children under eighteen lived in dual-income households. By 2012, this had increased to 60 percent (Pew Research Center 2015a). Among employed people in the United States, 5.2 percent hold two or more jobs (Davidson 2016).

6. Henly and Lambert (2014).

7. An estimated 10 percent of the workforce is assigned to irregular and on-call shift times. Another 7 percent is made up of people who work split or rotating shifts (Golden 2015).

8. Children in low-income families are more likely to be cared for by relatives and less likely to be cared for in formal childcare centers (Chaudry et al. 2017; Ruzek et al. 2014).

9. Wajcman (2015).

10. Merkus et al. (2015); Strazdins et al. (2006); Wight et al. (2008).

11. Henly and Lambert (2014).

12. Poor and working-class mothers place a high premium on educational attainment because they hope it will allow their children to have more opportunities than they had (Elliott, Powell, and Brenton 2015; Hays 1996). Black community leaders have long touted the value of education as an important part of racial uplift (Murtadha and Watts 2005). Ashley's parenting strategies are thus infused with gendered meanings about good mothering that intersect with racial and class meanings and inequities.

13. Hart and Risley (1995) found that by age three, children from low-income families have heard thirty million fewer words than children from wealthier families. A recent study suggests that the quality of parents' verbal interactions with children might be more important than the amount (Hirsh-Pasek et al. 2015).

14. Sadeh et al. (2003); Burdette and Whitaker (2005).

CHAPTER 9

1. Tara said that the reason she was making chicken teriyaki to go with spaghetti was to have a vegetable as a side dish. We are not sure if these kinds of food pairings were common in Tara's house; they didn't occur during other meals we had with her. It may be that, feeling watched by a researcher, she chose a side dish to emphasize her efforts to feed her children healthy foods like vegetables. Although we stressed to all the families that we wanted them to follow their usual routines and were not passing judgment on their food practices, some families may have felt that they were under the microscope and made decisions they wouldn't have otherwise; see Emerson, Fretz, and Shaw (1995) for how researchers' presence shapes what people

do and thus what researchers see. It may also be that, given the number of people she was feeding, Tara chose to include the chicken teriyaki to make sure there was enough food to go around, although that's not the explanation she offered.

2. Rashan and Tyree have different fathers. Tara left Rashan's dad when she got pregnant and she felt "the situation was going downhill," but he occasionally drops by with a Christmas or birthday gift, or to say hello. Tyree's dad has been in and out of prison and never comes by. "He wasn't there when I was pregnant. He wasn't there when I went into labor and none of that," says Tara. "But he was there when we made it. They always are."

3. In a powerful essay, Smarsh (2014) argues that poor teeth are associated with shame and intense scrutiny. They also "beget more poorness, [since] people with bad teeth have a harder time getting jobs and other opportunities." Tara felt stigmatized by her teeth and wanted better for her children. She explained, "I want my children to have pretty white teeth because I know mine are messed up. And I want them to have pretty smiles so when they do meet a girl or they do go in front of people's faces for jobs, stuff like that, they give a good persona about they-self.... That makes them look like something."

4. Sociologist Jennifer Jordan's (2015) concept of "edible memory" refers to the foods we grow attached to, both collectively, as communities and societies, and individually.

5. Experiments by Troisi and Gabriel (2011) found that comfort foods like chicken soup can actually trigger feelings of "belonging" in people.

6. College students in an experiment were asked to smell twelve scented oils, some associated with food (e.g., pumpkin pie spice, apple pie) and others not (e.g., lavender flowers, baby powder). Scent-evoked nostalgia predicted higher levels of self-esteem, optimism, and social connectedness, among other things (Reid et al. 2015: 157).

7. Although many of the mothers in our study had grown up in poverty, many recalled memories that were mostly positive.

8. Bugge and Almås (2006); DeVault (1991); Lupton (1996).

9. Hill and colleagues (2016) found that people who grew up poor have a harder time regulating their food intake and continue to eat even when they are not hungry.

10. Tara's household is one of the growing numbers of households in the United States getting by on less than $2 per person per day (Edin and Shaefer 2016).

11. See North Carolina Department of Health and Human Services (2018).

12. See Ventura and Birch (2008) and Shloim et al. (2015) for reviews. Critics note a lack of clarity in terms of whether pressuring children to eat results in pickier children or whether parents are more likely to pressure pickier children to eat (Farrow et al. 2009; Gregory et al. 2010). Many studies have focused on white, middle-class families. Kuyper et al. (2009) call for more attention to how feeding practices play out in poor and food-insecure households.

13. Daniel (2016).

14. Wilk (2010) argues that although the normative idea of the family meal is still ascendant in US culture, it is at odds with the "performative" or real way in which mealtimes play out in families, in which "conflict prevails."

15. David et al. (2010); Fishel (2015); Parrott and Parrott (2011); Weinstein (2006).

16. These findings come from two studies, conducted by sociologists Kelly Musick and Ann Meier, which draw on multiple waves of data from the National Longitudinal Study of Adolescent Health, a large, nationally representative dataset. In the first study, Musick and Meier find that associations between family meals and indicators of well-being weaken significantly after controlling for other factors. Musick and Meier (2012: 489) conclude: "The seemingly large effects of family dinners as estimated at the cross section (and in much prior research) are due mostly to unobserved factors." The ability to manage regular family meals may, in other words, be a proxy for other dimensions of the family environment, like strong family relationships. Musick and Meier's research also calls into question the idea that the benefits of family meals stretch into adulthood. In the second study, Meier and Musick (2014) "find that family dinners have little benefit when parent–child relationships are weak but contribute to fewer depressive symptoms and less delinquency among adolescents when family relationships are strong." Thus, family dinners can be beneficial but only if families have strong relationships to begin with; Musick and Meier find no evidence that the dinners themselves can create these strong bonds.

CHAPTER 10

1. Food is not the only source of friction between Leanne and her mother. Leanne attributes her mental health issues to moving in with her mother at the age of twelve and getting hooked on the same drugs her mom was using. According to Leanne, she stopped using crack cocaine when she overdosed and was sent to rehab at sixteen. Renata got clean too and things changed in their household. These days, Leanne depends a lot on Renata, for things like rides to the grocery store. Renata also manages Leanne's money.

2. Although these foods are often labeled junk food, they are ubiquitous in American diets (Chen 2016; Fielding-Singh 2017; Ochs and Kremer-Sadlik 2013). Their purchase and consumption have thus come to symbolize a form of belonging in US society (Perry and Calarco 2017; Pugh 2009). They are also an important way that low-income mothers "express their devotion to their children beyond basic survival needs" (Chen 2016: 163).

3. Between 1965 and 2008, the percentage of American men who cooked increased from 29 percent to 42 percent (Smith et al. 2013). Among men who cook, time spent cooking increased from thirty-seven minutes per day in 1965 to forty-five minutes per day in 2008 (Smith et al. 2013). A 2018 study suggests that the percentage of men who cook has continued to rise, to 46 percent in 2016 (Tailie 2018).

But while the percentage of men with a high school or college education who cooked increased between 2003 and 2016, the percentage of men with less than a high school education who cooked did not change (Tailie 2018).

4. 74 percent of American women report that they "usually prepare the meals" in their household, compared to 36 percent of men. Close to 10 percent of men and women said they split the meal preparation work evenly. See USDA (2016a).

5. Szabo (2012) reviewed the literature on the gendered division of cooking labor within households (see also Szabo 2014; Szabo and Koch 2017), concluding that men may find cooking more leisurely than women because they have autonomy in terms of when and if they do it, and because their cooking tends to be oriented toward leisure or self-care rather than the care of others.

6. Leanne's efforts to involve Latrell in cooking are one way that she creates the conditions for gendered family traditions, similar to when fathers are asked to carve the turkey at Thanksgiving. While people may remember their mothers as the primary cooks in the family (Best 2017), they may remember the public role their fathers played around food (such as preparing a signature dish), indicating the ways gender continues to organize and differentiate the domestic and public realms (Cairns, Johnston, and Baumann 2010).

CHAPTER 11

1. In general, married people exhibit better health and have lower mortality rates than unmarried people (Smith and Christakis 2008; Umberson, Crosnoe, and Reczek 2010). One reason may be because spouses—especially women—frequently monitor and attempt to control each other's health behaviors (Umberson 1992). However, not all of the health effects of marriage are positive. Married people also generally weigh more and exercise less than unmarried people (Umberson et al. 2010). Bove, Sobal, and Rauschenbach (2003) find that newly married couples' eating preferences tend to either converge or conflict, or that couples will eat separately. Typically, a woman plays the role of "food director," attempting to get her spouse to eat healthier, mirroring the role Rae took early in her marriage. This process is a negotiation, resulting in varying degrees of compromise and success (Bove et al. 2003).

2. Wilk (2010).

3. DeVault (1991) was the first to highlight how much work goes into feeding a family. Importantly, she found that some of it was invisible even to the women who did it.

4. Among American men, 46 percent do some cooking at home, compared to 70 percent of American women (Taillie et al. 2018). In a study that includes data from multiple countries, Hook (2010) finds that women spend less time cooking if they have a child under the age of five. Each paid hour of work is also associated with spending less time cooking.

5. Based on interviews with male and female "foodies," Cairns et al. (2010) found that women commonly framed their foodwork in terms of protecting family health. By contrast, men rarely mentioned health. Researchers also find key differences between how men and women feed their children (see Khandpur et al. 2014).

6. Rae's fears about Tyler's weight are informed by her own family history. But they also likely reflect the fact that mothers, individually and collectively, are positioned as responsible for children's health and weight (Boero 2007; Saguy 2013; Wright et al. 2015). Special scrutiny is reserved for poor mothers and mothers of color (Boero 2007), who are not only thought to feed their children less healthy foods but to have greater acceptance of larger bodies (Saguy 2013). Mothers must defend themselves in the face of these judgments (see Elliott and Bowen 2018).

7. Beagan et al. (2008) argue that current discourses about food and motherhood reinforce long-standing gendered divisions of labor by pressuring mothers to engage in intensive foodwork "through a new rationale": their families' health and that of the nation depends on it.

8. Ventura and Birch (2008); Shloim et al. (2015). See Chapter 9.

9. Bastwell et al. (2002).

10. Research on parental feeding practices has mostly focused on mothers, but researchers have begun comparing mothers' and fathers' feeding practices. As summarized by Khandpur et al. (2014), fathers are less likely to monitor children's food intake, track or limit snacks and desserts, or ensure that fruits and vegetables are available (Blisset et al. 2006; Hendy et al. 2009; Zhang and McIntosh 2011).

CHAPTER 12

1. A large body of research has investigated the "immigrant health paradox," the finding that newly arrived immigrants are often healthier than their native-born counterparts (Riosmena et al. 2013). They tend to eat better, have lower incidences of many diseases, and live longer. Over time, and especially across generations, however, their health deteriorates (Bates et al. 2008). Many studies show that over time, immigrants consume fewer fruits and vegetables and more junk food and soda (Ayala et al. 2008; Pérez-Escamilla 2011; Van Hook et al. 2016). Researchers posit that this is due to "acculturation"—that the lure of the American food culture proves too tempting.

2. Van Hook et al. (2016: 192).

3. Guendelman et al. (2011) conducted an experiment to test their hypothesis that "pressure felt by US immigrant groups to prove they belong in America" would lead them to eat "more prototypically American" foods. They found that Asian Americans were three times more likely to report an "American" food as their favorite after being asked whether they spoke English. Questioning the English abilities of white Americans did not affect their reported food preferences.

4. Latina immigrant mothers in our study often attributed their children's preferences for "American" food to the foods they were served at school meals. Most of the school-age children in the study received free or reduced price school lunches, which are designed to comply with US dietary guidelines. In our research sites, school lunches generally reflected stereotypical American taste preferences. This may be changing in some school districts, as menus are revamped to better reflect the taste preferences of diverse student populations (see Best 2017; Sparling 2017).

5. See Moss (2013) for a sobering exposé into the art and science of chemically crafted foods.

6. Other countries, including Sweden, Norway, and Chile, have instituted laws restricting companies from marketing junk food and other products to children. However, attempts to regulate food ads aimed at children have largely failed in the United States. In the late 1970s, the Federal Trade Commission (FTC) proposed to develop rules on restricting or banning food ads aimed at young children and solicited public comments on the proposed regulations. Critics charged that the FTC had overstepped its reach and turned into "a great national nanny" (*Washington Post* editorial 1978). Congress allowed the agency's funding to lapse and it was shut down briefly in 1980. In the same year, Congress passed a law prohibiting the FTC from addressing "unfair" advertising toward children, severely hampering the agency's scope and power. In recent years, some food companies have voluntarily pledged to reduce unhealthy food advertising to children, but the scope of the pledges is limited by the fact that they do not apply to television programming directed at children age 12 and older (Fleming-Milici and Harris 2016).

7. Federal Trade Commission (2012).

8. "The prevailing pattern of food and beverage products marketed to children and youth has been high in total calories, sugar, salt, fat, and low in nutrients," concluded McGinnis, Gootman, and Kraak (2006) in a report based on a comprehensive review of the scientific research on the effect of food advertising on children's nutritional beliefs, choices, practices, and outcomes.

9. Fleming-Milici and Harris (2016). Another study analyzed ads during Nickelodeon programming over a period of twenty-eight hours and found that 65 percent were for "foods of poor nutritional quality" (Center for Science in the Public Interest 2016).

10. Harris, LoDolce, Dembek, and Schwartz (2015). They note that this increase is despite the implementation of the Children's Food and Beverage Advertising Initiative in 2007, in which food companies voluntarily pledged to stop advertising unhealthy foods during "child-directed" programming.

11. Sadeghirad et al. (2016).

12. See Fleming-Milici and Harris (2016).

13. Takis were introduced to the United States in 2006; since then, they have become wildly popular, especially among kids and teenagers (Kiely 2013; PR Newswire 2014). Takis are produced by Barcel, a subsidiary of Grupo Bimbo (Caruso-Cabrera 2013).

14. Martínez (2013) argues that Latin American migrants' diets often began shifting even before they left their native countries as a result of the globalization of the food system and the modernization of food production and consumption practices since the 1980s.

15. Jacobs and Richtel (2017a) and Clark et al. (2012) attribute much of the increase in consumption of fast and processed food in Mexico to the North American Free Trade Agreement (NAFTA, implemented in 1994) and other free trade policies that lifted tariffs and rules restricting foreign investment, opening the "floodgates to cheap corn, meat, high-fructose corn syrup, and processed foods," and fueling the growth of American fast-food restaurants. See examples from Brazil and Ghana (Jacobs and Richtel 2017b; Searcey and Richtel 2017).

16. Van Hook et al. (2016).

17. It's important to Rosario to feed her children well as part of her identity as a good mom. But she also worries about her youngest daughter Gabi's weight. At her last checkup, Rosario was told by a health provider that Gabi was "a little small, but nothing to worry about yet." Although the health provider reassured Rosario not to worry, she still does. In a context of poverty and possibly food shortages, low-income mothers worry that their children's small bodies might signal to others that their mothers are not feeding them enough (Elliott and Bowen 2018).

CHAPTER 13

1. Coleman-Jensen et al. (2017). Rates of food insecurity in the United States were at 12 percent in 2016. Seventeen percent of households with children report experiencing food insecurity, compared to 11 percent of households without children (Coleman-Jensen et al. 2017). Rates of food insecurity were even higher during the years when we conducted this research (14.5%, on average).

2. Martin and Lippert (2012); Stevens (2010).

3. Household food insecurity seems to affect women's dietary quality more than children's or men's (Hanson and Connor 2014; Larson and Story 2011). Women without children and men living in food-insecure households do not tend to make the same nutritional sacrifices. In households facing food shortages, it is women living with children who give up their own food needs (Martin and Lippert 2012; Olson 2005; Stevens 2010).

4. We interviewed Mia during the fifth year of the project, not long after her seventh birthday. Mia told us that her mom and grandma often don't eat when she eats. She also expressed worries about not having enough to eat and concerns about how hard it is for her family to get enough food.

5. For research on children in food-insecure households, see Fram et al. (2011). Older children may even take it upon themselves to chip in resources for food.

6. This meal was unusual among the meals we observed because the kids didn't complain about the food or leave food uneaten.

7. During the time we observed Patricia Washington's family, her son Doug brought over takeout for Patricia twice. Patricia was uncomfortable talking about her family's food hardships. We don't know whether Patricia asked Doug to bring her food during the times we observed meals, in order to reinforce the image that the family was not food-insecure, or whether Doug commonly did this. Patricia's reticence to talk about the family's food supply means we were unable to clarify this.

CHAPTER 14

1. MacKendrick (2014, 2018) argues that in the face of inadequate regulatory oversight of the chemicals used to grow food, make processed foods, and manufacture consumer goods, people increasingly engage in "precautionary consumption" in order to mitigate their exposure to potentially harmful chemicals.

2. Whole Foods is the tenth largest supermarket chain in the United States and the largest to specialize in certified organic foods and so-called health foods (MacKendrick 2018: 23).

3. On conscious consumerism and "voting with your fork," see MacKendrick (2018) and DeLind (2011). Importantly, Greely never used the word "vote" or "politics" when describing her food practices and philosophy (see MacKendrick 2018), although she saw her shopping actions as having broad collective implications. For example, she emphasized the importance of buying from small, local farmers in order to "support our culture here [in this area] and, over time, influence [farming] practices."

4. MacKendrick (2018).

5. Food now comes from "a global everywhere, yet from nowhere" (Kloppenburg et al. 1996: 34), such that people increasingly aim to connect with the people and places that produce their food. The "eating for change" movement generally takes two forms. First, local food systems (e.g., farmers' markets and community-supported agriculture) try to create social ties between producers and consumers, conveying values such as care, community, and stewardship (Hendrickson and Heffernan 2002; Hinrichs 2000). Second, ethical and place-based labels (e.g., organic, fair trade) seek to re-embed food systems in their social and ecological contexts, incorporating a variety of values (e.g., ethical, cultural, environmental) (Barham 2002; Bowen 2015; Raynolds 2000).

6. Johnston and Szabo (2009) use Whole Foods as a case study to examine the motivations that underlie "shopping for change" and the associated tensions and limitations of this credo.

7. Walmart announced a new focus on procuring local foods in 2006, although its definition of "local" has shifted over time. Consistent with its overall strategy, Walmart has generally opted to "centralize and standardize local food from the top down" (Bloom and Hinrichs 2017: 180).

8. Funk and Kennedy (2016).

9. United States Department of Agriculture (2018a).

10. Funk and Kennedy (2016).
11. Som Castellano (2016) found that women who engage in alternative food practices exert more physical labor in food provisioning than women who do not engage in alternative food practices. See also Allen and Sachs (2007); Cairns and Johnston (2015); Little et al. (2009); and MacKendrick (2018).
12. Delind (2011).
13. In 2012, the year that we interviewed Greely, the median household income in the United States was $51,371. In North Carolina, it was $45,150 (https://www.census.gov/prod/2013pubs/acsbr12-02.pdf).
14. Being able to purchase organic foods and protect their children's health can give mothers a sense of control and accomplishment, but mothers who don't have the money, time, or energy to live up to these middle-class feeding ideals feel like failures (MacKendrick 2018; see also Cairns et al. 2010).
15. In response to Adelle's protests about the hot dogs they serve at the café, Greely says the café "is working on it," by which she means they hope to start sourcing their hot dogs from small local producers, but she has found it harder to enact her food philosophy at the café than she initially anticipated (see Chapter 20). Informing children about where their food comes from is important to many foodie mothers, according to Cairns and Johnston (2018), but meat poses a particular dilemma for these mothers, who want their children to understand the ethical connotations of the foods they eat but not to be exposed to animal slaughter. Indeed, Greely has shied away from taking Adelle to a conventional meat producer.
16. For discussions of food and belonging in other contexts, see Guendelman et al. (2011) and Wills et al. (2011).
17. Cairns and Johnston (2015).
18. For examples, see Bowen (2015) and Seidman (2007).
19. DeLind (2011).
20. See MacKendrick (2018).

CHAPTER 15

1. Researchers recommend repeatedly exposing children to new and disliked foods in order to foster healthy eating habits later in life (Sullivan and Birch 1990; Wardle et al. 2003).
2. Brenton (2017) documents how standards for feeding children have ramped up in recent decades, mirroring the "intensive mothering" phenomenon documented by Hays (1996).
3. For example, The Family Dinner Project suggests that parents avoid controversial topics, tell kids to take a "deep breath," and focus on developing select table manners to avoid conflict at the table (DeRosa 2016).
4. On parental feeding styles and child eating and weight status, see Faith et al. (2004). On parental control and child feeding practices, see Ventura and Birch (2008). On

the number of times foods must be presented for children to develop a taste for them, see Sullivan and Birch (1990) and Daniel (2016). Through repeated exposure, infants and children can learn to like foods that are not inherently palatable or calorific (Birch 1999; Wardle et al. 2003).

5. The United States has the highest prevalence of obese fifteen-year-olds (31%) in the countries that are members of the Organization for Economic Cooperation and Development (OECD 2017a).

6. The highest prevalence of obese adults in the OECD is in the United States (38.2%), followed by Mexico (32.4%). A person with a body mass index (BMI) of 30 of higher is considered obese. A person with a BMI between 25 and 30 is considered overweight. Mexico has the highest percentage of adults who are overweight (a category that includes people who are classified as obese or overweight): 70 percent, compared to 67 percent in the United States (OECD 2017a).

7. One study finds that middle-class mothers view the daily act of packing a lunchbox as a symbolic display of their commitment to classed ideas about good mothering and health (Harman and Cappellini 2015).

8. A study of English teens by Stead et al. (2011) found that teenagers (ages 13–15) used food to establish a popular social identity and made fun of other children who ate cheap or unpopular brands of food. The study shows teens engage in processes of judgment and distinction through food choices and consumption. See also Best (2017).

9. Marta's principles echo one of Pollan's (2009) key pieces of advice about food: "Don't eat anything your grandma wouldn't recognize as food." Laudan (2015) cautions foodies like Pollan against romanticizing the food of the past because "fast food has been a mainstay of every society."

10. Marta's point about the high cost of fruits and vegetables is supported by research. One study concluded that low-income households would have to allocate 70 percent of their average food-at-home budget just to meet federal recommendations for fruits and vegetables (Cassady, Jetter, and Culp 2007). Another study found that a family of four with two young children would need to spend $374 on top of their food stamps to meet federal guidelines for a healthy diet, even when choosing the most affordable options (Mulik and Haynes-Maslow 2017). However, as Guthman (2011) and Kirkland (2011) argue, although arguments focusing on the high costs of healthy food or whether people in poor neighborhoods have access to supermarkets seem like they are tackling structural problems in the food system, they ultimately focus more on food consumption than food production. In the end, the conclusion is that obesity could be prevented by changes in individual consumers' behavior, without fundamentally overhauling the food system.

11. Mothers' desire to protect their children's health and purity is a primary motivation for purchasing organic food (Cairns et al. 2013; see also Brenton 2017). Mothers attempt to protect children's health even before they are born (MacKendrick 2014, 2018; Waggoner 2017).

12. Bourdieu (1984) famously argued that food and eating are tied to processes of distinction and the preservation of social hierarchies. Beagan and her colleagues (2015) demonstrated that what seems correct to our taste buds is not natural, but is deeply intertwined with gendered and classed identities.

13. Food offers upper-class parents a vehicle for fulfilling ideals of responsible parenting that are centered around self-restraint, health, and appreciation for healthy foods, Fielding-Singh (2017) argues. "Using food this way also allows high-SES [socioeconomic status] parents to feel and signal to others that they are successful, invested caregivers," she writes (442).

14. In the past, high-brow tastes in food, art, and music were defined by their exclusivity. But Khan (2011: 134) argues that "the 'highbrow snob' is almost dead." The new mark of culinary sophistication is not exclusive consumption, but omnivorous consumption—exemplified by those who are both knowledgeable about diverse foods and willing to try anything (Johnston and Baumann 2010).

15. Some wealthy parents are so committed to ensuring that their children develop a diverse palate that they are willing to hire an expensive "nanny consulting service" to teach their nanny how to prepare sophisticated, healthy food from scratch, according to the *New York Times* (Tell 2013). Fielding-Singh (2017) notes that just as high-SES parents took pride in their children's healthy eating habits, they expressed guilt and shame when their children did not adhere to eating ideals.

16. Fielding-Singh (2017: 425) states that for high-SES parents, "food offers an ongoing medium for teaching restraint and delayed gratification." She finds that these parents regularly deny adolescents' requests for particular foods and drinks, in order to signal that they are transmitting the "right" values.

17. This answer comes in response to a parent's question about dealing with a "dinner dawdler." See http://itsnotaboutnutrition.com/2014/01/15/dawdler/. See also Rose (2014).

CHAPTER 16

1. The US Department of Agriculture (USDA) regularly estimates the costs of feeding a family of four according to federal nutrition guidelines. In May 2013, when we conducted the supermarket observation with Melanie, the USDA estimated that the "Thrifty Meal Plan" would cost between $552 and $632 per month for a family of four (USDA 2013). The USDA does not factor in the cost of home labor when making these estimates. Including labor costs, Mulik and Haynes-Maslow (2017) estimate that it would cost between $997 and $1,185 to feed a family of four according to the USDA's recommendations (and choosing the cheapest options).

2. Supplemental Nutrition Assistance Program (SNAP) guidelines state that "everyone who lives together and prepares meals together is grouped together as one household" (USDA 2018b). To be eligible for SNAP, a household may not have

$2,250 in countable resources, such as a bank account, or $3,500 in countable resources if at least one person is age sixty or older, or is disabled. In some states, the fair market value of vehicles over $4,650 is counted. Households must also meet gross and net income tests, with some exclusions for households in which all members are receiving Temporary Assistance for Needy Families (TANF) or Supplementary Security Income (SSI), or households with an elderly person or a person receiving disability payments.

3. Melanie's household income is under the federal poverty level of $27,560 per year for a family of five (https://aspe.hhs.gov/2013-poverty-guidelines).

4. In North Carolina, most households receiving food stamps have to "recertify" every six months (https://www2.ncdhhs.gov/info/olm/manuals/dss/ei-30/man/FSs400.htm). Household income is averaged over the six-month period. Melanie's average monthly income over the six-month period that includes the summer is about half of her average monthly income during the school year, so she gets more food stamps during this period. During the period of our observations with Melanie, she was working and getting $189 in food stamps per month.

5. The percentage of Americans who say they "actively try to include" organic foods in their diet is relatively similar across income groups (Rifkin 2014). However, higher-income households are more likely to actually purchase organic products (Dettmann and Dimitri 2009; Dimitri and Dettmann 2012).

6. Soda is a big source of tension between Melanie and her husband. Melanie despises soda because she believes it's unhealthy, and she doesn't want the kids drinking it. After many arguments with Kevin about soda, she has let it go, for now. Given that Kevin's health condition and lack of employment make him grumpy, Melanie understands that soda is a bright spot in Kevin's day and that it gives him a boost of energy.

7. Food can be a "symbolic antidote to a context of deprivation" for low-income parents, Fielding-Singh (2017: 442) argues. See also Chen (2016); and Perry and Calarco (2017).

8. See Brenton (2017); Fielding-Singh (2017); and Wright et al. (2015).

9. Food stamps also cannot be used for beer, wine, liquor, cigarettes, or tobacco (USDA 2017a).

CHAPTER 17

1. See, for example, Prasertong (2014). Additional tips include checking store circulars, shopping with cash, and buying generics.

2. Even though buying in bulk saves money, it creates an added logistical challenge as Ashley tries to calculate her monthly food budget.

3. Veit (2013: 1) argues that during the first two decades of the twentieth century, "modern food science, Progressive impulses, and U.S. involvement in World War I all came together to fundamentally change American thinking on food." For

analyses of more recent messages to women about cost-saving strategies, see DeVault (1991) and Koch (2012).

4. Post–World War I inflation led to rising food prices and other living expenses and exacerbated long-standing social tensions (Deutsch 2012).

5. Deutsch (2012: 48).

6. Proponents of "rational eating" in the early twentieth century focused on getting the most nourishment for the least amount of money. Foods that offered the most calories per dollar were considered a better value. As late as 1911, a US government nutritionist argued that fruits and vegetables were nutritionally void (Veit 2013).

7. Koch (2012).

8. Koch (2012) notes that stores employ a variety of overt and covert practices to increase profitability, concluding that the idea of consumer sovereignty is a fiction. See also Ken (2014) and Hussein (2017).

9. These strategies are discussed by Hussein (2017); Kendall (2014); Koch (2012); and Patel (2007).

10. Patel (2007: 224).

11. Patel (2007: 224) concludes, "Everything, including the smell of the air, the kind of lighting, the positioning of product and wall coverings, has been pored over and dissected."

12. These data allow stores to target their direct marketing materials to individual consumers—for example, by sending emails that highlight sales on products that consumers normally buy. Stores also use this information to help them determine what products to stock and how much of each they need (Patel 2007).

13. See, for example, Chen (2016); Fielding-Singh (2017); Karmarkar and Bollinger (2015); and Pugh (2009).

14. Researchers analyzed store receipts from a large California chain grocery store over a long period of time. Because customers swiped their store loyalty cards and received a credit for bringing their own bags, researchers could analyze the same customers' purchases when they did and did not use cloth bags. They found that shoppers acted differently depending on whether they remembered their cloth bags or not (Karmarkar and Bollinger 2015).

15. At the time of our field research, celebrities had been recently photographed drinking Neuro Sonic, adding to the drink's cultural cachet. On consumption in US culture, see Pugh (2009).

CHAPTER 18

1. In 2004, the Bush administration announced that it had successfully changed an important aspect of food aid. Instead of paper coupons, food stamp recipients would now use an EBT (electronic benefits transfer) card (Pear 2004).

2. We have replaced the real fast-food restaurant where Leanne works with "McDonald's" to protect Leanne's identity.

3. Leanne's oldest two children were adopted by her aunt and uncle when the youngest was still in diapers. Leanne doesn't have much contact with them because she is scared to allow her aunt and uncle near her other children. "They always nitpick with me. That's how they got the girls. Like if there was a diaper rash they called Social Services on me," she says. As is the case for all low-income mothers, the stakes for Leanne to demonstrate that she is a good mother are high (see Elliott et al. 2015; Elliott and Bowen 2018; Reich 2005).

4. Food Town was founded in North Carolina in 1957, becoming Food Lion in 1983. As part of the larger study we conducted, Voices into Action, we surveyed mothers about the closest supermarket to their house and their preferred supermarket. MacNell (2016) analyzed this survey as part of her dissertation. For the vast majority of participants (71%), the closest supermarket was a Food Lion. Food Lion was also the most popular choice. Many of the mothers in our study mentioned Food Lion's sales as one of the reasons they shopped there. However, only 38 percent of participants listed Food Lion as their preferred store. A fifth of the women preferred to shop at Walmart, despite the fact that this was not the closest option for anyone.

5. The amount of the paycheck is what Leanne reported being paid, as recorded in the researcher's field notes. However, the researcher didn't ask Leanne how many hours she had worked and did not see the check to confirm the amount.

6. In poor families experiencing multiple forms of material hardship, women adopt a range of strategies to prevent or mitigate the consequences of hardship, including making calculated tradeoffs, such as weighing the utility of paying one bill over another (Heflin et al. 2009).

7. According to the USDA, in 2016, 12.3 percent of US households were "food insecure," meaning that they did not have access at all times to enough food for an active, healthy life for all household members. Between 2008 and 2014, the food insecurity rate ranged from 14 percent to 14.9 percent (Coleman-Jensen et al. 2017).

8. Heflin et al. (2007); Olson et al. (1996); and Rose (1999).

9. Food insecurity is associated with events such as difficulty paying medical bills, unexpected expenses in the last year, or having a lower than usual income in the last year (Olson et al. 1996). Food insecurity is also associated with unstable and vulnerable housing situations such as living "doubled up" or having to move frequently (Cutts et al. 2011; Kirkpatrick and Tarasuk 2011). Kushel et al. (2006) find that both food insecurity and housing insecurity are related to lower access to or utilization of healthcare.

10. Desmond (2016).

11. Desmond (2016) offers a powerful analysis of why a woman who had been evicted used her entire monthly allotment of food stamps to buy lobster tails and other seafood. For people living on the economic margins, and who, like Leanne, face "compounded limitations," Desmond writes, "it was difficult to imagine the amount of good behavior or self-control that would allow them to lift themselves

out of poverty." According to Desmond, people cope with grinding poverty by "surviving in color, to season the suffering with pleasure." Similarly, Leanne finds ways to brighten her day and the days of her children; see also Chen (2016) and Fielding-Singh (2017).

CHAPTER 19

1. The food stamp program was temporarily expanded in 2009, as part of the Recovery Act. The boost expired on November 1, 2013. The USDA reported that a family of three, like Tara's, would see a $29 cut in food stamps, assuming no other changes in household size, income, or expenses (Concannon 2013). The shopping trip discussed in this chapter took place in early December, a few days after the Thanksgiving dinner described in Chapter 26. She was concerned about the costs of the upcoming Christmas dinner, almost a month away.

2. Philpott (2017) and Soss (2017).

3. In an article in the *Washington Post*, Dewey (2017) characterizes some of the most common myths about the SNAP program as follows: "It's rife with fraud; it's abused by immigrants; it's typically used to buy junk food." Among Americans surveyed, 54 percent think people should not be allowed to use food stamps to buy expensive items such as crab legs; 45 percent think that people should be allowed to use food stamps to buy junk food, like potato chips, candy, and soda (Delaney and Swanson 2013).

4. The social safety net available to poor families in the United States was severely cut by the 1996 Personal Responsibility and Work Opportunity Reconciliation Act. Twenty-three out of every one hundred poor families with children now receive cash assistance from Temporary Assistance for Needy Families (TANF), also known as "welfare" (Floyd et al. 2017). In 1996, sixty-eight out of every one hundred poor families with children received TANF. North Carolina's TANF-to-poverty ratio is one of the lowest in the country; for every one hundred poor families with children, only seven receive assistance from TANF (Floyd et al. 2016). At the same time, Moffit (2015) argues that total welfare spending has actually increased in recent decades. TANF has been cut, but Medicaid has expanded, the Earned Income Tax Credit (which gives tax breaks for low-income families) was started in 1998, and the food stamp (SNAP) program has ebbed and flowed with economic cycles. Moffit argues, importantly, that these spending shifts have been accompanied by distributions away from the poorest families to those with higher incomes, from single-parent families to families with married parents, and from non-elderly and nondisabled families to families with older adults and disabled members.

5. The USDA estimates that the SNAP program provided benefits to 44.2 million people living in 21.8 million households each month across the United States (USDA 2017b). The population of the United States in 2016 was approximately 323.1 million people (United States Census Bureau 2016).

6. Morin (2013).
7. Harris (2018) writes about the stigma and shame she felt when she had to use food stamps. She even kept it a secret from her daughter.
8. The New York State Senate, Senate Bill S6761, 2015–2016 Legislative Session. Available at https://www.nysenate.gov/legislation/bills/2015/s6761 (retrieved June 5, 2017).
9. Landsbaum (2016).
10. Olson et al. (2016). The quote comes from a press release on the study (http://news.ubc.ca/2016/03/08/ubc-study-welfare-recipients-seen-as-immoral-for-buying-ethical-products/).
11. Poppendieck ([1986] 2014: 21).
12. This history comes from Poppendieck ([1986] 2014).
13. President Hoover, a firm believer in the superiority of the American way of "neighborly concern," was initially hesitant to organize a coordinated relief effort. But as millions of Americans swallowed their pride and applied for relief from local governments or private charities, the inadequacy of pre-Depression relief arrangements became obvious (Poppendieck [1986] 2014). Farm prices fell more than 18 percent during 1932, after having fallen more than 50 percent over the previous two years. Although 1932 was a particularly bad year for farmers, the crisis was not new, with roots stretching back more than a decade. Huge surpluses of corn, cotton, and wheat began to accumulate.
14. Poppendieck ([1986] 2014: xvi).
15. In the foreword to Poppendieck's book, Marion Nestle emphasized how these policies aimed to resolve two pressing social issues with one stroke: breadlines, the masses of people who lined up for free food; and surpluses, the "great bounty of American agriculture that was available at the time but unaffordable and allowed to rot or be intentionally destroyed" (Poppendieck ([1986] 2014: ix).
16. Plumer (2014).
17. USDA (2017b). SNAP households received an average of $255 per month in food stamps, which can be used for most types of food and drinks. WIC, discussed in Chapter 23, is another important food assistance program (USDA 2017a).
18. For example, when President Trump revealed his proposed 2018 budget, it aimed to slash funding for food stamps by decreasing the number of people eligible for this program, imposing stricter time limits and work requirements on recipients, and allowing states to cut the amount of benefits individuals receive (Dean 2017). Many of these featured were included in the draft of the Farm Bill released in April 2018 and discussed below.
19. Dewey (2018a). Perdue made this statement in February 2018, in reference to an announcement that the USDA would begin looking for ways to increase the work requirements associated with receiving SNAP.
20. Existing SNAP rules already required that able-bodied adults work at least a part-time job, but gave exemptions to people with children under eighteen. The Farm Bill

proposal "would establish a single work standard for adults ages 18 to 59," requiring them to hold at least a part-time job or participate in an employment training program within a month of receiving benefits (Dewey 2018a, 2018b). Pregnant and disabled people and those with children under six would be exempt, but people with school-age children would not. People who fail to get a job or join a training program could lose SNAP benefits for twelve months for the first violation and thirty-six months for the second violation under the new proposal (Booker and Charles 2018). Preliminary analyses from the Congressional Budget Office suggested that the new rules could lead to one million people leaving the SNAP rolls over the next ten years (Dewey 2018b).

21. Booker and Charles (2018).
22. Sixty-five percent of people receiving food stamps are unable to work, because they are either children, elderly adults, or disabled. Among families with children who use food stamps, 55 percent have at least one person in the household working, and 44 percent of all SNAP households have at least one person working (USDA 2017b).
23. See Bartfeld et al. (2015) and Hoynes et al. (2016).
24. A significant source of stress, stigma is "the co-occurrence of labeling, stereotyping, separation, status loss, and discrimination in a context in which power is exercised" (Link and Phelan 2001: 377). Stigma can even be considered a fundamental *cause of* health inequalities as it "inhibits access to multiple resources—structural, interpersonal, and psychological—that could otherwise be used to avoid or minimize poor health" (Hatzenbuehler, Phelan, and Link 2013: 819). See Puhl and Heuer (2009) for a review of how weight stigma, for example, contributes to negative psychological effects and diminished opportunities for obese people.
25. Generally, retailers do not charge taxes at the point of sale on food paid for with food stamps (USDA 2017c).

CHAPTER 20

1. The "eating for change" movement is discussed in more detail in Chapter 14.
2. Bowens's (2015) book *The Color of Food* aims to showcase the diversity of the food and farm movement. She notes that people of color aren't represented in the books, conferences, and conversations about how to reform the food system. Regarding inequality in the restaurant industry, see Harris and Giuffre (2015); Jayaraman (2013); and Ray (2016).
3. Alkon and Agyeman (2011); Alkon (2012); Broad (2016).
4. Alkon (2012) and Alkon and Agyeman (2011) make the argument that the food justice movement is rooted in the environmental justice movement (e.g., Bullard 1990).
5. Alkon (2012: 21).
6. In response to the wide-ranging assumptions, values, and concerns of the diverse people and organizations that have mobilized under the umbrella of "food justice,"

Alkon and Agyeman (2011) call for a "broad definition of food justice" (5). See also Alkon (2012) and Broad (2016).

7. White (2011: 204). As discussed by Edge (2017), these ideas are not new. For example, civil rights activist Fannie Lou Hamer argued that black southerners would not achieve full citizenship "until they claimed sovereignty over their diet" (58). She founded Freedom Farm in 1969 in order to "give farmers land to work and poor people food to eat" (59).

8. See Mares and Peña (2010, 2011); White (2011); and many other examples in Alkon and Agyeman (2011).

9. Mares and Peña (2011: 208). See also Mares and Peña (2010). Mares and Peña explain that the plots can be understood as indigenous communities' attempts to replicate hometown kitchen gardens from Mexico, Central America, the Dominican Republic, Puerto Rico, and Cuba. However, some crop varieties were no longer being cultivated in the farmers' home countries; thus, these heirloom varieties are preserved only by farmers' efforts in the United States.

10. White (2011: 19).

11. Guthman (2011: 154). Guthman argues that many food justice efforts focus on donating, selling, or growing fresh produce in "food deserts" and/or educating the people who live there about the importance of eating locally grown, seasonal, organic produce.

12. Guthman (2008: 432).

13. Guthman (2011: 154).

14. Cairns (2017) notes that efforts to connect low-income children with the foods they eat—for example, by creating school gardens—tend to convey a message of salvation, painting these children as uniformly in need of saving from nutritionally poor diets.

15. Slocum (2007) argues that the markets where organic and local foods are sold—places like Whole Foods and farmers' markets, and possibly the Lotus Café—can be exclusionary. Although these venues do not intentionally try to exclude people of color or poor and working-class customers, they are designed in ways that aim to be comfortable and aesthetically pleasing to middle-class shoppers.

16. Biltekoff (2013): Dupuis et al. (2011).

17. Guthman (2008). Guthman (2011) discusses her experience supervising college students who were required to do a six-month field study with a social justice organization. Many of her students wanted to, as she puts it, "enable people to make healthy choices" and even "to teach people how to eat" (4). At the end of the field study, many of the students returned with stories about "how little the food or the mode of delivery resonated with the target population" (156). Mares and Peña (2010) note that even food scholars often overlook how many of the practices they frame as "alternative"—for example, preserving heirloom seeds and eating seasonally—are precisely the traditional, place-based practices of Native, Chicano, and other marginalized communities.

18. A comfort food can technically be anything that a person uses to feel better, but as Romm (2015) notes, American comfort foods are typically rich, warming, and indulgent, such as mashed potatoes or macaroni and cheese. Experiments by Troisi and Gabriel (2011) show that comfort foods can actually have psychological effects.

CHAPTER 21

1. We didn't ask Patricia why she gave her room card to the hotel receptionist. She might have suspected that Doug would get back from the grocery store before her, since her asthma and gout make walking slow-going. In case Saundra and the kids were not in the room, she may have wanted Doug to have a way to get in.
2. Patricia did not explain why she was buying self-rising flour. She didn't have access to an oven, but there are microwave recipes that call for self-rising flour.
3. Stores say that they lock up certain products, like formula, because they are an attractive target for shoplifters (Associated Press 2005). During the time of our fieldwork, we noticed that the baby formula was not locked up in the supermarkets in Raleigh's wealthier neighborhoods, including stores that are just a few miles from Patricia's hotel.
4. Ramsdell (2012).
5. As the USDA notes, there are many ways to define food deserts, or "low food access" neighborhoods. Most take into account accessibility to sources of healthy food (e.g., distance to stores), individual-level resources that affect accessibility (e.g., household income or access to a vehicle), and neighbor-level resources (such as the average income of the neighborhood or the availability of public transportation). See USDA (2017d) for additional details.
6. USDA (2017e). As noted above, the USDA defines food deserts as places that are both low income and experiencing low food access. In 2015, 18.9 percent of the residents of Wake County, the county that includes Raleigh, were classified as having "low access" to supermarkets, meaning that they lived more than one mile from a supermarket for an urban neighborhood or more than ten miles for a rural neighborhood. This rate is much higher than that of the counties that include New York (0.0%) or Chicago (7.2%), although it is important to note that county-level data obscure neighborhood-level patterns. The share of residents experiencing low food access in Wake County is similar to that of the county that includes Houston (18.1%) (USDA 2017f).
7. Raleigh residents averaged 7.2 bus trips per capita in 2012, a fraction of the bus ridership of large cities like New York (229.8 trips per capita), but also much lower than many small cities like Athens, Georgia (99.5 trips per capita) or Champaign, Illinois (87.4 trips per capita) (Fischer-Baum 2014).

8. See MacNell et al. (2017). The Kroger closed in January 2013. Variety Wholesalers opened a discount store, Roses, in the former Kroger space in 2015, along with a small Save-A-Lot discount grocery store (Barr 2015).

9. Sims (2012).

10. We organized this meeting, which aimed to bring people together to discuss and map assets related to food access in southeast Raleigh, as part of the participatory outreach objectives of our project. For more information, see Jakes et al. (2015).

11. Cummins and Macintyre (2002).

12. Morland et al. (2002a); Walker et al. (2009); Zenk et al. (2005).

13. Morland et al. (2002a); Moore and Diez Roux (2006).

14. According to Zenk et al.'s (2005) research in Detroit, race did not influence distance to supermarkets when considering wealthier neighborhoods. However, among the poorest neighborhoods, black neighborhoods were, on average, 1.1 miles farther from the nearest supermarkets than were white neighborhoods.

15. See Guthman (2011); Kirkland (2011).

16. Guthman (2011).

17. See Centers for Disease Control and Prevention (n.d.).

18. Office of Community Services (2017).

19. The White House of President Obama (2010).

20. Ken (2014) analyzed Walmart's "meaningful commitment" to implementing policies in order to improve food access, concluding that companies like Walmart make these commitments not because of their dedication to food justice but because they represent "an opportunity for increased revenue disguised as a social problem" (28).

21. Morland et al. (2002b); Moore et al. (2008).

22. An et al. (2012); Pearson et al. (2005).

23. Zick et al. (2009).

24. Shier et al. (2012).

25. For example, in a review article of existing research on the food environment-diet linkages, Caspi et al. (2012: 1174) noted that studies "overwhelmingly used a cross-sectional design." There are exceptions; for example, see Shier et al. (2012), which looked at children's BMI percentiles at two points in time (fifth grade and eighth grade).

26. The opening of the store in Philadelphia did not affect changes in fruit and vegetable intake or body mass index (Cummins et al. 2014). Likewise, the new store in Pittsburgh was not associated with an improvement in fruit and vegetable intake, whole grain consumption, or body mass index (Dubowitz et al. 2015).

27. Larsen and Gilliland (2009).

28. USDA (2017d).

29. MacNell (2016); MacNell et al. (2017).

30. Chapter 13 discusses in detail how Patricia and Saundra Washington cope with food shortages.

CHAPTER 22

1. This timing—going to the food pantry at the end of the month—was common among the low-income participants in our study and is discussed by Kaufman and Karpati (2007).

2. The group of people waiting at the food pantry is fairly representative of the demographics of the neighborhood and also indicative of demographic patterns in the prevalence of food insecurity. Households with children are more likely to be food insecure, particularly when headed by a single woman (Coleman-Jensen et al. 2017). In terms of total numbers, more than half of food-insecure households are white, but rates of food insecurity are higher among households headed by a black or Hispanic person (Coleman-Jensen et al. 2017). Differences in the prevalence of food insecurity on the basis of gender and race/ethnicity reflect the ways that gender, race, and social class intersect and structure income, wealth, and opportunity in the United States (Collins 2000; Gordon 1994; Hays 2003).

3. Citing data from Feeding America, Fisher (2017: 42) notes that each year, 37 million people receive charitable food assistance from at least one of the approximately 61,000 food pantries and soup pantries in the Feeding America network.

4. Fisher (2017: 42).

5. See Fisher (2017) and Poppendieck (1998) for a history of the development of the charitable food system. Soup kitchens began in England in the eighteenth century but became popular in the United States during the Depression. According to Fisher (2017), food pantries can be traced to the Depression, when people would line up to receive free bread and other foods. Eventually, these breadlines evolved into more formal initiatives, typically linked to churches.

6. Fisher (2017).

7. Gibson (2015); Goldrick-Rab (2018); Loftus-Farren (2016).

8. Fisher (2017: 3).

9. Poppendieck (1998: 4).

10. Fisher (2017: 46). See also Poppendieck (1998).

11. Poppendieck (1998: 5–6). Both Poppendieck and Fisher argue that the structure of the charitable food system—a network of food banks that distributes surplus food to pantries—means that food banks necessarily have a stake in feeding hungry people, while the root causes of hunger often go unexamined. Fisher (2017) argues that because anti-hunger organizations are beholden to corporations for donations, they are less likely to advocate systemic changes that would reduce hunger but might cut into corporate profits, such as raising the minimum wage.

12. Fisher (2017); Poppendieck (1998).

13. Food pantries generally set their own policies, including the types of food they distribute, guidelines for determining who qualifies, and the frequency of services. If they distribute food from federal commodity programs, there are additional regulations that they must follow. Food banks also impose regulations on pantries

to ensure things like fairness and food safety. Pantries typically pay food banks a "shared maintenance fee" to cover the costs of the food, no more than 18 cents a pound (Fisher 2017).

14. Fisher (2017).

15. See Hardison-Moody et al. (2015). As part of Voices into Action, we surveyed food pantries in three counties in North Carolina, including southeast Raleigh. Three-quarters (24 out of 31) of food pantry directors reported that their pantry relied entirely on unpaid volunteer labor. Almost all (28 out of 29) stated that demand for their services had increased in the past year, and more than half (17 out of 29) felt they were falling short of meeting people's needs. Reflecting how food pantries have come to serve as a semi-permanent fixture rather than a temporary stopgap, food pantry directors estimated that about two-thirds (62%) of their recipients, like Leanne, have been coming regularly over the last two years.

CHAPTER 23

1. Although WIC provides vouchers for infant formula to nonbreastfeeding mothers, WIC's official policy is to promote breastfeeding (USDA 2017g).

2. USDA (2016b).

3. USDA (2015).

4. As discussed below, "normal growth curves" and Body Mass Indices (a function of height and weight) are frequently used by healthcare providers to assess children's health and well-being (Timmermans and Buchbinder 2012). Children's body size is also understood as a proxy for their mothers' ability to properly care for them (Elliott and Bowen 2018).

5. This is discussed in more detail in Elliott and Bowen (2018). Growth curves and BMIs are often presented as objective measures of health and development (Timmermans and Buchbinder 2012), even though there is significant debate about the value of these measurements in assessing growth or measuring fat, especially beyond infancy (Armstrong 1995; Saguy 2013).

6. Elobid and Alison (2008); Guthman (2011); Mason et al. (2014). See also Klass (2018).

7. Elliott and Bowen (2018). See also Boero (2012); Maher, Fraser, and Lindsay (2010); Warin et al. (2012); Wright et al. (2015).

8. Casual comments on children's appearance are common. The WIC nutritionist, for example, says that Jade is "cute." In the previous chapter, in another example, Leanne Armstrong's mother, Renata, describes Leanne's one-year-old daughter as "a fat girl."

9. Social support is now often contingent on paid work (Hays 2003; Soss et al. 2011). Social welfare programs reflect the neoliberal state's focus on individual responsibility and wage work, with an ultimate goal of creating "compliant and competent worker-citizens" (Soss et al. 2011: 297). See also Spross (2017).

10. Reich (2016) argues that wealthy parents, in contrast, can easily opt out of state-mandated vaccinations.

11. Soss et al.'s (2011) research suggests that decisions about sanctions may display patterns of racial bias, even when caseworkers do not overtly express discriminatory beliefs. In particular, they find that welfare caseworkers are more likely to sanction black than white welfare recipients for the same violation.

12. Some states automatically take away food stamps when welfare sanctions are imposed, a consequence that reflects the interconnected surveillance associated with public assistance (Soss et al. 2011).

13. Michener (2018). She clarifies, "Not all beneficiaries were treated this way, but those who were felt 'no one listens' to people like them" (Michener 2017).

14. This may be in part due to the structure and requirements of the WIC program. According to focus groups conducted with WIC counselors (Chamberlin et al. 2002), the counselors worried that their advice wasn't adequately addressing the needs of the low-income mothers they worked with. However, they felt constrained by their lack of time; the protocols of the WIC program, which did not allow for flexibility; and the administrative burdens of the WIC certification process.

15. Crawford (1980) describes the emergence of a culture of "healthism"—a cultural preoccupation with personal health as a primary indicator of social status—starting in the 1970s. Rather than seeing health outcomes as linked to structural inequalities, good health is believed to be accomplished through individual actions. Health promotion efforts in the United States frequently affirm neoliberal values of personal responsibility and risk management (Ayo 2012). See also Elliott and Bowen (2018); Gómez and López (2013); Guthman (2011); Sered (2014).

16. In rejecting the WIC counselor's assessment, Melanie draws on an alternative conceptualization of weight and health (Elliott and Bowen 2018). Critical obesity scholars have similarly noted that ideal weights or BMIs do not take into consideration different body types (Campos et al. 2006; Guthman 2011; Saguy 2013; Strings 2015).

CHAPTER 24

1. Chapter 3 discusses in detail Rae's conflicted feelings about soul food.

2. Putnam (2000: 99).

3. Both statistics in this paragraph come from Fischer (2011) finds that the percentage of respondents who "gave or attended a dinner party" in the previous year decreased from about 80 percent in 1980 to 70 percent in 2003. The percentage of respondents who hosted or attended at least five dinner parties decreased from about 50 percent to 30 percent.

4. Julier (2013) interviewed and observed a small sample of thirty-five American households. Contrary to findings from quantitative analyses, she finds that people are investing considerable time and effort in maintaining relationships through the

sharing of food. But the boundaries around how we define and describe our social eating experiences are blurry.

5. Hochschild (1997); McPherson, Smith-Lovin, and Brashears (2006); Putnam (2000).

6. Putnam (2000).

7. Putnam (2000).

8. An analysis of the nationally representative General Social Survey by McPherson et al. (2006) shows that Americans are "far less socially connected" than we were in the 1980s. We have fewer people in whom we can confide. "The largest losses," they write, "have come from the ties that bind us to community and neighborhood" (371).

9. This analysis comes from Genadek, Flood, and Roman (2016). Time spent taking care of children as a primary activity doubled over the same period, and much of the increase comes from spending more time taking care of children together with a spouse. Shared time spent in leisure and while watching television also increased.

10. Sayer (2005).

11. Fischer (2011) argues that although Americans are entertaining friends in their homes less often, they are seeing their friends in person about as often as before. But now it is more likely to be while doing something else, such as going to the movies with friends.

12. To give an example of Americans' diverging diets, the number of Americans following a gluten-free diet has tripled since 2009 (Kim et al. 2016). 3.3 percent of Americans identify as vegetarian or vegan (defined as never eating meat, fish, seafood, or poultry or, for vegans, adopting a plant-based diet) (Vegetarian Resource Group 2016). A 2017 poll done by the University of Michigan found that one in six US families had a teen who was on a special diet (Aubrey 2017). See Crawford (2006) on the modern focus on health behaviors.

CHAPTER 25

1. Incarceration affects entire families, including children (Haskins, Amorim, and Mingo 2018). Alexander (2010) traces the ways seemingly race-neutral policies over three decades have disproportionately harmed black communities. She argues that mass incarceration of black people was a new form of racial segregation, disenfranchisement, and dispossession, akin to Jim Crow–era laws in the twentieth century.

2. See Comfort (2007) on how female partners of incarcerated men accomplish the work of family and intimacy "in the shadow of the prison." See also Elliott and Reid (2016) and Goffman (2014).

3. See Williams-Forson (2006); Edge (2017); and Twitty (2017) on the role that food has played in how African Americans survive and resist oppressive conditions.

4. On average, adult Americans live within eighteen miles of their mother, according to a University of Michigan survey (Bui and Cain Miller 2015).

5. On social ties as a strategy of survival, see Desmond (2016); Domínguez and Watkins (2003); Edin and Lein (1997); Hansen (2005); Roy and Burton (2007); Stack (1974); Stack and Burton (1993).

6. On the ways modern work and family policies create challenges and conundrums for parents, see Blair-Loy (2003); Hansen (2005); Hays (1996, 2003); Hochschild (1997, 2012); Pugh (2015); Thistle (2006).

7. Hansen (2005: 210).

8. di Leonardo (1987); Stack and Burton (1993); West (2009).

9. Cairns and Johnston (2015); DeVault (1991).

10. We see this gendered division of labor in the fact that even though Marquan is involved in the cupcake making, Ashley is in charge and it was her brainchild. See Cairns and Johnston (2015); DeVault (1991); di Leonardo (1987).

CHAPTER 26

1. Pleck (2000: 23). By the mid-1800s, people worried that, with jobs shifting out of the home and more people migrating to urban centers in search of work, family ties would grow weaker, as families started spending less time together at home. Thanksgiving was an opportunity to "bolster national unity," "restore the religious morals of an earlier generation," and reaffirm the primacy of family and kin ties (Pleck 2000: 22).

2. On the history and practices of American Thanksgiving, see Lyles and Roberts (2015) and Pleck (2000). Canadians celebrate Thanksgiving on the second Monday of October.

3. A 2013 poll found that 85 percent of Americans celebrated Thanksgiving, and almost half of the Americans who celebrated Thanksgiving started cooking the meal ahead of the actual day (YouGov 2013). Stores are increasingly opening their doors and holding sales on Thanksgiving Day (Jones and Ell 2017).

4. This information comes from Gallup Polls conducted in 1990, 1996, 2000, and 2014. That Americans report Thanksgiving as among the happiest days of the year is from a Gallup Poll conducted in 2014 (McCarthy 2015).

5. According to a 2017 representative survey of Americans conducted by Marist Poll in collaboration with NPR and the PBS *NewsHour*, 58 percent of people who planned to celebrate Thanksgiving said they dreaded having to talk about politics with family and friends (Marist Poll 2017). It's not just politics that causes stress for Americans at Thanksgiving; one in six families has teens who are on restrictive diets, adding to the complex logistics of the meal (Aubrey 2017).

6. See Leonard (2014); Ossola (2015); and Pleck (2000).

7. The history of the labor to prepare the first Thanksgiving meal comes from Braswell (2016). Almost half of women surveyed by the American Psychological Association in 2006 reported heightened stress during the holidays (APA 2006).

8. Pleck (2000: 24). Norman Rockwell's famous World War II–era painting of a Thanksgiving dinner, *Freedom from Want*, reflected and further reinforced the anchoring of women, domesticity, and the Thanksgiving meal, observes Pleck.

9. Oleschuk, Cairns, and Johnston (2016) note, "The holiday season generates mythical images of culinary abundance that are seldom matched in reality, and these myths leave many feeling stressed and inadequate." In our Voices into Action interviews with poor and working-class mothers, quite a few cited the costs of holiday meals as a major source of stress.

10. As discussed in Chapter 19, Tara's decreased food stamps were part of a nationwide reduction in food stamps in 2013.

11. Commentators have long noted the onerous, and impossible, ideal of excess that Thanksgiving represents to many poor Americans (Schmidt 2016).

12. Macaroni is a more common side dish in the southeastern United States than in the rest of the country. See Miller (2013) and Purvis (2017) for discussions of the central role that macaroni and cheese plays at Thanksgiving and how this tends to differ between black families and white families.

13. Here Tara sounds a lot like the poor urban mothers interviewed by Edin and Kefalas (2005), who said their children were the center of their lives.

CHAPTER 27

1. Espejel Blanco et al. (2012).

2. We were not present when Rosario prepared the chicharrón and only have her brief explanation of how she cooked it to go on here. She described barbecuing it with banana leaves to "give flavor." When Rosario made tamales to sell in the neighborhood, she also wrapped them in banana leaves, infusing them with a subtle, sweet grassy aroma.

3. The seven sacraments in the Catholic Church are Baptism, Confirmation, the Eucharist (also known as communion), Penance, the Anointing of the Sick, Holy Orders, and Matrimony (Libreria Editrice Vaticana 2018). The age at First Communion historically varied, but a 1910 papal decree to reinforce the religious components of the celebration "held that children should receive communion when they acquired a basic religious knowledge, typically at around age seven" (Pleck 2000: 170).

4. Donoso (2014).

5. Cline (1993: 455) argues that the "spiritual conquest" was "the attempt by Spanish clergy to convert the indigenous peoples of the New World to Christianity," and notes that spiritual conquest was seen as a necessary companion to military conquest. According to Treviño (2004: 15), the style of Catholicism practiced in Mexico and by Mexican Americans is unique in its home- and community-centeredness, its strong popular expression, its centrality to people's identity, and its historical marginality within the institutional Catholic Church.

6. Many Mexican and Mexican American people pay homage to Guadalupe in their homes and at church on a daily basis, and there are also important celebrations on Guadalupe's feast day, December 12 (García 2008).

7. According to García (2008: 268), among Mexican and Mexican American Catholics, the "living witness and faith of the people," primarily through symbol and ritual, is just as important as written texts. See also Treviño (2004).

8. García (2008: 270). Treviño (2004: 209) states that Catholicism "structures family and community life and expresses ethnic identity" and plays an important role in helping Mexican Americans and Mexican immigrants meet the challenges of modern life.

9. The *narcocorrido* genre emerged in the 1990s. Like earlier *corridos*, which can be traced to fourteenth-century Spanish ballads and had become a vehicle for telling stories of "defiant and heroic exploits" by the nineteenth century, narcocorridos feature "archetypal heroes." However, these heroes are the leaders of the drug cartels and other "big men" in the drug trade (Edberg 2004: 25).

10. Pinche is a common Mexican curse word; it would be most closely translated as "fucking" in this case. The meaning of gringo is ever-evolving and context-dependent but, according to Ramírez (2013), "gringo denotes the idea of otherness."

11. Güero is a Mexican slang term that means light-skinned or light-haired.

12. This conversation shows how common it is in the United States to conflate "American" with whiteness. Even though the United States is a racially and ethnically diverse nation, its long history of white supremacy and privilege means that even today many associate being an American with being white (Espiritu 2001; Golash-Boza 2006; Tuan 1998).

13. As discussed in Chapter 6, Rosario and Samuel are undocumented, although their children, all born in the United States, are US citizens. Rosario sometimes thinks about going back to Mexico by choice, but she also fears that she might be forced to return there one day. Her fears intensified over the course of our five-year study, as anti-immigrant sentiment gained momentum and became more publicly visible with the election of President Donald Trump.

14. Some of these critiques have come from the Catholic Church in their efforts to reinforce the religious roots of celebrations that have long been "religious, familial, and social events" (Pleck 2000: 170). The tensions are perhaps best exemplified in discussions of the quinceañera, a celebration, common in Mexico and among Mexican Americans, of a girl's fifteenth birthday. A quinceañera typically begins with a religious service, followed by a party that can be equivalent to a wedding in terms of time and cost (Treviño 2004). According to a 2006 survey by *Quince Girl* magazine, families spent, on average, $5,000 on the quinceañera (Alvarez 2007). Davalos (1996) argues that the quinceañera is an occasion when gender and ethnic identities are created and solidified.

15. See Desmond (2016), discussed in Chapter 18. See also our discussion of debates about using food stamps to buy "luxury" products in Chapter 19.
16. See, for example, Huntington (2004), who believed that the slow pace or lack of cultural assimilation among Mexicans (and other immigrant groups) in the United States would lead to a "bifurcated" America, destroying American culture and values. For a discussion of the ways Latino Americans experience discrimination in the United States, see Golash-Boza (2006).
17. Treviño (2004) notes that several families usually share the expenses of celebrations like these. Rosario did not tell us whether she and Samuel contributed financially to the party, but it is plausible.

CHAPTER 28

1. Trubek (2017).
2. See Cairns and Johnston (2015); DeVault (1991); Little et al. (2009); MacKendrick (2018); Allen and Sachs (2007); and Som Castellano (2016). All highlight the need for a gendered perspective on foodwork.
3. Demonstrating that she is a good mom may be especially important to Leanne considering that she lost custody of her first two children after accusations of neglect (see Reich 2005).
4. According to time use surveys, women spent 0.82 hours a day preparing food, 0.50 hours cleaning the house, and 0.29 hours doing laundry, compared to 0.35, 0.18, and 0.07 hours, respectively, for men (Bureau of Labor Statistics 2016a). In total, including both indoor and outdoor chores, women spent 2.24 hours per day doing household work, compared to 1.38 hours per day for men.
5. Today, 71 percent of mothers with children under age 18 are employed or actively looking for work, up from 47 percent in 1975 (United States Department of Labor 2018).
6. Sayer (2005).
7. Parker and Livingston (2016); Sayer (2005).
8. Researchers find that the division of housework, including cooking, has become more even in American households over time (Carlson et al. 2018). Policy changes can promote more equal divisions of labor. Hook (2010) found that the division of household labor was more equal in countries where there is more public childcare and men are eligible (and/or encouraged) to take parental leave.
9. Sixty-nine percent of children live in two-parent households today, compared to 87 percent in 1960 (Pew Research Center 2015b).
10. On how American families at all income levels have dealt with the anxiety and uncertainty associated with the recent economic recession, see Cooper (2014); for an analysis of these stresses and the new economy, see Pugh (2015).

11. Since the 1980s, the state has dismantled many social safety nets built up over the twentieth century (Collins and Mayer 2010). See also Moffit (2015) and Soss et al. (2011), as well as the additional discussion in Chapter 19.

12. Since the mid-1960s, the American economy has experienced severe wage stagnation (DeSilver 2014).

13. Brady and Burroway (2012).

14. Between 1999 and 2010, households with higher education and higher incomes experienced significant improvements in their "diet quality"—how healthy their diets were—while poorer and less-educated households experienced no improvement (Wang et al. 2014).

15. Rehm et al. (2016).

16. Bureau of Labor Statistics (2016b).

17. Smith et al. (2013).

18. USDA (2017h).

19. Best (2017) finds that young adults view their mothers' cooking as a symbol of their mothers' love for them.

20. The *Leave It to Beaver* family didn't reflect the majority of families in the 1950s (Coontz 1992). And it doesn't capture the realities of American families today. The majority of mothers of small children are employed, and many are single parents, some raising children with very little support or help.

21. According to a national survey, 48 percent of households cooked dinner six or seven times per week. Another 44 percent of households cooked dinner between two and five times per week (Wolfson and Bleich 2015).

22. Tailie (2018).

23. Musick and Meier (2012); Meier and Musick (2014).

24. As Abarca (2006) argues, food can be a source of both empowerment and oppression. Recognizing this means valuing the people who keep us fed and acknowledging and celebrating the other aspects of their identities and lives.

25. Guthman (2011).

26. Healthy, tasty school lunches are already happening in some schools, notes Best (2017). See also Poppendieck (2010), who calls for universal school lunches as a solution to many of the problems with school meals, and Oostindjer et al. (2016), for an analysis of school meals around the world and their potential to contribute to healthier and more sustainable diets. To give an idea of potential costs, in Sweden, where all children receive free hot lunches, the estimated cost is 5,900 Swedish kronor per person per year, or about $700, which covers the ingredients, personnel, and transportation (Livsmedelsverket 2015). This works out to about $3.87 per meal (assuming 185 days of school per year). The USDA already reimburses schools between $3.23 and $3.46 per meal for students eligible for free lunch, between $2.83 and $3.06 for students eligible for reduced-price lunch, and between $0.31 and $0.45 per meal for students who pay for their lunch (see https://www.federalregister.gov/documents/2017/07/28/2017-15956/

national-school-lunch-special-milk-and-school-breakfast-programs-national-average-paymentsmaximum; AK, HI, and PR not included).

27. These dinners take a variety of forms; they are as diverse as the food itself. Many churches host community suppers, open to all. The People's Supper provides a toolkit for people to host dinners in their homes, bringing together people from different political and cultural backgrounds to share "meaningful stories" and build understanding (https://thepeoplessupper.org/our-impact/). Master Chef contestant Amanda Saab started "Dinner with your Muslim Neighbor" as a way of countering hateful messages (https://www.muslimneighbor.com/#eat-together).

28. Although we don't discuss the topic in this book, Voices into Action had a substantial participatory outreach component (see Hardison-Moody et al. 2015). The first step was to bring community residents and organizational representatives together to think about the food and health assets in their communities and develop long-term strategies for change. From this process, each county developed a community action group, which met to design collaborative projects and advise the selection process for the mini-grants we funded. In total, we funded fifty-six mini-grant projects to improve access to healthy food and places to be active. Mini-grantees reported directly serving 38,998 adults and children, through innovative programs like yoga in childcare centers, $1 Zumba classes in a local church, garden-based entrepreneurship programs with youth, school and church gardens, and promotion for a local farmers' market. Each project reflected the priorities identified in community asset mapping workshops, by community stakeholders, and in our interviews and observations with mothers and grandmothers.

29. Coleman-Jensen et al. (2017).

30. Wang et al. (2014).

31. Poppendieck ([1986] 2014).

32. The proposal, released in April 2018, is discussed in more detail in Chapter 19.

33. See Chilton and Rose (2009).

34. At the 1996 Declaration on World Food Security, only the United States and Australia failed to adopt the notion "that food is a basic human right" or pledge to make efforts to cut world hunger in half by 2015 (Chilton and Rose 2009: 1204).

35. Chilton and Rose (2009).

36. Food insecurity rates did not change between 1995 and 2007, increased from 2008 to 2012, during the Great Recession, and began a gradual decline starting in 2012. They are still higher than pre-2008 levels (Coleman-Jensen et al. 2017).

37. The share of SNAP families that are working while receiving SNAP has risen considerably over the last three decades (Rosenbaum 2013).

38. Brady et al. (2017).

39. Brady and Burroway (2012).

40. Konczal (2013) argues that Universal Basic Income is a proposal both conservatives and liberals can get behind, since evidence points to its effectiveness at reducing poverty and finds that it does not discourage people from working.

41. Shaefer et al. (2018).
42. McLaughlin and Rank (2018) estimate that the annual aggregate cost of child poverty in the United States is $1.0298 trillion. Costs are associated with losses of economic productivity, increased health and crime costs, and increased costs as a result of child homelessness and maltreatment.
43. See Holmes (2013); Jayaraman (2013). In North Carolina, 31 percent of workers are employed in occupations where the median wage is less than $11.34 per hour. Among low-wage sectors in North Carolina, restaurants are the largest and fastest-growing industry. The median hourly wage among restaurant workers is $6.89 per hour (UNC-Chapel Hill Department of City & Regional Planning 2018).
44. Holmes (2013).
45. See Estabrook (2011). The documentary *Food Chains* also covers the work of the Coalition of Immokalee Workers in detail.
46. Jayaraman (2013). See also http://rocunited.org/about-us/#our-history.
47. The most recognized movement is the Fight for $15.
48. Glass et al. (2016). The study included nineteen European countries and three additional English-speaking countries (Australia, New Zealand, and the United States).
49. Glass (2016).
50. The United States spends more as a percentage of gross domestic product (GDP) on healthcare than any other OECD country: 17.2 percent. (Switzerland spent the next highest, with 12.4% of GDP.) Despite its high spending, the United States also has lower life expectancies than many OECD countries (OECD 2017b). It is also one of the only industrialized countries without universal health coverage and has "the largest share of unmet health-care needs due to financial costs, based on a comparison of 35 industrialized countries" (Kontis et al. 2017). To give additional examples of how social policies benefit people and families, Brady and Burroway (2012) find, based on a comparison of eighteen wealthy democratic countries, that the United States has the highest rate of poverty among single mothers by far. Engster and Stensöta's (2011) comparative study finds that family policies—for example, paid family leave and subsidized childcare, which the United States lacks— have a significant impact on improving children's well-being.

APPENDIX

1. We interviewed grandmothers only when they were the primary caregivers of the children; the sample included 12 grandmothers and 156 mothers. All participants completed a semi-structured interview about food routines and daily life, described in this chapter. Voices into Action participants also completed three food recalls, which asked them to recall all of the foods and drinks consumed over the previous twenty-four hours, and an additional semi-structured interview about one of the recalls. Prior to the first interview, all participants completed a short survey about

basic demographic and household characteristics. See Elliott and Bowen (2018) for more details about sample characteristics.

2. Participants in Voices into Action received $25 for completing one interview. (Participants were compensated separately for completing the food recalls.) The other participants received $20.

3. This project was supported by Agriculture and Food Research Initiative Competitive Grant no. 2011-68001-30103 from the USDA National Institute of Food and Agriculture. It aimed to better understand the complex factors that influence families' food beliefs, decisions, and practices. Although we started by interviewing 138 women, 124 women completed all parts of the Year 1 study and were included in the full longitudinal study. We also organized asset-mapping workshops, spearheaded community food assessments, and funded mini-grants to improve access to food in the three North Carolina counties that were part of the study.

4. The two rural counties comprised a combination of white, black, and Latino/a residents, while the urban neighborhoods had mostly black and Latino/a residents. North Carolina has seen a recent influx of Latino/a immigration. The Latina participants in our study are thus predominantly new immigrants.

5. See Esterberg (2002) on qualitative research methods, in general, and snowball sampling, in particular.

6. On the complexities of gauging social class, see Lareau (2011).

7. For a discussion of recruiting participants and other aspects of qualitative research, see Esterberg (2002).

8. See Charmaz (2006) and Corbin and Strauss (2015) for discussions of grounded theory approaches to qualitative research.

9. For example, a low-income black mother of three told Sarah Bowen, who is white, that she was worried about her daughter's slim body size for health reasons. However, in her next interview, with a black interviewer, Tashara Leak, she went further, explaining that she was worried that Child Protective Services (CPS) might identify her as a neglectful mother because of the child's small stature. This suggested she was more comfortable sharing her fears about CPS targeting young black mothers with a black, rather than white, interviewer.

10. Simply matching interviewers and interviewees on the basis of race doesn't address the complexities of people's intersecting identities, though. For example, a black interview participant told Sinikka Elliott, a white person, that she "cling[s] to white people quicker than . . . black people." This mother was pursuing a four-year degree, and her class aspirations may have informed her stated preference for whites.

11. For a comprehensive guide to ethnographic fieldwork, see Emerson, Fretz, and Shaw (1995).

12. As we discuss in Elliott et al. (2017), this sometimes meant that both we and the families shared a perception that something *should* happen during the observations,

imposing a temporal purposefulness and structure that may not characterize typical family life.

13. For a thorough discussion of writing fieldnotes, see Emerson et al. (1995).

14. In all, the fieldnotes totaled 1,553 single-spaced typed pages.

15. Ethnography helps researchers understand and explain what people actually do, because it is situated in people's lived experiences (Jerolmack and Khan 2014).

16. Kleinman and Copp (1993).

17. Recurring fieldwork, the opportunity to return again and again to the field is an important aspect of fieldwork (Elliott et al. 2017; Whyte 2013).

18. Ochs and Kremer-Sadlik (2013).

19. Ochs and Beck (2013: 64, emphasis in original).

REFERENCES

Abarca, Meredith. 2006. *Voices in the Kitchen: Views of Food and the World from Working-Class Mexican and Mexican American Women.* College Station: Texas A&M University Press.

Afflerback, Sara, Shannon K. Carter, Amanda Koontz Anthony, and Liz Grauerholz. 2013. "Infant-Feeding Consumerism in the Age of Intensive Mothering and Risk Society." *Journal of Consumer Culture* 13(3): 387–405.

Alexander, Michelle. 2010. *The New Jim Crow: Mass Incarceration in the Age of Colorblindness.* New York: New Press.

Alkon, Alison. 2012. *Black, White, and Green: Farmers Markets, Race, and the Green Economy.* Athens: University of Georgia Press.

Alkon, Alison Hope, and Julian Agyeman. 2011. *Cultivating Food Justice: Race, Class, and Sustainability.* Cambridge, MA: MIT Press.

Allen, Patricia, and Carolyn Sachs. 2007. "Women and Food Chains: The Gendered Politics of Food." *International Journal of Sociology of Agriculture* 15(1): 1–23.

Alvarez, Julia. 2007. *Once upon a Quinceañera.* New York: Penguin Group.

American Psychological Association (APA). 2006. "APA Survey Shows Holiday Stress Putting Women's Health at Risk." APA, December 12, 2006. Retrieved April 17, 2018, http://www.apa.org/news/press/releases/2006/12/women-stress.aspx.

An, Ruopeng, and Roland Sturm. 2012. "School and Residential Neighborhood Food Environment and Diet among California Youth." *American Journal of Preventive Medicine* 42(2): 129–135.

Annable, Kristin. 2012. "McDonald's Drops Use of 'Pink Slime' Ammonium Hydroxide in Hamburger Meat." *National Post,* January 26. Retrieved on January 15, 2018, http://nationalpost.com/news/mcdonalds-drops-use-of-pink-slime-in-u-s-meat.

Apple, Rima D. 2006. *Perfect Motherhood: Science and Childrearing in America.* New Brunswick, NJ: Rutgers University Press.

Armstrong, David. 1995. "The Rise of Surveillance Medicine." *Sociology of Health & Illness* 17(3): 393–404.

Associated Press. 2005. "Baby Formula? The Locked Case at the Front of the Store." *New York Times*, June 5. Retrieved February 2, 2018, http://www.nytimes.com/2005/06/05/us/baby-formula-the-locked-case-at-the-front-of-the-store.html.

Aubrey, Allison. 2013. "Family Dinner: Treasured Tradition or Bygone Ideal?" NPR, The Salt, February 26. Retrieved January 11, 2018, https://www.npr.org/sections/thesalt/2013/02/26/172897660/family-dinner-treasured-tradition-or-bygone-ideal.

Aubrey, Allison. 2017. "It's Not Just Politics. Food Can Stir Holiday Conflict, Too." NPR, The Salt, November 20. Retrieved January 17, 2018, https://www.npr.org/sections/thesalt/2017/11/20/564901919/its-not-just-politics-food-can-stir-holiday-conflict-too.

Avins, Jenni. 2017. "This Genius Cooking System Will Help You Plan Ahead to Eat Well All Week Long." *Quartz*, January 8. Retrieved June 6, 2017, https://qz.com/877221/streamline-your-week-of-cooking-and-beat-dinnertime-decision-fatigue-with-this-genius-system/.

Avishai, Orit. 2007. "Managing the Lactating Body: The Breast-Feeding Project and Privileged Motherhood." *Qualitative Sociology* 30(2): 135–152.

Ayala, Guadalupe, Barbara Baquero, and Silvia Klinger. 2008. "A Systematic Review of the Relationship between Acculturation and Diet among Latinos in the United States: Implications for Future Research." *Journal of the American Dietetic Association* 108(8): 1330–1344.

Ayo, Nike. 2012. "Understanding Health Promotion in a Neoliberal Climate and the Making of Health Conscious Citizens." *Critical Public Health* 22(1): 99–105.

Bailey, Sarah Pullman. 2018. "How the Mom Internet Became a Spotless, Sponsored Void." *Washington Post*, January 26. Retrieved February 6, 2018, https://www.washingtonpost.com/outlook/how-the-mom-internet-became-a-spotless-sponsored-void/2018/01/26/072b46ac-01d6-11e8-bb03-722769454f82_story.html?utm_term=.b2c7987bf848.

Bank Muñoz, Carolina. 2008. *Transnational Tortillas: Race, Gender, and Shop-Floor Politics in Mexico and the United States*. Ithaca, NY: Cornell University Press.

Barham, Elizabeth. 2002. "Towards a Theory of Values-Based Labeling." *Agriculture and Human Values* 19(4): 349–360.

Barr, Sarah. 2015. "Roses to Open in Former SE Raleigh Kroger Space." *News and Observer*, January 29. Retrieved February 2, 2018, http://www.newsobserver.com/news/local/community/midtown-raleigh-news/article10236242.html.

Bartfeld, Judith, Craig Gundersen, Timothy M. Smeeding, and James P. Ziliak. 2015. *SNAP Matters: How Food Stamps Affect Health and Well-Being*. Redwood City, CA: Stanford University Press.

Bastwell, Robert W., Alan S. Brown, Matthew E. Ansfield, and Gayla Y. Paschall. 2002. "'You Will Eat All of That!': A Retrospective Analysis of Forced Consumption Episodes." *Appetite* 38(3): 211–219.

Bates, Lisa M., Dolores Acevedo-Garcia, Margarita Alegría, and Nancy Krieger. 2008. "Immigration and Generational Trends in Body Mass Index and Obesity in the

United States: Results of the National Latino and Asian American Survey, 2003–2003." *American Journal of Public Health* 98(1): 70–77.

Beagan, Brenda, Gwen E. Chapman, Andrea D'Sylva, and B. Raewyn Bassett. 2008. "'It's Just Easier for Me to Do It': Rationalizing the Family Division of Foodwork." *Sociology* 42(4): 653–671.

Beagan, Brenda L., Gwen E. Chapman, Josée Johnston, Deborah McPhail, Elaine M. Power, and Helen Vallianatos. 2015. *Acquired Tastes: Why Families Eat the Way They Do*. Vancouver, BC: UBC Press.

Beck, Margaret E., and Jeanne E. Arnold. 2009. "Gendered Time Use at Home: An Ethnographic Examination of Leisure Time in Middle-Class Families." *Leisure Studies* 28(2): 121–142.

Becker, Howard S. 1963. *Outsiders: Studies in the Sociology of Deviance*. New York: Free Press.

Best, Amy. 2017. *Fast-Food Kids: French Fries, Lunch Lines, and Social Ties*. New York: New York University Press.

Biltekoff, Charlotte. 2013. *Eating Right in America: The Cultural Politics of Food and Health*. Durham, NC: Duke University Press.

Birch, Leanne L. 1999. "Development of Food Preferences." *Annual Review of Nutrition* 19(1): 41–62.

Bittman, Mark. 2011. "Is Junk Food Really Cheaper?" *New York Times Sunday Review*. Retrieved June 6, 2017, http://www.nytimes.com/2011/09/25/opinion/sunday/is-junk-food-really-cheaper.html.

Bittman, Michael, and Judy Wajcman. 2000. "Rush Hour: The Character of Leisure Time and Gender Inequality." *Social Forces* 79(1): 165–189.

Black, William R. 2014. "How Watermelons Became a Racist Trope." *The Atlantic*, December 8. Retrieved April 9, 2018, https://www.theatlantic.com/national/archive/2014/12/how-watermelons-became-a-racist-trope/383529/.

Blair-Loy, Mary. 2003. *Competing Devotions: Career and Family among Women Executives*. Cambridge, MA: Harvard University Press.

Blissett, Jacqueline, Caroline Meyer, and Emma Haycraft. 2006. "Maternal and Paternal Controlling Feeding Practices with Male and Female Children." *Appetite* 47(2): 212–219.

Bloom, J. Dara, and C. Clare Hinrichs. 2017. "The Long Reach of Lean Retailing: Firm Embeddedness and Wal-Mart's Implementation of Local Produce Sourcing in the US." *Environment and Planning* A 49(1): 168–185.

Blum, Linda. 2016. *Raising Generation Rx: Mothering Kids with Invisible Disabilities in an Age of Inequality*. New York: New York University Press.

Boero, Natalie. 2007. "Fat Kids, Working Mothers, and the 'Epidemic of Obesity': Race, Class, and Mother Blame." In *The Fat Studies Reader*, edited by Esther Rothblum and Sondra Solovay, pp. 113–119. New York: New York University Press.

Boero, Natalie. 2012. *Killer Fat: Media, Medicine, and Morals in the American "Obesity Epidemic."* New Brunswick, NJ: Rutgers University Press.

Bologna, Caroline. 2015. "Campaign Reminds Families Why It Is Important to Eat Together." *Huffington Post Canada*, September 15. Retrieved January 17, 2018, http://www.huffingtonpost.ca/entry/campaign-reminds-families-why-its-important-to-eat-together_us_55f862cde4b09ecde1d9eb32.

Booker, Brakkton, and Dan Charles. 2018. "Republican Farm Bill Calls on Many SNAP Recipients to Work or Go to School." NPR, The Salt, April 12. Retrieved April 20, 2018, https://www.npr.org/sections/thesalt/2018/04/12/601900588/republican-farm-bill-calls-on-some-snap-recipients-to-work-or-go-to-school.

Bordo, Susan. 2004. *Unbearable Weight: Feminism, Western Culture, and the Body*, Tenth Anniversary Edition. Berkeley: University of California Press.

Bourdieu, Pierre. 1984. *Distinction: A Social Critique of the Judgement of Taste*. Cambridge, MA: Harvard University Press.

Bove, Caron, Jeffery Sobal, and Barbara S. Rauschenbach. 2003. "Food Choices among Newly Married Couples: Convergence, Conflict, Individualism, and Projects." *Appetite* 40(1): 25–41.

Bove, Caron F., and Jeffery Sobal. 2006. "Foodwork in Newly Married Couples: Making Family Meals." *Food, Culture & Society* 9(1): 69–89.

Bowen, Sarah. 2015. *Divided Spirits: Tequilla, Mezcal, and Politics of Production*. Berkeley: University of California Press.

Bowen, Sarah, Sinikka Elliott, and Joslyn Brenton. 2014. "The Joy of Cooking?" *Contexts* 13(3): 20–25.

Bowens, Natasha. 2015. *The Color of Food: Stories of Race, Resilience and Farming*. Gabriola Island, BC: New Society.

Brady, David, and Rebekah Burroway. 2012. "Targeting, Universalism, and Single-Mother Poverty: A Multilevel Analysis across 18 Affluent Democracies." *Demography* 49(2): 719–746.

Brady, David, Ryan M. Finnigan, and Sabine Hügben. 2017. "Rethinking the Risks of Poverty: A Framework for Analyzing Prevalences and Penalties." *American Journal of Sociology* 123(3): 740–786.

Branch, Enobong Hannah. 2011. *Opportunity Denied: Limiting Black Women to Devalued Work*. New Brunswick, NJ: Rutgers University Press.

Braswell, Sean. 2016. "Thanksgiving's Well-Intentioned War on Women." *OZY*, November 24. Retrieved January 17, 2018, http://www.ozy.com/opinion/thanksgivings-well-intentioned-war-on-women/66140.

Brenton, Joslyn. 2017. "The Limits of Intensive Feeding: Maternal Foodwork at the Intersections of Race, Class, and Gender." *Sociology of Health & Illness* 39(6): 863–867.

Bridges, Khiara M. 2011. *Reproducing Race: An Ethnography of Pregnancy as a Site of Racialization*. Berkeley: University of California Press.

Broad, Garrett. 2016. *More Than Just Food: Food Justice and Community Change*. Berkeley: University of California Press.

Bugge, Annechen Bahr, and Reidar Almås. 2006. "Domestic Dinner: Representations and Practices of a Proper Meal among Young Suburban Mothers." *Journal of Consumer Culture* 6(2): 203–228.

Bui, Quoctrung, and Claire Cain Miller. 2015. "The Typical American Lives Only 18 Miles from Mom." *New York Times*, December 23. Retrieved February 2, 2018, https://www.nytimes.com/interactive/2015/12/24/upshot/24up-family.html.

Bullard, Robert. 1990. *Dumping in Dixie: Race, Class, and Environmental Quality.* Boulder, CO: Westview Press.

Bureau of Labor Statistics. 2016a. "Average Hours Per Day Spent in Selected Household Activities, 2016." Graphics for Economic News Releases. Retrieved April 19, 2018, https://www.bls.gov/charts/american-time-use/activity-by-hldh.htm.

Bureau of Labor Statistics. 2016b. "High-Income Households Spent Half of Their Food Budget on Food Away from Home in 2015." TED: The Economics Daily, October 5. Retrieved February 7, 2018, https://www.bls.gov/opub/ted/2016/high-income-households-spent-half-of-their-food-budget-on-food-away-from-home-in-2015.htm.

Burdette, Hillary L., and Robert C. Whitaker. 2005. "Resurrecting Free Play in Young Children: Looking beyond Fitness and Fatness to Attention, Affiliation, and Affect." *Archives of Pediatric and Adolescent Medicine* 159(1): 46–50.

Burkhauser, Richard V., Shuaizhang Feng, Stephen P. Jenkins, and Jeff Larrimore. 2009. "Recent Trends in Top Income Shares in the USA: Reconciling Estimates from March CPS and IRS Tax Data." National Bureau of Economic Research (NBER) Working Paper 15320. Retrieved January 31, 2018, http://www.nber.org/papers/w15320.

Cairns, Kate. 2017. "Connecting to Food: Cultivating Children in the School Garden." *Children's Geographies* 15(3): 304–318.

Cairns, Kate, Josée Johnston, and Shyon Baumann. 2010. "Caring about Food: Doing Gender in the Foodie Kitchen." *Gender & Society* 24(5): 591–615.

Cairns, Kate, and Josée Johnston. 2015. *Food and Femininity.* London: Bloomsbury.

Cairns, Kate, and Josée Johnston. 2018. "On (Not) Knowing Where Your Food Comes From: Meat, Mothering, and Ethical Eating." *Journal of Agriculture and Human Values*, https://doi.org/10.1007/s10460-018-9849-5.

Cairns, Kate, Josée Johnston, and Norah MacKendrick. 2013. "Feeding the 'Organic Child': Mothering through Ethical Consumption." *Journal of Consumer Culture* 13(2): 97–118.

Campos, Paul, Abigail Saguy, Paul Ernsberger, Eric Oliver, and Glenn Gaesser. 2006. "The Epidemiology of Overweight and Obesity: Public Health Crisis or Moral Panic?" *International Journal of Epidemiology* 35(1): 55–60.

Carroll, Abigail. 2013. *Three Squares: The Invention of the American Meal.* New York: Basic Books.

Carlson, Daniel L., Amanda Jayne Miller, and Sharon Sassler. 2018. "Stalled for Whom? Change in the Division of Particular Household Tasks and Their Consequences for Middle- to Low-Income Couples." *Socius* 4: 1–17.

Caruso-Cabrera, Michelle. 2013. "Grupo Bimbo: Meet the Mexican CEO Who Made Your English Muffin." CNBC, June 7. Retrieved February 1, 2018, https://www.cnbc.com/id/100798699.

Caspi, Caitlin E., Ichiro Kawachi, S. V. Subhramanian, Gary Adamkiewcz, and Glorian Sorensen. 2012. "The Relationship between Diet and Perceived and Objective Access to Supermarkets among Low-Income Housing Residents." *Social Science & Medicine* 75(7): 1254–1262.

Cassady, Diana, Karen M. Jetter, and Jennifer Culp. 2007. "Is Price a Barrier to Eating More Fruits and Vegetables for Low-Income Families?" *Journal of the Academy of Nutrition and Dietetics* 107(11): 1909–1915.

Castañón, Alfredo. 2010. "Tránsito de la Cocina Mexicana en la Historia. Cinco Estaciones Gastronómicas: Mole, Pozole, Tamal, Tortilla, y Chile Relleno." In *Saberes y Sabores en México y el Caribe*, edited by Rita De Maeseneer and Patrick Collard, pp. 23–55. Amsterdam: Rodopi.

Center for Science in the Public Interest. 2016. "Milkshakes, Sugary Cereals, Candy: What Nickelodeon Is Peddling to Kids." Retrieved June 5, 2017, https://cspinet. org/sites/default/files/attachment/Nickelodeon%20brief.pdf.

Centers for Disease Control and Prevention (CDC). 2017a. "Long-Term Trends in Diabetes." April 2017. Atlanta, GA: CDC. Retrieved April 9, 2018, https://www. cdc.gov/diabetes/statistics/slides/long_term_trends.pdf.

Centers for Disease Control and Prevention (CDC). 2017b. "Obesity and Overweight." Atlanta, GA: CDC. Last updated May 3, 2017. Retrieved April 14, 2018, https:// www.cdc.gov/nchs/fastats/obesity-overweight.htm.

Chamberlin, Leigh A., Susan N. Sherman, Anjali Jain, Scott W. Powers, and Robert C. Whitaker. 2002. "The Challenge of Preventing and Treating Obesity in Low-Income, Preschool Children: Perceptions of WIC Health Care Professionals." *Archives of Pediatric & Adolescent Medicine* 156(7): 662–668.

Charmaz, Kathy. 2006. *Constructing Grounded Theory: A Practical Guide through Qualitative Analysis.* Thousand Oaks, CA: Sage.

Chaudry, Ajay, Taryn Morrissey, Christina Weiland, and Hirokazu Yoshikawa. 2017. *Cradle to Kindergarten: A New Plan to Combat Inequality.* New York: Russell Sage Foundation.

CHD Expert. 2017. "CHD Expert Evaluates the Mexican Restaurant Industry, the Second Most Popular Menu Type in the USA." CHD Expert, April 24. Retrieved February 6, 2018, https://www.chd-expert.com/blog/press_release/chd-expert-evaluates-mexican-restaurant-industry-second-popular-menu-type-usa/.

Chen, Wei-ting. 2016. "From 'Junk Food' to 'Treats': How Poverty Shapes Family Food Practices." *Food, Culture & Society* 19(1): 151–170.

Chetty, Raj, David Grusky, Maximilian Hell, Nathaniel Hendren, Robert Manduca, and Jimmy Narang. 2017. "The Fading American Dream: Trends in Absolute Income Mobility since 1940." *Science*, Early Online View, April 24. doi: 10.1126/science.aal4617.

Chetty, Raj, and Nathaniel Hendren. 2018. "The Impacts of Neighborhoods on Intergenerational Mobility II: County-Level Estimates." *Quarterly Journal of Economics*, Early Online View, February 10. doi: 10.1093/qje/qjy006.

Chetty, Raj, Nathaniel Hendren, Patrick Kline, Emmanuel Saez, and Nicholas Turner. 2014. "Is the United States Still a Land of Opportunity? Recent Trends in Intergenerational Mobility." *American Economic Review: Papers & Proceedings* 104(5): 141–147.

Chilton, Mariana, and Donald Rose. 2009. "A Rights-Based Approach to Food Insecurity in the United States." *American Journal of Public Health* 99(7): 1203–1211.

Cinotto, Simone. 2006. "'Everyone Would Be Around the Table': American Family Mealtimes in Historical Perspective, 1850–1960." *New Directions for Child and Adolescent Development* 2006(111): 17–33.

Clark, Sarah E., Corinna Hawkes, Sophia M. E. Murphy, Karen A. Hansen-Kuhn, and David Wallinga. 2012. "Exporting Obesity: US Farm and Trade Policy and the Transformation of the Mexican Consumer Food Environment." *International Journal of Occupational and Environmental Health* 18(1): 53–64.

Cline, Sarah. 1993. "The Spiritual Conquest Revisited: Baptism and Christian Marriage in Early Sixteenth-Century Mexico." *Hispanic American Historical Review* 73(3): 453–480.

Cohn, D'Vera, Gretchen Livingston, and Wendy Wang. 2014. "After Decades of Decline, a Rise in Stay-at-Home Mothers." Pew Research Center, April 8. Retrieved June 2, 2017, http://www.pewsocialtrends.org/2014/04/08/after-decades-of-decline-a-rise-in-stay-at-home-mothers/.

Coleman-Jensen, Alisha, Matthew P. Rabbitt, Christian A. Gregory, and Anita Singh. 2017. *Household Food Insecurity in the United States in 2016*. Economic Research Report Number 237. Washington, DC: USDA Economic Research Service. Retrieved February 1, 2018, https://www.ers.usda.gov/webdocs/publications/84973/err-237.pdf?v=42979.

Colen, Cynthia, David. M. Ramey, Elizabeth C. Cooksey, and David R. Williams. 2018. "Racial Disparities in Health among Nonpoor African Americans and Hispanics: The Role of Acute and Chronic Discrimination." *Social Science & Medicine* 199: 167–180.

Collins, Jane, and Victoria Mayer. 2010. *Both Hands Tied: Welfare Reform and the Race to the Bottom in the Low-Wage Labor Market*. Chicago: University of Chicago Press.

Collins, Patricia Hill. 2000. *Black Feminist Thought: Knowledge, Consciousness, and the Politics of Empowerment*. 2nd ed. New York: Routledge.

Comfort, Megan. 2007. *Doing Time Together: Love and Family in the Shadow of the Prison*. Chicago: University of Chicago Press.

Concannon, Kevin. 2013. "Helping SNAP Recipients Prepare for November 1st Benefit Changes." United States Department of Agriculture, October 28. Retrieved February 1, 2018, https://www.usda.gov/media/blog/2013/10/28/helping-snap-recipients-prepare-november-1st-benefit-changes.

Coontz, Stephanie. 1992. *The Way We Never Were: American Families and the Nostalgia Trap*. New York: Basic Books.

Cooper, Marianne. 2014. *Cut Adrift: Families in Insecure Times.* Berkeley: University of California Press.

Corbin, Juliet, and Anselm Strauss. 2015. *Basics of Qualitative Research: Techniques and Procedures for Developing Grounded Theory.* 4th ed. Thousand Oaks, CA: Sage.

Craig, Lyn, and Judith Brown. 2017. "Feeling Rushed: Gendered Time Quality, Work Hours, Nonstandard Work Schedules, and Spousal Crossover." *Journal of Marriage and Family* 79(1): 225–242.

Crawford, Robert. 1980. "Healthism and Medicalization in Everyday Life." *International Journal of Health Services* 10(3): 365–389.

Crawford, Robert. 2006. "Health as a Meaningful Social Practice." *Health: An Interdisciplinary Journal for the Social Study of Health, Illness, and Medicine* 10(4): 401–420.

Cummins, Steven, Ellen Flint, and Stephen A. Matthews. 2014. "New Neighborhood Grocery Store Increased Awareness of Food Access but Did Not Alter Dietary Habits or Obesity." *Health Affairs* 33(2): 283–291.

Cummins, Steven, and Sally Macintyre. 2002. "'Food Deserts'—Evidence and Assumption in Health Policy Making." *British Medical Journal* 325(7361): 436–438.

Currid-Halkett, Elizabeth. 2017. *The Sum of Small Things: A Theory of the Aspirational Class.* Princeton, NJ: Princeton University Press.

Cutts, Diana Becker, Alan F. Meyers, Maureen M. Black, Patrick H. Casey, Mariana Chilton, John T. Cook, Joni Geppert, Stephanie Ettinger de Cuba, Timothy Heeren, Sharon Coleman, Ruth Rose-Jacobs, and Deborah A. Frank. 2011. "U.S. Housing Insecurity and the Health of Very Young Children." *American Journal of Public Health* 101(8): 1508–1514.

Daniel, Caitlin. 2016. "Economic Constraints on Taste Formation and the True Cost of Healthy Eating." *Social Science & Medicine* 148: 34–41.

Davalos, Karen Mary. 1996. "'*La Quinceañera*': Making Gender and Ethnic Identities." *Frontiers: A Journal of Women Studies* 16(2/3): 101–127.

David, Laurie, Kirstin Uhrenholdt, Maryellen Baker, Jonathan Safran Foer, and Harvey Karp. 2010. *The Family Dinner: Great Ways to Connect with Your Kids, One Meal at a Time.* New York: Grand Central.

Davidson, Paul. 2016. "The Job Juggle Is Real. Many Americans Are Balancing Two, Even Three Gigs." *USA Today*, October 17. Retrieved June 6, 2017, https://www.usatoday.com/story/money/2016/10/17/job-juggle-real-many-americans-balancing-two-even-three-gigs/92072068/.

Dean, Stacy. 2017. "President's Budget Would Shift Substantial Costs to States and Cut Food Assistance for Millions." Center for Budget Policy and Priorities, July 19. Retrieved April 14, 2018, http://www.cbpp.org/research/food-assistance/presidents-budget-would-shift-substantial-costs-to-states-and-cut-food.

De León, Jason. 2015. *The Land of Open Graves: Living and Dying on the Migrant Trail.* Berkeley: University of California Press.

Delaney, Arthur, and Emily Swanson. 2013. "Americans Feel Strongly about How Poor People Should Spend Their Food Stamps." *Huffington Post*, August 16. Retrieved

February 1, 2018, https://www.huffingtonpost.com/2013/08/16/food-stamp-poll_n_3763755.html.

DeLind, Laura. 2011. "Are Local Food and the Local Food Movement Taking Us Where We Want to Go? Or Are We Hitching Our Wagons to the Wrong Star?" *Agriculture and Human Values* 28(2): 273–283.

DeRosa, Bri. 2016. "How to Beat Tension and Conflict from Your Family Dinner." The Family Dinner Project, February 19. Retrieved January 10, 2018, https://thefamilydinnerproject.org/food-for-thought/how-to-beat-tension-and-conflict-from-your-family-dinner/.

DeSilver, Drew. 2014. "For Most Workers, Real Wages Have Barely Budged for Decades." Pew Research Center, October 9. Retrieved February 8, 2018, http://www.pewresearch.org/fact-tank/2014/10/09/for-most-workers-real-wages-have-barely-budged-for-decades/.

Desmond, Matthew. 2016. *Evicted: Poverty and Profit in the American City*. New York: Crown.

DeSoucey, Michaela. 2016. *Contested Tastes: Foie Gras and the Politics of Food*. Princeton, NJ: Princeton University Press.

Dettmann, Rachael L., and Carolyn Dimitri. 2009. "Who's Buying Organic Vegetables? Demographic Characteristics of U.S. Consumers." *Journal of Food Products Marketing* 16(1): 79–91.

Deutsch, Tracey. 2012. *Building a Housewife's Paradise: Gender, Politics, and American Grocery Stores in the 20th Century*. Chapel Hill: University of North Carolina Press.

DeVault, Marjorie. 1991. *Feeding the Family: The Social Organization of Caring as Gendered Work*. Chicago: University of Chicago Press.

Dewey, Caitlin. 2017. "What Americans Get Wrong about Food Stamps, According to an Expert Who's Spent 20 Years Researching Them." *Washington Post*, April 4. Retrieved February 1, 2018, https://www.washingtonpost.com/news/wonk/wp/2017/04/04/what-many-americans-get-wrong-about-food-stamps-according-to-an-economist/?utm_term=.852d832fe75f.

Dewey, Caitlin. 2018a. "The Trump Administration Takes Its First Big Step Toward Stricter Work Requirements for Food Stamps." *Washington Post*, February 22. Retrieved April 20, 2018, https://www.washingtonpost.com/news/wonk/wp/2018/02/22/the-trump-administration-takes-its-first-big-step-toward-stricter-work-requirements-for-food-stamps/?utm_term=.312e88e15753.

Dewey, Caitlin. 2018b. "The Republican Plan to Tighten Food Stamp Work Requirements is Advancing — Without a Single Democrat's Vote." *Washington Post*, April 18. Retrieved April 20, 2018, https://www.washingtonpost.com/news/wonk/wp/2018/04/18/the-republican-plan-to-tighten-food-stamp-work-requirements-is-advancing-without-a-single-democrats-vote/?utm_term=.107da9876c72.

di Leonardo, Micaela. 1987. "The Female World of Cards and Holidays: Women, Families, and the Work of Kinship." *Signs* 12(3): 440–453.

Dimitri, Carolyn, and Rachael Dettmann. 2012. "Organic Food Consumers: What Do We Really Know about Them?" *British Food Journal* 114(8): 1157–1183.

Domínguez, Silvia, and Celeste Watkins. 2003. "Creating Networks for Survival and Mobility: Social Capital among African-American and Latin-American Low-Income Mothers." *Social Problems* 50(1): 111–135.

Donoso, Juan Carlos. 2014. "On Religion, Mexicans Are More Catholic and often More Traditional than Mexican Americans." Pew Research Center, December 18. Retrieved February 2, 2018, http://www.pewresearch.org/fact-tank/2014/12/08/on-religion-mexicans-are-more-catholic-and-often-more-traditional-than-mexican-americans/.

Dotti Sani, Guilia, and Judith Treas. 2016. "Educational Gradients in Parents' Child-Care Time across Countries, 1965–2012." *Journal of Marriage and Family* 78(4): 1083–1096.

Dow, Dawn Marie. 2016. "Integrated Motherhood: Beyond Hegemonic Ideologies of Motherhood." *Journal of Marriage and Family* 78(1): 180–196.

Downey, Douglas B. 2008. "Black/White Differences in School Performance: The Oppositional Culture Explanation." *Annual Review of Sociology* 34: 107–126.

Dubowitz, Tamara, Madhumita Ghosh-Dastidar, Deborah A. Cohen, Robin Beckman, Elizabeth D. Steiner, Gerald P. Hunter, Karen R. Flórez, Christina Huang, Christine A. Vaughan, Jennifer C. Sloan, Shannon N. Zenk, Steven Cummins, and Rebecca L. Collins. 2015. "Diet and Perceptions Change with Supermarket Introduction in a Food Desert, but Not Because of Supermarket Use." *Health Affairs* 34(11): 1858–1868.

Dupuis, E. Melanie. 2002. *Nature's Perfect Food: How Milk Became America's Drink*. New York: New York University Press.

Dupuis, E. Melanie, Jill Lindsey Harrison, and David Goodman. 2011. "Just Food?" In *Cultivating Food Justice: Race, Class, and Sustainability*, edited by Alison Hope Alkon and Julian Agyeman, pp. 283-307. Cambridge, MA: MIT Press.

Edberg, Mark Cameron. 2004. *El Narcotraficante: Narcocorridos and the Construction of a Cultural Persona on the U.S.–Mexico Border*. Austin: University of Texas Press.

Edge, John T. 2017. *The Potlikker Papers: A Food History of the Modern South*. New York: Penguin Books.

Edin, Kathryn, and Laura Lein. 1997. *Making Ends Meet: How Single Mothers Survive Welfare and Low-Wage Work*. New York: Russell Sage Foundation.

Edin, Kathryn, and Maria Kefalas. 2005. *Promises I Can Keep: Why Poor Women Put Motherhood before Marriage*. Berkeley: University of California Press.

Edin, Kathryn, and H. Luke Shaefer. 2016. *$2.00 a Day: Living on Almost Nothing in America*. New York: First Mariner Books.

Ehrenreich, Barbara. 2001. *Nickel and Dimed: On (Not) Getting By in America*. New York: Henry Holt.

Elliott, Sinikka. 2012. *Not My Kid: What Parents Believe about the Sex Lives of Their Teenagers*. New York: New York University Press.

Elliott, Sinikka, and Sarah Bowen. 2018. "Defending Motherhood: Morality, Responsibility, and Double Binds in Feeding Children." *Journal of Marriage and Family* 80(2): 499–520.

Elliott, Sinikka, Josephine Ngo McKelvy, and Sarah Bowen. 2017. "Marking Time in Ethnography: Uncovering Temporal Dispositions." *Ethnography* 18(4): 556–576.

Elliott, Sinikka, and Megan Reid. 2016. "The Superstrong Black Mother." *Contexts* 15(1): 48–53.

Elliott, Sinikka, Rachel Powell, and Joslyn Brenton. 2015. "Being a Good Mom: Low-Income Black Single Mothers Negotiate Intensive Mothering." *Journal of Family Issues* 36(3): 351–370.

Elobid, Mai A., and David B. Allison. 2008. "Putative Environmental-Endocrine Disruptors and Obesity: A Review." *Current Opinion in Endocrinology, Diabetes, and Obesity* 15(5): 403–408.

Emerson, Robert, Rachel Fretz, and Linda Shaw. 1995. *Writing Ethnographic Fieldnotes.* Chicago: University of Chicago Press.

Engster, Daniel, and Helena Olofsdotter Stensöta. 2011. "Do Family Policy Regimes Matter for Children's Well-Being?" *Social Politics: International Studies in Gender, State & Society* 18(1): 82–124.

Espejel Blanco, Joel Enrique, Dena María Camarena Gómez, and Sergio Sandoval Godoy. 2012. "Alimentos Tradicionales en el Noroeste de México: Factores que Influyen en su Consumo." Presented at the Asamblea General de ALAFEC, October 9–12, Buenos Aires, Argentina. Retrieved February 2, 2018, http://www.alafec.unam.mx/docs/asambleas/xiii/ponencias/mercadeo/M_04.pdf.

Espiritu, Yen Le. 2001. " 'We Don't Sleep Around like White Girls Do': Family, Culture, and Gender in Filipina American Lives." *Signs: Journal of Women in Culture and Society* 26(2): 415–440.

Estabrook, Barry. 2011. *Tomatoland: How Modern Industrial Agriculture Destroyed Our Most Alluring Fruit.* Kansas City: Andrew McMeel.

Esterberg, Kristin G. 2002. *Qualitative Methods in Social Research.* Boston: McGraw-Hill.

Evans, Adrienne, and Sarah Riley. 2014. *Technologies of Sexiness: Sex, Identity and Consumer Culture.* Oxford: Oxford University Press.

Faith, Myles S., Kelley S. Scanlon, Leann L. Birch, Lori A. Francis, and Bettylou Sherry. 2004. "Parent-Child Feeding Strategies and Their Relationships to Child Eating and Weight Status." *Obesity* 12(11): 1711–1722.

Farrell, Amy Erdman. 2011. *Fat Shame: Stigma and the Fat Body in American Culture.* New York: New York University Press.

Farrow, Claire, Amy T. Galloway, and K. Fraser. 2009. "Sibling Eating Behaviours and Differential Child Feeding Practices by Parents." *Appetite* 52(2): 307–312.

Federal Trade Commission. 2012. "A Review of Food Marketing to Children and Adolescents." Follow-up report, December 2012. Retrieved May 208, 2018, https://www.ftc.gov/sites/default/files/documents/reports/review-food-marketing-children-and-adolescents-follow-report/121221foodmarketingreport.pdf.

Feriss, Timothy. 2007. *The 4-Hour Work Week.* New York: Harmony.

Fernández, Manny. 2017. "A Path to America, Marked by More and More Bodies." *New York Times*, May 4. Retrieved February 8, 2018, https://www.nytimes.com/interactive/2017/05/04/us/texas-border-migrants-dead-bodies.html.

Fernández-Aceves, Maria Teresa. 2003. "Once We Were Corn Grinders: Women and Labor in the Tortilla Industry of Guadalajara, 1920–1940." *International Labor and Working-Class History* 63: 81–101.

Fielding-Singh, Priya. 2017. "A Taste of Inequality: Food's Symbolic Value across the Socioeconomic Spectrum." *Sociological Science* 4: 424–448.

Fischer, Claude S. 2011. *Still Connected: Family and Friends in America since 1970.* New York: Russell Sage Foundation.

Fischer-Baum, Reuben. 2014. "How Your City's Public Transportation Stacks Up." *FiveThirtyEight*, July 31. Retrieved June 7, 2017, https://fivethirtyeight.com/datalab/how-your-citys-public-transit-stacks-up/.

Fishel, Anne. 2015. *Home for Dinner: Mixing Food, Fun, and Conversation for a Happier Family and Healthier Kids.* New York: American Management Association.

Fisher, Andrew. 2017. *Big Hunger: The Unholy Alliance between Corporate America and Anti-Hunger Groups.* Cambridge, MA: MIT Press.

Fitzgerald, Thomas. 1979. "Southern Folks' Eating Habits Ain't What They Used to Be . . . If They Ever Were." *Nutrition Today* 14(4): 16–21.

Fleming-Milici, Frances, and Jennifer L. Harris. 2016. "Television Food Advertising Viewed by Preschoolers, Children and Adolescents: Contributors to Differences in Exposure for Black and White Youth in the United States." *Pediatric Obesity* 13(2): 103–110.

Floyd, Ife, Ladonna Pavetti, and Liz Schott. 2017. "TANF Reaching Few Poor Families." Center on Budget and Policy Priorities, December 13. Retrieved April 14, 2018, https://www.cbpp.org/research/family-income-support/tanf-reaching-few-poor-families.

Fordham, Signithia, and John U. Ogbu. 1986. "Black Students' School Success: Coping with the 'Burden of "Acting White".'" *Urban Review* 18(3): 176–206.

Fragile Families. 2011. "Incarceration and Housing Insecurity among Urban Fathers." Fragile Families Research Brief, December 2011, Number 47. Retrieved January 7, 2018, https://fragilefamilies.princeton.edu/sites/fragilefamilies/files/researchbrief47.pdf.

Fram, Maryah S., Edward A. Frongillo, Sonya J. Jones, Roger C. Williams, Michael P. Burke, Kendra P. DeLoach, and Christine E. Blake. 2011. "Children Are Aware of Food Insecurity and Take Responsibility for Managing Food Resources." *Journal of Nutrition* 141(6): 1114–1119.

Funk, Cary, and Brian Kennedy. 2016. "Americans' Views about and Consumption of Organic Foods." Pew Research Council, December 1. Retrieved February 2, 2018, http://www.pewinternet.org/2016/12/01/americans-views-about-and-consumption-of-organic-foods/.

García, Mario T. 2008. *Católicos: Resistance and Affirmation in Chicano Catholic History.* Austin: University of Texas Press.

Genadek, Katie R., Sarah M. Flood, and Joan Garcia Roman. 2016. "Trends in Spouses' Shared Time in the United States, 1965–2012." *Demography* 53(6): 1801–1820.

Gibson, Jodi. 2015. "School Pantries: Helping Kids Thrive in School." Feeding America, August 29, 2015. Retrieved February 2, 2018, http://www.feedingamerica.org/hunger-blog/school-pantries-helping.html.

Glass, Jennifer. 2016. "CCF Brief: Parenting and Happiness in 22 Countries." Brief Report, Council on Contemporary Families News, June 15. Retrieved June 7, 2017, https://contemporaryfamilies.org/brief-parenting-happiness/.

Glass, Jennifer, Robin W. Simon, and Mathew A. Andersson. 2016. "Parenthood and Happiness: Effects of Work-Family Reconciliation Policies in 22 OECD Countries." *American Journal of Sociology* 122(3): 886–929.

Goffman, Alice. 2014. *On the Run: Fugitive Life in an American City.* Chicago: University of Chicago Press.

Golash-Boza, Tanya. 2006. "Dropping the Hyphen? Becoming Latino(a)-American through Racialized Assimilation." *Social Forces* 85(1): 27–55.

Golden, Lonnie. 2015. "Irregular Work Scheduling and Its Consequences: Briefing Paper 394." Economic Policy Institute. Retrieved June 6, 2017, http://www.epi.org/publication/irregular-work-scheduling-and-its-consequences/.

Goldrick-Rab, Sara. 2018. "It's Hard to Study if You're Hungry." *New York Times*, January 14. Retrieved February 2, 2018, https://www.nytimes.com/2018/01/14/opinion/hunger-college-food-insecurity.html.

Gómez, Laura E., and Nancy López. 2013. *Mapping "Race": Critical Approaches to Health Disparities Research.* New Brunswick, NJ: Rutgers University Press.

Gordon, Linda. 1994. *Pitied but Not Entitled: Single Mothers and the History of Welfare.* New York: Free Press.

Gosse, Van. 2005. *The Movements of the New Left, 1950–1975: A Brief History with Documents.* New York: Palgrave Macmillan.

Gregory, Dick. 1973. *Dick Gregory's Natural Diet for Folks Who Eat: Cookin' with Mother Nature.* New York: Harper and Row.

Gregory, Jane E., Susan J. Paxton, and Anna M. Brozovic. 2010. "Pressure to Eat and Restriction Are Associated with Child Eating Behaviours and Maternal Concern about Child Weight, but Not Child Body Mass Index, in 2- to 4-Year-Old Children." *Appetite* 54(3): 550–556.

Guendelman, Maya, Sapna Cheryan, and Benoît Monin. 2011. "Fitting In but Getting Fat: Identity Threat and Dietary Choices among U.S. Immigrant Groups." *Psychological Science* 22(7): 959–967.

Gustafson, Kaaryn. 2009. "The Criminalization of Poverty." *Journal of Criminal Law and Criminology* 99(3): 643–716.

Guthman, Julie. 2008. " 'If They Only Knew': Color Blindness and Universalism in California Alternative Food Institutions." *Professional Geographer* 60(3): 387–397.

Guthman, Julie. 2011. *Weighing In: Obesity, Food Justice, and the Limits of Capitalism.* Berkeley: University of California Press.

Guthman, Julie, and Sandy Brown. 2015. "Whose Life Counts? Biopolitics and the 'Bright Line' of Chloropicrin Mitigation in California's Strawberry Industry." *Science, Technology, and Human Values* 41(3): 461–482.

Hamal Gurung, Shobha. 2015. *Nepali Migrant Women: Resistance and Survival in America*. Syracuse, NY: Syracuse University Press.

Hansen, Karen V. 2005. *Not-So-Nuclear Families: Class, Gender, and Networks of Care*. New Brunswick, NJ: Rutgers University Press.

Hanson, Karla L., and Leah M. Connor. 2014. "Food Insecurity and Dietary Quality in US Adults and Children: A Systematic Review." *American Journal of Clinical Nutrition* 100(2): 684–692.

Hardison-Moody, Annie, Sarah Bowen, J. Dara Bloom, Marissa Sheldon, Lorelei Jones, and Brandi Leach. 2015. "Incorporating Nutrition Education Classes into Food Pantry Settings: Lessons Learned in Design and Implementation." *Journal of Extension* 53(6).

Hardison-Moody, Annie, Lillian MacNell, Sinikka Elliott, and Sarah Bowen. 2018. "How Social, Cultural, and Economic Environments Shape Infant Feeding for Low-income Women: A Qualitative Study in North Carolina." *Journal of the Academy of Nutrition and Dietetics*, Early Online View, April 11. doi: 10.1016/j.jand.2018.01.008.

Harman, Vicki and Bendetta Cappellini. 2015. "Mothers on Display: Lunchboxes, Social Class and Moral Accountability." *Sociology* 49(4): 1–18.

Harris, Deborah A., and Patti Giuffre. 2015. *Taking the Heat: Women Chefs and Gender Inequality in the Professional Kitchen*. New Brunswick, NJ: Rutgers University Press.

Harris, Janelle. 2018. "How I Stopped Being Ashamed of My EBT Card." *BuzzFeed News*, January 23. Retrieved February 1, 2018, https://www.buzzfeed.com/janelleharris/i-was-ashamed-to-use-food-stamps-but-no-one-should-be?utm_term=.lwGMgw1ny#.kuaLl0odw.

Harris, Jennifer L., Megan LoDolce, Cathryn Dembek, and Marlene B. Schwartz. 2015. "Sweet Promises: Candy Advertising to Children and Implications for Industry Self-Regulation." *Appetite* 95: 585–592.

Harris, Jessica B. 2011. *High on the Hog: A Culinary Journey from Africa to America*. New York: Bloomsbury.

Hart, Betty, and Todd R. Risley. 1995. *Meaningful Differences in the Everyday Experience of Young American Children*. Baltimore, MD: Paul H. Brookes.

Haskins, Anna, Mariana Amorim, and Meaghan Mingo. 2018. "Parental Incarceration and Child Outcomes: Those at Risk, Evidence of Impacts, Methodological Insights, and Areas of Future Work." *Sociological Forum* 12(3): e12562.

Hatzenbuehler, Mark L., Jo C. Phelan and Bruce G. Link. 2013. "Stigma as Fundamental Cause of Population Health Inequalities." *American Journal of Public Health* 103(5): 813–821.

Haws, Kelly, L., Rebecca Walker Reczek, and Kevin Sample. 2017. "Healthy Diets Make Empty Wallets: The Healthy = Expensive Intuition." *Journal of Consumer Research* 43(6): 992–1007.

Hays, Sharon. 1996. *The Cultural Contradictions of Motherhood*. New Haven, CT: Yale University Press.

Hays, Sharon. 2003. *Flat Broke with Children: Women in the Age of Welfare Reform*. New York: Oxford University Press.

Heflin, Colleen, Mary E. Corcoran, and Kristine A. Siefert. 2007. "Work Trajectories, Income Changes, and Food Insufficiency in a Michigan Welfare Population." *Social Service Review* 81(1): 3–25.

Heflin, Colleen, Andrew S. London, and Ellen K. Scott. 2009. "Mitigating Material Hardship: The Strategies Low-Income Families Employ to Reduce the Consequences of Poverty." *Sociological Inquiry* 81(2): 223–246.

Hendrickson, Mary, and William Heffernan. 2002. "Opening Spaces through Relocalization: Locating Potential Resistance in the Weaknesses of the Global Food System." *Sociologia Ruralis* 42(4): 347–369.

Hendy, Helen M., Keith E. Williams, Thomas S. Camise, Nicholas Eckman, and Amber Hedemann. 2009. "The Parent Mealtime Action Scale (PMAS): Development and Association with Children's Diet and Weight." *Appetite* 52(2): 328–339.

Henly, Julia R., and Susan J. Lambert. 2014. "Unpredictable Work Timing in Retail Jobs: Implications for Employee Work-Life Conflict." *Industrial & Labor Relations Review* 67: 986–1016.

Hesser, Amanda, and Merrill Stubbs. 2016. *Food 52—A New Way to Dinner: A Playbook of Recipes and Strategies for the Week Ahead*. Berkeley: Ten Speed Press.

Hill, Sarah E., Marjorie L. Prokosch, Danielle J. DelPriore, Vladas Grisckevicius, and Andrew Kramer. 2016. "Low Childhood Socioeconomic Status Promotes Eating in the Absence of Energy Need." *Psychological Science* 27(3): 354–364.

Hinrichs, C. Clare. 2000. "Embeddedness and Local Food Systems: Notes on Two Types of Direct Agricultural Markets." *Journal of Rural Studies* 16(3): 295–303.

Hirsh-Pasek, Kathy, Lauren B. Adamson, Roger Bakeman, Margaret Tresch Owen, Roberta Michnick Golinkoff, Amy Pace, Paula K. S. Yust, and Katharine Suma. 2015. "The Contribution of Early Communication Quality to Low-Income Children's Language Success." *Psychological Sciences* 26(7): 1071–1083.

Hochschild, Arlie Russell. 1997. *The Time Bind: When Work Becomes Home and Home Becomes Work*. New York: Holt Paperbacks.

Hochschild, Arlie Russell. 2012. *The Outsourced Self: Intimate Life in Market Times*. New York: Metropolitan Books.

Holmes, Seth M. 2013. *Fresh Fruit, Broken Bodies: Migrant Farmworkers in the United States*. Berkeley: University of California Press.

Hook, Jennifer. 2010. "Gender Inequality in the Welfare State: Sex Segregation in Housework, 1965–2003." *American Journal of Sociology* 115(5): 1480–1152.

Hoynes, Hilary, Diane Whitmore Schanzenbach, and Douglas Almond. 2016. "Long-Run Impacts of Childhood Access to the Safety Net." *American Economic Review* 106(4): 903–934.

Huntington, Samuel P. 2004. "The Hispanic Challenge." *Foreign Policy* March/April: 30–45.

Hussein, Jennifer. 2017. "All the Ways Grocery Stores Trick You into Spending More Money." *Business Insider*, September 25. Retrieved January 25, 2018, http://www.businessinsider.com/ways-grocery-stores-trick-you-into-spending-more-money-2017-9/#free-samples-1.

Jackson, Peter. 2015. *Anxious Appetites: Food and Consumer Culture*. London: Bloomsbury.

Jacobs, Andrew, and Matt Richtel. 2017a. "A Nasty, NAFTA-Related Surprise: Mexico's Soaring Obesity." *New York Times*, December 11. Retrieved February 1, 2018, https://www.nytimes.com/2017/12/11/health/obesity-mexico-nafta.html.

Jacobs, Andrew, and Matt Richtel. 2017b. "How Big Business Got Brazil Hooked on Junk Food." *New York Times*, September 16. Retrieved February 1, 2018, https://www.nytimes.com/interactive/2017/09/16/health/brazil-obesity-nestle.html.

Jakes, Susan, Annie Hardison-Moody, Sarah Bowen, and John Blevins. 2015. "Engaging Community Change: The Critical Role of Values in Asset Mapping." *Community Development* 46(4): 392–406.

Jayaraman, Saru. 2013. *Behind the Kitchen Door*. Ithaca, NY: Cornell University Press.

Jensen Wallach, Jennifer. 2014. "How to Eat to Live: Black Nationalism and the Post-1964 Culinary Turn." *Study the South*, July 2. Retrieved February 2, 2018, https://southernstudies.olemiss.edu/study-the-south/how-to-eat-to-live/.

Jensen Wallach, Jennifer, and Rebecca Sharpless. 2015. *Dethroning the Deceitful Pork Chop: Rethinking African American Foodways from Slavery to Obama*. Fayetteville: University of Arkansas Press.

Jerolmack, Colin, and Shamus Khan. 2014. "Talk Is Cheap: Ethnography and the Attitudinal Fallacy." *Sociological Methods and Research* 43(2): 178–209.

Johnston, Josée, and Shyon Baumann. 2010. *Foodies: Democracy and Distinction in the Gourmet Foodscape*. New York: Routledge.

Johnston, Josée, and Michelle Szabo. 2009. "Reflectivity and the Whole Foods Market Consumer: The Lived Experience of Shopping for Change." *Agriculture and Human Values* 28(3): 303–319.

Jones, Charisse, and Kellie Ell. 2017. "Thanksgiving Day Grows in Importance for Shoppers." *USA Today*, November 24. Retrieved January 17, 2018, https://www.usatoday.com/story/money/retail/2017/11/23/thanksgiving-day-grows-importance-shoppers/885996001/.

Jordan, Jennifer A. 2015. *Edible Memory: The Lure of Heirloom Tomatoes and Other Forgotten Foods*. Chicago: University of Chicago Press.

Julier, Alice. 2013. *Eating Together: Food, Friendship, and Inequality*. Champaign: University of Illinois Press.

Kalleberg, Arne L., and Till M. von Wachter. 2017. "The U.S. Labor Market during and after the Great Recession: Continuities and Transformations." *RSF: The Russell Sage Foundation Journal of the Social Sciences* 3(3): 1–19.

Karmarkar, Uma R., and Bryan Bollinger. 2015. "BYOB: How Bringing Your Own Shopping Bags Leads to Treating Yourself and the Environment." *Journal of Marketing* 79(4): 1–15.

Kaufman, Leslie, and Adam Karpati. 2007. "Understanding the Sociocultural Roots of Childhood Obesity: Food Practices among Latino Families of Bushwick, Brooklyn." *Social Science & Medicine* 64(11): 2177–2188.

Ken, Ivy. 2014. "A Healthy Bottom Line: Obese Children, a Pacified Public, and Corporate Legitimacy." *Social Currents* 1(2): 130–148.

Kendall, Graham. 2014. "The Science That Makes Us Spend More in Supermarkets, and Feel Good While We Do It." *Conversation*, March 4. Retrieved February 1, 2018, https://theconversation.com/the-science-that-makes-us-spend-more-in-supermarkets-and-feel-good-while-we-do-it-23857.

Keremitsis, Dawn. 1983. "Del Metate Al Molino: La Mujer Mexicana de 1910 a 1940." *Historia Mexicana* 33(2): 285–302.

Khan, Shamus Rahman. 2011. *Privilege: The Making of an Adolescent Elite at St. Paul's School.* Princeton, NJ: Princeton University Press.

Khandpur, Neha, Rachel E. Blaine, Jennifer Orlet Fisher, and Kirsten K. Davison. 2014. "Fathers' Child Feeding Practices: A Review of the Evidence." *Appetite* 78: 110-121.

Kiely, John. 2013. "Rise of the Takis." *Houston Press*, October 8. Retrieved April 12, 2018, http://www.houstonpress.com/restaurants/rise-of-the-takis-6411512.

Kim, Hyun-seok, Kalpesh G. Patel, Evan Orosz, Neil Kothari, Michael F. Demven, Nikolaos Pyrsopoulos, and Sushil K. Ahlawat. 2016. "Time Trends in the Prevalence of Celiac Disease and Gluten-Free Diet in the US Population: Results from the National Health and Nutrition Examination Surveys 2009–2014." *JAMA Internal Medicine* 176(11): 1716–1717.

Kimmel, Jean, and Rachel Connelly. 2007. "Mothers' Time Choices: Caregiving, Leisure, Home Production, and Paid Work." *Journal of Human Resources* 42(3): 643–681.

Kirkland, Anna. 2011. "The Environmental Account of Obesity: A Case for Feminist Skepticism." *Signs: Journal of Women in Culture and Society* 36(2): 463–485.

Kirkpatrick, Sharon I., and Valerie Tarasuk. 2011. "Housing Circumstances Are Associated with Household Food Access among Low-Income Urban Families." *Journal of Urban Health* 88(2): 284–296.

Klass, Perri. 2018. "Do Parents Make Kids Fat?" *New York Times*, January 8. Retrieved January 20, 2018, https://www.nytimes.com/2018/01/08/well/family/do-parents-make-kids-fat.html?_r=0.

Kleinman, Sherryl, and Martha A. Copp. 1993. *Emotions and Fieldwork.* Thousand Oaks, CA: Sage.

Kloppenburg, Jack, John Hendrickson, and G. W. Stevenson. 1996. "Coming In to the Foodshed." *Agriculture and Human Values* 13(3): 33–42.

Kneebone, Elizabeth. 2014. "The Growth and Spread of Concentrated Poverty, 2000 to 2008–2012." Brookings, July 31. Retrieved February 7, 2018, https://www.brookings.edu/interactives/the-growth-and-spread-of-concentrated-poverty-2000-to-2008-2012/.

Koch, Shelley. 2012. *A Theory of Grocery Shopping: Food, Choice, and Conflict.* London: Berg.

Kochhar, Rakesh, Richard Fry, and Paul Taylor. 2011. "Wealth Gaps Rise to Record Highs between Whites, Blacks, Hispanics." Pew Research Center, July 26. Retrieved April 23, 2018, http://www.pewsocialtrends.org/2011/07/26/wealth-gaps-rise-to-record-highs-between-whites-blacks-hispanics/.

Konczal, Mike. 2013. "Thinking Utopian: How About a Universal Basic Income?" *Washington Post*, May 11. Retrieved April 23, 2018, https://www.washingtonpost.com/news/wonk/wp/2013/05/11/thinking-utopian-how-about-a-universal-basic-income/?utm_term=.f59220a8cd58.

Kontis, Vasilis, James E. Bennett, Colin D. Mathers, Guangquan Li, Kyle Foreman, and Majid Ezzati. 2017. "Future Life Expectancy in 35 Industrialised Countries: Projections with a Bayesian Model Ensemble." *Lancet* 389(10076): 1323–1335.

Kornrich, Sabino. 2012. "Hiring Help for the Home: Household Services in the Twentieth Century." *Journal of Family History* 37(2): 197–212.

Kornrich, Sabino, and Frank Furstenberg. 2013. "Investing in Children: Changes in Parental Spending on Children, 1972–2007." *Demography* 50(1): 1–23.

Kraus, Michael W., and Jacinth J. X. Tan. 2015. "Americans Overestimate Social Class Mobility." *Journal of Experimental Social Psychology* 58: 101–111.

Kushel, Margot B., Reena Gupta, Lauren Gee, and Jennifer S. Haas. 2006. "Housing Instability and Food Insecurity as Barriers to Health Care among Low-Income Americans." *Journal of General Internal Medicine* 21(1): 71–77.

Kuyper, Edith M., Dorothy Smith, and Lucia L. Kaiser. 2009. "Does Food Insecurity Influence Child Feeding Practices?" *Journal of Hunger & Environmental Nutrition* 4(2): 147–157.

Kwan, Samantha, and Jennifer Graves. 2013. *Framing Fat: Competing Constructions in Contemporary Culture.* New Brunswick, NJ: Rutgers University Press.

Landsbaum, Claire. 2016. "The 'Steak and Lobster' Food-Stamp Myth Refuses to Die." *New York Magazine*, February 19. Retrieved June 5, 2017, http://nymag.com/daily/intelligencer/2016/02/steak-and-lobster-food-stamp-myth-lives-on.html.

Lareau, Annette. 2011. *Unequal Childhoods*, 2nd ed. Berkeley: University of California Press.

Lareau, Annette. 2014. "Schools, Housing, and the Reproduction of Inequality: Experiences of White and African-American Suburban Parents." In *Choosing Homes, Choosing Schools*, edited by A. Lareau and K. Goyette, pp. 169–206. New York: Russell Sage Foundation.

Larsen, Kristian, and Jason Gilliland. 2009. "A Farmers' Market in a Food Desert: Evaluating Impacts on the Price and Availability of Healthy Food." *Health & Place* 15(4): 1158–1162.

Larson, Nicole I., and Mary T. Story. 2011. "Food Insecurity and Weight Status among U.S. Children and Families: A Review of the Literature." *American Journal of Preventive Medicine* 40(2): 166–173.

Laudan, Rachel. 2015. "A Plea for Culinary Modernism." *Jacobin*, May 22. Retrieved February 2, 2018, https://www.jacobinmag.com/2015/05/slow-food-artisanal-natural-preservatives/.

Leonard, Kimberly. 2014. "Thanksgiving Woes: Anxiety, Depression." *U.S. News & World Report*, November 26. Retrieved January 17, 2018, https://www.usnews.com/news/articles/2014/11/26/thanksgiving-reality-for-some-stress-anxiety-depression.

Levenstein, Harvey. 2003. *Revolution at the Table: The Transformation of the American Diet*. Berkeley: University of California Press.

Libreria Editrice Vaticana. 2018. "Catechism of the Catholic Church: The Seven Sacraments of the Church." Retrieved February 2, 2018, http://www.vatican.va/archive/ENG0015/__P3E.HTM.

Link, Bruce G. and Jo C. Phelan. 2001. "Conceptualizing Stigma." *Annual Review of Sociology* 27: 363–385.

Little, Jo, Brian Ilbery, and David Watts. 2009. "Gender, Consumption, and the Relocalisation of Food: A Research Agenda." *Sociologia Ruralis* 49(3): 201–217.

Livsmedelsverket. 2015. "School Lunches." Last updated March 5, 2015. Retrieved April 23, 2018, https://www.livsmedelsverket.se/en/food-habits-health-and-environment/maltider-i-vard-skola-och-omsorg/skola.

Loftus-Farren, Zoe. 2016. "Mobile Pantries Get Fresh Food to Where People Need It Most." *Civil Eats*, June 13. Retrieved February 2, 2018, https://civileats.com/2016/06/13/mobile-pantries-get-food-where-people-need-it-most.

Lupton, Deborah. 1996. *Food, the Body and the Self*. Los Angeles: Sage.

Lupton, Deborah. 2012. *Fat*. New York: Routledge.

Lyles, Toby, and Amy Roberts. 2015. "Thanksgiving by the Numbers." CNN, November 25. Retrieved January 17, 2018, http://www.cnn.com/2012/11/21/living/thanksgiving-by-the-numbers/index.html.

MacKendrick, Norah. 2010. "Media Framing of Body Burdens: Precautionary Consumption and the Individualization of Risk." *Sociological Inquiry* 80(1): 126–149.

MacKendrick, Norah. 2014. "More Work for Mother: Chemical Body Burdens as a Maternal Responsibility." *Gender & Society* 28(5): 705–728.

MacKendrick, Norah. 2018. *Better Safe Than Sorry: How Consumers Navigate Exposure to Everyday Toxics*. Berkeley: University of California Press.

MacNell, Lillian. 2016. "Exploring Race, Class, and Food Access across Different Geographic Scales." PhD dissertation, Department of Sociology and Anthropology, North Carolina State University.

MacNell, Lillian, Sinikka Elliott, Annie Hardison-Moody, and Sarah Bowen. 2017. "Black and Latino Urban Food Desert Residents' Perceptions of Their Food Environment and Factors That Influence Food Shopping Decisions." *Journal of Hunger and Environmental Nutrition* 12(3): 375–393.

Maher, Jane Marie, Suzanne Fraser, and Jo Lindsay. 2010. "Between Provisioning and Consuming? Children, Mothers, and 'Childhood Obesity.'" *Health Sociology Review* 19(3): 304–316.

Mares, Teresa M., and Devon G. Peña. 2010. "Urban Agriculture in the Making of Insurgent Spaces in Los Angeles and Seattle." In *Insurgent Public Space: Guerilla Urbanism and the Remaking of Contemporary Cities*, edited by Jeffrey Hou, pp. 241–254. New York: Routledge.

Mares, Teresa M., and Devon G. Peña. 2011. "Environmental and Food Justice: Toward Local, Slow, and Deep Food Systems." In *Cultivating Food Justice: Race, Class, and Sustainability*, edited by Alison Hope Alkon and Julian Agyeman, pp. 197–219. Cambridge, MA: MIT Press.

Marist Poll. 2017. "Civility in America Poll Findings." NPR/PBR NewsHour/Marist Poll, November 21. Retrieved April 17, 2018, http://maristpoll.marist.edu/wp-content/misc/usapolls/us171112_PBS/NPR_PBS%20NewsHour_Marist%20Poll_Nature%20of%20the%20Sample%20and%20Tables_Civility%20and%20Politics_November%202017.pdf#page=3.

Martin, Molly A., and Adam Lippert. 2012. "Feeding Her Children, but Risking Her Health: The Intersection of Gender, Household Food Insecurity and Obesity." *Social Science & Medicine* 74(11): 1754–1764.

Martínez, Airín D. 2013. "Reconsidering Acculturation in Dietary Change Research among Latino Immigrants: Challenging the Preconditions of US Migration." *Ethnicity & Health* 18(2): 115–135.

Mason, Susan M., Alan J. Flint, Andrea L. Roberts, Jessica Agnew-Blais, Karestan C. Koenan, and Janet W. Rich-Edwards. 2014. "Posttraumatic Stress Disorder Symptoms and Food Addiction in Women by Timing and Type of Trauma Exposure." *JAMA Psychiatry* 71(11): 1271–1278.

Matthew, Dayna Bowen. 2015. *Just Medicine: A Cure for Racial Inequality in American Healthcare*. New York: New York University Press.

Mattingly, Marybeth J., and Suzanne M. Bianchi. 2003. "Gender Differences in the Quantity and Quality of Free Time: The U.S. Experience." *Social Forces* 81(3): 999–1030.

Mattingly, Marybeth J., and Liana C. Sayer. 2006. "Under Pressure: Gender Differences in the Relationship between Free Time and Feeling Rushed." *Journal of Marriage and Family* 68(1): 205–221.

McCarthy, Justin. 2015. "Holidays, Weekends Still Americans' Happiest Days of Year." Gallup News, January 13. Retrieved January 17, 2018, http://news.gallup.com/poll/180911/holidays-weekends-americans-happiest-days-year.aspx.

McGinnis, J. Michael, Jennifer Appleton Gootman, and Vivica I. Kraak (eds.). 2006. "Food Marketing to Children and Youth: Threat or Opportunity?" Report prepared for the Institute of Medicine of the National Academies. Washington, DC: National Academies Press. Retrieved May 31, 2017, https://www.stopcorporateabuse.org/sites/default/files/resources/food_marketing_to_children_and_youth_threat_or_opportunity_iom_report_2005.pdf.

McLaughlin, Michael, and Mark R. Rank. 2018. "Estimating the Economic Cost of Child Poverty in the United States." *Social Work Research*, Early Online View, March 30. doi: https://10.1093/swr/svy007.

McPherson, Miller, Lynn Smith-Lovin, and Matthew E. Brashears. 2006. "Social Isolation in America: Changes in Core Discussion Networks over Two Decades." *American Sociological Review* 71(3): 353–375.

Meier, Ann, and Kelly Musick. 2014. "Variations in Associations between Family Dinners and Adolescent Well-Being." *Journal of Marriage and Family* 76(1): 13–23.

Merkus, Suzanna L., Kari Anne Holte, Maaike A. Huysmans, Willem van Mechelen, and Allard J. van der Beek. 2015. "Nonstandard Working Schedules and Health: The Systematic Search for a Comprehensive Model." *BMC Public Health* 15: 1084.

Michener, Jamila. 2017. "People Who Get Medicaid Are Made to Feel Powerless. That Pushes Them out of Politics and toward Fatalism." *Washington Post*, August 17. Retrieved February 2, 2018, https://www.washingtonpost.com/news/monkey-cage/wp/2017/08/17/people-who-get-medicaid-are-made-to-feel-powerless-that-pushes-them-out-of-politics-and-toward-fatalism/?utm_term=.7b77cd07a7ee.

Michener, Jamila. 2018. *Fragmented Democracy: Medicaid, Federalism, and Unequal Politics*. Cambridge: Cambridge University Press.

Miller, Adrian. 2013. *Soul Food: The Surprising Story of an American Food, One Plate at a Time*. Chapel Hill: University of North Carolina Press.

Mishel, Lawrence, Josh Bivens, Elise Gould, and Heidi Shierholz. 2012. *The State of Working America*. 12th ed. Ithaca, NY: Cornell University Press.

Mitchell, Tamra. 2015. *North Carolina's Greatest Challenge—Widespread Struggles Remain a Grave Threat to Economic Growth and Us All*. Raleigh: North Carolina Justice Center. Retrieved February 7, 2018, http://www.ncjustice.org/?q=budget-and-tax/btc-reports-north-carolinas-greatest-challenge-widespread-struggles-remain-grave.

Moffit, Robert A. 2015. "The Deserving Poor, the Family, and the U.S. Welfare System." *Demography* 52(3): 729–749.

Montoya, Michael. 2011. *Making the Mexican Diabetic: Race, Science, and the Genetics of Inequality*. Berkeley: University of California Press.

Moody, Aaron. 2017. "NC Cities among the Most (and Least) Educated in the Nation." *News and Observer*, July 25. Retrieved February 7, 2018, http://www.newsobserver.com/news/local/article163516688.html.

Moore, Latetia, and Ana V. Diez Roux. 2006. "Associations of Neighborhood Characteristics with the Location and Type of Food Stores." *American Journal of Public Health* 96(2): 325–331.

Moore, Latetia, Ana V. Diez Roux, Jennifer A. Nettleton, and David R. Jacobs. 2008. "Associations of the Local Food Environment with Diet Quality—A Comparison of Assessments Based on Surveys and Geographic Information Systems." *American Journal of Epidemiology* 167(8): 917–924.

Moore, Mignon R. 2011. *Invisible Families: Gay Identities, Relationships, and Motherhood among Black Women.* Berkeley: University of California Press.

Morin, Rich. 2013. "The Politics and Demographics of Food Stamp Recipients." Pew Research Center, July 12. Retrieved February 1, 2018, http://www.pewresearch.org/fact-tank/2013/07/12/the-politics-and-demographics-of-food-stamp-recipients/.

Morland, Kimberly, Steve Wing, Ana Diez Roux, and Charles Poole. 2002a. "Neighborhood Characteristics Associated with the Location of Food Stores and Food Service Places." *American Journal of Preventive Medicine* 22(1): 23–29.

Morland, Kimberly, Steve Wing, and Ana Diez Roux. 2002b. "The Contextual Effect of the Local Food Environment on Residents' Diets: The Atherosclerosis Risk in Communities Study." *American Journal of Public Health* 92(11): 1761–1767.

Moss, Michael. 2013. *Salt Sugar Fat: How the Food Giants Hooked Us.* Toronto: McClelland & Stewart.

Mulik, Kranti, and Lindsey Haynes-Maslow. 2017. "The Affordability of MyPlate: An Analysis of SNAP Benefits and the Actual Cost of Eating According to the Dietary Guidelines." *Journal of Nutrition Education and Behavior* 49(8): 623–631.e1.

Murray, Erin Byers. 2016. "The Classic Meat and Three." *The Local Palate*, February 1. Retrieved April 9, 2018, http://thelocalpalate.com/articles/the-classic-meat-and-three/.

Murtadha, Khaula, and Daud Malik Watts. 2005. "Linking the Struggle for Education and Social Justice: Historical Perspectives of African American Leadership in Schools." *Educational Administration Quarterly* 41(4): 591–608.

Musick, Kelly, and Ann Meier. 2012. "Assessing Causality and Persistence in Associations between Family Dinners and Adolescent Well-Being." *Journal of Marriage and Family* 74(3): 476–493.

National Agricultural Workers Survey. 2014. "Demographic Characteristics." Retrieved February 6, 2018, https://naws.jbsinternational.com/table/2/10.

National Public Radio (NPR). 2013. "A Poll about Children and Weight: Crunch Time during the American Work and School Week – 3pm to Bed." National Public Radio, Robert Wood Johnson Foundation, and Harvard School of Public Health, February 25. Retrieved April 11, 2018, https://media.npr.org/documents/2013/feb/Children%20and%20Weight_Summary.pdf.

Nelson, Margaret K. 2010. *Parenting Out of Control: Anxious Parents in Uncertain Times.* New York: New York University Press.

Newman, Sarah L., Rachel Tumin, Rebecca Andridge, and Sarah E. Anderson. 2015. "Family Meal Frequency and Association with Household Food Availability in United States Multi-Person Households: National Health and Nutrition Examination Survey 2007–2010." *PLoS ONE* 10(12): e0144330. https://doi.org/10.1371/journal.pone.

Newport, Frank. 2015. "Americans' Perceived Time Crunch No Worse Than in Past." Gallup News, December 31. Retrieved April 11, 2018, http://news.gallup.com/poll/187982/americans-perceived-time-crunch-no-worse-past.aspx.

North Carolina Department of Health and Human Services (NC DHHS). 2018. "Low Income Energy Assistance." Retrieved February 1, 2018, https://www.ncdhhs.gov/assistance/low-income-services/low-income-energy-assistance.

Ochs, Elinor, and Margaret Beck. 2013. "Dinner." In *Fast-Forward Family: Home, Work, and Relationships in Middle-Class America*, edited by Elinor Ochs and Tamar Kremer-Sadlik, pp. 48–66. Berkeley: University of California Press.

Ochs, Elinor, and Tamar Kremer-Sadlik (eds.). 2013. *Fast-Forward Family: Home, Work, and Relationships in Middle-Class America*. Berkeley: University of California Press.

Office of Community Services. 2017. "Healthy Food Financing Initiative." Office of Community Services, Administration for Children & Families, US Department of Health and Human Services. Last updated June 14, 2017. Retrieved April 14, 2018, https://www.acf.hhs.gov/ocs/programs/community-economic-development/healthy-food-financing.

Oleschuk, Merin, Kate Cairns, and Josée Johnston. 2016. "Let's Rethink the Pressure of Cooking Family Meals during the Holidays." *Huffington Post Canada*, December 20. Retrieved January 17, 2018, http://www.huffingtonpost.ca/merin-oleschuk/family-meal-holidays_b_13729720.html.

Oliver, Jamie. 2010. "Teach Every Child about Food." TED Talk, February. Retrieved June 7, 2017, https://www.ted.com/talks/jamie_oliver/.

Olson, Christine. 2005. "Food Insecurity in Women: A Recipe for Unhealthy Tradeoffs." *Topics in Clinical Nutrition* 20(4): 321–328.

Olson, Christine M., Barbara S. Rauschenbach, Edward A. Frongillo Jr., and Anne Kendall. 1996. "Factors Contributing to Household Food Insecurity in a Rural Upstate New York County." Institute for Research on Poverty Discussion Paper no. 1107-96. Madison, WI: Institute for Research on Poverty. Retrieved June 6, 2012, http://www.ssc.wisc.edu/irpweb/publications/dps/pdfs/dp110796.pdf.

Olson, Jenny G., Brent McFerran, Andrea C. Morales, and Darren W. Dahl. 2016. "Wealth and Welfare: Divergent Moral Reactions to Ethical Consumer Choices." *Journal of Consumer Research* 42(6): 879–896.

Oostindjer, Marije, Jessica Aschemann-Witzel, Qing Wang, Silje Elisabeth Skuland, Bjørg Egelandsdal, Gro V. Amdam, Alexander Schjøll, Mark C. Pachucki, Paul Rozin, Jarrett Stein, Valerie Lengard Almli, and Ellen Van Kleef. 2016. "Are School Meals a Viable and Sustainable Tool to Improve the Healthiness and Sustainability of Children's Diet and Food Consumption? A Cross-National Comparative Perspective." *Critical Reviews in Food Science and Nutrition* 57(18): 3942–3958.

Organic Trade Association (OTA). 2017. "Organic Industry Survey." Retrieved April 10, 2018, https://ota.com/resources/organic-industry-survey.

Organization for Economic Development (OECD). 2017a. "Obesity Update 2017." Retrieved February 2, 2018, https://www.oecd.org/els/health-systems/Obesity-Update-2017.pdf.

Organization for Economic Development (OECD). 2017b. "OECD Health Statistics 2017: Frequently Requested Data." Last updated November 10, 2017. Retrieved February 7, 2018, http://www.oecd.org/els/health-systems/OECD-Health-Statistics-2017-Frequently-Requested-Data.xls.

Ossola, Alexandra. 2015. "Why Are Holidays with Your Family So Stressful?" *Popular Science*, November 25. Retrieved January 17, 2018, https://www.popsci.com/why-are-families-particularly-stressful-during-holidays.

Parker, Kim, and Gretchen Livingston. 2016. "6 Facts about American Fathers." Pew Research Center, June 16. Retrieved June 8, 2017, http://www.pewresearch.org/fact-tank/2016/06/16/fathers-day-facts/.

Parrott, Les, and Leslie Parrott. 2011. *The Hour That Matters Most: The Surprising Power of the Family Meal*. Carol Stream, IL: Tyndale House.

Patel, Raj. 2007. *Stuffed and Starved: The Hidden Battle for the World Food System*. Brooklyn, NY: Melville House.

Pear, Robert. 2004. "Electronic Cards Replace Coupons for Food Stamps." *New York Times*, June 23. Retrieved April 11, 2018, https://www.nytimes.com/2004/06/23/us/electronic-cards-replace-coupons-for-food-stamps.html.

Pearson, Tim, Jean Russell, Michael J. Campbell, and Margo E. Baker. 2005. "Do 'Food Deserts' Influence Fruit and Vegetable Consumption?—A Cross-Sectional Study." *Appetite* 45(2): 195–197.

Pérez-Escamilla, Rafael. 2011. "Acculturation, Nutrition, and Health Disparities in Latinos." *American Journal of Clinical Nutrition* 93(5): 1163S–1167S.

Perry, Brea L., and Jessica McCrory Calarco. 2017. "Let Them Eat Cake: Socioeconomic Status and Caregiver Indulgence of Children's Food and Drink Requests." In *Food Systems and Health*, edited by Sara Shostak, pp. 121–146. Vol. 18 in *Advances in Medical Sociology*. Bingley, UK: Emerald Publishing.

Pew Research Center. 2015a. "The Rise in Dual Income Households." Last updated June 18, 2015. Retrieved June 6, 2017, http://www.pewresearch.org/ft_dual-income-households-1960-2012-2/.

Pew Research Center. 2015b. "Parenting in America: The American Family Today." Last updated December 17, 2015. Retrieved June 8, 2017, http://www.pewsocialtrends.org/2015/12/17/1-the-american-family-today/.

Pfeffer, Carla A. 2016. *Queering Families: The Postmodern Partnerships of Cisgender Women and Transgender Men*. New York: Oxford University Press.

Philpott, Tom. 2017. "It's Time to Stop Shaming Poor People for What They Buy with Food Stamps." *Mother Jones*, January 18. Retrieved June 5, 2017, http://www.motherjones.com/environment/2017/01/food-stamps-snap-soda-nyt.

Piketty, Thomas, and Emmanuel Saez. 2003. "Income Inequality in the United States, 1913–1998." *Quarterly Journal of Economics* 118(1): 1–39.

Pilcher, Jeffrey M. 1998. *Que Vivan Los Tamales! Food and the Making of Mexican Identity*. Albuquerque: University of New Mexico Press.

Pilkauskas, Natasha V., Irwin Garfinkel, and Sara S. McLanahan. 2014. "The Prevalence and Economic Value of Doubling Up." *Demography* 51(5): 1667–1676.

Pleck, Elizabeth. 2000. *Celebrating the Family: Ethnicity, Consumer Culture, and Family Rituals*. Cambridge, MA: Harvard University Press.

Plumer, Brad. 2014. "The $956 Billion Farm Bill, in One Graph." *Washington Post*, January 28. Retrieved June 5, 2017, https://www.washingtonpost.com/news/wonk/wp/2014/01/28/the-950-billion-farm-bill-in-one-chart/?utm_term=.9faeea817701.

Polaski, Sandra. 2004. "Mexican Employment, Productivity and Income a Decade after NAFTA." Brief Submitted to the Canadian Standing Senate Committee on Foreign Affairs, February 25. Retrieved February 6, 2018, http://carnegieendowment.org/2004/02/25/mexican-employment-productivity-and-income-decade-after-nafta-pub-1473.

Pollan, Michael. 2009. *Food Rules: An Eater's Manifesto*. New York: Penguin Books.

Pollan, Michael. 2013. *Cooked: A Natural History of Transformation*. New York: Penguin Press.

Poppendieck, Janet. 1998. *Sweet Chairty: Emergency Food and the End of Entitlement*. New York: Penguin Books.

Poppendieck, Janet. 2010. *Free For All: Fixing School Food in America*. Berkeley: University of California Press.

Poppendieck, Janet. [1986] 2014. *Breadlines Knee-Deep in Wheat: Food Assistance in the Great Depression*. Berkeley: University of California Press.

Porter, Jane. 2015. "North Carolina's Historic Preservation Tax Credits Could Be Coming Back." *Indy Weekly*, September 3. Retrieved February 7, 2018, https://www.indyweek.com/news/archives/2015/09/03/north-carolinas-historic-preservation-tax-credits-could-be-coming-back.

PR Newswire. 2014. "Barcel USA Awarded the Nielsen 2014 U.S. Breakthrough Innovation Award for Takis." PR Newswire, July 11. Retrieved February 1, 2018, https://www.prnewswire.com/news-releases/barcel-usa-awarded-the-nielsen-2014-us-breakthrough-innovation-award-for-takis-266812241.html.

Prasertong, Ajali. 2014. "15 Money-Saving Ways to Outsmart Your Supermarket." *Kitchn*, January 27. Retrieved February 1, 2018, https://www.thekitchn.com/15-moneysaving-ways-to-outsmart-your-supermarket-199531.

Pugh, Allison J. 2009. *Longing and Belonging: Parents, Children, and Consumer Culture*. Berkeley: University of California Press.

Pugh, Allison J. 2015. *The Tumbleweed Society: Working and Caring in an Age of Insecurity*. New York: Oxford University Press.

Puhl, Rebecca M., and Chelsea A. Heuer. 2009. "The Stigma of Obesity: A Review and Update." *Obesity* 17: 941–964.

Puhl, Rebecca M., and Chelsea A. Heuer. 2010. "Obesity Stigma: Important Considerations for Public Health." *American Journal of Public Health* 100(6): 1019–1028.

Puhl, Rebecca M., Melanie M. Wall, Chen Chen, S. Bryn Austin, Marla E. Eisenberg, and Dianne Newmark-Sztainer. 2017. "Experiences of Weight Teasing in Adolescence and Weight-Related Outcomes in Adulthood: A 15-Year Longitudinal Study." *Preventive Medicine* 100: 173–179.

Purvis, Kathleen. 2017. "This American Comfort Food Leads a Double Life—But Only Some of Us Know the Secret. Do You?" *Charlotte Observer*, November 15. Retrieved February 2, 2018, http://www.charlotteobserver.com/living/food-drink/article184866748.html.

Putnam, Robert D. 2000. *Bowling Alone: The Collapse and Revival of American Community*. New York: Simon & Schuster.

Ramírez, Aida. 2013. "Who, Exactly, Is a Gringo?" NPR, Code Switch, August 7. Retrieved February 2, 2018, https://www.npr.org/sections/codeswitch/2013/08/07/209266300/who-exactly-is-a-gringo.

Ramsdell, Laura. 2012. "Neighbors Upset after News of Kroger Closings in SE Raleigh." *Raleigh Public Record*, December 13. Retrieved June 5, 2017, http://raleighpublicrecord.org/news/2012/12/13/neighbors-upset-after-news-of-kroger-closings-in-se-raleigh/.

Ray, Krishnendu. 2016. *The Ethnic Restaurateur*. New York: Bloomsbury Academic.

Raynolds, Laura. 2000. "Re-embedding Global Agriculture: The International Organic and Fair Trade Movements." *Agriculture and Human Values* 17(3): 297–309.

Rehm, Colin D., José L. Pennílvo, Ashkan Afshin, and Dariush Mozaffarian. 2016. "Dietary Intake among U.S. Adults, 1999–2012." *Journal of the American Medical Association* 315(23): 2542–2553.

Reich, Jennifer. 2005. *Fixing Families: Parents, Power, and the Child Welfare System*. New York: Routledge.

Reich, Jennifer. 2016. *Calling the Shots: Why Parents Reject Vaccines*. New York: New York University Press.

Reid, Chelsea A., Jeffrey D. Green, Tim Wildschut, and Constantine Sedikides. 2015. "Scent-Evoked Nostalgia." *Memory* 23(2): 157–166.

Reynolds, Gretchen. 2013. "The Scientific 7-Minute Workout." *New York Times*, May 9. Retrieved June 6, 2017, https://well.blogs.nytimes.com/2013/05/09/the-scientific-7-minute-workout/?_r=0.

Rifkin, Rebecca. 2014. "Forty-Five Percent of Americans Seek Out Organic Foods." Gallup News, August 7. Retrieved February 2, 2018, http://news.gallup.com/poll/174524/forty-five-percent-americans-seek-organic-foods.aspx.

Riosmena, Fernando, Rebeca Wong, and Alberto Palloni. 2013. "Migration Selection, Protection, and Acculturation in Health: A Binational Perspective on Older Adults." *Demography* 50(3): 1039–1064.

Roberts, Dorothy. 2010. "The Social Immorality of Health in the Gene Age: Race, Disability, and Inequality." In *Against Health: How Health Became the New Morality*, edited by J. M. Metzl and A. Kirkland, pp. 61–71. New York: New York University Press.

Rodríguez-Alegría, Enrique. 2012. "From Grinding Corn to Dishing Out Money: A Long-Term History of Cooking in Xaltocan, Mexico." In *The Menial Art of Cooking: Archaeological Studies of Cooking and Food Preparation*, edited by Sarah Graff and Enrique Rodríguez-Alegría, pp. 99–117. Boulder: University Press of Colorado.

Romm, Carl. 2015. "Why Comfort Food Comforts." *Atlantic*, April 3. Retrieved February 2, 2018, https://www.theatlantic.com/health/archive/2015/04/why-comfort-food-comforts/389613/.

Rose, Dina. 2014. *It's Not About the Broccoli: Three Habits to Teach Your Kids for a Lifetime of Healthy Eating*. New York: Perigree.

Rose, Donald. 1999. "Economic Determinants and Dietary Consequences of Food Insecurity in the United States." *Journal of Nutrition* 129(2): 517S–520S.

Rosenbaum, Dottie. 2013. "The Relationship between SNAP and Work among Low-Income Households." Center on Budget and Policy Priorities, January 30. Retrieved April 20, 2018, https://www.cbpp.org/research/the-relationship-between-snap-and-work-among-low-income-households.

Roy, Kevin M., and Linda Burton. 2007. "Mothering through Recruitment: Kinscription of Nonresidential Fathers and Father Figures in Low-Income Families." *Family Relations* 56(1): 24–39.

Runfola, Cristin D., Ann Von Holle, Christine M. Peat, Danielle A. Gagne, Kimberly A. Brown, Sara M. Hofmeier, and Cynthia M. Bulik. 2013. "Characteristics of Women with Body Size Satisfaction at Midlife: Results of the Gender and Body Image Study (GABI)." *Journal of Women's Aging* 25(4). doi: 10.1080/08952841.2013.816215

Rutherford, Markella. 2011. *Adult Supervision Required: Private Freedom and Public Constraints for Parents and Children*. New Brunswick, NJ: Rutgers University Press.

Ruzek, Erik, Margaret Burchinal, George Farkas, and Greg J. Duncan. 2014. "The Quality of Toddler Child Care and Cognitive Skills at 24 Months: Propensity Score Analysis Results from the ECLS-B." *Early Research Childhood Quarterly* 28(1). doi: 10.1016/j.ecresq.2013.09.002.

Saad, Lydia. 2013. "Most U.S. Families Still Routinely Dine Together at Home." Gallup News, December 26. Retrieved February 6, 2018, http://news.gallup.com/poll/166628/families-routinely-dine-together-home.aspx.

Sadeghirad, B., T. Duhaney, S. Motaghipisheh, N. R. C. Campbell, and B. C. Johnston. 2016. "Influence of Unhealthy Food and Beverage Marketing on Children's Dietary Intake and Preference: A Systematic Review and Meta-Analysis of Randomized Trials." *Obesity Reviews* 17(10): 945–959.

Sadeh, Avi, Reut Gruber, and Amiram Raviv. 2003. "The Effects of Sleep Restriction and Extension on School-Age Children: What a Difference an Hour Makes." *Child Development* 74(2): 444–455.

Saguy, Abigail C. 2013. *What's Wrong with Fat?* New York: Oxford University Press.

Salatin, Joel. 2014. "'Slate' Criticizes the 'Home-Cooked Family Dinner': Joel Salatin Responds." *Mother Earth News.* Retrieved June 7, 2017, http://www.motherearthnews.com/real-food/slate-family-dinner-zb0z1409zsie#axzz3COJm4yiK.

Sandberg, Sheryl. 2013. *Lean In: Women, Work, and the Will to Lead.* New York: Alfred A. Knopf.

Sayer, Liana. 2005. "Gender, Time, and Inequality: Trends in Women's and Men's Paid Work, Unpaid Work, and Free Time." *Social Forces* 84(1): 285–303.

Sayer, Liana C., Suzanne M. Bianchi, and John P. Robinson. 2004. "Are Parents Investing Less in Children? Trends in Mothers' and Fathers' Time with Children." *American Journal of Sociology* 110(1): 1–43.

Schmidt, Leigh Eric. 2016. "Thanksgiving, a Celebration of Inequality." *Atlantic,* November 22. Retrieved January 19, 2018, https://www.theatlantic.com/business/archive/2016/11/thanksgiving-a-celebration-of-inequality/508346/.

Schulte, Brigid. 2014. *Overwhelmed: Work, Love, and Play When No One Has the Time.* New York: Farrar, Straus & Giroux.

Searcey, Dionne, and Matt Richtel. 2017. "Obesity Was Rising as Ghana Embraced Fast Food. Then Came KFC." *New York Times,* October 2. Retrieved April 12, 2018, https://www.nytimes.com/2017/10/02/health/ghana-kfc-obesity.html.

Segal, Laura M., Jack Rayburn, and Stacy E. Beck. 2017. "The State of Obesity: Better Policies for a Healthier Tomorrow." Washington, DC: Trust for America's Health. Retrieved April 9, 2018, https://stateofobesity.org/files/stateofobesity2017.pdf.

Seidman, Gay. 2007. *Beyond the Boycott: Labor Rights, Human Rights, and Transnational Activism.* New York: Russell Sage Foundation.

Sered, Susan. 2014. "Suffering in an Age of Personal Responsibility." *Contexts* 13(2): 38–43.

Severson, Kim. 2017. "Black Vegans Step Out, for Their Health and Other Causes." *New York Times,* November 28. Retrieved November 28, 2017, https://www.nytimes.com/2017/11/28/dining/black-vegan-cooking.html.

Shaefer, H. Luke, Sophie Collyer, Greg Duncan, Kathryn Edin, Irwin Garfinkel, David Harris, Timothy M. Smeeding, Jane Waldfogel, Christopher Wimer, and Hirokazu Yoshikawa. 2018. "A Universal Child Allowance: A Plan to Reduce Poverty and Income Instability among Children in the United States." *RSF: The Russell Sage Foundation Journal of the Social Sciences* 4(2): 22–42.

Sharpless, Rebecca. 2003. *Cooking in Other Women's Kitchens: Domestic Workers in the South, 1865–1960.* Chapel Hill: University of North Carolina Press.

Shier, Victoria, Ruopeng An, and Roland Sturm. 2012. "Is There a Robust Relationship between Neighbourhood Food Environment and Childhood Obesity in the USA?" *Public Health* 126(9): 723–730.

Shloim, Netalie, Lisa R. Edelson, Nathalie Martin, and Marion M. Hetherington. 2015. "Parenting Styles, Feeding Styles, Feeding Practices, and Weight Status in 4–12-Year-Old Children: A Systematic Review of the Literature." *Frontiers of Psychology* 6: 1849.

Sims, Julia. 2012. "Kroger Closings Highlight Needs in Southeast Raleigh." WRAL, November 29. Retrieved June 5, 2017, http://www.wral.com/kroger-stores-closing-in-southeast-raleigh/11826959/.

Slaughter, Anne-Marie. 2012. "Why Women Still Can't Have It All." *Atlantic*, July/August. Retrieved February 1, 2018, https://www.theatlantic.com/magazine/archive/2012/07/why-women-still-cant-have-it-all/309020/.

Slocum, Rachel. 2007. "Whiteness, Space, and Alternative Food Practice." *Geoforum* 38(3): 520–533.

Smarsh, Sarah. 2014. "Poor Teeth." *Aeon*, October 23. Retrieved June 6, 2017, https://aeon.co/essays/there-is-no-shame-worse-than-poor-teeth-in-a-rich-world.

Smith, Kirsten P., and Nicholas A. Christakis. 2008. "Social Networks and Health." *Annual Review of Sociology* 34: 405–429.

Smith, Lindsey P., Shu Wen Ng, and Barry M. Popkin. 2013. "Trends in US Home Food Preparation and Consumption: Analysis of National Nutrition Surveys and Time Use Studies from 1965–1966 to 2007–2008." *Nutrition Journal* 12: 45. doi:10.1186/1475-2891-12-45.

Smith-Spangler, Crystal, Margaret L. Brandeau, Grace E. Hunter, J. Clay Bavinger, Maren Pearson, Paul J. Eschbach, Vandana Sundaram, Hau Liu, Patricia Schirmer, Christopher Stave, and Dena M. Bravata. 2012. "Are Organic Foods Safer or Healthier Than Conventional Alternatives? A Systematic Review." *Annals of Internal Medicine* 157(5): 348–366.

Snider, William D. 1985. *Helms and Hunt: The North Carolina Senate Race, 1984.* Chapel Hill: University of North Carolina Press.

Som Castellano, Rebecca. 2016. "Alternative Food Networks and the Labor of Food Provisioning: A Third Shift?" *Rural Sociology* 81(3): 445–469.

Soss, Joe. 2017. "Food Stamp Fables." *Jacobin*, January 16. Retrieved June 5, 2017, https://www.jacobinmag.com/2017/01/food-stamps-snap-welfare-soda-new-york-times/.

Soss, Joe, Richard C. Fording, and Sanford F. Schram. 2011. *Disciplining the Poor: Neoliberal Paternalism and the Persistent Power of Race.* Chicago: University of Chicago Press.

Sparling, Nina. 2017. "From Phở to Fajitas, School Lunches Feed a Diverse Nation." *Civil Eats*, November 2. Retrieved February 1, 2018, https://civileats.com/2017/11/02/why-culturally-relevant-food-matters-in-school-lunch/.

Spross, Jeff. 2017. "Welfare's Customer Service Problem." *Week*, August 21. Retrieved February 2, 2018, http://theweek.com/articles/719246/welfares-customer-service-problem.

Stack, Carol. 1974. *All Our Kin: Strategies for Survival in a Black Community.* New York: Basic Books.

Stack, Carol B., and Linda M. Burton. 1993. "Kinscripts." *Journal of Comparative Family Studies* 24(2): 157–170.

Stead, Martine, Laura McDermott, Anne Marie MacKintosh, and Ashley Adamson. 2011. "Why Healthy Eating Is Bad for Young People's Health: Identity, Belonging and Food." *Social Science & Medicine* 72(7): 1131–1139.

Stepler, Renee, and Mark Hugo López. 2016. "Ranking the Latino Population in the States." Pew Research Center, September 8. Retrieved January 31, 2018, http://www.pewhispanic.org/2016/09/08/4-ranking-the-latino-population-in-the-states/.

Stevens, Christine A. 2010. "Exploring Food Insecurity among Young Mothers (15–24 Years)." *Journal for Specialists in Pediatric Nursing* 15(2): 163–171.

Strazdins, Lyndall, Mark S. Clements, Rosemary J. Korda, Dorothy H. Broom, and Rennie M. D'Souza. 2006. "Unsociable Work? Nonstandard Work Schedules, Family Relationships, and Children's Well-Being." *Journal of Marriage and Family* 68(2): 394–410.

Strings, Sabrina. 2015. "Obese Black Women as 'Social Dead Weight': Reinventing the 'Diseased Black Woman.'" *Signs: Journal of Women in Culture and Society* 41(1): 107–130.

Sue, Derald Wing, Christina M. Capodilupo, Gina C. Torino, Jennifer M. Bucceri, Aisha M. B. Holder, Kevin L. Nadal, and Marta Esquilin. 2007. "Racial Microaggressions in Everyday Life: Implications for Clinical Practice." *American Psychologist* 62(4): 271–286.

Sullivan, Shannon. 2015. *The Physiology of Sexist and Racist Oppression*. New York: Oxford University Press.

Sullivan, Susan A., and Leann L. Birch. 1990. "Pass the Sugar, Pass the Salt: Experience Dictates Preference." *Developmental Psychology* 26(4): 546–551.

Szabo, Michelle. 2012. "Foodwork or Foodplay? Men's Domestic Cooking, Privilege and Leisure." *Sociology* 47(4): 623–638.

Szabo, Michelle. 2014. "Men Nurturing through Food: Challenging Gender Dichotomies around Domestic Cooking." *Journal of Gender Studies* 23(1): 18–31.

Szabo, Michelle, and Shelley Koch. 2017. "Introduction." In *Food, Masculinities, and Home: Interdisciplinary Perspectives*, edited by Michelle Szabo and Shelley Koch, pp. 1–28. New York: Bloomsbury Academic.

Tailie, Lindsay Smith. 2018. "Who's Cooking? Trends in US Home Food Preparation by Gender, Education, and Race/Ethnicity from 2003 to 2016." *Nutrition Journal* 17: 41. doi: 10.1186/s12937-018-0347-9.

Tell, Carolina. 2013. "The Nanny Recipes: Skip the Microwave." *New York Times*, November 13. Retrieved April 23, 2018, https://www.nytimes.com/2013/11/14/fashion/chef-run-service-teaches-nannies-recipes-that-skip-the-microwave.html.

Thistle, Susan. 2006. *From Marriage to the Market: The Transformation of Women's Lives and Work*. Berkeley: University of California Press.

Thompson, Julie R. 2017. "ABC's Lawsuit Is a Reminder That We're Still Eating 'Pink Slime.'" *Huffington Post*, March 22. Retrieved April 12, 2018, https://www.huffingtonpost.com/entry/abc-pink-slime-court_us_58d27adae4b02d33b7473d17.

Throop, Elizabeth M., Asheley Cockrell Skinner, Andrew J. Perrin, Michael J. Steiner, Adebowale Odulana, and Eliana M. Perrin. 2014. "Pass the Popcorn: 'Obesogenic' Behaviors and Stigma in Children's Movies." *Pediatric Obesity* 22(7): 1694–1700.

Timmermans, Stefan, and Mara Buchbinder. 2012. *Saving Babies? The Consequences of Newborn Genetic Screening*. Chicago: University of Chicago Press.

Tipton-Martin, Toni. 2015. *The Jemima Code: Two Centuries of African American Cookbooks*. Austin: University of Texas Press.

Trebay, Guy. 2012. "Guess Who's Not Coming to Dinner." *New York Times*, November 29. Retrieved June 5, 2017, http://www.nytimes.com/2012/11/29/fashion/saving-the-endangered-dinner-party.html.

Treviño, Roberto R. 2004. *The Church in the Barrio: Mexican American Ethno-Catholicism in Houston*. Chapel Hill: University of North Carolina Press.

Troisi, Jordan D., and Shira Gabriel. 2011. "Chicken Soup Really Is Good for the Soul: 'Comfort Food' Fulfills the Need to Belong." *Psychological Science* 22(6): 747–753.

Trubek, Amy B. 2017. *Making Modern Meals: How Americans Cook Today*. Berkeley: University of California Press.

Tuan, Mia. 1998. *Forever Foreigners or Honorary Whites? The Asian Ethnic Experience Today*. New Brunswick, NJ: Rutgers University Press.

Twitty, Michael W. 2017. *The Cooking Gene: A Journey through African American Culinary History in the Old South*. New York: HarperCollins.

Umberson, Debra. 1992. "Gender, Marital Status, and the Social Control of Health Behavior." *Social Science & Medicine* 34(8): 907–917.

Umberson, Debra. 2017. "Black Deaths Matter: Race, Relationship Loss, and Effects on Survivors." *Journal of Health and Social Behavior* 58(4): 405–420.

Umberson, Debra, Robert Crosnoe, and Corinne Reczek. 2010. "Social Relationships and Health Behavior across Life Course." *Annual Review of Sociology* 36: 139–157.

United States Census Bureau. 2016. "Quick Facts: United States." Retrieved February 1, 2018, https://www.census.gov/quickfacts/fact/table/US/PST045216.

United States Census Bureau. 2017a. "Maricopa County Added Over 222 People per Day in 2016, More Than Any Other County." CB17-44. Retrieved February 7, 2018, https://www.census.gov/newsroom/press-releases/2017/cb17-44.html.

United States Census Bureau. 2017b. "Quick Facts: Wake County, North Carolina." Retrieved February 7, 2018, https://www.census.gov/quickfacts/fact/map/wakecountynorthcarolina/IPE120216.

United States Department of Agriculture (USDA). 2013. "Official USDA Food Plans: Cost of Food at Home at Four Levels, U.S. Average, May 2013." Retrieved February 2, 2018, https://www.cnpp.usda.gov/sites/default/files/usda_food_plans_cost_of_food/CostofFoodMay2013.pdf.

United States Department of Agriculture (USDA). 2015. "WIC at a Glance." Last updated February 27, 2015. Retrieved February 2, 2018, https://www.fns.usda.gov/wic/about-wic-wic-glance.

United States Department of Agriculture (USDA). 2016a. "Table 3: Usual Grocery Shopper and Usual Meal Preparer in the Household, on an Average Day in 2016, Age 18 and Older." USDA Economic Research Service Eating and Health Module (ATUS), 2016. Retrieved April 12, 2018, https://www.ers.usda.gov/webdocs/DataFiles/48782/Table3_2016.xlsx?v=43076.

United States Department of Agriculture (USDA). 2016b. "Snapshot of the WIC Food Packages." Retrieved June 5, 2017, https://www.fns.usda.gov/sites/default/files/wic/SNAPSHOT-of-Child-Women-Food-Pkgs.pdf.

United States Department of Agriculture (USDA). 2017a. "Supplemental Nutrition Assistance Program (SNAP): What Can SNAP Buy?" Last updated November 17, 2017. Retrieved February 1, 2018, https://www.fns.usda.gov/snap/eligible-food-items.

United States Department of Agriculture (USDA). 2017b. "Characteristics of Supplemental Nutrition Assistance Program Households: Fiscal Year 2016." Report No. SNAP-17-CHAR (November 2017). Washington, DC: USDA. Retrieved February 1, 2018, https://fns-prod.azureedge.net/sites/default/files/ops/Characteristics2016.pdf.

United States Department of Agriculture (USDA). 2017c. "SNAP Retailer Notice." Last updated August 23, 2017. Retrieved April 14, 2018, https://fns-prod.azureedge.net/sites/default/files/snap/Retailer-Sales-Tax-Notice.pdf.

United States Department of Agriculture (USDA). 2017d. "Food Access Resource Atlas: Documentation." Lasted updated December 5, 2017. Retrieved February 2, 2018, https://www.ers.usda.gov/data-products/food-access-research-atlas/documentation/.

United States Department of Agriculture (USDA). 2017e. "Food Access Resource Atlas: Go to the Atlas." Lasted updated May 18, 2017. Retrieved February 2, 2018, https://www.ers.usda.gov/data-products/food-access-research-atlas/go-to-the-atlas.aspx.

United States Department of Agriculture (USDA). 2017f. "Food Environment Atlas: Go to the Atlas." Lasted updated September 18, 2017. Retrieved February 2, 2018, https://www.ers.usda.gov/data-products/food-environment-atlas/go-to-the-atlas/.

United States Department of Agriculture (USDA). 2017g. "Women, Infants, and Children (WIC): Breastfeeding Is a Priority in the WIC Program." Retrieved February 2, 2018, https://www.fns.usda.gov/wic/breastfeeding-priority-wic-program.

United States Department of Agriculture (USDA). 2017h. "Poorest U.S. Households Spent 33 Percent of Their Incomes on Food in 2015." USDA Economic Research Service, last updated May 19, 2017. Retrieved February 7, 2018, https://www.ers.usda.gov/data-products/chart-gallery/gallery/chart-detail/?chartId=83579.

United States Department of Agriculture (USDA). 2018a. "National Count of Farmers Market Directory Listing." Retrieved February 2, 2018, https://www.ams.usda.gov/sites/default/files/media/NationalCountofFMDirectory17.JP.

United States Department of Agriculture (USDA). 2018b. "Supplemental Nutrition Assistance Program (SNAP): Am I Eligible for SNAP?" Last updated January 16, 2018. Retrieved February 2, 2018, https://www.fns.usda.gov/snap/eligibility.

United States Department of Labor. 2018. "Women in the Labor Force." Retrieved January 31, 2018, https://www.dol.gov/wb/stats/NEWSTATS/facts/women_lf.htm#one.

University of North Carolina–Chapel Hill Department of City and Regional Planning. 2018. "The State of Low-Wage Work in North Carolina. Occupations." Retrieved February 7, 2018, http://www.lowwagenc.org/occupations/.

Van Hook, Jennifer, Susana Quiros, Michelle L. Frisco, and Emnet Fikru. 2016. "It Is Hard to Swim Upstream: Dietary Acculturation among Mexican-Origin Children." *Population Research and Policy Review* 35(2): 177–196.

Vegetarian Resource Group. 2016. "How Many Adults in the U.S. Are Vegetarian and Vegan?" Retrieved February 2, 2018, http://www.vrg.org/nutshell/Polls/2016_adults_veg.htm.

Veit, Helen Zoe. 2013. *Modern Food, Moral Food: Self-Control, Science, and the Rise of Modern American Eating in the Early Twentieth Century*. Chapel Hill: University of North Carolina Press.

Ventura, Alison K., and Leann L. Birch. 2008. "Does Parenting Affect Children's Eating and Weight Status?" *International Journal of Behavioral Nutrition and Physical Activity* 5(15):1–12.

Waggoner, Miranda R. 2017. *The Zero Trimester: Pre-Pregnancy Care and the Politics of Reproductive Risk*. Berkeley: University of California Press.

Wajcman, Judy. 2015. *Pressed for Time: The Acceleration of Life in Digital Capitalism*. Chicago: University of Chicago Press.

Walker, Renee E., Christopher R. Keane, and Jessica G. Burke. 2009. "Disparities and Access to Healthy Food in the United States: A Review of Food Deserts Literature." *Health & Place* 16(5): 876–884.

Wang, Dong, Cindy Leung, Yanping Li, Eric Ding, Stephanie Chiuve, Frank Hu, and Walter Willett. 2014. "Trends in Dietary Quality among Adults in the United States, 1999 through 2010." *JAMA: The Journal of the American Medical Association* 174(10): 1587–1595.

Wardle, J., M. L. Herrera, L. Cooke, and E. L. Gibson. 2003. "Modifying Children's Food Preferences: The Effects of Exposure and Reward on Acceptance of an Unfamiliar Vegetable." *European Journal of Clinical Nutrition* 57(2): 341–348.

Warin, Megan, Tanya Zivkovic, Vivienne Moore, and Michael Davies. 2012. "Mothers as Smoking Guns: Fetal Overnutrition and the Reproduction of Obesity." *Feminism & Psychology* 22(3): 360–375.

Washington Post. 1978. "The FTC as National Nanny." Editorial in the *Washington Post*, March 1, 1978. Retrieved May 30, 2018, https://www.washingtonpost.com/archive/politics/1978/03/01/the-ftc-as-national-nanny/69f778f5-8407-4df0-b0e9-7f1f8e826b3b/?noredirect=on&utm_term=.4a0000ceec5b.

Weinstein, Miriam. 2006. *The Surprising Power of Family Meals: How Eating Together Makes Us Smarter, Stronger, Healthier and Happier*. Hanover, NH: Steerforth Press.

West, Emily. 2009. "Doing Gender Difference through Greeting Cards." *Feminist Media Studies* 9(3): 285–299.

White, Monica M. 2011. "Sisters of the Soil: Urban Gardening as Resistance in Detroit." *Race/Ethnicity: Multidisciplinary Global Contexts* 5(1): 13–28.

White House of President Obama, The. 2010. "Taking On 'Food Deserts.'" February 24, 2010. Retrieved June 1, 2017, https://obamawhitehouse.archives.gov/blog/2010/02/24/taking-food-deserts.

Whitten, Sarah. 2016. "America's Favorite Comfort Food Is . . ." CNBC, January 25. Retrieved February 6, 2018, https://www.cnbc.com/2016/01/25/americas-favorite-comfort-food-is.html.

Whyte, Michael. 2013. "Episodic Fieldwork, Updating, and Sociability." *Social Analysis* 57(1): 110–121.

Wight, Vanessa R., Sara B. Raley, and Suzanne M. Bianchi. 2008. "Time for Children, One's Spouse, and Oneself among Parents Who Work Nonstandard Hours." *Social Forces* 87(1): 243–271.

Wilk, Richard. 2010. "Power at the Table: Food Fights and Happy Meals." *Cultural Studies* 10(6): 428–436.

Williams-Forson, Psyche A. 2006. *Building Houses Out of Chicken Legs: Black Women, Food, and Power*. Chapel Hill: University of North Carolina Press.

Wills, Wendy, Kathryn Backett-Millburn, Mei-Li Roberts, and Julia Lawton. 2011. "The Framing of Social Class Distinctions through Family Food and Eating Practices." *Sociological Review* 59(4): 725–740.

Wise, Timothy A. 2010. "Agricultural Dumping under NAFTA: Estimating the Costs of U.S. Agricultural Policies to Mexican Producers." Mexican Rural Development Research Report 7. Washington, DC: Woodrow Wilson Center for International Scholars. Retrieved April 9, 2018, http://www.ase.tufts.edu/gdae/Pubs/rp/AgricDumpingWoodrowWilsonCenter.pdf.

Witt, Doris. 2004. *Black Hunger: Soul Food and America*. Minneapolis: University of Minnesota Press.

Wolfson, Julia A., and Sara N. Bleich. 2015. "Is Cooking at Home Associated with Better Diet Quality or Weight-Loss Intention?" *Public Health Nutrition* 18(8): 1397–1406.

Wright, Jan, Jane Maree Maher, and Claire Tanner. 2015. "Social Class, Anxieties and Mothers' Foodwork." *Sociology of Health & Illness* 37(3): 422–436.

YouGov. 2013. "Poll Results: Thanksgiving Dinner." YouGov/Huffington Post Survey, November 18–19, 2013. Retrieved April 18, 2018, https://today.yougov.com/news/2013/11/20/poll-results-thanksgiving-dinner/.

Young, Iris Marion. 2005. *On Female Body Experience: "Throwing Like a Girl" and Other Essays*. New York: Oxford University Press.

Zagorsky, Jay L., and Patricia Smith. 2017a. "No, Poor People Don't Eat the Most Fast Food." CNN, June 12. Retrieved April 9, 2018, https://edition.cnn.com/2017/07/12/health/poor-americans-fast-food-partner/index.html.

Zagorsky, Jay L., and Patricia K. Smith. 2017b. "The Association between Socioeconomic Status and Adult Fast-Food Consumption in the U.S." *Economics & Human Biology* 27(A): 12–25.

Zenk, Shannon N., Amy J. Schulz, Barbara A. Israel, Sherman A. James, Shuming Bao, and Mark L. Wilson. 2005. "Neighborhood Racial Composition, Neighborhood Poverty, and the Spatial Accessibility of Supermarkets in Metropolitan Detroit." *American Journal of Public Health* 95(4): 660–667.

Zhang, Li, and William A. McIntosh. 2011. "Children's Weight Status and Maternal and Paternal Feeding Practices." *Journal of Child Health Care* 15(4): 389–400.

Zick, Cathleen, Ken R. Smith, Jessie X. Fan, Barbara B. Brown, Ikuho Yamada, and Lori Kowaleski-Jones. 2009. "Running to the Store? The Relationship between Neighborhood Environments and Risk of Obesity." *Social Science & Medicine* 69(10): 1493–1500.

Zick, Cathleen D., and Robert B. Stevens. 2010. "Trends in Americans' Food-Related Time Use: 1975–2006." *Public Health Nutrition* 13(7): 1064–1072.

INDEX

Abarca, Meredith, 250n11,
  251n14, 282n24
access to food
  and choice of neighborhood, 33–34
  and food deserts, 11, 165–69, 271n11,
    272nn5–6, 273n20
  and foodie ideal, 5
  and mobile markets, 226
  African American food culture, 8,
    26–29, 197–98, 245n5, 277n3. *See
    also* soul food
African foods, 28, 240n26,
  245n5, 246n16
African Heritage Cookbook, The
  (Mendes), 245n7
agricultural labor, 9, 111, 228–29, 240n34
agricultural subsidies, 241n35
Agyeman, Julian, 270n4, 271n6
Alexander, Michelle, 277n1
Alkon, Alison Hope, 270n4, 271n6
alternative food movement. *See* "eating
  for change" movement
AmazonFresh, 125
American Academy of Pediatrics, 249n4
American Time Use Survey, 281n4
Annie's HomeGrown, 113
Apple, Rima D., 247n5

Armstrong, Leanne
  and challenges of poverty, 1–3,
    11, 137–48
  drug addiction, 256n1
  education, 6, 22
  fast-food restaurant job, 140–41,
    266n2, 267n5
  food assistance, 137, 171–79, 267n11
  food environment, 166–67
  Fourth of July celebration, 84–90, 234
  and gendered food labor, 6–7,
    86, 257n6
  importance of home-cooked meals to,
    1–6, 84–86, 220
  parenting strategies, 6, 84–86, 88–90,
    137–38, 171, 173–76, 267n3, 281n3
Asian Americans, 233, 258n3
Atlantic, 220, 252n6
"Aunt Jemima" stereotype, 246n20

barbecue restaurants, 10–11
Best, Amy, 257n6, 259n4, 263n8,
  282n19, 282n26
birth centers, 31–37
Bittman, Mark, 50
black nationalism, 245n10
Blue Apron, 125